D1481975

The South Carolina Diary of
Reverend Archibald Simpson

PART 2

Here begins the Eleventh Volume of my Diary, which I find to be so
very useful in the ... life that I cannot think of giving it over tho the very
bad state of health now renders writing very painful to me, and I have some
I am now so infirm, that I do but little to write. I have no prospect of
Livery to finish this volume, and no desire to live beyond the Lords
appointed time, Each growes more & more tiresome to me. May the Lord
of His infinite grace & mercy make me ready And take me thro a
Redeemers righteous merits to Himself, And Enable me at my ...
parting Moment to say with His servant of old, Now lettest thou
thy Servant depart in peace for my Eyes have been thy salvation

Port Glasgow — Lords day October: 22: 1780 ys has been a very comfortable day both
to my ... thaven in ... measure what it was t worship ... in spirit & in truth, to have a ...
from a dabbs blessing In ye forenoon Mr Colhoun Lectur on ysaiah 55 first ... verses ...
... one of ye plainest ... most spiritual discourses ... speak I ever hrd, ... and apt to be a ...
of refreshing from ye presence of ye Mst High, In ye afternoon ... preacd A very ...
from Romans 13.6 last clause, full of rich spiritual matter, ye very manner of ... ...
a most excellent delivery, ... very rich & Copious And preaches ... great ... & feeding the ...
... presence apptd to be ... its Item, ye ... a glory of ye Lord was displayed in ye sanctuary ...
... has proved a great a good day of ye son of Man among us. there's ... ... Auditory more than ...
attentive And many with affect, there truly Evangelical discourses we rejoyce ye Lord ... prov ... me
most particularly ... ... my ... sg man appears plead fair for being a great ... ...
light in ye ch. of Scotland, May ye Lord spare & abundantly bless him ... & ... ...
... Even to ye ... himself help, Lord at last bless ye Lord for His grant t yeach ... ...
word th a number of very pious promising youths under ye Ministry And that ye ...
... ... th a prospect of ye Gspl being faithfully preachd among And Espeacly ... to ... & the ...
others of us, as apparantly soon to pass of ye stage of time and going down to ye silent grave, ...
... Every ... sch familyes wd blend in pray & ... Althou' I spent this ... ...
... ye Lords dutys, here in a ... Sryth, promising some of ob — Hor day ... ...
ye day spent at Mr Colhoun And tho ye Lord wd bless & ... ... whereas ... ...
day in a ... lively serious frm of ob, was mostly engaged in ... ...
... very quite a ... frm pious ... among ... distrss; So mdes ... only ... ...
... the ... ... in my br ... stomack, ye weather Extream ...
exceedingly Storing, Constant violent winds, sleet, hail, a ye ... ...
... ... myself toberable — ... ... October 23 ... ...
... of a bd, I ... ... I have been ... ...
... ... familyes ... being a ... ... at other times ... ...
... ... in several ... ... As ... ...
... ... day ... ... God ... ...

The South Carolina Diary
of
Reverend Archibald Simpson

Part 2, April 1770–March 1784

Edited by Peter N. Moore

THE UNIVERSITY OF SOUTH CAROLINA PRESS

© 2012 University of South Carolina

Published by the University of South Carolina Press
Columbia, South Carolina 29208

www.sc.edu/uscpress

Manufactured in the United States of America

21 20 19 18 17 16 15 14 13 12
10 9 8 7 6 5 4 3 2 1

Library of Congress Cataloging-in-Publication Data
Simpson, Archibald, ca. 1734–ca. 1795.
The South Carolina diary of Reverend Archibald Simpson / edited by Peter N. Moore.
p. cm.
Includes bibliographical references and index.
ISBN 978-1-61117-046-7 (cloth : alk. paper) — ISBN 978-1-61117-047-4 (cloth : alk. paper)
1. Simpson, Archibald, ca. 1734–ca. 1795—Diaries. 2. Presbyterian Church—South
Carolina—Clergy—Biography. 3. Presbyterians—South Carolina—Biography. 4.
Presbyterians—South Carolina—History—18th century—Sources. 5. Presbyterian
Church—South Carolina—History—18th century—Sources. 6. South Carolina—
Church history—18th century—Sources. 7. South Carolina—History—18th
century Sources. 8. South Carolina—Social conditions—18th century—
Sources. I. Moore, Peter N., 1961– II. Title.
BX9225.S465A3 2012
285'.1092—dc23
[B]
2011043950

Frontispiece: Representative image of an original page from Reverend Archibald Simpson's
diaries. Courtesy of the Charleston Library Society, Charleston, South Carolina.

Contents

Introduction
vii

Introduction

THIS SECOND AND FINAL PART OF *The South Carolina Diary of Reverend Archibald Simpson* covers Simpson's final years in South Carolina (1770–72) as well as his brief return immediately following the Revolutionary War (1783–84). It incorporates material from volumes 7, 8, and 11 of his diary, which were among the most detailed and revealing of his surviving volumes. Together these diaries paint an intimate, complex, and in places fascinating portrait of the rural lowcountry during the era of the American Revolution.

On the whole I have sought to preserve the emotion, intimacy, and dailiness of Simpson's diary while minimizing its tedium and redundancy. Throughout his life Simpson used the diary as a "record of God's mercies" and a barometer for his soul, but since I provided ample amounts of this introspective material in part 1, I have largely omitted it here. I have also cut most of the stock descriptions of Sabbath services along with his more-or-less daily complaints about poor health, although I have retained his detailed descriptions of more severe bouts of illness. As in the preceding volume, I have included most of his visits to the sick, dying, and distressed—indeed one great feature of Simpson's diary is how it takes us into the homes and intimate lives of his neighbors—but I have omitted the more routine social calls. On the other hand, I have retained all of Simpson's references to his slaves, mainly because he so rarely noticed them.

One new and significant theme that emerges here is courtship. Simpson's first wife died in 1765, and his oldest child a year later. By 1769, when he began volume 7 of his diary, Simpson was the sole parent of two young girls and had already unsuccessfully courted four women. Though the details of these suits are lost along with volume 6 of his diary, at least one of them, to Mary Cater, ended disastrously for Simpson and fueled the enmity of the anti-evangelical faction at Indian Land. This failed proposal forms the backdrop for the series of suits Simpson undertook beginning in the spring of 1770 to win the affections of Mrs. Green, Mrs. B, Mrs. P.C., and Miss Sally Murry, successively. When this last proposal to Sally Murry exploded, Simpson's reputation was tarnished yet again, placing his "future usefulness" as a minister in jeopardy. By 1772 his declining health, his failure to find a

mother for his children, and his damaged reputation convinced him to
return to Scotland. These intersecting lines of religion, gender, courtship,
and social conflict are dense and complicated, so I have included here nearly
all of the material relating to Simpson's search for a second wife.

Simpson evidently intended to return to South Carolina, for he made no
effort to sell his extensive plantation on the Saltcatcher River, leaving his
affairs instead in the hands of friends, factors, and lawyers. The Revolutionary War intervened, however, and Simpson was forced to remain in Scotland
for eleven years, serving the congregation at Newark Chapel in the parish of
Port Glasgow. He left a detailed record of these years in Scotland in volumes
10 and 11 of his diary, both of which have survived. When he finally returned
to South Carolina in the late summer of 1783, he was dismayed and disillu-
sioned by what he found, and he left a remarkable picture of both Charleston and the rural lowcountry in the immediate aftermath of the war. I have
included most of that material here, although I have been forced to exclude
materials from his years in Scotland along with nearly eighty pages of journal entries from his 1783 voyage.

A Brief Note on Editorial Policies

As I noted in part 1, I have tried to balance readability with faithfulness to
the original manuscript. Simpson, like most eighteenth-century diarists, was
not consistent in matters of punctuation, spelling, capitalization, and abbreviations. His penmanship itself presented problems as it was often difficult
to distinguish his capital *A*'s, *C*'s, *M*'s, *N*'s, *P*'s, and *W*'s from his lowercase
versions, and although he nearly always capitalized initial *E*'s, he was inconsistent in capitalizing initial *S*'s. When in doubt, I have used a lowercase
letter. I have also silently capitalized proper names and the first words of sentences. With punctuation, he rarely used periods and commas in the early

Facing: Henry Mouzon, *An Accurate Map of North and South Carolina With their
Indian Frontiers, Shewing in a distinct manner all the Mountains, Rivers, Swamps,
Bays, Creeks, Harbours, Sandbanks and Soundings on the Coasts; with The Roads and
Indian Paths; as well as The Boundary or Provincial Lines, The Several Townships and
other divisions of the Land in both the Provinces; the whole from Actual Surveys. . . .*
London: Printed for Robt. Sayer and J: Bennett, 1775, detail. Courtesy of the
Charleston Library Society, Charleston, South Carolina.

diaries, but by 1769 he was using them very liberally. I have retained as much of the original punctuation as possible, though I have silently inserted commas when needed for clarity, and periods at the end of sentences (unless Simpson used a comma, in which case I have retained his original punctuation). Spelling is rather more problematic. Simpson's education made him a good speller, but in volumes 7 and 8 he used a shorthand form that omitted most vowels. In these volumes I have silently expanded abbreviated words and retained the eighteenth-century spellings (favour, publick, physick) to maintain consistency with the earlier volumes.

I have also made additional minor changes as follows:

Apostrophes. Simpson rarely used them. I have silently inserted them only for abbreviated names (e.g., Mr. D's house).

Superscripts. I have been brought them down to the line, and the thorn has been replaced with *th*.

Abbreviations. I have silently expanded abbreviations, including abbreviated names when known, except for books of the Bible, which Simpson abbreviated even when not writing in shorthand.

Insertions and deletions. Inserted words appear with no special marks; marked-through words have been omitted in most cases.

Corrections and emendations. I have silently corrected obvious errors, such as words that were inadvertently repeated. I have inserted words that were obviously omitted and placed them in brackets. I have also placed uncertain words in brackets unless they are illegible, in which case I designated them [illegible].

Page numbers. Simpson did not number his pages. I have inserted page numbers in brackets.

Ellipses. Because Simpson paid little regard to punctuation and frequently used long, run-on sentences, the use of ellipses is problematic. However, in adhering to the style guide of the University of South Carolina Press, I have used a four-dot ellipsis when the excised material follows the end of a sentence, and a three-dot ellipsis for excisions within a single sentence or for longer omissions of several sentences.

Line breaks. Simpson did not use indentation, paragraphs, or line breaks. I have inserted line breaks to separate the entries and enhance readability.

For my approach to annotations, see the introduction to part 1. I have not re-annotated items that were annotated in part 1; consult the previous volume for the many names and places that appear here without annotations.

The South Carolina Diary of
Reverend Archibald Simpson

PART 2

VOLUME 7

April 6, 1770–April 22, 1771

1770

[65 (III)][1] *Friday April 6 1770* . . . After breakfast proceeded for Port Royal. Got to my old acquaintances & friend Mr. Bowmans about ten O Clock, having rode about fourteen miles with the way I went. After had rested myself a little, desired to retire, when Mrs. Bowman went upstairs, to conduct me to the room, and with a great deal of cheerfulness in her countenance, told me she had very good news to tell me, and hoped they would be welcome ones, after Sitting down she told me, that for some time she had some reason to think my addresses would be acceptable, if paid to the excellent & amiable Mrs. G, widow of the late unhappy Reverend Mr. G of this place,[2] Daughter to Dr. Cuthberts wife, that it would be most acceptable to her Mother & the Doctor her Father in law, and from several other considerations besides her person, temper, education, family & fortune, pressed it upon me, and further told me, that she had already Spoken, to the Lady herself & obtained her liberty for me to wait upon her, & also to her Mother & the Doctor, who were very desirous of its taking place, if agreeable to Mrs. Green herself. This information from so worthy a person, very much surprized & pleased me, for though it was most unexpected yet had no reason to doubt of it, after getting over my first Surprize I promised her to take every proper step, to make myself agreeable to the Lady herself, that was consistent with my station, & begged her advice, which she in the most free & prudent manner gave me, and then retired, but repeatedly insisted I should go into Beaufort, and make some beginning tomorrow, which I was not very willing to do as it was Saturday. After was left alone, this affair still filled me with amazement, I was certain that Mr. & Mrs. Bowman were very Sincere in it, I was as certain, that Doctor Cuthbert & his wife, were too good to have any mean or Sinister design and were above all design to deceive or impose on me. As for the Lady herself, her mind was not yet known, but I have all possible reason to believe her a person of great Sincerity, great prudence and discretion, I once had thoughts of her about three years ago but laid it aside as thinking it impractical to Succeed, and now so unexpected encouragement from her parents, & those who have the greatest influence over her, and no discouragement from herself when spoken to, I could not but wonder, how this would End, and went to prayer about it, humbly begging for direction from above, and that it might Succeed or not as it would be for Gods glory & our good. . . . In the afternoon Mr. Bowman returned from Beaufort, where he had gone in the morning. He told us that Dr. Cuthbert had applied to the church minister or clergyman,[3] that as at present their church is rebuilding, & they have the use of a large empty private house, and the meeting house is scarcely tenable, for his leave for me, to preach there on Sabbath, as it was the clergymans time to preach Saint Helena, but He refused it because, as He expressed it in his letter, we were dissenters from the church of England & did not use the same forms of prayer with them, and therefore ought not to worship in the Same place, that he had no disrespect to my person, but only because of our profession, I would not be admitted into his pulpit, nor they who joined with me in worship according to the Presbyterian form, to perform it in the same place where He & the members of the church of England worshiped although at a different time. This refusal of his, had not only affronted the Dissenters, but all his own people in general, and the more so, as the Dissenters, had often lent their meeting house when in repair, to the church ministers, and very lately they had the use of it for Several weeks. This affair gave me some concern, lest it should cause any easiness, and resolved while at Beaufort to do all I could to excuse the clergyman, who is a very young man and already very little thought of by his parishioners. Sat up late with my good old friends, who are very desirous of the connection above mentioned, & let me know, that it will be expected I shall preach a third part of my time in Beaufort if it takes place, and at present there seems a door opening for great usefulness in that place, whether I ever should have such connection or not, and believe it will be my duty to preach as often to them as possible, and drop

Ponpon entirely. May the Lord give me counsel and direction, & and do what will be most for his glory and honour.

[66 (113)] *Saturday April 7 1770* This day in a sweet humble frame of soul. . . . I took a short walk in the Town, to let people see I was come, and returned it being just dusk. I then took an opportunity to speak to the Doctor, and ask the liberty of his family to pay my respects to his Daughter in law Mrs. Green, which he very readily granted, and assured me of his friendship and of the great esteem the whole family had for me, and that they would be all much pleased, if it should be agreeable to the Lady herself, who is a most Judicious person but very reserved, and would be very cautious, as she had been most cruelly imposed upon in her first marriage, and since the Death of her very profligate husband though a Clergyman, she had never entertained any thoughts of again entering into that state, though she had had many offers, & some of them Gentlemen of good fortune, but that she had a very favourable opinion of me, and both He & her mother a most worthy pious Lady, would rejoice at the connection, if agreeable to the party concerned. After some conversation with him, I waited upon Mrs. Cuthbert, & asked her liberty, which she not only granted, but with great affection told me, I had her most hearty approbation, that though her Daughter, would be left entirely to Judge for herself, yet she would do all for me, that she could, and added further, that at Mrs. Bowmans desire, she had talked with her daughter about it, and found no very material objection, but believed perseverance would gain her consent, we then conversed on the matter for near an hour in the most friendly manner. I told her as it was Saturdays night, and my mind was much engaged with my subject, I would delay waiting on Mrs. Green till Monday, which she very much approved of. After this we were all in company together, till near Eleven at night, and had much serious useful conversation, Mrs. Cuthbert & I persuading the Doctor to take no further notice of the Clergymans ill natured very foolish letter & that we would use our influence to soften others & especially to excuse him to his own people, which the Doctor agreed to. . . .

Lords Day 8 . . . The Lord very mercifully favoured us in the weather, so that our old house which was neither wind nor water tight was very commodious, and was not only crowded within, as close as they could press together, but also a great many out of doors seated upon chairs, which were brought from many houses, so that had a very fine Congregation, all the Genteel people in

Town, & many from the Country were present, both forenoon & afternoon.
Preached both parts of the day, from Jhn 10:17:18 and never was better helped,
nor had more of Gods most gracious & comfortable presence in preaching
the glorious Gospel than this day. . . . The auditory were most serious and
eagerly attentive, & not a few were almost constantly in tears both parts of
the day. The whole Sermon was on the Lord Jesus Christ, his Death & Sac-
rifice, which was the great thing they were struck & delighted with, and many
of them even filled with admiration, & wonder, as I learned after Service was
over. Their poor young Minister, preaches never longer than fifteen minutes,
& the Sermons consist only of the few moral sentences, taken out of Some
ancient heathen, for in many Sermons the name of Jesus Christ is not mentioned under any one of all his characters, nor can it be found by his Sermons,
that Man is a fallen creature, or that there is any Saviour, either needed or
provided, which many of them make great complaints of, so that what was
preached today was most acceptable to many. . . .

[67 (115)][4] *Monday April 9 1770* . . . This morning in a humble thankful frame
of soul, praising the Lord for all his goodness mercy faithfulness & truth to
poor vile unworthy me. Was also engaged in prayer, particularly for direction & assistance in the affair I was to enter upon, for the blessing of success
if it be his holy will & would be for his glory & our good, and no other ways.
Was in some perplexity and anxiety for [am] truly backward, on such occasions, and am not at all Master of that address & politeness necessary [to
such] occasions. Perceived Her also perplexed & thoughtful. After breakfast
got an opportunity [to be] with her alone, and immediately acquainted her
with [my] design, She did not disguise her expecting it, but on the [whole]
was very Silent, giving me neither encouragement, nor discouragement, received me with kindness & respect. [I] mentioned her being a Mother, and
found her less averse to it, than I expected, discoursed [together about] her
being bred to the church of England having been wife to a clergyman of that
church, & long [a] communicant there, this was discoursed largely of, and
as I determined to leave her wholly to her own [choice], I found that she
looked upon the difference to be so small that had reason to think that would
be no [obstacle], she declaring herself a sincere lover of faithful Gospel
preaching whether in church or meeting and has always been attached to my
ministry even the few years she lived with her own husband. I [acquainted]
her of the many appointments at present on my mind of preaching in Distant places, [having] the Sacraments to give etc., which would prevent my

waiting on her so often as I most earnestly [wished] & hoped she would excuse. She declared herself very well satisfied, that my time was constantly employed [in] those things of the greatest importance and that she should not expect so much attendance as some [others] might give, hinted she would not have me give myself so much trouble about her, yet sufficiently showed she expected Sometimes to see me, if I really persisted. I also mentioned to her, that it would not suit me to wait upon her in publick places, as is usual on such occasions, for I would have little opportunity of seeing her in public but at those places of worship, where I preached, and there it did not [at] all suit me, she very readily admitted the excuse. Spent near an hour, very agreeably with [her] and let her know when I proposed to come over again, if some unforeseen call did not prevent me, and took my leave very well satisfied. Went down to the bay & did some business, & visited at several places, where heard much of the great pleasure there was in hearing the Gospel yesterday, the great & universal desire there was, I would preach as often as possible. Severals went & offered their Subscriptions for the building of a new meeting house, the Gentleman who has undertaken it declares he will endeavour to have it up in three months, if possible. . . . Met with the Clergyman & behaved civilly & well to each other, poor Creature saw him afterwards very foolishly employed in playing at hand ball or fives[5] as it is called, with very ordinary company, this it seems is [most] of his employment all day, and at night cards and dancing constantly, all which gives great dissatisfaction. Returned & Dined at the Doctors, after Dinner had some conversation with him about what had passed with Mrs. Green, with which he was pleased, & told me repeatedly to be sure to persevere, and to call as often as possible. . . .

Tuesday 10 . . . After an early breakfast proceeded homeward. Called at Mr. Grdns, and afterwards at Simmons plantation,[6] where learned, that the Negroes are destroying & carrying off what creatures both horses & cattle I could not get up [three illegible words] the rest over, called at Mr. DeSaussures, found her as low as anything possibly could be, but still clear of the [fever] & have hope may recover, found her calm and composed in mind, condemning herself and Justifying God. Spent near an hour with her, discoursing to & praying with her, she is able to speak very little. . . .

[68 (126)] *Thursday April 12* . . . In the afternoon got ready, & set off for Wilton, being to preach there next Sabbath, Mr. Maltby having desired me to change pulpits with him, as he has some business up this way . . . at the Savanna called to visit Mrs. Jackson . . . Stayed some time here, and proceeded to Mr. Hunts in company with Mrs. B & others.[7] Mr. Hunt informed me that he had found great relief by a prescription I had directed to as a palliative for the gout, so that he was able to ride abroad, this gave me a real pleasure, I know of no happiness equal to that of being useful to mankind, either to their bodies or souls, Spent the night very agreeably, was free & cheerful, & yet grave, watchful & circumspect. Was pleased on several accounts of spending this evening here, & particularly with Mrs. B, as had an opportunity of letting her friends & relations see, there is nothing of that connection between her & me, which is strongly suspected, & I believe much wished for, by most of them.

Friday 13 . . . After breakfast left this very agreeable company & proceeded, was assisted in prayer and praise while traveling. Got to Mr. Lamberts at the round O about Eleven O Clock, He was not at home, stayed and rested myself & horses about an hour & proceeded to Jacksonburgh, where met with Mr. Lambert & some other friends, Stayed & Dined with them, at the publick tavern, Captain Browns, being much pressed to it, afterwards visited several families in the Burrough, and proceeded over the river, Met Mr. Maltby & his wife, going up to Mr. Lamberts in their way to the Saltcatcher, rode to my good old friends Mr. Brandfords, where stayed the night, here I met with my very worthy & good friend Mrs. H, widow of Mr. W H in whose family I formerly lived,[8] and from whom I received the greatest kindness. Were very happy in meeting together, she at present lives mostly here with her Sister, Mr. B's daughter Hamilton that was, now again a widow was also here, had a very agreeable night, with these good old friends, we were all often much affected, when talking over old affairs & conversing of former matters, had much serious useful improving conversation. . . .

[69 (128)] *Lords day April 15 1770* . . . Found a large congregation, found my heart warmed & affected with the Sight of my old & first people, at the least their posterity, for many of my friends and acquaintances here are gone off the stage of time & the Congregation consists mostly of them, who were children when I lived in these parts. . . . Was concerned at hearing Something of the Presbyterys design to settle Ponpon congregation with a minister, who it is thought will not be very acceptable to the most serious Sort of the people, Some of the Brethren are much for carrying this matter, to strengthen their hands with the addition of one of their own stamp. This and some other designs which I heard of gave me, but little prospect of doing any good, by attending on the presbytery. May the Lord prevent my fears & direct me to my duty.

Monday 16 This morning though felt very sore and fatigued early intending for Port Royal, was so fatigued, that could not be employed in prayer. . . . About ten O Clock, after having rode about twenty miles, stopped at Mr. Jnstns an old acquaintance at Combahee ferry, and had some breakfast got, here I stayed & rested myself about an hour or more, then proceeded, to Port Royal ferry, where was obliged to wait near two hours for the tide, Dined at Mr. Hzls, late in the afternoon proceeded over & rode to Mr. Bowmans, on Broad River where stayed all night, was most exceedingly fatigued, sore & weary for had rode above fourty miles, here I learned that the devil was stirring up some opposition to settling the Gospel at Beaufort, but was not in the least discouraged by that, for it was what I expected, and was pleased to find, that the friends of that interest were resolved not to be soon discouraged, nor to give over so good a design for any opposition. I also learned, that there was one Captain Rd, making his addresses to Mrs. Green, that He had done so for some time, that her Mother was exceedingly averse to it, & so was her Father in law, but it was thought to be something agreeable to herself, had it also hinted that to prevent this, was the reason & perhaps the chief one, of the Encouragement, that was given me by the Doctor & his wife, this I knowed when I was last on the Island, that Captain R was waiting on her, & Saw him with her, on Saturday afternoon at Beaufort, & was also certain of its being very disagreeable to Mrs. Cuthbert as He is a Seafaring man, but had no notion of its being agreeable to Mrs. Green herself. This intelligence gave me no great concern on account of Mrs. Green, for although have great value for her, & would think myself very happy with her, yet have no particular attachment, nor are my passions in the least concerned in the matter, but I was not pleased to be called in on such an occasion, only to serve a purpose as it were, and though I can not at all blame the Doctor & his wife, but must regard them in giving me the preference, yet I could not bear the thoughts of anything that looked being made a tool of, and was resolved to give myself very little concern about it, and to be well satisfied, that I was really Mrs. Greens choice as well as her parents, before I give her my hand, the Doctor & his family are at present out at their plantation on Broad River, about three miles from this, Mr. & Mrs. Bowman visited them, on Friday last, and are very much of the opinion that I will succeed, as the parents are so very much for it, but I am now of quite a different opinion, and have not the least expectation to succeed, and the great concern that the Doctor & his Lady have for my succeeding convince me of their fears, and that they have good reason for being so. I am certain I shall not be able to act with any Spirit in it, as I am now sure, that they act as much through fear of her marrying Captain R as through any desire of her having me. May God direct me, to act wisely, prudently, & suitable to my character, and do what will be for His own glory & our good.

Tuesday 17 . . . After breakfast, rode to the Doctors, was very kindly received by the whole family, observed the Single ladies were dressed as expecting company. Soon after I went there, I observed Mrs. Cuthbert & her Daughter Green, walk into the Garden, and they continued there about an hour in very close conversation, Mrs. Cuthbert I observed once seemed very earnest & agitated. This I thought did not promise well. I imagined something uncommon to be the case, that required so much talking from the mother to the Daughter, I could not bear the thoughts of offering myself to a Lady, that needed so much talking to, and was convinced that she was averse to the affair, after this I had a good deal of conversation with the Doctor, and observed he spoke much of the folly & vanity of young people, the wrong choice they were apt to make and persuading me to perseverance, He also mentioned Captain R waiting on his Daughter in law, said he did not believe, she gave him any encouragement, yet he came very constantly. I observed him carefully & said little, only that I could not give long attendance, that it was contrary to my temper, to be troublesome to any person, that I could not marry any woman if I thought there was any other man in the world, she wished to have rather than myself, and that I could not bear the thoughts of having a woman teezed & talked into any such business, that Since I had come there I would again wait on Mrs. Green, but must be excused from persevering to follow any woman whatsoever . . . [70 (130)] In the evening when the heat was abated, I asked Mrs. Green if she would walk, which she very readily did, and we were by ourselves a full two hours, & the half of it after Dark. I then put it to her, at first she behaved much as before, making me little or no answer, but afterwards told me, it would not do, that it was not agreeable to her, this answer she repeatedly gave me, I insisted much to know her reason for its being disagreeable, but she would not give me any, and begged to be excused. I continued urging my suit, & intreating for her reason, I often asked her, if her objection was to my person, my children, my Circumstances, station of life, my character, the abuses I have met with or our difference in the profession of religion, she often & repeatedly after discoursing of each of these particulars assured me, she had no objection upon any of these accounts, but would not mention her reason, and at last told me, that the reason did not concern me, nor anything on my part, I then told her, that I had so great an opinion of her honour & ingenuity, that I did not begin my addresses with asking her, if she was entirely at liberty to receive addresses because I believed, if she was engaged to any person, she would not have given me liberty & encouragement to wait upon her, but that now I begged leave to put that question to her, and accordingly did so, she declared she was not engaged to any person. I then asked if her heart & affections were not engaged & disposed of, she answered no, they were still at her own disposal, I did not urge her on this point, thinking it too tender & delicate, Among other things she told me, that she really believed we would be happy as married persons but said, she was very happy as she was & had no desire to marry. I told her, I believed she was so, but that we were not born for ourselves and so forth. I repeatedly told her she might take longer time to think of it, and that I could not take this for an answer, she with some earnestness insisted that I must take it as my final answer, that she would think no more of the matter than she had done, and that no thinking would make her change her mind, and that reason that made my offer not acceptable to her, she could not tell me, I mentioned my design of waiting upon her next Monday, she repeatedly desired I would not, however I insisted I should, if my business would permit, & then we returned into the house, at first she behaved with distance, & I thought not so politely as I expected, which I took notice of to her, and afterwards she was more free & easy in her behaviour. Soon after our coming in, the Doctor & her Mother seemed very anxious to know my Success, & being by ourselves, I just told them, that although I had not the Smallest reason to hope for being ever connected with their family, yet I would not desert Beaufort, but would act for that infant Congregation in the very same manner as if I was to succeed, that I would preach for them soon after my Sacraments were over, & continue to supply them often without looking for any reward, and would think myself exceedingly happy if I could be the instrument of settling the Gospel there, where it was so much needed, I observed the first part of my discourse affected them very much, especially Mrs. Cuthbert, she seemed very much shocked & distressed, and could not recover herself for some time, it made a strong & a very visible impression on her which I imputed to more reasons than her Daughters refusing me, after supper, we sat up pretty late, Mrs. Cuthbert was melancholy, yet spoke much on the advantages of religion, & religious connections, when we were retiring, the Doctor lighted me to my room, and immediately told me, that the hint I had given them gave his wife the most sensible concern, & afflicted her much, that their resolution was to leave Mrs. Green to her own choice, but they were extremely grieved to see her act so foolishly, I excused her, & said there was no accounting for fancy. I repeated most of what had passed, only omitted her saying that the reason did not concern me or my connections, but herself, the Doctor insisted on my continuing my addresses & told me, that now her Mother, would take an opportunity to talk very seriously to her, & fully let her know, what was her Sentiments & her desire, I told him I had said something about coming back again, but I did not know if I would, and that I could by no means persist in it, but he insisted on my coming at least once, which I consented to but could not be positive if it would be next week or after Indian Land Sacrament, he desired to know, if I had asked her, if she was engaged to any Gentleman, & told him, I had & repeated her answer, he mentioned Several things to me, which he begged I would urge to her at my next meeting, as its being so agreeable to her Mother, that she would be settled near her relations, and very near a plantation which he intended to give his Eldest Son, her brother by the mothers side, & several other things of that kind. He then mentioned, a young Gentleman & friend of mine, & an intimate acquaintance whose Estate lies near mine, & said could I introduce him to get acquainted with Mrs. Greens younger sister, Miss N A W, that it would be extremely agreeable to the whole family, and would most certainly overcome all difficulties with Mrs. Green, that the two sisters being settled near each other, would be such a satisfaction, as would remove every obstacle, the young Gentleman, is Mr. R H,[9] son of the late Reverend & worthy Mr. Hutson my predecessor, this surprized me very much & looked like a double plot, I told him [71 (132)] I was indeed very intimate with that Gentleman, that He was a very Sober, virtuous, worthy person, & I had a good deal of influence with him, & should think him very happy in such a connection, but that matchmaking was out of my way, that was Mrs. Green to accept of me, it would no doubt bring him to be acquainted with her Sister, or was Miss Nancy ever where he sometimes comes, it might give any opportunity, to ask his Sentiments of her, which I should be ready enough to do, but nothing further. The Doctor declared, that was all he would desire, & that it was only a thought of his own, which he trusted to my honour, but insisted on my again visiting Mrs. Green. After was left alone, could not but admire the strangeness of these occurrences, could not blame these worthy persons, for desiring to have their daughters, so worthily provided for, yet the appearance of design was disgusting, & resolved to act with great caution & circumspection. . . .

Wednesday April 18 1770 . . . As had to return to Mr. Bowmans and intended to set away before breakfast, the Doctor was very early with me. He again began with telling me the concern & trouble his wife was in about Mrs. Green, her resolution to have some serious conversation with her about, her desire I would continue my addresses a little longer, and that insisted if coming back next Monday, I would write to Mrs. Green, that she would certainly show them the letter, which would afford them a further opportunity of discoursing with her, and that as my Sacraments were coming on, I need not require an answer for two or three weeks, which would be a gaining of time, and offered them further opportunity to deal with her, I told him, I was very averse to write upon such a Subject, as an ill use had been made of the only letter I wrote to Miss C on such an occasion[10] & that I had almost resolved never to write to any woman on such an affair, but as he continued to urge me I promised I would, & would enclose it to him, for his & her Mothers perusal before it was delivered. He then mentioned his & her Mothers concern about Captain R, & hoped she was not attached to him, but I saw plainly enough they were very much afraid of it, and now I was so fully confirmed in my former Sentiments, that I was sorry I had promised to write, but the Doctor held me to my promise, he again mentioned the affair of last night about Mr. Hutson & her Sister, and bid me think of it, I desired him to excuse me to the Ladies for going away before breakfast, & set off. Was well satisfied with my conduct in this affair, as had nothing to accuse myself with, but still it appeared a very strange providence. Rode to Mr. Bowmans praying to & praising the Lord, and rejoicing in God as my all in all forever more. Poor Mrs. Bowman was much pleased with my staying all night, & was in great hopes, I had succeeded but was greatly disappointed when I told her how it was, & immediately expressed her fears of an attachment to Captain R, & lamented poor Mrs. Cuthbert if it really should be so. She also blamed Mrs. Green and said she thought, that she had used her parents, & herself Mrs. Bowman very ill, in telling them she was willing, I should make my addresses to her, and that she had also used me ill, in not

telling me at first, as she did last night, but on the contrary encouraged me
to come back, & now the affair would be publick, as the Negroes & others
in the family would carry it abroad, I excused Mrs. Green as well as I could,
but Mrs. Bowman blamed her much, & with a good deal of resentment, and
was much persuaded that her heart & affections were otherwise engaged, yet
she also joined in soliciting me, to come back or to write, & even entreated
me to it, as she thought it would be so great a step towards settling the Gospel in Beaufort. . . . Have learned one useful lesson from this affair, not to
be too hasty in forming any connections, but to wait & observe what providence may do for me as something may be in store, that will be for my advantage. Remembered how it was about my purchasing land, I had often
such near prospects of making a purchase, that it seemed hardly possible I
could miscarry, & yet was still disappointed, and at last God did better for
me, than either myself or friends could have expected or even wished for,
and I did not doubt, but God would do so in the article of my marrying if
I ever should. When got to Mr. Hzls on the Indian Land side of the ferry,
found them eating some shellfish crabs, which induced me to stay & take
some refreshment, calling for some Drink, chiefly that might be of some service to the house, as they charge me no ferriage. Stayed here about an hour,
and proceeded home. . . .

Thursday 19 . . . In the afternoon was sent for over to Mr. Donnoms, his
brother & brother in law Mr. Way, being returned from Ponpon, where they
had been about some business, and wanted to see me. Was obliged to Spend
the Evening here, was something melancholy at the Sight of my children,
who being at no school are losing what reading they had attained to, and
being under no government, are running quite wild, after the example of the
other children of this family, who are the most spoiled & worst brought up
children I most ever saw, to have no bad example set before them, Mine indeed are not so much indulged, but alas very different from what they were,
I am greatly distressed about them, this was but a disagreeable evening, the
general conversation not Edifying, till family prayer came on, in which had
a comfortable Season. . . .

[72 (134)] *Saturday 21* . . . Have lately been reading the History of Abelard
& Heloise with their letters,[11] seen much of the sinful, carnal affections of
my desperately wicked & deceitful heart, with respect to my Dear deceased,
this Idol of Jealousy is what I believe the Lord has contended with me for,

and by it he has been greatly offended, the power of memory & imagination in calling up past comforts, and still presenting to me, that once justly beloved Object, is my great Sin, my great grief & often makes me cry out, Oh wretched man that I am. This day blessed be God I was kept free from these carnal wanderings, and enjoyed Gods most gracious & comfortable presence. . . .

Lords Day April 22 1770 . . . The Congregation were late in coming, but was full & large when I began, preached both parts of the day from 1 Cor 11:26, with what to me was really Gods most remarkable presence & assistance. . . . The Congregation was numerous, several strangers, very serious & in general much affected, yet in the forenoon some young people behaved ill, so that was obliged repeatedly to call to take care, was grieved to see a young Gentleman not twenty one years of age very Drunk. He is almost always so, his parents are both dead, his mother was under my pastoral care at Wiltown, a very good sort of woman, but died when he was very young, & his Father in a few years after. I saw him in the morning before we went in, very much in Drink, & in the time of Service, his behaviour, was most extremely foolish. Was so grieved & distressed for him, that took notice of it in the prayer, & prayed for him, without naming any person. In the afternoon, we had none of his company, the Congregation were very much affected, & so was I myself. . . .

Thursday 26 This morning in a humble Spiritual frame of soul, Sensible of the workings of sin. . . . Was in the forenoon over visiting the sick Negroes, & endeavouring [73 (136)] to assist them . . . Received a letter, containing an account from Dr. Reids estate,[12] against me to the amount of one hundred & fifty pounds currency for his attendance to me & my Dear deceased Jeany Muir, & Chevy Simpson fourteen & fifteen years ago, I had repeatedly asked for my account from the Doctor, & he always declared both to me, & to many others in the most publick manner, that He never did nor would make any charge against me, but that He gave all he had done for me & my family for his supporting of the Gospel, so that though I had at different times offered him money, he never would receive any, but once twenty pounds, which he said he accepted as a token of my gratitude, and that he would be more than that in my way,[13] as I pressed it upon him, but never would give me any account & openly valued himself in his generosity to me, receiving the thanks of my friends in those parts for the same. I have been often with him, even since my circumstances were sufficiently able to pay for all the kindness he showed me in my distress, but he never would hear of my paying him, & always said though his attendance on me & mine, was in the way of his business, in his books yet he would or had crossed it out, and it should never come against me, but never offered me a receipt nor could I ask it of him, as it seemed to doubt his honour & veracity, Some months ago, the Doctor died, and his widow & executors I suppose finding it on his books, have drawn out the above account & sent, requiring a speedy payment, which as things are circumstanced must be made and at present will distress me, as I have not sold any of my crop, and though am now entered on the fifth year at Saltcatcher, have not received two years salary, which with the great expense of settling and building makes me very much straitened, this affair surprized, & gave me some uneasiness as I have not the money, but most cheerfully will I pay it for my Dear, Dear very Dear deceased. About midnight sat down and looked over the particulars, which affected me, as it revived the distresses that I & my Dear family underwent at that time, all which brought me into a very humble lowly praying frame of spirit, when reviewing my weary pilgrimage through this wilderness of the time that I have been in this province, and the many great mercies God has shown to poor me & mine. . . .

Friday April 27:1770 Early this morning dispatched my boy to Beaufort with a letter to Doctor Cuthbert containing one to Mrs. Green, which I sent open, that the Doctor & his wife might, if they approve of it, seal & deliver it to her, but they did not approve of it they might destroy or send it back. Committed this important affair to God by prayer, & left with my heavenly Father, the Smallest anxiety about it. . . .

Saturday 28 . . . My boy returned, with a very kind & friendly letter from Dr. Cuthbert, letting me know, that he & his wife approved of my letter, he sealed & delivered it to Mrs. Green, who has not returned any answer, which was what both they & I expected, as we had desired her not to be hasty, but to take time & consider the affair, before she gave her answer, which must be final. . . .

[74 (138)] *Lords Day April 29:1770* . . . Preached all day from Thessalo: 1:10 last clause, the Lord was most graciously with me, and his everlasting arms round about me. . . . There was a very big old man in a mean dress, his head white as Snow, who had been the greatest part of his life in the Army, going about seeking a place to live at, on some Gentlemans plantation, he happened to come here, in order to apply to some of the Gentlemen in meeting. During the time of the first prayer & psalms, he was not in the least affected, but seemed rather careless, but soon after the text was given out, and I began to open it up & enter upon the Subject, he appeared like one thunderstruck, got up & stared with great amazement, & surprize, burst out in tears, which flowed down his aged cheeks, to the very floor. He was at first sitting at the whole length of the house from me, after he had stood some time, he began to move towards the pulpit very slowly, still pouring out great abundance of tears, & often stopping, then again moving towards, still staring at me, with surprizing mixture of terrour, astonishment, & satisfaction in his countenance, and being a very big strong made, coarse talking old man the whole auditory began to be amazed & severals in much pain, especially the women were much alarmed. Most of the people took him to be out of his Senses, and that he was coming up to lay hold of me, he kept coming along, though some made motions to him to stop. I was obliged to call to be attentive, and kept my eye much upon him, not knowing what to think, when he came up to the head of communion table, I made a sign with my hand to him to stop & sit down there, upon which he kneeled down on the floor, leaning his arms on the seat by the communion table and continued so all the time of sermon still weeping, it was a solemn affecting sight. Betwext sermons he spoke to Mr. James Donnom, who has had some knowledge of him these several years, then came to me, & begged to live in my plantation, with his wife an old woman and one Son, but as I had no possible conveniency to take them I spoke to some of the Gentlemen for him, and Mr. Jordan, promised to take him home to a place of his Employers Mr. Middletons, to make trial of his behaviour, & give him an opportunity to attend publick worship, which he earnestly desired. In the afternoon he was at the same place of the communion table mostly on his knees, and wept much, especially during the free & large offer of Salvation, & pressing call to come to the glorious deliverer, rush to make inquiry after him & take notice of him. . . .

[75 (140)] *Wednesday [May]* 2 This morning felt very poorly & indisposed . . . found the indisposition of my body, very much unfitted me for that study which had in view, was obliged also to be engaged in several little affairs which were perplexing & troublesome, and to complete all, Satan himself brought an affair in my way, which greatly troubled & distressed me as was

obliged repeatedly to correct the mulatto girl Mona with some severity, which
is very uncommon with me, and exceedingly painful, she had been left yesterday afternoon with the charge of the house in a hurry when I had not time
to lock up the Desk & closet, & the old wench Bess was not at hand, this
tempted her to get into the Desk & take out some trifling things, at the same
time there was a small piece of money amissing, which I put into the desk
yesterday, and as she has been often guilty of thefts of the Same kind, corrected her twice to make her confess, & dealt much with her. She discovered
some small things but denied any knowledge of the money which was afterwards found, & I believe of that she was innocent, this distressed & plagued
me a good deal, and very much unfitted me for study, and lost most of the
forenoon. Went at last to prayer, saw evidently that the hand of the Enemy
was against me, and was enabled with great tenderness of Spirit to pour out
my soul unto the Lord, and there my complaint was against myself, to the
Lord did I cry, & to the Lord did I make my Supplication, pleaded & wrestled earnestly for pardoning mercy & Sanctifying graces . . . got near unto
the Lord, & was admitted to sweet intercourse with Jehovah, found his presence refreshing & strengthening. . . .

Thursday May 3 1770 . . . Old Mrs. Lambright came & brought her Daughter Mrs. Vaux, to be admitted for the Lords Supper, after conversing with her,
I with pleasure & satisfaction agreed to receive her, was well assisted both in
discoursing with her and in prayer, and found this a very pleasant & comfortable duty. . . .

[77 (144)] *Wednesday 9* . . . This day was informed that a young man, whom
I married, at my own house last Thursday forenoon, was yesterday killed with
thunder. He was riding about his lawful & necessary business when there
came on a great thunder storm & heavy rain upon which he rode up to an
oak tree & stood under it, to be sheltered from the rain, when the thunder
struck the tree, and shattered it all to pieces, killed him and his horse, who
were both found soon after by a traveler. His clothes were tore & burnt in a
fearful manner, his skin in many places burnt and scorched, one arm & one
thigh broke, besides his shoulder. He was a sober, well inclined youth, was
present at sermon last Sabbath, both parts of the day and was very much
affected especially in the afternoon, the time of the most earnest & pressing
invitations, to come to Christ and Drink of the living waters, of Spiritual &
Eternal blessings, which were then offered in the fullest & freest manner, in

which the hearers were particularly & repeatedly pressed to accept of then, as it might be to some of the last call, and the expression was used, that for as near as it was to the Sacrament of the Lords supper, some there, might never live to see it or to hear the offer of grace & mercy that might then be given and therefore it was again & again urged upon them to accept of the present invitation, both him & his wife were much affected. He went home to a friends house in great concern, talking much about the Sermons, and especially that of the afternoons. On Monday morning he got up early and went to Secret prayer in the room imagining his wife asleep, which she observed with great pleasure. On Monday afternoon he read to the family a sermon of Russells upon Joshuas resolution to serve the Lord,[14] and often expressed his desire & resolution to do so with his family, as soon as he should be settled, on Monday afternoon, with some reluctance he parted with his wife, & rode about twenty miles or more, to meet a Gentleman with whom he was going to live till the fall of the year, when he intended to go with his wife & settle in Georgia, from whence he had come about three months ago, and yesterday was returning when it pleased the Lord to call him into Eternity, as above. Was much affected & concerned when heard the account of his Sudden & awful Death, though I hope in mercy to himself, was affected for the poor young woman his wife who is a very well disposed young body, the child of a very worthy friend of mine now in Eternity who will be my crown of rejoicing in the day of the Lord, having in a very remarkable manner been called under a [Sermon I] preached at Ponpon, and for some years before his Death, gave good evidences of a very remarkable conversion. Went to prayer for this poor distressed young woman, and the relations of the deceased, he having a very aged mother living somewhere down the Country, and a Sister Mrs. Frnr, living on Indian Land, also prepared to take notice of this awful providence tomorrow from the pulpit, or at the grave if buried there. The Lord prepare and make me ready for my great change. . . .

[78 (146)] *Thursday May 10:1770* . . . Should have mentioned yesterday, that agreed to admit to the Lords table Mr. James Ferguson, nephew to good old Mrs. Hatcher, who came over to my own house on that account. . . . When got to Mr. DeSaussures, was informed that the young mans corpse was at the meeting house, that his very disconsolate wife and Sister, with some of her relations were at the late Colonel Devauxs, upon which I rode there to visit the young woman, but she was gone forward to the meeting house, where I found her, exceedingly distressed yet behaving in a most Christian manner. I went into the study house and Sat some time with her, could not help shedding tears when saw her distress, she expressed herself in a very Sensible affected manner, and for some time she held me so fast that I could not get from her. After some time when I recovered my self was helped to speak suitably and freely to her. Afterwards had the corpse, which were very offensive, put into the grave covered over with bushes, till the Sermon should be Ended. There was a good Congregation, all much affected with this very alarming providence, preached from John 7:37 with most Gods most gracious and delightful presence. . . . This was a most blessed & comfortable season. Had some things particularly prepared for the poor mourning young woman, who attended with great & becoming decency, for the other mourners, and for all of us, on so melancholy an occasion. Was well assisted in prayer and preaching, and hope that no part of the word was lost. After the Service was over, and the tokens given to the communicants, we walked to the grave, where I discoursed on this melancholy occasion, with a view to these two texts of Scripture, all things come alike to all etc. and, Think ye that those eighteen, upon whom the tower in Siloam fell & a slew them, that they were sinners above all men, that dwelt in Jerusalem. I showed them, that the manner of his Death, was not to be looked upon as a Judgment, that we were not to apply providences in that manner to others, that nothing was to be known of a persons state, by the manner of their Death, that it was a very wrong notion of many, that if people died easy, quietly and willingly, that they were happy, showed them the folly of such a notion, and how contrary it was to the Scripture, which says, that in life the wicked are not plagued as other men, & in Death they have no lands, gave some account of the young man, which had informed myself of, directed to the proper improvement of the providence, put them in mind of the last Sabbaths afternoon sermon, and the expressions then made use of, pointed out to them how far such declarations from the pulpit, & so directly & immediately accomplished, might be looked upon as from the Spirit of God, warmly exhorted the Congregation, tenderly directed & instructed the mourning relations, and concluded with telling something of the nature of the Electricity fire, and showing them that in thunderstorms there was the greatest danger in going under trees, and that under the Divine protection their greatest safety lay in being in the open air, that the more open the place was, and the more they were wet, the less danger they were in. I thought it my duty to give them this warning and caution, and that I ought to embrace this opportunity to do it, all were very serious, & I was well assisted both in discoursing and praying. . . .

[79 (148)] *Saturday May 12 1770.* This is my birthday, I am now about thirty five or thirty six years of age.[15] Neither I nor my parents ever expected, I would have been so long in this world, nor Seen so many days, yet the Lord contrary to the expectations of those who know me, has hitherto spared & kept me alive, and blessed be his holy name, not altogether in idleness or to no purpose, yet also, how little have I done for God. . . .

Lords day May 13 This has been a most glorious & comfortable day to a poor creature, as one of the days of heaven to my soul, a day of heavenly & Divine Enjoyments, was in the Spirit on the Lords day, and worshiped God in Spirit & in truth. . . . There was a large congregation, my friends from Port Royal were all over. Dr. Cuthbert, his wife & Daughter Miss Nancy were present. Mrs. Green had always been used to attend on these occasions, but at this time stayed at home with the young part of the family. Mrs. Cuthbert joined with us, as an occasional communicant, reserving to herself a liberty to join in her own church, the Establishment, as she finds it will be for her Edification, this gave me very great satisfaction, as she is a person of a considerable rank & station, in life of an Eminent character, and has perhaps been a communicant in the church of England more than twenty years, her example will I hope prevail on others, to Drop the spirit of bigotry, the great thing I desire is to see good [80 (150)] Christians of every denomination, joining altogether as they have opportunity, and paying no regard to forms & Ceremonies. The Doctor applied for a token for his son after I got there, Mr. Daniel DeSaussure from Beaufort who communicated about three or four years ago and professes himself a member of the Established church and is at present one of their vestry at Beaufort, followed me out after the action sermon, for a token and joined with us. Admitted young Mrs. Bowman for the first time, in the morning before I went in. Preached from John 19:30 middle clause, It is finished . . . There was a very great weeping especially when was on the sufferings of Christ showing the difficulties the Lord of glory met in finishing the great work of our redemption . . . It was most pleasant & surprizing to observe the countenances of the poor Negroes of whom there was a great number present, I suppose near or about two hundreds, or perhaps more, for not only their own part of the house was crowded but there were crowds at every window. It was delightful to see the pleasing wonder and surprize they were filled with when I particularly addressed them, with an offer of Christ and finished redemption. There were numbers of them in tears with their eyes and their hands lifted up as with the greatest earnestness they were accepting the offer, which I believe many of them did. It was a delightful & stricking sight, to see the whole people lifting up their heads, and looking back upon the Negroes, with their countenances bathed in tears, while on the other hand to see the poor slaves also bathed in tears looking forward sometimes at the people, but mostly at me, with an eagerness, pleasure & surprize, as if I had been proclaiming liberty to them all from their slavery. The Lord continued his blessed, glorious and delightful presence with poor worthless me, and his people through every part of service. Was particularly full in covenanting, in their name & my own, at the time of the consecrating and praying for a blessing on the Elements. . . . My Strength and liveliness continued and so did the peoples though we were betwext five & six hours in the Service, there was hardly any went out during the communicating, as is the bad custom here, and very few went away till the whole was over, my inveterate Enemy poor unhappy Mrs. Broadbelt now Ferguson, was present all day, and though did not offer to be a communicant, yet was often in great agitation and wept very much, Mains sister in law with his children were present the whole time, she was also almost constantly in tears. . . . Just after I came out of the pulpit, I observed a young man, one Mr. Grmbl,[16] coming towards me from the other Side of the meeting but he said nothing, and I thought, had a strange wild like look. I Saw a hat on the steps of the pulpit, and thought I had been mistaken in his coming to speak to me, and that he was looking for his hat. I pushed by him to get into the Study house for some refreshment, but just I got in, I heard a great cry & noise in the meeting house, and was immediately called back, for there was a man in a strong convulsion fit, I went in and found him in the most violent Epileptic fit I ever saw, he was so driven and beat against the benches, that I thought he would have been killed, his countenance had the most dismal appearance I ever beheld, and he had bit his tongue, till the blood was running out of his mouth. The women were dreadfully frightened, and the men crowded so about him, that it was some time before I could get so much order, as to get him blooded, after a long & severe fit, he began to come to, and immediately called for me begging me to pray for him, which he said was what he wanted to say to me, when he came up, as I left the pulpit, but he could not speak, he begged earnestly to be baptized having never received that ordinance, but as he was not properly in his Senses I declined it, till another opportunity. It was near an hour before I could get away from him, at last got him Sent home in his own chaise, went & Dined with Dr. Cuthberts family, received a letter from the Doctor & Mr. Bowman at Port Royal to the presbytery acquainting them, with what we have done at Beaufort for erecting the Gospel ministry there, and desiring them to appoint me to supply them for the present, the Doctor also mentioned to me, that had received no manner of [81 (152)] Satisfaction from Mrs. Green, that her mother was very much for it, that she pretended not to choose to marry, I told him, that had no intention to talk of that matter at present, but I was persuaded she was inclined to Captain R, & that I wanted to drop it. He owned Captain R still visited there, but had never spoke to him nor her Mother, that they would never consent to it, and begged I would not be in too great a hurry, and that at least I would according to my letter, wait for my final answer till after the Saltcatcher Sacrament, I told him, I should. . . .

Monday May 14:1770 . . . Was very busy getting ready to set out for Charlestown, in order to meet the presbytery according to promise[17] . . . did not get to Mr. Lamberts at the round O till after Dark, exceedingly fatigued. Spent the night comfortably here, was informed Mr. Maltby at Wilton had the Sacrament last Sabbath, heard some things of a stranger young minister, who preached here two Sabbaths of a very Suspicious character, & improper behaviour, had heard of him yesterday from Dr. Cuthbert, he had been at Beaufort last week, but as they were all coming over to the Sacrament, they would not ask him to preach, though they pressed him much to come with them, but he would not, under the pretense of going to Wilton to assist Mr. Maltby, he indeed went there, but neither preached nor partook as a Christian, and on the whole appears to be a very ordinary person. . . .[18]

Tuesday May 15 . . . When got near to Charlestown gate, was stopped by an old acquaintance (Alxr Brns) & desired to visit his wife in childbed, & the child, who seemed to be a dying, stayed about half an hour, & prayed, exhorted the afflicted mother to be resigned to part with her Dear babe, they were exceedingly thankful, & I thought it a little time well spent, rode into town, put up my horses at Mrs. Cliffords, as usual, who informed me there was a Lady from the Country lying in, at her house, so that I could not have the room in which I used generally to sleep, the first night I go to Town, which made me think of looking out for lodgings as Mr. Mitchells family are at present in the country, called on Mrs. Holmes to see Mr. Donnom[19] who stays there, and has been sick, but is better, and was abroad. From thence went down on the bay hoping to see some of the ministers if any came to Town, as was passing along the street Mrs. Prioleau called out of a house to me, where she was visiting, and behaving exceeding kind & affable, this made me resolve to take lodgings at her house, as she continues to take in country Gentlemen as lodgers since Mr. Prioleau died, accordingly got directions from her, where she lives, having lately moved. Was informed at the book sellers shop, that the Reverend Mr. Richardson is in town, but could not tell where to find him, went to Mrs. Prioleaus & engaged my lodging, then went to Mrs. Holmes where supped with Mr. Donnom, found his fears about the presbyterys designs, to be much the Same with my own, as it was late before I went back to my lodgings, Mrs. Prioleau was gone to bed, so that had no opportunity of discoursing with her, was poorly & fatigued, but cheerful & hoping on the Lord my God, my Saviour & Redeemer, my all in all, my everlasting & unchangeable portion.

[82 (154)] *Wednesday May 16* This morning after breakfast Mrs. Prioleau had the Bible brought, & desired prayers as usual in the Country, this was satisfying, as I know her temper is to imitate the polite careless fashions, after breakfast & prayers I had Some conversation with her by herself about what had been told her by my vile lying persecuting Enemy unhappy Mrs. Broadbelt now Ferguson, and her very unfriendly behaviour on it, she acknowledged it, & excused herself, by saying her passions were so agitated at that time, that she knew not what she was doing, & was sorry she had not waited till she saw me herself, that she had been very soon after convinced by discoursing with some indifferent persons, that were present at the conversation, that she had been vilely imposed upon, & Mrs. Ferguson had done it designedly and with some bad views, which could be easily enough guessed at, and upon the whole hoped I would think no more of it, and accordingly I told her I should entirely forget, as I was quite easy since she was convinced of her being abused and imposed on in it. . . .

Friday May 18 1770 This morning got up early and went away without staying to take leave of Mrs. Prioleau. . . . Being very weary & exceeding thirsty called at the tavern at Ashepooh and drank part of a bottle of Northward beer, which found very refreshing, believe I greatly hurt myself, by being too abstemious when I am traveling, It was just dark when got to Godfreys

Savannah [85 (160)] to Mrs. Jackson, who was on the path, knew me & insisted on my coming in, which I did, & drank a little rum & water which found also very refreshing. How good & comfortable Gods creatures are, when used in moderation! How little satisfaction the Glutton & the drunkard have, to the person, who uses Meats & drink in moderation. . . . Had told the wenches that would be home this night, & desired them to have some broath for me, which I am fond of when very much fatigued, but they thought no more of it, so that found all asleep at my lonely habitation, & with difficulty got a light, and near midnight got some tea & my ordinary fare on these occasions, two eggs, had sweet peace & contentment of mind, & with my Servants returned praise & thanks to God for all his mercy, grace & goodness to poor, vile, unworthy me.

Saturday May 19 1770 . . . Late in the afternoon went over to Mr. Donnoms to Drink tea and to see my dear children . . . Was also informed that good old Mrs. Lambright, departed this life on Tuesday night in a most comfortable manner, soon after I left her, she began to talk to all about her of the grace, mercy, love & faithfulness of God to his children & people, of the pleasantness of religions ways, of the happiness of those who have an interest in the Lord Jesus Christ, she often called on her children to seek & to serve the Lord, gave them & all about her many exhortations, was full of peace, of joy & comfort in believing. Continued so all that day & night, often calling them to Sing psalms & hymns, which she pointed out to them, on the Tuesday, notwithstanding the use of the means, she grew evidently weaker & changed for Death, which filled her with great joy, as she had repeatedly expressed her fears, of being brought back to health, & to continue in the world. That day she hardly ever ceased speaking to all about her in the praises of God, of Christ, & religion, which was the more remarkable in her, as she was naturally of a very backward & bashful disposition, very seldom speaking, very timorous & fearful, and rather seemed kept under a Spirit of bondage. She was all her life a very hidden, self denied Christian, and died triumphing & rejoicing in the Lord her God, her Saviour & Redeemer with joy unspeakable & full of glory. She appeared as one in heaven before she got there, she triumphed over all fears of Death, Died without pain, & continued speaking & praising till the very last breath, have not heard of anything like it since my Dear Mrs. Simpson went triumphing to glory. Was greatly pleased to hear it, and was helped to bless & praise God therefore. . . .

Wednesday 23 This morning though still feel very fatigued, rode to Coosawatchy about thirteen miles, to visit & Baptize, Mr. Grimball, the distressed young man [86 (162)] who was so mad with the Epileptic fit at the Indian Land meeting house on Sabbath see night, he was with me last Sabbath at the Saltcatchers, & entreated me to come & visit him at his own house, he was obliged to go away betwext sermons, and in the afternoon had another very bad fit, and expects nothing but to be subject to them, although he is using of some means against so melancholy a disorder. Found him a much more intelligent person, than I expected, remarkably sober, very serious and I hope under such religious impressions as may End in his Eternal happiness. He has for five or Six months been very desirous of religious instruction, & to be baptized, by me, but his wifes relations, put him off, wanting to be baptized, by a minister of the Established church, he had consented to have his only child baptized by a church minister, but would not be baptized himself, unless I refused to do it. Spent all the forenoon with him, and had much more satisfaction than I expected, which made my way clear & easy. After dinner I baptized him in presence of his wife & her Father (old Mr. Roberts) & three relations who attended during the ordinance. Was well helped & assisted, through this solemnity & hope the Lord was with us, poor creature, he was very much affected. In the afternoon I called at Mr. Ddrgs, and sat about an hour, old Mr. Br and his wife being present, afterwards called at Dr. Bowers, & consulted with him about my stomach & breast, which has this day distressed me much and seems to grow worse. He advised to keep myself more cool than have for some time done, to bathe my breast, stomach & the whole chest of my body with artificial Salt water, & as soon as I can bear it, to use a Salt bath for my whole body as am labouring under a general relaxation & advised the use of some balsamicks, afterwards called at Mr. Browns, and had serious conversation with Mr. Brown about good old Mrs. Lambrights death & my baptizing Mr. Grimball, which although I expect to be abused by the Anabaptists, yet I believe will be very generally approved. Called on Mrs. DeSaussure, & had some serious conversation with Mr. DeSaussure himself who I think is under a great & I hope a Saving concern about his salvation, then proceeded home, where did not get till after Dark. Was Satisfied with this days employment, though so poorly in body, that could not be so lively, as wish to be. . . .

[87 (164)] *Lords day May 27 1770* . . . Preached from Philip: 2:12 last clause of the verse taking it in connection with the text from which the action Sermon was preached, our Lords words upon the cross, It is finished, had Gods gracious & comfortable assistance . . . After Sermon baptized a child in the Study house for one Miller, his wife seemed careless & stupid while he was affected & in tears. Consulted with the Doctor, about my own case, and received a balsamic Electuary to take, resolved to continue bathing with Salt water as above. Was spoke to by Mr. Els Roberts,[20] about admitting him to the Sacrament, which surprized me, & will be attended with some difficulty, but desired him to wait upon me next Thursday at my own house. was convinced after I came out from Sermon, by conversing with some, that it is by Special direction, had made choice of this subject. Dined at Mr. DeSaussures, & after Dinner was desired to retire with him where he acquainted me with the Strong work of conviction he has for some time been under, and I would fain hope a real work of grace, and his Desire to be admitted a communicant, at the Ensuing occasion, conversed about half an hour with him, and am persuaded & convinced, the Lord is blessing his word & doing in this place, by the Gospel . . . Sent over for my Dear children to come & stay all night with me, heard them read, Catechized and instructed them, with pleasure & delight. When I was hearing Susy read, I had their Dear Mothers Bible in my hand, and happening to tell her whose Bible it was, I saw it brought tears in her eyes, and after she was done reading, I observed her take it in her hand and often kiss it, and wetting it with tears. Afterwards she wept a good deal, her tenderness affected me, even when I spoke to her not to cry for her Dear mama, but she could not refrain. I was at the Same time, no less affected to see poor Dear Betsy, who knows nothing of a mama, she said, she wondered what made Susy cry at seeing her mama Bible, and that Susy always cried when anybody spoke about her mama. It was a tender and affecting scene to hear them, but poor Susy could not make any answer. This was a pleasant and comfortable evening to my soul. . . .

[88 (166)] *Tuesday May 29 1770* . . . Late in the afternoon went over to Mr. Donnoms, found my neighbour Mrs. F there, heard them have some talk, about moving Saltcatcher schoolhouse more this way and taking the school Master from the Meeting house, to teach there, which will be a great disappointment, to some families on the other side of the Meeting, who joined with Mr. Donnom & me in getting the present school Master, when the Saltcatcher neighbourhood would not join in moving their schoolhouse, and now we can do without them, they are for moving it, and Mr. Donnom is for joining them. This when mentioned to me, I opposed rather too positively, for saw Mrs. F offended. Was sorry I said anything about it, for as my children live at Mr. Donnoms, they must go wherever they send theirs, and I must in this as well as in other things Submit to their humours. The Saltcatcher Neighbourhood have greatly disappointed me, being of a very careless, weak, humoursome turn, as to the Education of their children, careless of their families, & many other concerns. . . .

Wednesday 30 . . . After breakfast set out to visit Mr. Richard Hutson oldest Son of the Reverend & worthy Mr. Hutson, who lives partly in Charlestown, & partly on his plantation about Six miles from this, called in at the School & saw the teacher for the [first] time. I wish, he may continue to answer expectation. After sitting a little, proceeded, found Mr. Hutson at home and Spent most of the day with him. He is about three or four & twenty years of age, a very sober quiet young man, but of no very bright parts, was sent to the Northward College, but would not take Education, not inclined to anything of activity, but as he possesses a great Estate by his Mother, chooses to live upon it, in a quiet easy manner, found him as weak in religion as in most other things, and labouring under many mistakes, yet his religious Education seems to have taken some effect, but his careless indolent temper, makes him indifferent almost to everything. Was concerned to see the Son of so active a Father, so very much the reverse of his disposition, yet it is a great mercy that he is perfectly sober, and not given to vice. Got him to subscribe fourty pounds currency towards paying for the meeting house, for which the Trustees are still in debt, & to engage to take a pew. He is of a kind, friendly disposition but somewhat close, and of a very narrow Contracted way of thinking, for his large fortune, & bringing up. Our conversation was all serious and improving and in the afternoon mostly on religious matters. Shall Endeavour to cultivate an intimacy with him, and if possible be of use to him. . . .

Thursday 31 . . . This forenoon married Adam Wilmer, to Ann Gates both Dutch living up the Saltcatcher, & I believe very poor, but surely the poor have a right to the lawful comforts & enjoyments of life, as well as others. In the afternoon, was visited by Mr. Elias Roberts a young man, from the Indian Land desiring to be admitted a communicant. He has at different times spoke to me, his disadvantages have been great, the family far from being reckoned religious, yet the young people have turned out remarkably well considering the example they have had. He attends very well upon Sermons and appears for some time to be serious and concerned about religion. I have not given him much encouragement, till last Sabbath, he was so pressing with me, that appointed him to come this day. Found him seemingly very serious, and even more knowing than I expected considering his opportunities. He professed his Sorrow & repentance from Sin, his earnest desires after an interest [in] Christ, and to grow in holiness & true religion, I should have wished for more satisfaction Considering what his own practice has been, and the light the family are looked upon in, yet found things so hopeful, and much beyond what I could have expected, that I could not refuse him. Accordingly agreed to receive him, if the church officers Do not make any material objection. . . .

[89 (168)] *Tuesday [June]* 5 . . . Had appointed to go over the river but for some time it rained, and kept me in suspense, at last it cleared off a little, and I set off, but had not gone three miles, till it rained very hard, however proceeded, as there was no thunder, I stopped about half an hour under a tree, with young Mr. Joseph Brlsfrd,[21] his wife, & mother in law who had come down to the river a fishing, & expected more company but were all disappointed by the rain. This young Gentleman, has lately married Miss Elizabeth McPherson, daughter to my good friend Captain John McPherson who died Some years ago. He is settled on a plantation of his own, up Coosawhatchy Swamp, He has always been brought up to the Established church, but has when residing on the Indian Land attended very Constantly at both meetings. After having stopped some time with them I proceeded up the river to old Mrs. McTiers, Mrs. Shaws Mother, where Mrs. Shaw at present lives, her house on her own place, not yet being finished for her to go into though her Negroes are planting there, Dined with Mrs. Shaw & her Sister Mrs. Melvin, their Mother was not at home. . . . Stayed about two hours here, and went over to Mr. John McTiers[22] where [90 (170)] stayed about two hours longer. My business in that and the other visits of this day, was to explain to them the nature of letting pews in the dissenting meeting houses, for the people this having never been used to any such thing, there are some persons Enemies to the Gospel, who have endeavoured to give them very strange notions about our having pews in the Saltcatcher Meeting house, which are now near finished, & are soon to be let. . . . As was riding out, from Mr. Mctiers, was stopped at his school house by Mr. Ptrsn,[23] the young man, who was formerly School to Main when my affair with Miss Cater happened, and who afterwards applied to me, to be admitted as a communicant, which was thought by many to be an extraordinary circumstance, and it was indeed a very extraordinary one, and highly favourable for me, had Some conversation with him, about two particular affairs, of what had been reported about the manner of my admitting him, which he utterly absolutely & with great seriousness denied, and about an oath which he had taken, about the affair betwext Miss Cater & me, he acknowledged his rashness, & great inconsiderateness and offered to make an oath, or make any Satisfaction I pleased, that what he swore to was the very reverse of what had been represented, and spoke with such seriousness, & solemnity, that I could not doubt of him, gave him some advice & directions, comforted & Encouraged him to persevere in well doing. . . .

[91 (172)] *Thursday June 7:1770* . . . Have heard nothing from Mrs. Green, nor do I expect that matter to be determined till after the Sacrament here, but every day hear vague reports of her supposed attachment to Captain R, but I know full well, that there is no regard to be paid to common fame, as it has of late been often & most [positively] reported, that I am just on the point of Marriage with the aimiable & good Mrs. B, for which there never was the Smallest reason, I have these two months or more avoided calling at her house because of this report, as thought it might be a disadvantage to her by keeping others off, who might intend what at present was neither in my power, nor my inclination. Yet instead of lessening the report it has rather increased it, she told me this evening several troubles she has lately met with, and kindly complained of my unkindness in not calling upon her as I used to do because of such groundless idle reports. I made the best answer I could, assured her, it was not for want of respect but I was afraid of being a disadvantage to her, however promised to call as soon as convenient. Was at times much perplexed & uneasy in my mind but kept almost continually offering ejaculatory petitions that might be preserved from right & left hand errors, at this time, and that might be preserved from a circumstance, which has once already cost me very Dear, Dear indeed, the very thoughts fill me with terrour, & makes me tremble. . . .

Friday June 8 . . . Was much urged & talked to, by Mr. & Mrs. Donnom to go & wait on or rather, to renew an offer made, about eight months ago to Mrs. B, which perplexed & disturbed me, as they are entire strangers to my offer to Mrs. Green & indeed so are all the world except her Mother, the

Doctor, and Mr. & Mrs. Bowman, nor was it at all proper, I should inform them, they thought me obstinate, but I could not undeceive them. . . .

Lords day 10 . . . Preached in the forenoon from Eph: 4:27 and had Gods most gracious & comfortable presence . . . The Subject was Somewhat Singular & engaging, So that although we had a good number of young gay people, Strangers, yet they were remarkably attentive. . . . [92 (174)] After Sermon I was obliged, to go & marry a couple who were published in the afternoon (Philip Wilmer & Ann Holmes). It was about two miles out of my way, was much pleased to find, there was no company present, there being only the Mr. & Mrs. of the house, who is Sister to the young woman, & myself. Stayed & Dined with them, and though soon vomited, as usual the most of what I eat, yet found myself refreshed & nourished. . . .

Tuesday June 12 . . . About twelve O Clock was interrupted by Mrs. Windsor, who came to be discoursed with in order to be admitted a Communicant. Discoursed with her accordingly, and had good hopes that there was a real work of grace begun on her soul. She some months ago appeared to have strong convictions, and appears still to be in a very humble gracious way. I agreed to receive her, talked largely with her, gave her the best instructions & advices I was able, & prayed with her, she was much affected & shed many tears, & very reservedly hinted at some of her late troubles. . . . Drank tea with my children & with the School Master at Mr. Donnoms, & alas, already observed, the old Spirit prevailing of slighting & despising the School Master, and that before the children. It gave me great concern, poor old man He is not what I could wish, yet He is too good for some of his Employers, and his treatment is far below what He deserves. It makes me very unhappy with respect to my children, that their lot is cast [93 (176)] where Education is so little prized, am grieved & distressed & know not how to help myself, O that God may guide counsel & direct me. . . .

Tuesday June 19 1770 . . . On Wednesday 13 . . . rode to Mr. Jordans, where Dined, & after Dinner, discoursed with a young woman a relation of his, who at present lives in his family, It would have been my desire to have discoursed with her in private, but he chose to have his Daughter & himself present & have it in the hall. As the young person is a poor relation, & under obligations to him, and as I know his temper, & odd way, I acquiesced, although was not pleased, However was very large & full in my discoursing with her, and never was more assisted on such an occasion in my life, and put the questions in such a way as to be very close to her conscience, & yet to give no advantage against her making a plain & Sincere answer, although in the presence of them who looked upon themselves as her Superiours because her present benefactors, I look upon her as a very sencible, sincere & I hope a truly gracious young person, and far Superiour to Many I have conversed with, yea very much so to them that presumed to sit in Judgment upon her. Yet I could not be so well satisfied as if had been alone with her, was very large & full in my exhortation and directions to her, and had various reasons for being so, agreed to receive very freely & prayed with & for her as usual. Afterwards set off down the parish. . . . Found by some conversation from Mr. Hunt that he believed I was Soon to be married to his Cousin Mrs. B, which I contradicted in the plainest terms, but still saw it was believed. It has given me some uneasiness that he should think so lest the disappointment should give him some bad impressions with respect to me or her. Returned back again & rode to Mrs. B according to promise last week, got there before Sun Set, found her Mother in law, Mrs. Jackson who at present lives with her, Miss P F or the young woman who lives with her, she told me, that had looked for me all this week, stayed here all night, was very free & cheerful with the company present, but carefully avoided being much with her alone, though her company and conversation was as always, exceeding agreeable, took an opportunity, when with her, to ask if she could give me any account of the rise of the report of our going to be married, and of the reasons, why her Cousin Hunt and his family so firmly believed & expected it. She told me, that some things which she had said in jest, she believed had made her Cousin think so, that had explained the matter to his wife, & would take care to do so to himself, at the same time, she sufficiently confirmed what I had no longer any reason to doubt of. I begged her to undeceive her Cousin, lest he should take up any prejudices to my disadvantage, by imagining I had not used her well, or as the common phrase is, had Jilted her, which she knew very well was very far from being the case, which she very readily acknowledged, and assured me, in that case she would do me justice. I also Signified to her, that at present I was not at my own disposal, & did not know if I ever should, but should ever have the most friendly regard and Esteem for her. She professed the same for me, but was melancholy, & I was also under Some considerable concern. I asked her how she explained the matter to her Cousin Mrs. Hunt, she said, that she told her, I

had offered myself to her about seven or eight months ago, that she had refused the offer, that after twice being with her, I had accepted of her refusal
and that although at her request I visited her as I had done before, yet not
at all upon that footing, and that I had faithfully kept my promise, and never
offered myself to her since, and that if I ever did she was fully determined to
____. I heard her with a tender concern, but made no immediate answer,
but Signified to her as above, told her so in plain, but tender terms without
explaining myself, how or on what way I for the present was not at my own
disposal, nor did she ask me. Her behaviour during this delicate and tender
Conversation, was most engaging, every way becoming & worthy of the
Noblest of her Sex, as we were sitting at the door, the rest of the Company
being in the hall, I was so affected that was often obliged to get up, and walk
out in the yard a few turns & come back to her. Her delicate behaviour, en-
deared her more than ever, and had I been entirely free should have immediately put her to the trial. It was to me a trial, I never expected to have been
put to, even after the Information I gave her, she behaved to me the very same
as ever, nor could I through the whole evening observe the smallest alteration from what has always been her behaviour to me, except for two nights
when I courted her, during which time she was more reserved than usual,
but as soon as I assured her I dropped all such thoughts, she resumed a most
free, tender, endearing behaviour, when by ourselves and as much so this
night after the above conversation as ever, only appeared to be very melancholy. I sat up a little with her after the family were retired, but a very short
time, to what used to do, & had a very tender parting. After was got by myself, could not but wonder at the strange providences I meet with, & the surprizing dilemmas I am brought into, as a Single man. I think I may Sincerely
& truly say, without any thought or design of my own, Could I have imagined what I am now very sure of, both her & I might have been very happy
months ago, but I could not have thought of any such thing, till once I was
engaged in waiting on Mrs. Green. Why Mrs. B should have refused what
she seems by some hints to have desired, even at the time the offer was made,
is what I cannot understand. Sometimes I am apt to think it not so much
from a real passion, as for conveniency, or some disappointment she has met
with, at other times I know not how to be so uncharitable. I know that at
this time she has some Gentlemen waiting on her, but gives them no encouragement, nor any of that entertainment, which made her formerly sometimes be reflected on as guilty of Coquetry, and as what has now happened,
I could never have thought of, so not even this, surprizes me more, than

when I was invited & encouraged to wait upon Mrs. Green. As there was
another person sleeping in the Same room with me, I could not go to my
knees, but kept walking about in earnest ejaculatory petitions to God, to
counsel, guide & direct both her & me, to preserve me from suffering from
this strange affair, which I was afraid of producing some evil consequences,
though she is not in the least [94 (178)] to be suspected of being capable of
such resentments as I met with from the unhappy Mrs. Broadbelt now Mrs.
Ferguson whom I never offended, though I never could return her passion,
was in hopes that the Lord who knows my conscience would not suffer
me, to meet with any ill treatment from this affair. . . . On the morning of
Thursday 14 I awaked with a great pain & stiffness in my throat, & difficulty
to swallow, & a violent pain all over my head, which as it increased to a most
dangerous quinsy, I shall speak something more of its rise, About three or
four months ago I was all of the sudden seized with a swelling in my throat
and choaking so that in less than half an hour I was like to strangle, but Mr.
Hamilton being in the plantation, took a large quantity of blood from me,
which relieved me, & afterwards taking a purge, I thought myself quite well,
as felt no more of it, but believe, there must have still been something in
my blood tending to the disorder. On Tuesday last in the forenoon while I
was shaving, the black ribbon I wear Sewed around my throat all winter un-
ripped & there being nobody at hand to sew it again, and the weather being
most excessively hot so that it was disagreeable, & being about the time, I
always take it off, I did so, and at the same time washed my throat with Salt
water, & afterwards with campherated spirits, before I rode, & found no bad
effect that night. Yesterday before I came from home found a stiffness &
soreness in my throat but after washing it with the Spirits it went off, though
I was somewhat uneasy in being obliged to be abroad, so soon after taking
off that ribbon, as have been apt to catch cold at such occasions, this is all
the account I can give, of what brought this disorder so suddenly & violently
upon me, though am convinced & all my friends are, that the Inflammation
must have been long working in my blood. As felt myself much disordered,
was very desirous to get home. . . . When got home betwixt twelve & one O
Clock, felt hungry as had eat very little breakfast, and having nothing dressed,
eat two boiled eggs, as is common with me, when I come home & have
nothing provided, had some difficulty in swallowing but thought I growed
easier, and being very much overcome, and fatigued with the excessive heat,
lay down & fell asleep, but before two O Clock, awaked strangling & in
the most distressing pain, my throat almost closed, my tongue amazingly

Swelled, my pallate swelled down in my very throat. Went & got a glass, to look into my throat, but found it impossible to open my Jaws. I immediately took a double dose of physick, which soon worked both as a vomit and a purge, and that expressly for Several hours, so that thought myself something easier, and wrote about an hour in the evening to conclude the forenoon Sermon, but was Soon obliged to give over, as a violent fever came on and all the distress of my throat & Soreness of the tonsils increased, so that about eight O Clock, I sent to Mr. Donnoms, who came over and took a large quantity of blood from my left arm, my greatest distress and most excruciating pains were in my left ear, and in the left side of my throat. After the bleeding I breathed something easier, had a strong gargle prepared, with which I often washed very low in my throat with a rag on a stick, and gargled with the Anther mouth water, had a preparation of the peruvian bark, and small snake root got, & took largely of that in the substance, and kept frequently Swallowing some liquids though with great pain, Mr. Donnom sat about an hour with me & would have stayed all night, but chose rather to be alone. Saw plainly that had a violent quinsy and sore throat coming, what might very probably end in Death. Endeavoured to be prepared for it, was in a very humble, heavenly resigned frame of soul, could quietly leave my Dear children in the assurance of Gods Fatherly care of them. . . . On Friday 15 Mrs. Donnom came over, when prepared an Emolient of the Spirits of harts horn, sweet oyl & muck and put it under my chin from ear to ear, my throat & whole neck was now very much swelled, kept all day washing, gargling & often Swallowing Something or another, and as was unable to read, to write, or doing any thing of that kind, and one of Mrs. Donnoms children sick obliged her to go home, I laid it on myself as a task to bottle off, and cork a Cask of Lisbon wine, which [95 (180)] with great difficulty, and amidst the most distressing pains I performed, my resolution and fortitude was often ready to fail me, especially when I began to chew the Corks, which having been boiled, & standing by me in hot water, I imagined would be of service to me, by keeping my Jaws moving, and believe it really was. It was with great pain & difficulty I could thrust my little finger at first, between my teeth and yet by repeated efforts, I forced & obliged myself to go through this very painful & difficult, so that bottled off & corked in the [lightest] manner ten dozen of bottles of wine and never in all my life, had my resolution, and fortitude put to a greater trial, at the last the fever came on, had another visit from Mr. & Mrs. Donnom, who stayed with me, till the evening, at which time, my fever had abated a little. Mrs. Donnom did me several

Services by rubbing & chasing the Emollient into my throat, and pinning cloths about my head & neck, but her own indisposition obliged her to go home . . . through the greatest part of this night, I was much out of my head, when ever, I began to dose, I waked starting, & much terrified, so that for some time could not know, where I was, towards [morning] the fever abated, as could not keep in bed got up very early on Saturday & sent off for the Doctor, who was not at home, but the boy followed him, & brought him in the afternoon, when my disorder was most dreadfully increased, he with difficulty, got looking into my throat, where were two large ulcers one on the left side, one on the pallate & another forming on the right side, all very deep in the throat about the remotest part of the tongue, he approved of all that been done, & though looked on my case as yet would try his Endeavour & exhorted me to resolution & perseverance, had all this day kept using the Same means much as yesterday, only added the use of camphere, & receiving the steam of hot vinegar, through a funnel into my throat, My friends now began to gather about me, and both men [&] women were in the utmost concern, lamenting & bewailing the destitute condition they would be left for the Gospel & at the same time expressing the most tender Sympathy with me, at seeing me in such inexpressible distress. I could now on Saturday afternoon hardly been understood when I spoke, & with the utmost pain & difficulty forced out a Single word at time, yet was in a most joyful frame of soul, at the near prospect of Entering into Eternal glory, Endeavoured what I could to comfort & compose them, assured them of the comforts which overflowed in my soul, and that yet I was very willing to live & labour in the Gospel, and that although Death to me would be the greatest gain, yet I would use every mean & medicine & exert myself with the utmost resolution, while my strength & senses remained, told them not to be surprized if I died very hard for I expected to die, either of hunger, or in strong fits, which I told them, would I believe soon be the case, for now the pain of swallowing was so great, that every time I attempted to swallow my spittle or any thing else, it shook my whole frame, affected my nerves and evidently convulsed me, told them that no doubt the wicked & my Enemies might think & call it a Judgment like Death, but I was as willing to Die in that manner if God required, as ever I had been to serve him in my life, all were in tears. I told them that I freely forgave all my Enemies, that I had never in thought word nor deed been guilty of what they laid to my charge, that I adhered to the answers & account of these matters which I had written and could alter nothing, and that so innocent was I of all their vile charges, that

I had never yet seen any one thing, for which I had to ask forgiveness from the Searcher of hearts before whose awful tribunal I expected in a few hours to appear, in all that affair of Main, & Mrs. Broadbelt that was now Ferguson concerning her and Miss Mary Cater that was, now Mrs. Dupont. Was seized with a shivering & chilly fit & afterwards with great burning heat, my whole throat & neck was swelled & puffed up, my face was much swelled & inflamed with a high red colour, my whole head was swelled, my anguish and torment was inexpressible, my strength failed me much, my looks were much altered, my eyes looked dead & heavy & sometimes wildish, yet my soul was full of peace, quietness, heavenly comforts & joy in the Holy Ghost. In this condition I was when my good friend Mr. James Donnom came, his astonishment & grief was unspeakable nor was he able to conceal, I thanked him for all his kindness, recommended my Dear children to him, begged him to look to God for another Minister, but he was inconsolable and lamented poor Saltcatcher & Indian Land as broken & ruined, as I intreated him to be resigned, & to go immediately & draw up my will, & gave him directions for the same, my Dear children were brought to me, about Six this Evening, I had desired to have them with me yesterday & often this day called to have them sent for, but my friends had purposely kept them out of my sight, lest it should hurt me, but now at last they were brought, I cannot describe my feelings, when I saw them, I could not weep but my heart was ready to burst, my bowels [glared] & yearned over them, I tenderly pressed them [to my] distressed breast, & yet was afraid to kiss them their Dear lips lest my distemper should have become infectious. They wept & cried bitterly. I retired with them, prayed over & blessed them as well as I could, gave them some advices as to love God & Christ, to pray, to read their books, to be good children, to love the Gentleman that would take care of them, all of which they promised with sobs & cries, I then brought them back to the company, & desired them [96 (182)] to be carried home to Mr. Donnoms, they begged me to send for them, in the morning, which I promised, & they went away in tears. About Dark, the Medicines came, which was much the same I had been using. I set to and forced myself, though with the most excruciating pain, to take them. Retired with my friend Mr. James Donnom & acquainted him of the affair betwixt Mrs. Green & me, & how he should act, if he ever heard it talked of. Repeated also to him what I had before said of the affair betwixt my Enemies above mentioned & me, continued hourly taking the Medicines, & almost constantly gargling washing or attempting to swallow some liquid or another, which was resolved to do as long as possible, even if

there no reason to have any hopes of success, which yet neither my friends
nor I had given entirely over, as it was possible my distemper was hastening
to a Crisis & would soon take a favourable turn, which was really the case,
though this afternoon and evening it seemed a hoping against hope. The
unexpressible agony, anguish & torment I was in kept the Sweat continually
pouring off me, was also in a Constant motion, almost walking, about ten
at night, I remembered it was the time to wind up the Clock, I went & did
it, and turned round & said with great difficulty I believe I am now near
done with all time things, I expect my Eternity, a glorious Eternity will begin,
& before this clock needs again to be wound up, I expect to be putrifying in
my grave, Continued without any sensible ease, till about Eleven O Clock
at night, when being quite spent, I with great pain, & inexpressible torment
got a tumbler of warm wine & water Swallowed down after had been taking
some of the Medicines, I found immediate relief, by my pallate turning up
& something broke in my throat. I was at first confused & amazed like one
that dreamed, my Overseer[24] & Mr. James Donnom were sitting by me, he
looked very attentive on me and imagining by my looks & motions there
was something extraordinary the matter with me, imagined by my breath-
ing easier, that I was relieved. I desired him to go to prayer, which he did,
and made an excellent prayer in which he showed his great Concern for this
poor Congregation, I felt more & more easy, and could join very distinctly
with the prayer, whenever we got up, I told him I was relieved, & felt surprizingly easy, and desired to go to bed, he persuaded me to sit up about an
hour longer & to keep stirring about, in which time, he was more confirmed
of the Lords goodness to him & to me. I went to bed betwixt twelve & one
O Clock, but did not sleep till near the morning, had a slight fever, was in
a humble thankful frame, blessing & praising the Lord for his mercy &
goodness to a poor unworthy creature . . . This morning Tuesday 19 my good
friend Mr. James Donnom went away very early, having taken leave of me
last night, and stayed constantly with me since Saturday Evening. . . .

Thursday 21 . . . [97 (184)] Was so weak & poorly, and the day showery, that
was almost afraid to go out, yet duty required it. Found the people very
hearty, in Subscribing to raise rights for the choice of pews, I discoursed
about a quarter of an hour and more, & prayed, in which was well assisted
& enlarged. As there was not near pews enough, and a good many worthy
friends and well wishers to the Interest were obliged to go without pews, it
was immediately concluded to Enlarge the house by another addition, and

about nine hundred pounds was subscribed for that and other purposes, there was the greatest peace, harmony, and unanimity, everything was carried on truly becoming the Gospel. It was a most pleasant & comfortable sight, to see no strife, but who would give most for the advancement of the Gospel. A large number of Trustees were chosen and agreed to act, all were greatly pleased, and much affected to see so happy an alteration, wrought in this wilderness in a few years, that where a Sermon had never been preached, and Gospel ordinances never seen, there is now a flocking to the Gospel, which shines here, as a light in a dark place, as a light set up on a hill, and I hope, there is not only a flocking to Sermons & ordinances, but a flying to the Lord Jesus, and that numbers of poor souls are receiving Eternal Salvation . . . My short & severe illness seems to have had this good effect on the people in general, that being alarmed at the prospect of losing the Gospel, they have been very liberal in doing all they can to have it secured & provided for, hitherto indeed I have received very little from this Congregation, which now distresses, and straitens me much, but it is to be hoped, that after this that part of my Salary, which comes from this Side, will be better paid. Unhappy Mrs. Broadbelt now Ferguson was present all the time, she had taken a great deal of pains to set the people against taking pews, which she knew would oblige them to contribute to the Support of the Gospel, and set out this morning to go to Mr. David Fergusons to persuade him against it, but being too late, she went to meeting where both he & his wife her last husbands Sister were, and this Mortification to see him amongst the highest subscribers for a right, received as a Trustee, and act accordingly and also of being witness to the whole transaction, which raised her Spite, malice & madness to the greatest degree, so that she employed her tongue constantly against me, against the Gentlemen, who had been the chief encouragers of the Gospel here & getting the pews built, telling the people, they were flattered in order to have their pockets picked, that they were abused, imposed upon & deceived, only to enrich me & some others, and kept calling me everything that was bad, thus lest I should have been exalted above measure, she as a Messenger of Satan came to buffet me, poor wretched creature, she made no impression, but was more hated & despised than ever, It is Surprizing that she will not stay away, but attends very constantly at both meetings, she perpetually abuses me, and still attends on my Ministry. . . .

[98 (186)] *Lords day 24* A very Damp Cloudy Drisling morning, was assisted in Secret duties, had a Sabbaths frame of soul. . . . Got to meeting without getting wet, and found a good Congregation much larger than I expected, about ten O Clock the whole heavens were overcast with the thickest Darkest clouds, and it began to thunder & lighten in a very awful manner, and poured Down the heaviest rain. As the people were all shut up in the meeting house, and no more could be expected, I began earlier than usual, acquainting the people that if they would endeavour to be composed & easy in their minds, that as soon as it cleared up, I would dismiss the Congregation, and give them an opportunity of returning home, without being exposed to such weather. Put them also in mind that we were engaged in the worship & service of a gracious & merciful God, and had good reason to hope for his presence & protection, notwithstanding the violence of the storm, & the threatening Elements. Begun with prayer as usual, in which Enlarged more than common, and was well assisted, then Sung the 29 psalm Watts version long meter, entitled, Storm and Thunder,[25] afterwards prayed again, with fervency & melting affections, then Sung the 116 psalm, common meter second part, with a particular view to my recovery from my late illness, then preached from Mark 13:33 with great fullness, freedom & enlargement. . . . The rain continued till betwixt one & two O Clock, at which time I dismissed the Congregation, the Mother of the young man who was lately killed with thunder, married & buried in eight days, was in the meeting, and the violent storm of thunder & rain, my encouraging the people & praying for protection, and also preaching of the Shortness & uncertainty of life, of sudden Deaths, made it a very affecting time to her, and his pious Sister, the Sight of the old Lady, together with the subject and circumstances of the time, made it really moving & affecting to the most who were present. . . .

Monday June 25 . . . After breakfast sent my horses round by the ferry, and was put over myself in a Canoe to the other Side, where met the horses, and proceeded on my way to Beaufort, my chief business there, is to be determined in my affair with Mrs. Green. It is now two months since she had my letter, and this is the week on which I was to wait on her. Am Sufficiently convinced that at present her mind is towards Captain R, and as it is very disagreeable to be waiting on a person, whose heart is otherways engaged, I have longed much for this day to come, that might be off from such a disagreeable employ. Had I known anything of the affair betwixt Captain R & her, I never would have been persuaded to paid any addresses to her, and Since I have been informed of it, I have been anxious to come genteely off, as I cannot bear to be made a tool of, and should be very unhappy did she consent to have me, only to please her parents & friends. I am very confident she will continue her refusal & return me my letter this night, in which case I shall say nothing to her of pleasing herself nor give the least hint of Captain R, but if she contrary to my expectation should declare her acceptance of me, I shall be much distressed lest, it should only be to please her relations, & shall think myself obliged to put it to her if it is her real choice, got to Doctor Cuthberts at Beaufort about ten O Clock . . . he told me that Captain R, was gone off, to the West Indies, but was to be in Soon again, that he & his wife, had assured Mrs. Green, of their most absolute displeasure, if ever she married that Gentleman and that she gave them no Satisfaction, one way or another. I assured him of my resolution to be Determined this evening, but made no complaints of my being ill used in only being called in to prevent her throwing herself away on a person no ways deserving of her, nor to be my Rival . . . [99 (188)] As soon as prayers were over, Mrs. Green & I was left alone, she at first behaved very silent to any questions I put to her but at last, told me she could not accept of my offer, but would give no reasons, nor was I very pressing to know them. As have good reason to believe it is nothing else than a predelection or favour of the above Gentleman, I told her I expected for many good reasons especially her at first approving among her friends, or at least consenting to my waiting on her, but that received her refusal, & desired her to return me the letter I had sent her, which she promised to do, & afterwards Sent it to my room. We were near three hours together, from Eleven till near two, & parted in a most friendly and affectionate manner. I would have thought myself exceedingly happy to have been husband to Mrs. Green had she in her heart & affections really chosen & preferred me, but as matters were situated, I rejoiced to be off, and trembled at the thoughts of her giving her consent to please her friends, without the approbation of her heart, which would have made me completely wretched, I did not give her the most distant hint of what I knew. After I retired to my room, could not but look back on this providence with Surprize & amazement, that I should be drawn into this courtship, which I neither desired, nor thought of, and that I should again be talked of, & for no other purpose on my side that I can yet see into, than to divert me for about three months from courting anywhere else, and to prevent my being in a capacity of receiving the offers & advances lately made me, what End providence may serve with respect to Mrs. Green I know not, but to me it appears a very strange providence. I doubt not but God has infinitely wise & good purposes to serve by it, though at present I cannot comprehend the use or End thereof. It put me in mind of the conduct of providence towards me, in the purchase of land, many places seemed just cast in my way to raise my expectations & give me the Sight of them, and were presently removed, and yet at last, God did better for me than ever I could have wished or expected, and incomparably more so than all the advantageous purchases that had so often appeared to be laid in my way before, & may be the Lord may do so, with respect to marriage if I ever am to Enter into that state. It also put me in mind of the Lords dealing with me, about going from Indian Land & off the province, Several advantageous offers presented themselves to me, both in this & other provinces, & some of them in a very remarkable manner, & yet all of them, as soon as expected & as it were embraced in design, were immediately removed, so that I was often as my Dear wife was, amazed & surprized to think why unsought for, they were put in my way, as it were only to raise & disappoint my expectations, and now I have for these four years been made to see, that my not removing was the best thing ever happened to me, and that my staying has been in great mercy to myself & to many others. I this night viewed the now concluded Surprizing providence in the Same light, and was fully Satisfied, that all these strange providences about marriage will End in the same way, unspeakably more for my advantage, than if any of the former designs had taken place. . . .

Tuesday June 26 1770 . . . About Six O Clock went downstairs, when the Doctor soon came & asked how it went last night, he seemed not much surprized at informing him of the refusal, but after asking if my letter was returned & if I had taken my final Denial, he was much concerned, for I found neither He nor Mrs. Cuthbert expected, that I would have determined the matter, the Doctor retired & acquainted his wife who was greatly concerned & grieved, and all the time at breakfast, & while I stayed she appeared to be exceedingly troubled. Mrs. Green observed, & was also in great Confusion, saw when she looked at her Mother the tears often started in her eyes, I was the most free, easy & composed among them. Was in a most heavenly cheerful frame of soul. . . . Stayed till about eight O Clock & took a very affectionate leave, assuring them I would continue as much concerned for the Success of the Gospel in Beaufort as if I had had the greatest success. . . .

[100 (190)] *Wednesday June 27* . . . Rode over to the Indian Land, about five miles, to visit Mrs. Threadcraft, Miss B Wilkins, that was,[26] she was last

Friday delivered of a dead child, to the great danger of her life, was prayed for on Sabbath as still very low, found her in a very distressed condition, had suffered greatly from the ignorance & unskillfulness of the person who was with her as Midwife, found her melancholy & dejected. Spent several hours here, was assisted both in conversing & praying with her. . . .

[101 (192)] *Monday Jully 2:1770* . . . The thoughts of Sickness & indisposition distresses me on account of my lonely condition. Some of my most intimate friends make use of it as an argument to be more in earnest about marrying than ever I have been, & I acknowledge it is of some weight with me, for perhaps a kind & tender wife is never more necessary for any person, than in the decline of life, and though not come near to that age which might be called the decline of life, yet from my tenderness in childhood & youth and from my excessive labours, for these Seventeen years I have reason to expect an early old age, and it may already be begun, and in such a case, a pious, prudent, discreet, kind, affectionate wife would be a great comfort. But, on the other hand, may not increasing infirmities, and an early old age bring on an early Death, and should not the apprehensions of such a circumstance make me lay off all thoughts of marriage, even though I should be sure, of success & happiness? After breakfast, as I have the greatest ease & freedom from the pain in my back, when I am on horseback, Mr. Donnom[27] insisted on my riding with him, over to the plantation, and into the fields which he is going to look over, this employed us about two hours with his giving orders & directions about the affairs of the plantation, found the Crop much hurted by the great rains so that a good part of it is a likely to be lost. This is the Condition of most planters through the whole province. . . .

Tuesday 3 . . . After an early Dinner, set out to go up the river on the Indian Land Side. Called at old Mrs. Mctiers and sat about an hour with Mrs. Melvin, her Mother is still among her relations Down the Country, and Mrs. Shaw was gone to her plantation. Afterwards sat about half an hour at Mr. John McTiers, had some very serious conversation with his wife he being abroad. . . . Proceeded some miles further up, to Mr. E J, he & his wife were rode over to Mr. J R's lately married to Mrs. J sister.[28] I went there, & drank tea with them altogether, then returned back to Mr. Jaudons, my visit being chiefly to him, and on his account, who has for some time been in a very extraordinary condition, being I am afraid much under the power of Satan, but cannot at present write his very extraordinary case, During his first wifes time, who was a most excellent Christian, he turned very sober & serious so that most Christians thought him in a very promising way, and I had great hopes of his [being] a useful Christian. After her Death and during his widowhood, he turned very loose, and took up much with bad Company, and gave up himself much to drink which was a great affliction to me and all his friends but still he had great convictions, & often set about reforming and at last seemed entirely to quit excess in Drink & bad Company, and before his late marriage, lived to all appearance very soberly, though it was thought at first to be rather a political than a religious reformation, his health & his Character making it necessary, as for his worldly interest providence continued Surprizingly without any care or conduct of his, to increase it. In the first week of his marriage, he was siezed with the most unaccountable Jealousy I ever heard of, so that for some weeks though he never tasted liquor, he seemed in a frensy, I had visited him, but knew nothing of it, and after I heard of it, I thought it best to deal with some of his relations, but not to appear forward in making inquiry into so delicate, a matter. Of late I have had several letters from him intreating me to visit him at his own house, & also Some [102 (194)] conversation with him, at both meeting houses, from which he absented himself for some Sabbaths, by these conversations I found the distress of his mind, was all turned into a religious concern, this night had a great deal of conversation with him, but not so much to my Satisfaction as I could have wished, he appears to be under great Concern about religion, but I think, not yet in so right a way, as he ought to be. He has in a great measure thrown up the care of his worldly affairs & really neglects them, the Sin & danger of which I took great pains to convince him of. He is almost continually employed in religious exercises & often very improperly, which I endeavoured to let him [know] Satan himself might drive him to. He is persuaded that he was formerly converted, but has fallen from grace, I laboured to convince of his mistake, & that I was fully persuaded, he never has been in a converted state, He is a strange mixture of spiritual pride & a sort of bastard humility, of vain confidence & deep despair, talks much of impressions, sometimes of raptures, of former communion with God, of answers of prayer, & also of his great and unthought of wickedness. He appears still to be full of himself & very self righteous, yet I hope God, who brings good out of evil, & order out of confusion may yet make it End well. I took great pains with him, and all present, in opening up the nature of a true work of grace, the dupes & wiles of Satan, and his many [ways] of deluding & deceiving souls as an angel of light, was well assisted in discoursing for hours together, and enabled to deal very faithfully & yet most tenderly with him. At family prayer, I read and expounded the 2nd chapter of the Ephesians, was well assisted in prayer, he was much in tears, & so was another present. I hope this may prove a good evenings work. I this afternoon as riding up here met Mr. P R and had about an hours conversation with him, greatly to my comfort & satisfaction, and am fully convinced that there is something very extraordinary in the work I hope of grace, that has for several months been in the family of old Mr. R, which used to be looked on in the very worst light.[29] I think, if ever there was a great & a real work of grace on any person, it is on Peter Roberts. I never heard a more satisfying account given of a work of Conviction, and I hope of Conversion in all my life, he told me also of his younger Brother Elias speaking to his parents, putting them in mind of the wicked life the whole family had lived, which brought them to tears, and of his proposing to have family worship set up, which was done accordingly, and is kept up very regularly, the old Gentleman since the Sacrament in May last attends very constantly, & is often in tears, Peter I hope is really brought to Jesus Christ. Elias another Son I have great & good hopes of also. John Roberts another son has long had many convictions, but at present seems to have but little if any religious impressions. Mr. Grimball the Son in law whom I lately Baptized has set up family religion, and have great reason to think well of him, Peters wife sister to Mr. Grimball is under great convictions & in a very hopeful way. Almost everyone in the family seems deeply affected, I hope by the Spirit of God, O how comforting, & encouraging is it to see the Gospel blessed & have success. . . .

Wednesday Jully 4 1770 This morning in a humble Spiritual, thankful frame of soul, earnestly desirous to be useful to this family. Got up early and renewed the conversation again with Mr. Jaudon, found him something more teachable, humble, & evangelical, after breakfast, I desired him to walk out by ourselves, and had about an hours conversation, concerning the affair between him and his wife. He was not very free. Justified himself more than he ought, yet declared, he now believed her innocent, but her behaviour was very foolish, as he thought, & I believe she was to blame. This conversation was of so delicate a nature, that cannot narrate it. Upon the whole he seemed in a more calm, composed frame of mind when I came here, and he often declared his great satisfaction from this visit. Gave him the most suitable directions I could think, both with respect to himself and his conduct in his family. Afterwards discoursed with Elias Roberts who is here, found he is meeting with some discouragements from self righteous professors of religion, and with great temptations from Satan. Endeavoured to direct, to strengthen, & encourage him. Afterwards called on Mr. John Roberts, & desired him to ride with me, which he did for about an hour, during which time I discoursed very closely to him, about the state of his soul, the many convictions which he formerly had, and now when the grace of God, seemed to come into his Fathers family in a very remarkable manner, he was to appearance, the most backward in the family. He acknowledged it, made some excuses, and told me his resolutions. I exhorted him to set up family worship, and gave some directions, he was very serious. Hope the Lord is not passing him by. One thing I observed with great concern, that both he & Mr. Jaudon have in their marriages met with nothing to help them in religion, but rather a great hindrance. The two women seem to have no knowledge of it, no love to it, but the greatest dislike, & seem to sneer at the very mentioning of it. Mrs. Jaudon is I think the most Simple Sort of woman I ever knew, Simple very Simple, and I think in prudent hands would be of a very pliable disposition, and easily brought to conform to all the outward forms of religion. Mrs. Roberts appears to be much more sharp, & of stronger natural parts, but not so good natured & very obstinate. I think both their husbands are much more the objects of pity than Envy, and are both unhappy though on different accounts. Proceeded some miles by myself, blessing the Lord, and praying for these persons I have been with. . . .

[103 (196)] *Lords day 8* The weather still exceeding wet & rainy, yet got over to Indian Land without being much exposed. Was in a humble, Spiritual frame of soul. . . . Preached from Mark 13:33 . . . there was great seriousness & attention among the hearers, the Word of God, was very suitable to the present aspect of providence, for as have had a very rainy Season, there is much reason to expect, great & general Sickness and already it is begun, both among whites & blacks, almost all the Congregation looked very poorly & everybody Complaining, the heat was excessive, the whole auditory seemed to faint & succumb under it, as preached long, giving only one Sermon, was very much fatigued. Sweated most excessively, was very Sick before concluded the last prayer, and in the time of the last psalms heaved up much bile in the pulpit but it was a good, & comfortable Season to my soul, pleasant to see Something of the Divine power attending his word. Called at Mr. DeSaussures & took some refreshment, afterwards conversed with a Negro fellow belonging to Dr. Cuthbert who seems to be under some real exercise of soul, about his Eternal Salvation. Satan seems also very busy with him, he is an African & has not been many years in the Country, the work seems very mechanical, yet from what I have learned & known among these poor Africans, I have good hopes that it is a real work of the Holy Ghost. It is pleasant work to be dealing with souls whether of freemen or slaves, methinks there is a peculiar pleasure, in seeing these poor Africans, stretching out their hands to the Lord Jesus Christ. . . .

Monday July 9 . . . [104 (198)] In the afternoon I went over to Mr. Donnoms, where spent about an hour talking to poor Joe D,³⁰ in the closest & most serious manner I could, giving him, the best & most necessary advices I could think of, and then rode up to his Father with him, having before prepared the way for carrying back this very wicked prodigal youth, who having left the ship to which he was bound has been wandering about, living the most wicked prophane life that can be imagined, and although now driven back to his distressed Father through want, necessity, and the great hardships he has exposed himself to, yet seems noways reformed. The good worthy Father was much affected with the Sight of his prodigal before him on his knees, and having spoke suitably to him, he told him, that he took another trial of him, & exhorted him to humble himself before God, and to implore his mercy, grace & pardon. Colonel Glover,³¹ a friend of Mr. Donnom was present & joined me in this good work. . . .

Tuesday July 10 1770 . . . As have lately heard from some of my good friends much of Mrs. B's attachment & regard etc., and knowing I must have some conversation with her cousin Mr. Hunt to explain matters to him, lest he should take any prejudice, which might be hurtful to the cause of religion in this place, He being one of the first note, and having a real regard for Mrs. B, as a very aimiable & worthy person, a very remarkable instance of the Success of the Gospel in this place, I thought, it might be proper to have some further conversation with her before I spoke to Mr. Hunt, and as have many reasons, to alter my state, & being persuaded that can never do it, with a person more agreeable & more deserving than her, though her circumstances far from affluent, I judged that by conversing again with her, I could know whether or not it would be proper to let her know, I would renew my offer, if according to her own declaration, she would accept of it, without further ceremony, yesterday I wrote her a few lines in a free manner, letting her know I wanted as Soon as the Sacrament was over, to have some serious

conversation with her about old affairs, this day I received a very Sensible
free letter, yet mixed with Some things, that I could not avoid waiting upon
her Sooner than I intended. Accordingly Set out a little before Sun set, &
rode hard so that got there about dark, found her brother Mr. Joseph Hunt,
with her, & her Cousin Mrs. H, was received, with the utmost ease & affa-
bility, & in the kindest manner. Spent the evening altogether, in useful improving conversation. After Supper & prayers, when the rest retired, we sat
up together till about two O Clock, our conversation together was tender &
affectionate, she acknowledged her former declaration, when I was last here,
& her willingness to stand to it, but desired me to postpone a more particular & solemn engagement till after the Sacrament, when I asked why she
refused me formerly when I offered myself, she answered, she hardly thought
me in earnest, had no particular intention to marry & did not imagine I
would have been so easily denied, that her refusals were only according to
form, and that she could not do less than what she did, that since that time
she had heard I was waiting on others & did not expect I would have ever
returned to her, that she was now fully Satisfied of my being in good earnest,
and had she known so much of my conduct in these matters at first, that
it might have been otherwise, but still she desired that there should be no
solemn engagements till after the Ordinance, as she wanted to give me a full
account of the circumstances of her & her childs Estate, which she was
desirous to do in writting (of which she is very capable) & that afterwards I
might proceed or not as I pleased, that she would then grant me, whatever
I would ask, that she did not intend to make any conditions, but leave everything to her Cousin Hunt & myself, for she was very willing to trust herself,
her child & all they had entirely in my hands, she then told me of her affairs
in general, which I found to be much better, than common report has represented, and in many things opened her mind very freely to me, which I received in the most respectful manner, and endeavoured to make her Sensible
of the Sense I had of her goodness, & of the Esteem I had for her, all this &
much more to the same purpose, passed, in the most cool & rational conversation, affectionate & tender, without any passionate [feelings] on either
side, and according to her repeated request we parted without any positive
conclusion till after the Solemnity is over as to her estate, but as to her person repeatedly engaged to be positively mine which she often declared. . . .[32]

[105 (200)] *Thursday Jully 12* . . . In the forenoon Mr. Peter Roberts from the
Indian Land came to be admitted a communicant, He stayed about four

hours with me, & had very great Satisfaction in conversing with and in admitting him. I think the work of the Holy Ghost upon him, is the most plain, clear, deep, full, solid and Evangelical I have almost ever met with. It appears to be a great work indeed. He gave me some very particular accounts. It was in the time of the last action Sermon at Indian Land, that he was entirely brought out of himself into the Lord Jesus Christ, he told me of the Lords work at much the same time on his Father & mother, his younger brother, & his own wife, he gave me some discouraging accounts of his brother in law Mr. Grimball, the Anabaptists among whom Grimball was brought up, are doing all they can to draw him not only from the baptism I administered to him, but from every serious concern under my ministry, seeming as if, they would rather, he should have no religion at all, than not have it among them, O they are both ministers & people an unknown set of people. I instructed, examined, exhorted, charged, directed & prayed with him as usual, and hope he will be my crown of rejoicing in the day of the Lord. . . .

Friday 13 A good and comfortable morning. Was just proceeding to preparatory duties after prayer & wrestling with God when was informed by a Messenger that James Donnom Esquire & Colonel Glover were coming to spend the forenoon with me, I could have been glad to had the day to myself as wanted to spend the afternoon in writting the preparation Sermon, but Mr. Donnom being my special friend, & the Colonel being his friend, a very worthy Gentleman of great Credit & fortune, I could not avoid it, they accordingly came & stayed all the forenoon with me, which was spent in useful improving Conversation. The Colonel was much pleased with my Situation and Circumstances, & is very capable of being friendly & useful both to me & to my Dear children. With this view Mr. Donnom brought him, that I might get acquainted with him. We went all over to Mr. Jonathan Donnoms & Dined together, after Dinner, we came back to my house, walked over to my plantation, where the Colonels horses & chair met him, & he proceeded homewards, to Ponpon where he lives. . . .

Saturday 14 This has been a good & comfortable day to my soul. . . . Was at times much concerned about the weather, as there is every day, most constant heavy rains so that the whole Earth is socked in water, the Crops greatly hurted, the roads almost impassable and the river up, this evening there was the heaviest rain I think has been this Summer, was very earnest with God in pleading for fair & favourable tomorrow, on Thursday and the Communion Sabbath. . . . This evening I was informed that poor Miss Cater that was now Mrs. Dupont, is lying in of her first child at Mains, has been exceedingly bad, and now no life is expected for her, this gave me the greatest concern on her account, revived all my tenderness for her, and notwithstanding her base vile usage to me, and all the evils she endeavoured to bring upon me, or rather suffered herself to be made the tool & instrument of doing, yet my soul bled for her, went directly to solemn prayer on her account, pleaded earnestly, for her life, wrestled with God for pardon & forgiveness to her, and for her [106 (202)] Eternal salvation, humbly begged & intreated the Lord to open her eyes, to enlighten her conscience, to sprinkle her with the blood of Jesus Christ, that she might not die with a lie in her right hand but might give glory to God & honour to his holy name, which she had caused, to be so evil spoken, so blasphemed & abused, cried fervently to the Lord, cried & made supplication on her account, and found it a good time to my own soul. . . .

Lords day Jully 15:1770 This morning very wet & rainy. Was concerned for the people, it grows very Sickly, and is discouraging to attend amidst such weather . . . found a Surprizingly good Congregation, It is pleasant to see people so eager after the word of God, preached both parts of the day from 1 Corinth: 11:27:28:29:30 with great enlargement, fullness, freedom & affection . . .was on the verse showing what it is to receive the Lords supper unworthily, or when Christians may be said to do so, 2ly the greatness of the Sin of unworthy communicating as here expressed by the apostle, such are guilty of the body & blood of the Lord. In afternoon was shewing the great danger, that attends, or the dreadful punishment of unworthy communicating, such cast & bring Damnation or Judgment to themselves, and then, what improvement all Christians should make of the sin & danger of receiving this ordinance in a rash, ignorant, careless, prophane or hypocritical manner, even to make the most careful & diligent preparation for it, that they may partake thereof, in a humble, suitable, becoming manner, to their benefit & comfort. . . . Between sermons received a letter from good worthy Mr. Potter, who is successfully proclaiming the Gospel of peace, was very much fatigued, yet had to ride about two miles out of my way to marry a Couple whom I had published at the dismission of the Congregation, I published them out at once as I usually do, when I am well acquainted with the parties, and I kept it back to the very last dismission, because of the Surprize it gave people, and the occasion it afforded them to talk idly. It was the same young woman whom I married the third day of May last, whose husband was killed with thunder & whom I buried on the 10 of May, and this afternoon the 16th of Jully I married her again, such things are shocking & shameful. . . .

Monday 16 . . . All the morning & early part of the day was very busy with the Trustees of Saltcatcher settling accounts about my salary & the meeting house, afterwards with much satisfaction admitted Mr. Cully the blacksmith, whose pious wife, was admitted & buried last summer. He was bred an Irish papist & is publickly to renounce the Romish religion & be received a member of the Protestant church on Thursday and then into communion with us, God willing on Sabbath, I hope to have much comfort in him. . . . Betwixt Eleven & twelve at night I was writting in my Diary what had been my exercise on Saturday night for poor Mrs. Dupont, I received a letter from a friend on the Indian Land desiring me to attend the funeral of a relations child tomorrow, and acquainting me that last night, she sat up with poor Mrs. Dupont, whom she accounts, is in the most melancholy condition with a most violent Histerical disorder, and it is thought cannot possibly live out this night, this, with the melancholy peculiarity of her distracted Condition, gave me most inexpressible concern, had just been at prayer for her, if in the land of the living, as I did not then know. Afterwards went again to prayer for her and was earnest with God for her salvation if still in time, but my apprehension of her Death, much amazed me. . . .

Tuesday Jully 17 . . . [107 (204)] At the Indian Land was informed that poor Mrs. Dupont died last night, about half an hour after Eleven, much about the time I was on my knees for her, I have not time at present to write the particulars I heard from a good hand of her most melancholy Death, but it was the most melancholy I ever heard, she had many fits, was for several days in the most raving distracted condition, full of terrour, and in the most fearful despair, and died so, but I shall be more particular after the Sacrament. . . . Was much affected with the dismal End that poor Dear Mary Cater made & yet I hope & believe she has got her soul for a prey, that the Lord thus chastened her, that she might not be condemned, she never declared what put her into such despair & horrour, indeed she had little opportunity to do it, being almost constantly in fits & in the most distracted raving madness, went to prayer for a Sanctifying use of this amazing providence to me & to others, especially to the family where it has happened. . . .

Thursday 19 In a humble lively spiritual frame of soul, comfortable in morning duties, the morning & forenoon raining and showery yet found a good Congregation there, as had several people to discourse with, & to give an account to the officers of the church, of the persons I had received as new communicants, among whom were this morning Mr. Thomas Timmons & his wife, I was very busy before I went in, preached the preparation Sermon [108 (206)] from 1 Corinth: 11:27:28:29:30 with great fulness . . . after prayer & Singing I acquainted the congregation with Mr. Cullys design, & desired him to stand up, where he sat in my pew & answer to such questions as I put to him, & declare his renunciation, & also his declaring himself a protestant, which I read to him, and as I went through many of the particular errors of the church of Rome & took his renunciation & abjuration of every one of them, and his declaring his faith & belief of the contrary truths, it took about three quarters of an hour or more, the Congregation were much pleased. I also received him as a member of this Congregation. Then, I proceeded to baptize a negro fellow belonging to Mr. Blakes named Isaac, and as many people are greatly against instructing negroes in the knowledge of Christianity & baptizing them, I was obliged to Enlarge in the introductory discourse, & [found] it to be our duty, I then discoursed from Col: 3:11, Explained the Epistle to Philemon & to confirm the paraphrase I gave upon it I read Sir Richard Steels translation of that Epistle into the *Style of a Modern letter,* from his Christian Hero,[33] afterwards expatiated again upon the duty of Encouraging them to become Christians, then discoursed to the Negroes in general from Eph: 6:5:6:7:8 & was very particular in laying the obligations upon the Negro who was brought in very young, has always behaved remarkably well, has learned to read most surprizingly well, & has a great deal of Christian knowledge, and lived a most Christian life, then baptized him. After pronouncing the blessing I came down & gave out the tokens, was betwixt three and four hours in the pulpit, was most exceedingly fatigued. . . .

Saturday Jully 21 . . . Late in the afternoon received a line from Mr. Donnom that Mrs. Bee from Ponpon and Mrs. Ohear were there & would be very glad to see me, I could not go just then but in the evening, went and staid about half an hour, found them both well & their families, was informed, that good worthy Mr. Maltby was in [109 (208)] great distress in his family, Mrs. Maltby has been very ill, the children very Sick, the youngest of whom He buried last Wednesday, being obliged to speak at the grave himself, their Servants have also been very Sick, was sincerely concerned for him and his

Dear family, as I well know his trouble & distress both of body & mind, was much pleased to hear of his own exercise, and of the kindness of his people. . . .

Lords day Jully 22 1770 This through the Infinite riches of Divine grace has been one of the days of heaven to my soul, a day of grace, a day of glory, an high communion Sabbath . . . Found a large & numerous Congregation, though the badness of the roads, & the prevailing Sickness, kept back many at the Indian Land, had severals to Converse with about various cases, & others to serve with tokens after got there, went into publick worship in the most humble, heavenly & Spiritual frame. Preached the action Sermon from 1 Peter 3:18 with great fulness, freedom, earnestness and tender affections . . . [110 (210)] I was exceedingly Spent in the action Sermon, and after a short prayer, I gave out a double quantity of verses to Sing, and retired to the School house, having no other place at present which being at a great distance, walking in the burning Sun without any shade, increased my fatigue, Served one with a token and put off another who offered himself for the first time, was ready to Sink against I got to the house, and after drank some wine & water, was exceeding Sick & reached often to vomit, when brought some phlegm & much bilious froath, which relieved me much. As was near a quarter of a mile from the meetinghouse, was much delighted with their Singing, which made the most pleasant & heavenly musick I ever heard, returned to the Congregation in the most humble & Elevated frame of soul, went up to the pulpit and after discoursing a little of the nature, use & Ends of this holy ordinance, I fenced the tables, as usual in the church of Scotland and in this Congregation, was larger & more full than I intended, then went down to the table, where the Lord was with me, was well assisted in Consecrating the Elements, in exhorting & in communicating . . . Was also well assisted in exhorting and directing the communicants, there was another full table, of whom nine or ten were Negroes, in all about Eighty or Eighty one communicants, and few of them from the Indian Land, during the Second Service, my strength failed me so much, that I was obliged often to sit down, and would fain have spoke sitting, but did not, I am not much for a minister speaking a great deal to the Communicants at the table and I would direct my people to transact immediately with God & Jesus Christ, and if they can be sufficiently employed to take no heed to the discourse of the minister, but as many truly gracious & very worthy persons, are either so weak, or so fearful and confused at the Lords table, that they cannot be suitably employed without assistance from the minister, and for that reason I generally speak a good deal, with pauses and intervals. Was this day obliged to make these intervals longer than usual, and was concerned, that could not speak more, by way of ejaculations, such as I would have the communicants repeat after me, for saw many young & weak people at this table, and had been requested to speak in that manner, what I thought expressed such exercises as they ought to be employed, after this Second Service, returned to the pulpit, took notice of the Lords great goodness and comfortable presence to us through the day. . . .

[III (212)] *Tuesday 24* . . . In the forenoon rode to Mr. Strains, whose daughter a young woman, has been bad with a sore throat, visited a poor family in the Same plantation, lately come into the parts, who have been all very Sick, and as common with strangers, of the lower class of people, are very obstinate, in refusing every thing that is proper for them, I said a great deal to the husband who has been very ill, both with respect to their souls, & their health, he seemed to take it well, found them ignorant & self conceited, though bred under the Gospel . . . Proceeded riding fast, to Mrs. B's, thinking to bring our matter to a conclusion. Just before I got to the house, was informed, that Mr. Jonathan W[34] was with her & had been there from Dinner time, He is a very young man, at least eight years younger than her, I believe ten years, and Some months ago waited very constantly upon her, but got no encouragement, & had dropped it, of late, he has renewed his Suit & spends a great deal of his time with her, though she denies that she gives him any encouragement & her relations, dislike the very thoughts of it, however her letting him have so much of her company seems not very Justifiable. It was after dark before I got there, Observed her very much disconcerted, at my coming, so much, that she did not receive me as usual, soon afterwards, Observed her & Miss Polly F often talking & laughing together as if concerting some measure which pleased them much, after candles were lighted, I was much Surprized to find Mrs. B exceedingly shy of me, & uneasy when I was near her, but giving more of her company to Mr. Wilkins, with whom I jocked & was very good company. Upon Mrs. B's walking out, I stepped after, & mentioned her behaviour. She would not allow that she was reserved to me. I insisted to have Some conversation with her that night, which she at first refused, but afterwards consented, and promised me her company, after the rest should be retired, with which I was fully satisfied, notwithstanding she behaved still in the Same manner, & Mr. Wilkins, who is not only young in years, but very young every way, could not help dropping Some hints of his great expectations of Success, which I did not think worth taking notice of, Supper & prayers were at the ordinary time, Soon after which, half an hour after ten, Mrs. B ordered candles, and upon letting us know in what rooms, we were to lodge, Her & Miss Polly went upstairs to their own room, & bid us good night. This amazed me, nor could I believe it to be real. Mr. Wilkins lodged upstairs also in a room opposite to theirs, the Overseer & her little Son sleeping in the Same room with him, I lodged down stairs, in the room off the hall, and as I was not at all disposed to sleep, I went to the book desk, and got a book, first volume of Torques works.[35] I amused myself reading till after three O Clock, I for Sometime expected she would have come down again into the hall, but upon her not coming, I concluded either she had lately given Mr. Wilkins some encouragement when she did not expect me back & had not yet got an opportunity to break with him, and was afraid to let him see how matters stood between her & me, for I could not harbor the least suspicion, that she was abusing me, Or, I imagined that she & Miss Polly had taken this opportunity to make me more assiduous & pushing by making me Jealous of Mr. Wilkins, & upon the whole I thought it most probable, but, at the same time, thought it very foolish conduct, If Mr. Wilkins had been a Gentleman any ways equal to myself either in years or character, I would have passed it over, but as He is in a manner a boy, and known to be a very Simple youth, I thought myself very ill used, & resolved to resent it, after my Candle was burnt out, I walked about the room for some time, had not the least passion, but was cool, calm, free from anger, trouble or concern, only thought it incumbent on me to Sift this matter to the bottom & to act with Spirit, went to prayer, and composedly presented my Supplications to God, with freedom & affection. About four O Clock I went to bed, & slept about half an hour.

Wednesday 25:1770 Having slept about half an hour which I found refreshing, I got up before five O Clock, and walked about. As none but the Overseer was up, I would have made my boy get the horses at Eleven in the night, & gone away, but did not chuse to set Mr. Wilkins a talking about me, I would have gone away this morning, but as I had always stayed to give prayers, I thought it might be said that while I had some selfish views, I stayed & gave [112 (214)] but when I had no longer any such prospects, then I could go away, and show no manner of regard to morning family worship, this determined me to stay till breakfast & prayers were over, however went out and ordered my horses to be got ready betwixt Six & Seven O Clock. Mrs. B & Miss Polly came down stairs, the common compliments passed, with ease & cheerfulness on my side, but Observed Mrs. B to be greatly confused & exceedingly troubled. She often & very narrowly eyed me & watched my every motion, and after breakfast insisted to know, what I meant by having my horses so early ordered, & intreated me much to stay, I told her my business called me away, for it really was So, I intended to have set off early, even if every thing had been according to my wish, and after prayers I called my boy & horses, she again repeated her pressing me to stay, & when she could not prevail, she asked me, if I intended to call & see her Sister Jacksons child, which is bad with the Hooping Cough, I told her, I believed I should not go that way, she then told me, that the child was thought bad, and as her Sister had lost all her children young, she was very uneasy, and would have Sent for me, if I had not been expected at her house, and that both she & her Sister would take it as a favour, if I would visit the child. I told her I would go on purpose, and accordingly set off, made my boy, gather in the woods as I was riding along, some colts foot, & carry with me, to Mr. Jacksons as good for the childs disorder, found the child likely to be bad with the Cough, but not dangerous as yet, Sat about an hour and proceeded to old Mr. Atkins, who was taken very Sick on Sabbath after communicating, and carried home with a violent fever, found still very poorly, & I am afraid likely to be worse, Stayed here, till about the middle of the afternoon, had a very agreeable day in serious useful improving conversation, Sometimes with Mr. Atkins but mostly with his wife, who is a very Sensible, Conversable woman, and I think a worthy good woman, and to me very agreeable company, except when making remarks on her Neighbours, she is somewhat unhappy in her temper, critical & critisising, being herself in general very nice & unexceptionable. In the afternoon rode back to Mr. H, who was not home from Charlestown, & his Lady gone a visiting, Stayed about half an hour with Mrs. H's brother, chiefly to rest my horses, it being exceedingly hot. As I passed Mr. Jacksons, Mr. W Ferguson married to another Sister of Mrs. B's, stopped me, & said he was come to ask me to go up to his house on the other Side of the Salt-catcher, & baptize his youngest child about two months old, who was very ill with the Hooping Cough, I told him I would, & we appointed to meet tomorrow afternoon at Mr. John Mctiers, this stopped me, at Mr. Jacksons, where stayed about an hour or more, it being still most excessively hot, the young Lady Miss A Jackson, who lives with Mrs. B was here, & Jesting said she expected Soon to be a boarder with me, I told her no, I did not expect but probably she might be so with Mr. Wilkins. She answered no, it was impossible, Mrs. Jackson repeatedly said the same, but on observing me, more serious than ordinary on such discourses, she asked me what was the matter, & if I really thought So, I told her, I did not know what to think, but her Sister & I had parted that morning in an odd manner, and that I had no intention to go back, she expressed great concern, and said it was impossible her Sister could deny me her company & give it to Mr. Wilkins, I answered I did not know, what she did with Mr. Wilkins, but she had used me very ill, in promising me her company, yea had brought me there at her own desire, & after all disappointed me, Mrs. Jackson was greatly affected, as soon as it cooled I rode homewards, where got about an hour after dark. . . .

Thursday Jully 26 1770 This morning found my self much refreshed & strengthened with sleep . . . Late in the afternoon I set out for Mr. Fergusons, to meet him at Mr. John Mctiers, when I got Mrs. C's, near the bridge,[36] was informed that Mr. James Jordans only daughter in her twentieth year, had on Wednesday run away with Mr. G T,[37] a young man of no great character, to the great grief & distress of her Father, this gave me great concern on her Fathers account, but more especially that she had been at the Lords Table last Sabbath, & that very night made a fruitless attempt to run off, to get married to that person, whom her Father hated & abhorred. O the mystery of iniquity that works in the human heart, O the Enmity of Satan at a Gospel interest. This melancholy affair is very distressing to me, as attended with Several Circumstances, which will undoubtedly cause the Lords work here to be evil spoken of, & the holy name of Jesus to be blashphemed, proceeded to Mr. McTiers, where met with Mr. Ferguson, who told me that his Sister in law Mrs. B was gone up, and Mr. Wilkins with her in the chair having kept her company since Tuesday. . . . About Sun down Set off with Mr. Ferguson having near about nine miles to ride, and about fifteen from my house, had a good deal of conversation with Mr. Ferguson, found him sensible especially about worldly business , and of a very Saving turn, am told, that he thrives and gets up in the world, he is very sober & industrious, diligent, & careful to keep what he makes, we did not get there till above an hour after dark, found both their children with the hooping Cough, but the youngest very bad with a constant violent fever, Soon after I got there I was desired to walk into a room where Mrs. B was with her Sister & the Sick Infant, after the usual compliments Mrs. B said something about, she believed I did not expect we would meet [113 (216)] so soon which

brought on a conversation about Tuesdays night, when she expressed herself
with great concern & tenderness as exceedingly troubled & grieved for her
foolish Conduct, that she perceived her error immediately, Observed I did
not go to bed, which gave her great anxiety, and that she slept as little as I
did, that she spoke of it to Miss Polly, who insisted upon it, that I could not
take it amiss as Mr. Wilkins was there and that she could give me her company next day, & make an apology if I seemed to think any thing of it, she
after some time mentioned again to Miss Polly, & told her how she had
promised me her company, that I had also come by appointment, and that
by my sitting up I was [certainly] uneasy & would resent it, the other assured
her, that it was usual with me, to sit up very late & persuaded her not to
come down, as she had not stayed or done it at first, that she continued full
of anxiety & concern, and was confirmed in the morning by my reservedness
& having my horses ready So Soon, that I was affronted, and that her having behaved so foolishly had ever since given her the utmost concern. I told
her in very strong terms, how ill I thought myself used, and that I thought
myself obliged to resent it, or she herself must have despised me, she wanted
to say, that she thought it was later than it was, and that it was thought-
lessness, I told her, by no means to say so, and begged her if there was any
connection between Mr. Wilkins & her to be true & faithful to him, that I
acquitted her of all obligations to me, she often assured me, in the strongest
terms, that there was no such thing between them, and that she had never
given him any encouragement. I told her she did very ill, to keep him spending his time about her, and that no person of Sense, would believe she could
not dismiss him when she had a mind, she silently acknowledged it, I told
her, if that was not the case, I knew what must have been her design, that I
did not think her capable of acting so weakly as to make me Jealous of him,
& to make me more assiduous lest he should cut me out, that I despised the
mean [and artifice], and should never look upon such a youth, as a Rival or
fit to be set up in opposition to me, She was greatly affected, & often begged
my pardon, begged I would forgive her, owned she had acted very foolishly
& wrong, and intreated me to be assured she did not intend to use me ill,
or in the least affront me, begged whatever I did not to entertain any such
thoughts of her, that she now and before I had spoke to her, saw her conduct
in such a light, as made her exceedingly angry with herself and that though
she could not forgive herself, she intreated my forgiveness, that I might keep
her company for what time I pleased, and if I did not desire it, yet not to
think, she intended to affront me, or had any connection with Mr. Wilkins.

I told her, I firmly & truely believed her, but could not easily forget, her using me so meanly, that I was satisfied, & would intirely pass it over, and would take an opportunity either this night, or tomorrow morning to have some further conversation with her, this was a tender moving scene on her part, & though I felt a good deal of resentment, yet was obliged to express rather what I had felt before, than at that very time, after being about an hour with her in which hardly ever took notice of her Sister being present with us, I went out to the Gentlemen, Mr. Ferguson and Mr. [Dvs] who is executor for this Estate of which Mr. Ferguson has the care, & Mr. Wilkins. Mrs. B did not come till Supper was on the table, when she appeared more composed & easy, At Supper I observed I had a ring of hers upon my finger, which I had not thought of, nor did I remember of my putting it on, though I remembered having it in my hand while I was with her & holding her hand in mine, Mr. Wilkins I saw observed it before I did, and seemed very much Surprized & concerned, upon which I pulled it off & slipped it into her hand, as I could not willingly give uneasiness to any person, she behaved with great freedom & compliance, and after prayers when Candles were called for, she put herself in my way, but as I observed the child was very bad, and she looked very much fatigued with her long ride in the hot Sun, I told her I could not be so cruel as to keep her up, when she seemed to have so great need of rest, & was to get up before today to relieve her Sister & sit up with the child, therefore I advised her to go to sleep, which she did. After went into my room, & reflected on the day, had Satisfaction in reviewing the greatest part of it, and particularly what had passed between Mrs. B & me, found the works of the truly famous & very worthy John Bunyan,[38] & read for some time in his pilgrims progress with great Satisfaction, I never meet with that valuable book, but I receive benefit by it. Sat up till near midnight, & after a short prayer went to bed, in a sweet humble frame of soul.

Friday 27 . . . I got up early, and yet when I came out found Mr. Wilkins had gone very early without taking leave, although he had promised to stay breakfast & ride down with me, the Gentlemen breakfasted before the Ladies got up, which was late, when we had prayers, as I saw the child was very ill, I thought it would be improper to take Mrs. B apart for our Conversation, & thought it better to omit it, till some other opportunity, Accordingly I took my leave of them all, without saying anything in particular to Mrs. B. . . . Proceeded to Mr. Jordans,[39] where stayed dinner, found him still in an odd strange way but to all appearance not the least real concern about religion, but falling back very fast into an excess of concern about the world, full of himself, full of self conceit, Endeavoured to discourse usefully to him, but could not make any impression on him & was melancholy to see him, in what I think a very evil condition, So that did not Speak so much or stay long, as I intended, Immediately after Dinner, I proceeded, called & sat a little at Mr. Mctiers, who is himself very poorly, and seems to me as if he had Some great Sickness coming on. I gave him some advice about his health, afterwards called at his Mothers, with whom and her two Daughters Mrs. Melvin and Mrs. Shaw I spent about two hours or better in free cheerful conversation & drank tea. Thought I was rather too free & cheerful with them, they were all very kind, they are in many respects a worthy family but excessively set upon the world, and have very little, or no regard for the publick ordinances of religion, very seldom ever attending on them though both families have a pew in the Saltcatcher meeting house, poor Mrs. Shaw, her promising day seems past & gone and she has now almost intirely given up publick worship, I may say altogether. It made me melancholy to think of her, I once had some good hopes of her, and had her relations consented to the connection, which she herself desired & wished of, she might have been in a very different way, from that which she is now in, and yet perhaps, it might not have been so, and then I would have been very miserable, with her it might have been a merciful providence, to me it might have been a very distressing one, I adore & bless God, that the connection never took place. . . .

[114 (218)] *Lords day 29* . . . After Sermon, was stopped at the blacksmiths & baptized a child for Dutch parents, both Lutherans, then proceeded through a small rain to Mr. DeSaussures where Dined, had some further conversation, with the Negro fellow of Doctor Cuthberts who is under religious concern, and I hope in a good way, was Sorry, that spoke so freely with Mrs. Graves on a particular affair about Betsy Cliffords husband, as it might have been full as well omitted, though my design was good & to testify against a very evil custom, yet have formerly experienced, that Mrs. Graves is apt to make a bad use of such free conversations.[40] After Dinner proceeded homewards, Mr. Martin, brother to the Reverend Mr. John Martin on Wando[41] was with me, & spent the night at my house in his way to James Donnoms, we did not get home till just dusk, had useful & improving conversation with him. . . .

Tuesday 31 . . . About the middle of the forenoon Mr. Jordan called on me, expressed his satisfaction at my concern for & sympathy with him in his trouble, was in general pleased with his behaviour, as it was really other than I expected, yet was troubled to see him have so much resentment against the young man, who is now his Son in law, who is very sober Genteel well behaved young person, of a family equal if not Superiour to Mr. Jordans, & thought by every person to be deserving of his daughter, though not such a match as Mr. Jordan expected being but in low Circumstances. Was grieved to see Mr. Jordan, of such an unchristian spirit, and so little himself under the rod, he stayed dinner with me, & went to Mr. Donnoms, I spoke very little to him, as was afraid he could not yet bear any advice, and I was busy getting ready to go to the Indian Land, to bury a child of Mr. C B's of better than a year old, who died last night of the Hooping Cough.[42] Accordingly rode there, was helped in Ejaculations by the way, was detained a good while at the house, as usual. Could not help remembering that the last time I buried a child from this house poor Miss Mary Cater was there, and had my Scarf in her hand, but at the Sight of me, dropped it, & could not put it on. Main & his family were here today, the child was interred in the church yard, Mr. Brown in his letter of invitation, desired me to bury his child in what way was most agreeable to myself, I read the funeral Service of the church of England, according to the form used by their own Ministers without adding a Single word after it, my reason for doing so was, that I had been informed, that by many insinuations, they were not pleased with the discourse I made at their last childs funeral, and as both parents are professed members of the church of England I was determined not to displease them, at this time by anything I should say. The people seemed surprized I did not join the two Services together, but I believe the Father who was the only parent out, was better pleased as it was. . . .

Wednesday first day of August 1770 . . . [115 (220)] Mrs. B wrote a very handsome kind & affectionate letter, excused herself for not writting according to her promise, and in her letter hinted, at Some uneasiness in her mind, about a rash which she had made in her husbands life time, about her ever marrying again, which he at that very moment checked her for, & would not allow her to say or promise any such thing. This is the case of conscience she once spoke to me of, long enough before I had any thoughts of paying my addresses to her, this I thought, might perhaps be real, as she now had a nearer prospect of marriage that ever she had Since her husband died, or, it might only be a finess, but her letter, was so tender, affectionate & respectful, that as it would be too late before I could get there, I would go up in the morning. . . .

Thursday August 2 1770 . . . Got there before nine O Clock . . . Got an opportunity of being near two hours with Mrs. B, who received me as usual in the most kind and affectionate manner. After sometime I asked her, what she meant by the hint, of her being uneasy & almost ready to conclude never to marry, and if that old affair, was really a matter of conscience to her, she answered, that she could not say positively it was so, though formerly it had made her uneasy, but, as she had never, although often courted, thought seriously of marrying any person except myself, that since what passed between her & me before the Sacrament, it seemed to give her some concern. I told her, I was well satisfied, it need not in the least trouble her, for if I thought, there was anything in it, I would not for all the world desire a connection with her, that I should think it would be an entailing evil upon any posterity we might have, but although I was clear in the matter, & was fully satisfied, if it was so as she had related to me, yet if she was not satisfied also, if it was a matter of conscience with her not to marry, that I would now drop the affair intirely, & never mention it more. She was for sometime Silent, & then said she could not say it was a matter of Conscience to her, & was Satisfied that although it was a rash saying, yet it noways bound her, as Mr. B had at that very time made her unsay it, after various affectionate conversations, I asked her, if her mind was not the Same as before the Sacrament, she said it was, I asked her, if she did not at that time and afterwards look upon herself as Engaged to me, she answered, yes, she looked upon herself as partly engaged to me, I asked her if she did not intend now to confirm it by engaging herself wholly & absolutely to me, to be married as Soon as convenient, Still reserving, that if her relations & I could not to her Satisfaction settle any concerns about her & her childs Estate, that we might by mutual consent be free, after declaring she wanted no settlements, & wishing me to delay it, till she got home, & some other womanish excuses, she freely & fully consented to be mine, our word & truth to one another, and exchanged rings, I having one in my pocket as a pledge & token thereof. Thus I am once more, for a third time engaged & Contracted, whither be accomplished, or like the two former broke off, time will discover. I was very cool & deliberate and with concern remembered, the two former engagements, I silently prayed that if it was for Gods glory, for her good & mine, & the advantage our children, it might prosper, and be happily finished but if God saw that it would not, I humbly & earnestly begged it might be stopped & broke off. I also mentioned so much to her, which she said was the very desire & language of her heart, she was very serious, & yet easy, free, & cheerful in it. May God glorify himself in it & to his holy will I entirely submit, whatever comes of me or mine, let his glorious name be honoured & exalted. After this I was about an hour with her, all which time, she was very cheerful, free & easy in her conversation, but in some things rather more reserved than she has sometimes formerly been, which I approved of, we talked of several things, as about my children getting of some new things for them, about some additions to my house, about the time of being married, which I proposed to be in October, or the latter End of September, among other things, she asked me about my Engagement to poor Miss Mary Cater & told me, what shocking fearful things she had heard of her despairing Death. I told her it was too true, I also told her of the Intelligence I received & how I was exercised about her, & by all that a very worthy person who was with her in all her illness, & I could think by comparing things together, that at the time she expired, I was upon my knees in earnest prayer for her Salvation. She seemed considerably affected with this discourse. She at last put me in mind, that we forgot there was company in the house, and begged me to go into the hall, where the company was, & leave her alone, as she wanted to be by herself, & wished that no body might come into her directly, which I accordingly did, she was sometime alone and when the Door was opened she appeared to me to have been crying which Surprized me, but I soon forgot it, afterwards were in company together [116 (222)] with the rest of the family & the visitors, till near Sun down, when after drinking tea I set out for home. . . .

Lords day August 5 In a very humble, spiritual frame of soul this day . . . When I went first to the meeting & was early out, I saw among other Gentlemen, Mr. Thomas Timmons Brother to the young man, who has carried off, & married Mr. Jordans daughter, they had got a License out Some time ago and were married next morning after they run away, by the Reverend Mr. Tong, Rector of St. Bartholomews,[43] & have returned to Mr. Thomas Timmons, being to go and live in Georgia, where Mr. George Timmons the young man is settled. I saw also Mr. Jordan walking at a distance in the woods, his looks were very uncommon, wild, distracted & furious like. I went up to him, & gave him the common Salutations. He immediately asked me, if I had seen, any of the wretched beggarly Crew the Timmons, I tried to Moderate him, but he behaved most shamefully, threatening to go & shoot Mr. Timmons saying he had brought his pistols, & prepared a load for that very purpose, I was shocked to hear him, he continued to use a great deal of very indecent language, I put him in mind of the consequences of murder, he said it was no murder to destroy such wretches, he then vowed in very strong gross language, he would cut a stick and come into the meeting house & beat Mr. Timmons while he could stand over him, he would do it, in the face of the whole congregation & the time of Service. I put him in mind of the law, he raved like a madman, saying he despised the law, he was above the law, he had money enough, he would take his revenge of the wretches, and they would pay for it, I asked him, if he was above the law of God, he answered no, I asked if the law of God did not forbid such behaviour on the Sabbath, he then broke out again in very indecent language, that it was no breech of the Sabbath to do so, & he would do it, I warned him to take care what he did, or he would be ill used if he offered any such thing in meeting, he answered he would do it, he would do in that meeting house what he pleased, that we used him ill, in suffering such a wretch to come to meeting, that we were all against him and he would take his revenge, and a great many more such expressions, I told him he was acting a very Sinful part, that I was Sorry to see him in such a condition (for he was like a raving mad person), & took my leave of him, I then went & spoke to Mr. Jonathan Donnom, to try to Moderate him, & keep an eye on him. I then went to Mr. Thomas Timmons & desired him, not to come in Mr. Jordans way, and if Mr. Jordan used him rudely not to regard it, as he knowed himself in no danger from a man so much older than himself, and an infirm [117 (224)] person, & to consider, how he was chafed in his mind & at present not himself. Mr. Timmons expressed himself with the utmost Moderation, Said he was exceedingly sorry for Mr. Jordan and that he had been obliged to assist his Brother, to carry off his daughter, things were so situated & Mr. Jordan so obstinately against his Brother, that there was a necessity for it, or things would have been much worse, all this I knew to be very true, that He would keep out of Mr. Jordans way and would bear any thing from him, even to some blows, he spoke so much like a Gentleman & Christian, that I was much pleased with him & glad to see, what a Contrast there was between him, and my poor old friend, after this I retired to the School house & was sometime alone, still uneasy about this affair, and after I went into the pulpit, continued uneasy, Observed

Mr. Jordan did not come in till I was in prayer, and then behaved very inde-
cently, his looks were still wild & furious, he had one pistol in his hand in a
threatening posture, the other on his arm, as usual in this part of the world,
he did not go into his own pew but ran to the window opposite to it, and
knocked it open, as if he would have broke it to pieces, & kept looking out
at the window, as if watching for Some body, sometimes turning about &
looking over all the people, all which made me very uneasy and most of the
Congregation were so, having stayed about ten or twelve minutes he went
out & got his horse & rode homewards, which made me easy & Satisfied.
Preached from Gen: 5:24 with Gods most gracious & comfortable presence.
. . . After the last Sermon I was informed that poor Mr. Jordan before he
came in, went to the window opposite to my pew where Mr. Thomas Timmons sat, and there kept looking at Mr. Timmons with the most diabolical
looks, changing his posture, & making as if taking sight at him with his pistol in his hand, his finger at the trigger, & his thumb upon the Cock in an
horizontal posture, but did not directly present it, which greatly terrified several of the people, especially my informant Mrs. Donnom, who sat very nigh
Mr. Timmons with her own, & my children, and that the Gentlemen intended to have bound him over, or confined him, but there happened no
Magistrate to be at meeting, Mr. James Donnom being Sick & Mr. Hunt
gone to Charlestown, this increased my concern & uneasiness for him, poor
man his pride has received a most severe shock, for most people think his
daughter has not done much amiss, but he expected great worldly things for
her. After had refreshed myself at home, I rode up to Campbells hill, to see
Mr. James Donnom, and consult with him about Mr. Jordan. He was very
angry when he heard of his Conduct and insisted upon it, he must have been
in liquor, which I never thought of, but am afraid was the case, Mr. Donnom mentioned an Instance of it before, and considering Mr. Jordans prudent behaviour when the affair happened, it appears to have been certainly
the case, this affected Mr. Donnom & me very much, lest as he is now a solitary person, he should take to that abominable practice to keep up his Spirits, and we resolved to do what we could to prevent it. . . .

[118 (226)] *Wednesday August 8 1770* . . . [119 (228)] Between Eleven & twelve
O Clock, I set out for Mr. Thomas Timmons to visit Mr. Jordans daughter,
Miss Polly Jordan that was, now wife to Mr. George Timmons, this visit was
partly at her Fathers request & partly my own desire, had also consulted both
Her Fathers friends & mine about it, who all thought it might be very proper

that I should discourse with and advise her before she leaves the parts, I found both her & her husband at home & all the family, I behaved to her & to all of them with Some reserve, but at the Same time, let them see, though I could not approve of her conduct, yet I came with friendly intentions, and not as an Enemy. Their behaviour to me was very becoming, hers was modest and decent yet she did not seem much affected with what she had done, only was troubled that her Father was so obstinate and full of resentment against her husband & Brother in law. We dined together, after which I took out Mr. Thomas Timmons and had a long discourse with him, pointing out to him, wherein I thought he had acted amiss and Especially the evil of his being a communicant at that time, He said it grieved him greatly that things should so fall out at that very time, but it was not design, and on the whole, he condemned himself much, was so humble, & Submissive, & spoke so much like a Christian, and a man of sense that I was much pleased and Satisfied. Afterwards I desired Mr. Jordans daughter to walk into a room with me, and laid before her the heinous Sin of disobedience to parents, and a parent, who had been at so great expense about her Education, the baseness of her conduct, her ingratitude & unkindness to her Father, the vileness of her conduct in carrying on Such a design at so solemn occasion, & attempting it, that very night after coming from the Lords table, of the many lies, & falsehoods which she was guilty of in carrying it on, etc etc etc all which she owned & acknowledged, she wept grievously at mentioning her conduct about the Sacrament, and mentioned some things which seemed to carry the face of some excuse more than I thought was possible, & told me very particularly with tears the frame & temper of her mind that day, bewailed the woeful necessity she was under of lies, falsehoods, and studied equivocations, acknowledged what I said of her disobedience & unkindness to her Father, in General, but said many very strong & affecting things for her excuse, and which indeed greatly lessened & alleviated her fault, she pled the necessity of her case, his harshness, severity, and unreasonable prejudices, against her husband, his inexorable inflexible temper, and a great deal more, she also very modestly [hinted] at some necessities of a private nature, for her taking the step she did, of her having taken every step she could to inform her Father, of the desperateness of her Condition, hoping he would consent to its being done openly & in a Credible manner, but that she could not prevail, and was under the most unavoidable necessity to do as she did, or much worse Consequences must have followed, and that it could be delayed no longer. She lamented her having no mother, lamented my not being a married man, or by means of my wife, she would long ago have let me know the misery which an unconquerable passion, and an inexorable parent had reduced her to, that she often prayed God to give her courage to tell me, but could never do it, and all this Mingled with so many tears, that I was quite disarmed, and affected, and could say but little to her, I remembered former times, she sometimes spoke of her Father, with acrimony & resentment, which I checked & reproved. She had agreed to her Brother in law binding her Father over before a Magistrate to keep the peace, this she said was to prevent his doing Mischief to her husband or Brother in law, & bringing himself to disgrace, but I made her sensible she was wrong to consent to any such thing, and convinced the Gentlemen, there was no need of it, I then gave her, all the best advices I could, both with respect with repentance towards God, her behaviour towards her Father, & towards her husband and the Christian society among whom she is going to live. I sent for her husband, & spoke to him, giving him & her both the best advices I could think of, for their behaviour towards God, one another, and the world. They were both very thankful especially her husband was exceedingly so, I advised them both to write to her Father, but not to persist in Seeing him if he continued Obstinate, to set off for their home in Georgia as soon as possible, to write to me whenever they got there, when I would give them further directions, assured them of my friendship, that all my interest in their Father, should be employed for their good if I saw or heard they deserved it, took a kind and affectionate leave of them and left the family, with hopes that this piece of service will turn out for good, may the Lord grant it for Christs sake. I returned home directly, where found a letter from Mr. Jordan acknowledging his great Misconduct on Sabbath, and begging it might be looked over, as his boy was gone & I had not time to write a proper answer, I thought it best to delay writting him till I return from Beaufort, Spent the evening in writting and finished next Sabbaths Sermons, may the Lord help in further preparing & delivering them. . . .

[120 (240)] *Friday August 10 1770* Early this morning about two O Clock, after I had slept about a quarter of an hour, I heard a rapping at my room door which alarmed me very much, as it was Some time before I could speak or know where I was, when I could speak, was told it was my boy from my house with a letter, when got up found it was Primus, with a letter from the Reverend Mr. Maltby of Wilton, letting me know, that it had pleased a Sovereign God, to take his wife off by Death, yesterday morning about nine O clock and He earnestly intreated me to attend the funeral this afternoon. This melancholy providence affected me much, yet thought it would not be possible for me to get there & be able to preach as would be expected, and also doubted if it was my duty, to disappoint Beaufort. Returned to bed in some suspence, but could not sleep, got up again & examined what papers I had brought out with me, then returned to bed & endeavoured to think of something proper & suitable, to this melancholy occasion, and resolved to leave the determination of my going or not going till the morning, was for some time awake and suitably employed, at last fell asleep and continued so, till after Sun up. When I first got up felt something of a backwardness to undertake so great a fatigue, as am but poorly, and the weather is now most excessively hot, besides from this place to Mr. Maltbys is at about fourty miles, but again, when I reflected on the melancholy providence, and that five years ago the Reverend Mr. Gordon, performed the Same kind office for me, I could not think of indulging myself, and after morning and family prayer I determined to go, accordingly wrote a letter to Doctor Cuthbert, informing him of the Melancholy providence, & desiring him to excuse me, to the good people of the Island & promising to preach soon. After breakfast, good Mrs. Hatcher supplied my pockets with what would be refreshing by the way, and I set off, resolved not to ride too fast, but a quick steady gait as my horses are poor, rode by way of Combahee ferry, and got to Mr. Brandfords, the other side of Ponpon ferry about two O Clock. They were both gone to the parsonage to assist in having things done but had left Dinner for me. Stayed here about an hour & three quarters, refreshing myself and making further preparation, and rode to the parsonage, where was a very good Company gathered together, mostly my friends, excepting old Mr. Stobo and his family. Found poor Mr. Maltby, in a very great distress, taking on, as it is called most excessively, a great deal too much so, was grieved & troubled for him, and attempted to comfort him but in vain, betwext five & Six O Clock, we went to the meeting house, a melancholy procession indeed, as poor Mr. Maltby attended and was almost beside himself, his kind & affectionate people mingled their tears with his, poor Gentleman, about a twelve month ago He lost his Eldest Son a promising youth, of Seventeen years. About three weeks ago he lost a child of about a year & a half old, & now his Dear wife miscarried of a living child & in a few days departed. Yet surely his grief should be within measure. The Corpse was taken into the meeting house. I begun with prayer, as usual, then Sung the 90th psalm third part common metre, then discoursed rather better than an hour, upon the necessity the benefit & advantage of affliction, from Psalm 119:170: It is good for me, that I was afflicted,[44] Spoke repeatedly and particularly to my afflicted Reverend Brother but he could take no notice, I never saw such a distressed behaviour, it was at times highly indecent & unbecoming but he was not Master of himself. Prayed largely & fervently for him, after the Discourse, Sung the concluding hymn at the Grave, the third hymn of the Second book, & there pronounced the blessing, was never better assisted in all my life than in this Service, was enabled to be full, large, suitable, tender and affectionate and to pour my soul in the most fervent supplications, the people were serious & attentive, but Mr. Maltbys great distress took off the attention very much. It was truly very affecting to see him standing by the grave and pouring tears into it, in great abundance, he kept both in the meeting & there, almost constantly talking to himself, and moving both hands & feet etc, He is left with five motherless children, the youngest about four or five years old, a stranger, in a strange place, yet his people most exceedingly kind. In returning from the grave, Old Mr. Stobo came and led him by the arm, which gave me occasion to observe by Mr. Stobos speeches to him, that there is a very great intimacy between them, which I was afterwards informed of by my good friend Mr. Brandford, & that it is like to prove very hurtful to poor Mr. Maltby, who although he has been often warned against that designing person, yet is like to fall into the Snare. I found at my first speaking to Mr. Maltby that he did not much expect me, & indeed seemed to me, as if he did not much desire me, and that it was largely his Congregation that insisted on his Sending for me. This surprized me, and made me almost wish myself in Beaufort, but when I found the intimacy between Mr. Stobo & Mr. Maltby, I saw the reason, as I was exceedingly fatigued and weary and things in great confusion at Mr. Maltbys, I left my friend Mr. Lambert with him, and rode home with Mr. & Mrs. Brandford where spent the evening very agreeably and with good Satisfaction. . . .

Lords day 12: This day four years my Dear little Jeany, was taken from this world of sin & misery to heavenly & Eternal glory. This life here was short, but full of pain, trouble & Sickness, but now she dwells in the Land of everlasting life, where the inhabitants are no more Sick, where there is no Sin nor Sorrow. Could not help, reflecting on this melancholy day four years. . . .

[121 (247)] *Monday August 13* . . . Proceeded to Jacksonburgh, where had some business to settle & stayed all the forenoon, had Some talk with Mr.

Mybnk,[45] about the account Sent in from Doctor Reids Estate by his widow, Mr. Mybnks Sister, which believe I must pay, though it is most unjust, and had many years ago Settled it with the Doctor. . . . Called at Mrs. Jacksons, to inquire for their little boy, who is better, also heard from Mrs. Jackson that her Sister Fergusons youngest child is also something better, inquired if her Sister Mrs. B was at home as I was going there. They were very kind & respectful as usual, but when I mentioned my going to Mrs. B's, I fancied Mrs. Jackson looked something more serious than usual, which made me think I would find some body or other with Mrs. B whom they wished was not there . . . I did not get to Mrs. B's till after Dark, about a mile before I got there, I met a Negroe who told me, that Mr. Wilkins was with his mistress & had been there from Saturday afternoon, this Confirmed me I was right in my Observation in Mrs. Jackson who is very much displeased with her Sister, for keeping his Company so much. Was also surprized Mrs. B should act such a part, but was determined to see it out, when I got there, both him & her were much surprized to see me, as they thought I was come from Beaufort. She received me more freely than the last time, him & I met here, & I saluted her more freely than ever I had done before company, After some time, she went out to order Supper. I met her before she came in, and asked if I should have her company tonight, or if I was to be used as last time, she said she was not well, had been feverish, kept her bed till twelve O Clock, & begged I would excuse her. I answered I suppose her rest had been broke these two nights past, as the Gentleman had been much with her, but certainly I had a right to some conversation this night and must insist upon it, she answered he had been there from Saturday, but she gave him no encouragement for he knowed he hated to hear him speak of such matters. I told her it was very strange that she hated to hear him speak & yet loved his company so much, but I must have it in my turn. She consented, and I was determined to be off if possible, or confirmed beyond a doubt. I observed she carefully avoided giving me any opportunity before him, but seemed to take opportunities to whisper him, her behaviour much amazed me, and though my passions are not at all concerned yet my pride & resentment was affected, after supper & prayers, my lodging as usual was in the room off the hall, Mr. Wilkins up stairs, where his Candle was carried up & he was acquainted with it, and went up accordingly, she stayed with me in the hall, about half an hour, but was very uneasy . . . [122 (248)][46] about marrying, I asked if she did not think herself absolutely & positively . . . & that she had changed her mind, & could not marry, I told her . . . returned such advances to me, her

answer was she could not help it, and that, she had changed her fancy, I told
. . . fancy was a very improper word betwixt her & me, and asked if it was
fancy, that made her profess such . . . me, when I was not thinking of making any addresses to her, she was silent, but said if I would let her . . . she
would give me her last & final answer tomorrow if I would stay, or Send it
in a letter to me in two days, I told her I was amazed to hear her speak of a
final answer after such repeated Engagements, and pledges passed between us,
that if she wanted to be off, she might do as she pleased, but I could not look
upon any thing she had to say or write as a final answer as she had given that
already, that I was most basely & cruelly used, after her taking such steps to
get me to offer myself to her, & so readily engaging herself to me, and after
. . . so many miles & undergone so much fatigue, I should be received in such
a manner, I told her, I was ready to wait . . . at any time either with or without her, she repeatedly said if she could be satisfied to marry, she . . . me, but
that she was now indisposed & tomorrow would determine the matter, I was
during part of this discourse making towards the room door, we were both
standing, and she held my hand long, and often pulled me towards her, begging me to be satisfied, but I thought her conduct so strange, that I parted
without turning to her, after she was gone upstairs, I walked about a little, &
resolved to see the bottom of this strange affair, and that if she should afterwards appear to be never so faithful, yet if she could not give me Satisfying
reasons for this conduct, that I never . . . the connection between us. Determined also to let as little resentment as possible, take place that I [might] be
more Satisfied as to her conduct, & search more narrowly into it. It was by
the good persuasion of my friends that I made the late offer & her engaging
behaviour had gained upon me, but have still been kept from having any
passion, excepting a sincere & hearty regard, had I been well used. . . .

Tuesday 14 Had a comfortable nights rest & was much refreshed by it, got
up early, and was about betwixt two or three hours up before I saw any but
the Overseer, who told me, it was his opinion & the opinion of the Sensible
[negroes] of the house that it would soon be a match between Mr. Wilkins
& Mrs. B, and that they were all much against it & was sorry to think I was
used so ill, which he really believed was the case . . . After breakfast & prayers,
she asked me to stay . . . She was shy & displeased . . . and never could look
me in the face, and was far from being so free as usual . . . I asked her, if she
did not think herself as much engaged to me, as she had been to Mr. B [be-
fore] they were married, she hesitated & answered no, I asked her where was

the difference, she said her engagement . . . was not so positive, that now she had changed her mind about marrying, I [asked if she] [123 (234)] thought her vow was binding, she answered she could not tell, but sometimes she thought it was, I told her if she had changed her mind about marrying, or changed her fancy from me, I begged her to return my letters etc. She was very much confused, was Sometime silent & at last said, Do you want your letters? I answered yes, I want them just now if you are of the mind, that you speak, and I promise upon honour to bring back yours, she was much affected & at last said she did not doubt my honour, but begged to keep mine till my boy came, which I agreed to then told her, I would go home & not disappoint her going to Mr. D's, she asked me to go with her, I excused myself. After this she was more cheerful & more free with me, all seems a Mystery, but I must go through with it. Took an affectionate leave of her, as do not know what I think, was willing to hope the best of her, though hardly wish to succeed with her, as am afraid she has made herself so mean in my opinion, that could not be happy with her, proceeded homewards amazed & Surprized at the Strange conduct of providence in promoting such things in my lot, & in a manner bringing them in my way, but with a full persuasion of the kindness of providence and that even this, would work for my good. . . .

[124 (236)] *Thursday August 16 1770* . . . According to agreement Sent my boy to Mrs. B last night for my letters etc, and wrote her, I still looked upon her as mine, and therefore addressed her as such for I could not think it possible, she designed to disappoint me, or to fall back from what she herself called being partly Engaged, but as I did not chuse to say any more, I left it to her own honour & conscience & had Sent my boy to wait for the letters or what she pleased to write me & to stay as long as she pleased. Was this forenoon a little concerned till he returned when he brought me a letter from her, which I may afterwards insert, letting me know she had company, her brother & Sister Miles, and as she did not chuse to send the letters and ring by the boy she would keep them till Sabbath week, & if she did not change her mind, she would deliver them to me at Meeting. Poor thoughtless woman, how much is she altered, to talk of delivering such things to me, at publick worship, how much I pity her, but this is the effects of her spending so many Sabbaths, playing so idly with poor young Mr. Wilkins. After this I applied myself to study & writting with great delight. . . .

Friday 17 . . . Yesterday my horse run away from Mrs. B's, and she lent my boy one, which I sent back this morning, and when he returned, he told me Mr. Wilkins was there, and had gone yesterday as he hinted at the tavern, that the Negroes told him, that their Mrs. used me very bad, & was next week going to Town, & then the week after that to be married to Mr. Wilkins etc. I did not much mind this information, but it was confirmed this evening by what I heard from a better hand. I rode over to Mr. Donnoms, & soon afterwards Mr. John Brown & his wife, Brother in law to Mrs. B & her next neighbour came there, Mrs. Brown confirmed what the boy told me, but said her Sister in law told her I was too late in making my application or she would have accepted me according to her word, for she had told her Sister and all her relations that she would, Mrs. John Brown told me, that on Sabbath last she told her, that she had some letters of mine, (but did not mention the ring) and that she wanted to return them to me, but had lost one of them or accidentally tore it up, and that she had positively refused me & wished I would not come again, this with other information of her idly spending the Sabbaths with poor Mr. Wilkins, turned my resentment & pride into pity & contempt, I gave Mrs. Donnom & Mrs. Brown a short general account of what had passed since the tenth of Jully which amazed & confounded them, and engaged them both to go to her next week and get my letters from her, and the ring as I do not want either to write to or visit her, which they promised to do. Thus have I been Served as the great Mr. Halyburton was before me.[47] Poor creature how much I pity & compassionate her, O the dupes of Satan! O what Enmity he has at precious souls! that he thus hurries them on to wickedness without any temptation! She can give no reason unto her intimates why she has so used me. Stayed Supper, was by this information made quite easy and Satisfied & delivered from a great burthen, was cheerful and returned home after prayers. . . .[48]

129 [118] *Tuesday 21* . . . Being informed that Several of my Neighbours & Congregation, were at the publick [illegible word] about two or three miles from my house a fishing & dining there together, upon which I rode to the [illegible word]. I found severals of them there, among others Mrs. Donnom, who told me, she went down yesterday to see Mrs. B but she had heard of it, & went abroad to shun Mrs. Donnom, her & Mr. Wilkins went abroad on Sabbath & though Mrs. Donnom sent to her where she was, and with Mrs. John Brown dined at her house, the two young [illegible word] being

at home, yet Mrs. B refused to come home by Sending them word she had
the fever, Mr. & Mrs. [Dunlap], Mrs. B's next neighbours were also there,
Mrs. Donnom told me, that had wanted much to see me, to let me know
how matters were betwixt Mrs. B & Mr. Wilkins, she told me, that Mrs. B
sometime said I had come too late, at others said she had the greatest regard
for me, but could not be a ministers wife, denied that she was positively engaged before the Sacrament, but never told Mrs. Dunlap what passed at her
Brother in laws, when the rings were exchanged, Sometimes even that she had
loved me, but before I offered myself of the 10 of last month had changed
her fancy, & now loved none but Mr. Wilkins, & must have him, but still
spoke exceeding [illegible word] of me, had shown Mrs. Dunlap my letters,
& said she wanted to send them back, but did not tell, I had demanded them,
Mrs. Donnom told me many other such things, as that Mr. Hunt forbid his
niece ever to come into his house, & forbid Mr. Wilkins to come where he
was, that all her relations were enraged with her, & concerned for me . . .
Was concerned for poor Mrs. B & very thankful for my deliverance, much
like that of a man, who has narrowly escaped Shipwreck or being taken by
a turkish [130 (120)] Galley. Stayed about four hours here, Dined on fish
dressed in different ways, and as had my Chair box full of the finest apples,
gave away several dozen among friends & their children both before & after
Dinner, which was exceedingly acceptable, we were all very cheerful, and I
thought myself very happy in making so acceptable a present among my
friends, Had them from my good Mother Mrs. Hatcher. Sometime ago she
sent me nine dozen, Six dozen of which I sent down to Mrs. B, and intended
to have sent her twelve or fourteen dozen this afternoon, but they were much
better disposed of. It was my design, if she had used Mrs. Donnom well yesterday & sent up my letters, & not acted so meanly to have Sent three or
four dozen, but her acting in so Sneaking a manner, has made me resolve to
have no correspondence with her, that I can avoid, any more than in my
publick character, gave Mrs. Dunlap some directions what advice to give her,
as soon as she shall be married so that she may not fall off, from the religious
profession, which she had made. As I would fain impute her conduct to
weakness, for that she was very much in love with the writter, for Several
months or above a year is what she owns to Some, and as that was certainly
a great weakness so the Same reason may have occasioned the frenzy she is
now in, for the young man, and think it would be best for her to marry as
soon as possible, lest her fancy take another turn, I hope and pray it may
never turn back to me. . . .

Wednesday August 22 . . . In the afternoon I rode over the Indian Land to visit old Mrs. Mcpherson. As I passed Mrs. Clarks the tavern at the bridge Mr. Hunt was there driving Some Cattle down from his cowpen. He asked me to light, after the common compliments we walked out to the woods by the river side and discoursed over the affair, between his Cousin and me, and gave me some information, which much affected me. He told me, that the whole family, that is, all the branches thereof, had for several months been acquainted with her strong passion for me, that she herself made no secret of it among them, that it had begun above twelve months ago, that they knew of the faint offer I had made her last fall, and had all been much concerned at my taking my answer so soon, that they had often been in hopes, I would have renewed my Suit, that all of them and He in particular had repeatedly given it out, that her & I were to be married, that He did it on purpose I would inquire of him, why he said so, which would have given him an opportunity to Inform me, of her violent passion for me, which he & the relations, as well as herself hoped would have brought me to renew of my offer, that Mr. Wilkins had been hanging about her most of last winter & spring but got no sort of Encouragement, that Mrs. B's going up to Mr. Donnoms the Sixth of June last, was contrived on purpose & known to the whole family, that is to him, his wife and some of Mrs. B's sisters, or to them all, to get into my Company in order to engage me to visit her again at her own house, I having at that time omitted it for about thirteen weeks, and that she with great satisfaction had acquainted them with her Success as she thought, for when she visited me, at my own house, she took a fancy to a fine china tea pot, having some cups which it suited remarkably well, which I made her a present of, and she carried it to his house & showed it to his wife, and that they had all great hopes from my visiting her the week after that on the thirteenth of June. He confirmed what she told me, that night of her having said to him, that I courted her & she was to have me, that after the 13th of June, she said not much about me, but concealed her disappointment from them by making them believe that affairs betwixt her & me was according to her wish, and he believes that about or soon after this, Mr. Wilkins who had left her returned & Mr. Hunt was afraid he was somehow sent for, that on the 10th of July, when I renewed my offer to Mrs. B or rather, asked her if she would now stand to her word which she had told to her own relations, to several of my friends & to myself, of accepting me, that after her & I parted which was about four O Clock in the morning, that either before his wife got up, or after breakfast, she i.e. Mrs. B told Mrs.

Hunt I had offered myself & that she had engaged herself to me, and that she said it with the greatest pleasure & satisfaction, & begged Mrs. Hunt to tell it to Mr. Hunt and that I had left all settling of the Estate to him, & that I was to wait on him after the Sacrament about it, and that she repeatedly mentioned it with great pleasure to his wife next day who dined with us at Mr. Dunlaps, that his wife seeing her so overjoyed in order to Mortify her, would not tell him, but insisted Mrs. B must come & do it herself, that in two or three days after that Mrs. B came to his house, with pleasure & satisfaction in her looks, & after Sometime took him into a room, and asked if his wife, had told him, that she was to be married soon, he told her, she had not told him and added I hope Patty, it is to Mr. S, she told him it was & how generous I was about [131 (122)] her Estate & her son, bidding her do with it what she pleased, that if she gave all up to me I would do the best I could for her & her child, that I would [bear the Estate] and Educate him as my own child, that he Mr. Hunt said he always expected I would do & advised her to make no settlement, but to put herself, her child, & what Estate into my hands, without any conditions, and that to show her what his Sentiments of me were, he would give up the mortgage he had of her Estate to me before we were married, if I mentioned any thing of it, to him, or he would give it to me on the day after marriage, whither I mentioned it, or not, that when she repeatedly said, and is there nothing to be done, shall I bring him here to talk with you about it, he answered, I shall be very glad to see him, but will tell him there is no need for any settlement, that you trust all to him, & upon her repeating it, you say then, there is nothing to be done about settlements, he answered no I tell you, there needs nothing to be done but let him, get a parson & be married, as soon as you can, and I suppose, you are old enough to go to bed together without being put [to] it, that all this & more to the same purpose on the thirteen or fourteen of Jully at his own house, that on the twentieth of Jully she came to his house, in the most afflicted condition, with horrour & distress in her looks & after sometime, appearing to be one distracted, she went into a room, where he followed her, and there after crying bitterly & throwing herself upon a bed, she in an agony of distress cried out to him, who had earnestly intreated her to know what was the matter, Oh I am ruined, I am ruined, I am the most wretched of all women, etc etc, that he was terrified to see & hear her, & said, what is the matter [two illegible words] Mr. S [two illegible words] has he gone from his Engagements? She cried out Oh no, no, that is not it, Mr. S is the best of Men, but I can never have him, he does not know me, or he would never

have me, & much more, to the Same purpose, that he was amazed & terrified & pressed to know who or what disturbed her, she cried in an agony
Wilkins, what of him says Mr. Hunt, I am engaged to him says she, O horrid cried he, Are you engaged to both? Yes, yes says she, Oh I am undone, I
am ruined, I am the most wretched creature alive. He asked her to whom
she was engaged first, she answered, to Wilkins. He asked her, how she came
not to tell me so, she said, she was so overjoyed with my offer, she could not,
and that she was in hopes to get off with Wilkins, but found she could not,
and added that there was an absolute necessity for her to have him, though
she knew she was to be most miserable, He asked, who she loved most, she
answered, Mr. S, Mr. S, but never expected him to come back, that she
thought she could spend herself comfortably with Wilkins till Mr. S offered,
that now she was completely wretched & was under the woeful necessity of
marrying the man whom now she could not be happy with, & could not
love, He asked her how she could serve me so, she answered, in greatest distress, I am drove to it, I can trust him with my character, he is a good man
& will not expose nor ruin me, but Wilkins is not to be trusted and will ruin
me and take every advantage against me, therefore I must forever quit all
thoughts of the worthy & best of men, whom I love, & shall always love, &
must marry one whom I can never esteem, because I am in his power, &
must marry him out of fear of being exposed & ruined by him and that there
was no help for it, Mr. Hunt says, her distress was inexpressible, that she
often fainted, tore her hair, & cried most grievously, that He insisted since
she could not have me for fear of Wilkins she should have none of us, that
he was sure, I did not value her fortune, that Wilkins if he had anything to
show from under her hand & prosecuted could recover no more than the
half of her fortune, and that she might still have me, or live Single, that after
much talking to her, she seemed to be something pacified, but often said,
that even that [illegible words] & that she would be obliged to marry Wilkins
whom now she despised, that she engaged him to write me that something
extraordinary was the case, and I must loose her from her engagements, that
the letter was wrote, & was to be Sent next day, that she recollected that it
was the day before the Sacrament Sabbath, & begged it might not be sent
me, as it would disturb me, which he agreed to, that after this Mrs. Hatcher,
sister Jackson & his wife kept exhorting her never to have Wilkins, that Mr.
Hunt would give him [illegible word] of her part of the Estate, as soon as it
was cleared, & in the mean time, give him security for it, get her entirely out
of his power, & upon Condition she married me, which she promised to

endeavour to bring Mr. Wilkins to consent unto, but still continued in the greatest distress with horrour & terrour in her looks while there. On Monday the 23 of Jully, he understood that she had insisted to her Sister & his wife, that there was an absolute necessity for her having Wilkins, and that her reasons could not be removed. Poor Mr. Hunt tore up the letter he had wrote, and discharged her his house, or ever to come where he was unless she would consent to live without either of us, at least for some time, that after this sometimes she seemed to comply with his advice, but again at other times fell into the greatest distresses, often calling herself most miserable & wretched of all women, & still urging some private reasons why she must marry Wilkins, that she had frequent fears, faintings, hystericks, & was often like a distracted person, all her relations were in the greatest confusion & distress that neither he nor they could take it on them to acquaint me, Mr. Hunt did not offer to tell me, what he thought to be the reason nor did I ask him, the matter seemed too delicate & tender, and we were both affected, He said [132 (121)] that though he had not seen her for Sometime, yet she still persisted that I was the object of her affections and that she knew, she was to be most miserable & wretched all her life, but must marry Wilkins, he could & would [illegible word] her if she did not, and that she doubted not but I would forgive & pity her, which poor Lady, I most Sincerely do, & shall not cease to pray that God may pity & forgive her, & make her more happy than she expects, this I most solemnly declare is the Substance of what Mr. John Hunt her own Cousin told me, although not conceived in such strong expressions as he generally used, and is but the sum & substance of what he told me, at much greater length. I acquainted him of the whole of my conduct, which He said was most exactly what she told him. I repeated my last letter to her, & hers to me, and acquainted him I had Sent down Mr. Donnom & Mrs. John Brown to get my letters & my ring and to return hers on Monday last but that she had gone from home to avoid them. He told me, he would do what he could to prevent her marrying Wilkins, & would write me in a few days, and though he could not expect I would ever think of her again, yet if I could bring myself to it, perhaps it might be possible for her to give me intire Satisfaction, by laying every thing before me, that had [happened] between her & Wilkins, which gave her so great uneasiness, to this I made little answer, only said there was no saying what time might bring about, this last supposition of his, I thought was very friendly toward her & was necessary enough, after what had been said. . . . Was very much affected with the account I had heard, was grieved & distressed to the very heart, for poor, poor, unhappy Mrs. B, whose agony & distress I believe is exceeding great, no wonder poor Lady, said she could not look me in the [eyes], no wonder, she often turned away from me & dropped tears, Now I understand the Mystery of her strange conduct, on the evening of Monday week, when standing on the floor of the hall, [near] the room door, when I was upbraiding her, and walking away from her, she held me a full quarter of an hour, often pulled me towards her, drawed me unto her breast, & still turned away her head from me, & when I drew off from her, she often said with the most Melancholy accents, will you leave me so, that was, as I understood her, would I leave her in anger and without saluting her, and indeed I was so distressed & shocked at her behaviour, that I could not look at her, let alone Salute her and on the day of [illegible word] her countenance seemed to me black as the very ground, was also very thankful for the kindness of providence to me & mine in this strange affair. . . .

Thursday August 23 . . . In the afternoon I rode over to Captain Mcphersons. As I passed Mrs. Clark at the bridge I saw Mr. Wilkins, observed his boy had a large portmanteau, beckoned him, he retired into the shoe makers shop, and Endeavoured to shun me. Mr. Ferguson, brother in Law to Mrs. B, was with him and came out & spoke to me, and afterwards Mr. Wilkins came out. He has been Sick, and looks very poorly. He had also a very dejected look, owing I suppose to his Mother & own relations being against his match with Mrs. B, as well as her relations, besides he is under age, and will find it somewhat difficult to get equipped for his wedding if his relations do not interpose their Credit for him, the Common compliments passed between Mr. Wilkins & me, he repeatedly admired to see me look so fat & hearty, as at this time I am fatter & lustier than ever I was in my life, for begin to be something gross over the belly, which gives me some uneasiness, for if it was [133 (119)] the divine will, I would rather Continue slender, it is very Surprizing, that I should grow so fat at this Season of the year, and at a time when I go through almost as much if not greater exercise, and very violent exercise, as I ever did in my life, my friends, as well as myself have been uneasy about it and are afraid I am growing to my grave as the Saying is. . . .

[134 (117)] *Tuesday 28* . . . Got up this morning blessing the Lord and desiring to spend this day among the Sick & afflicted on this Side of the river, accordingly after breakfast & morning duties, set out. Rode to Mr. Strains, but before I got there, was overtaken in a very heavy showery rain, and though

run my horse, and was well provided with my Cloak, yet got considerable
wet. It continued to rain all the forenoon, so that was obliged to stay here,
the children are troubled with fevers, this I think is as good & worthy a family as I am acquainted with, they are both serious, religious, Sensible & well
educated people, & are at great pains with their children, they are exceeding
friendly to me, & to the Gospel interest in this place. After Dinner, Mr. Strain
rode with me, we rode four miles, the worst ride that can be imagined, it is
from the Situation of the place, bad at any time but almost unpassable at
present, Every step to the horses belly, I could hardly have got there without
a guide, it was to visit Mr. Strbls a Dutch family on Gibs place, the Genteelest Dutch people I have ever been acquainted with. He is a very Sensible,
Genteel, well bred man, in very good easy Circumstances, their house furnished as if in Charlestown from which some months ago they moved, & live
very Genteely in their house, His wife I think a very pious, good, Sensible
worthy young woman, being his third venture, she is daughter to a Lutheran
clergyman, who is gone home to conform to the church of England,[49] She
has been very bad & miscarried, her sister a young Lady of about Sixteen has
been very ill, as also a girl a niece of his, had not heard of it till last Sabbath,
found them all something on the recovery. . . .

[140 (246)] *Wednesday September 5 1770* . . . In the forenoon wrote a letter
to the Gentlemen from whom I purchased my new Negroes last year, their
worthy Father, Colonel Smith, is lately dead on Rhode Island where he had
gone for health. He was my very worthy & good friend, ever since I have
been in the province, and am apprehensive Since his Death Some or other
of my Enemies, has been doing me some ill offices with them, or they would
not have wrote me so soon as uneasy about their money, the most of which
I would have paid them [by] now had my rice been sold, or had I received
money due to me, in very good security, afterwards transcribed from my
pocket Diary. . . . About Eight O Clock, I took a vomit of [illegible word]
grains of merc: vitae which in about an hours time began to work, made me
very sick, and worked me exceeding hard till late after midnight, gave me a
great many vomits, chiefly of bile very black thick & rancid, and was exceeding hard to be brought up, I hardly remember ever to have been more Sick
in my life, or worked with greater severity. I have often vomited a larger quantity but never so much black deep coloured bile, at last after many hard vomits in which I was often like to faint & was prodigiously Scalded with the
hotness of the bile after it was put in motion, it [began] to work downwards

& worked me till near morning, though at times I slept a little, but cannot express the sickness & distress I went through, was not able to take any nourishment after the operation was over, as I usually do, but Continued Sick at my stomach & overpowered with sleep till the morning. Before I took the vomit had gone to praying particularly for a blessing upon it, & safety of it, which comforted me in my very uncommon Sickness, & after it abated the Lord helped me to praise & bless his holy name for his mercy & goodness to me in this Severe operation.

Thursday 6 . . . Set about study & writting for Sabbath forenoon, designing another Subject for the afternoon and was well assisted in study & writting, had the Lords most comfortable presence, directing me to many suitable, awful, & very important truths, especially in the introduction, which chiefly designed for ignorant, careless, hypocritical & formal professors of religion, & was chiefly occasioned by a fresh instance of defection in a young communicant, had never had so much pain & uneasiness in my life, about the unbecoming lives & practices of some religious professors, as of late about some who have within these two years, made a profession in this new Congregation, Severals of whom have since the last Sacrament here acted & behaved, in such a manner as to give me great distress, Miss Polly Jordan attempting that very night to run off with the man, whom actually went off on the Wednesday following & has for these two years been a communicant, Mr. Thomas Timmons & his wife, that day admitted for the first time, & yet both privy to such a matter, Mr. Jordans very undecent, & very unbecoming behaviour at publick worship that day fortnight, who has not only been a communicant for many years but a deacon & officer at the tables, Mrs. B's misconduct & misbehaviour known only to myself, & one or two friends, & have this week been informed, that young Miss Nancy F[50] a communicant these two years, is thought to be with child, such things have proved very grieving & distressing to my mind, have greatly distressed & affected me, have robed me of my peace & Satisfaction of mind, have broke my [slumbers] and deprived me of sleep, have not been able to eat or drink as usual Since heard of the last, her poor Mother is in great distress, and has been talking much to her, & some of the women that are neighbours have been doing the Same, at her Mothers desire, her condition looks much like one Some months pregnant but she denies it & says she has been Some months disordered, she is but young & has always had a modest behaviour & good character, [but] sometime last winter, she was at some dances, where there

was very bad company, & has since had [severe] [141 (241)] afflictions cast
upon her, the Lord knows whether she is innocent or guilty, time will soon
discover, [yet] the report & clamour made about it, greatly troubles & distresses me, & proves very hurtful to the cause of religion . . . Was surprized
with a visit from Mr. Jordan & Mr. [B] with, his business was to engage me
to marry him at Ponpon next Monday forenoon to Miss B Oswald, a young
Lady about twenty two years of age, who lives with her Mother in law, old
Mrs. Oswald, but has no fortune at all of her own, their Father dying very
poor, I thought her full too young for him but approved of her person &
character. His courtship has been very short, & she seems to be fond of him
for his money notwithstanding his being more than double her age, he was
highly elevated, & in the greatest flow of Spirits I ever saw him or any person else, to be in their Sober Senses, I am very well assured he was perfectly
so, as he was truly transported, with the thoughts of what he hoped so soon
to accomplish, I was grieved & sorry to see his great weakness, was distressed
to observe him so intirely to forget his children & former connections yet
could not but approve of his choice, though observed many things very rep-
rehensible in his present temper & conduct with respect to his former &
present family. Promised to go part of the way on Sabbath after Sermon, to
publish him three times at once after pronouncing the blessing, he was to go
down tomorrow to acquaint his intended bride, who had last night agreed
to be married as Soon as he pleased and was to send me notice before Sabbath morning. His Elevated behaviour afforded me many useful lessons &
made me see the great necessity of being much on my watch & guard, he
was so transported with confident expectations of spending all his future days
in great peace & happiness, as he expressed it, that I greatly pitied him, and
expect nothing less than some great disappointment, some great Misfortune
to happen him, though truly a good & gracious man I hope & believe him
to be. He was greatly pleased with my approving of his choice, which I could
not refuse as to the person & her character, since he chose so young a
person. . . .

Saturday September 8 . . . About breakfast time Mrs. B's overseer, R H, came
to my house, & after desiring to be in private with me, he [142 (229)] delivered me a bundle from Mrs. B containing all my letters except two which
she said, had got wet & were tore up, with my ring, desiring me to return
hers, her letter contained a seeming reflection, as if I had been talking of her,
but was wrote as if conscience had checked her, & concluded as usual, &

upon the whole was a more discrete letter than I expected, her Overseer told me, that she was not married, that the tailor was sick who was to make the wedding cloaths, that there seemed a little demur among them, but he expected they would be married next week, that her relations continued very obstinate against her & her marriage, that he heard her say, she wanted very much to come to meeting tomorrow, but could not do it, till she heard from me, and was very anxious to receive a letter from me, that when she delivered him the letter, she sent her love to me & to my children, and desired very particularly to know, how we were, I wrote her a very kind letter, in which I freely forgave her, fully disengaged her, wished her health & happiness in her designed connection & took my final leave of her, assuring her of my friendship. I may at another time, copy into this Diary, her last letter to me & mine to her. Sent all her letters & her ring by the Overseer, thus I hope am done with this troublesome affair . . . Late in the afternoon walked home with my children, who had come over to see a parrot Sent them in a present from Beaufort. . . .

Lords day September 9 1770 . . . Mrs. B was in meeting and seemed confused but about her I had no manner of thought nor concern, Mr. Wilkins was also there, I saw him in Company with his Brother in law Threadcraft who has turned out a very ordinary person, & with Ganolke who though a great tool of his Brother in law Mains against me yet attends very constantly on publick worship, & behaves well. As I was passing by, where they were, I went to them, asked how they were & gave them my hand as usual. Mr. Ganolke behaved very complaisant & with good manners but Mr. Wilkins & his brother in law were far from behaving so, Mr. Wilkins turned about his back yet turned again & gave his hand, but said little. Mr. Threadcraft gave his hand but not so complaisantly as usual. I observed their behaviour but took no notice of it, for I went up on purpose to observe them, poor Mr. Wilkins seemed very uneasy at the Sight of me, and his looks at me were full of wrath, he continued much the Same way during the Sermon, behaving in the most uneasy, careless like manner, and as if very discontented at being there, with frequent mad furious looks at me. I easily guessed the reason, that he imagined I had been doing him some ill turns, either with the widow or her relations, who are still against, but as I knowed myself perfectly innocent, I was very indignant about his unjust thoughts of me, or his ungenteel, unmanly behaviour, though at first it gave me Some uneasiness and concern, that he should take up such unjust prejudices against me, and endeavour to prejudice others, resolved to speak to him after Service if I had opportunity. After the Sermon I was a little among friends as usual, afterwards went up to the retiring house and changed my Robes for my Coat, at my coming away Mrs. B was right in my way and I could not get her shunned, upon which I asked her how she did, she was very complaisant & behaved as usual upon which I lighted & talked a little to her, told her I was glad she came to meeting as usual & hoped she would look upon me as one of her friends, which she said she always did & would do. I asked her if she believed what I wrote her yesterday, which she said she did & took very kindly. I then offered her my hand, which she accepted of very kindly, I told her that Mr. Wilkins was prejudiced against me, very unjustly, that he had not behaved well to me, & that I hoped she would undeceive him, as she knew in what a friendly manner I always spoke of him. She assured me, that she would. I then told her I much wished to see her business finished, and assured her I would do her any kindness with her relations I could. While I was with her, I observed Mr. Wilkins at a neighbouring chair very uneasy & much disturbed like, upon which after I parted with her, & taken my leave of some other company, I took an opportunity to speak with him, & told him was sorry to see him so uneasy, & to behave in so Strange a way to me, and assured him, that he had not the least reason, that I was intirely done with her, and that if she had let me known how [it stood] [betwixt] him & her, I never would have spoke to her on that head after the 10th of Jully, that he [143 (227)] could appeal to her & to all her relations, that I had always spoke well of him, he owned he had not behaved well to me, this morning, that he was very sorry for it, he owned she said I always spoke well of him but Said he imagined I had prejudiced her relations against him, but that after what I told him, he was Satisfied I had not, he repeatedly gave me his hand, said he would not give notice to anything he should hear, but would look upon me as his friend, which I assured him he might do and that I would endeavour to do him Service with her relations. He told me, he did not intend to have gone home with her but she had told him, she had Something to say to him, & that being Satisfied I used him honourably, he would go and hear what she had to say to him, It grieved me, that I was obliged to concern myself in such an affair, at this time but thought it necessary, and my duty. Just as I parted with him and mounted my horse, he seemed very uneasy to get home and before I got my feet fixed in the Stirrups, he set off with me. After riding a little and endeavouring to recover myself I found the girth very slack and that the Saddle came over the horses neck, he was still running with me. I then looked out for my boy & called for him, but he was gone far ahead out of hearing and took no notice of me, at this very time the horse, while I was looking & calling for my boy, my horse started at something & run to one Side, upon which I was thrown to some distance. As I felt myself going I endeavoured to throw myself off, and to fall on my right hand but it seems I struck the ground with my head with great violence and was laid Speechless. My horse stumbled at the same time & fell upon me, two men riding at some distance, saw my horse start & throw me. They immediately came up and found me lying to all appearance dead, they stood by sometime about a minute, at last one of them said I breathed when they lighted and lifted me up. I was positively limber and to all appearance dead, but in about five or ten minutes I began to come to, they kept holding me up for some time. When my horse had run past my boy, which was the first notice he had of my fall, he catched the horse & came up to them, crying very much, & said he would go to Mr. Donnoms for the chair which he did. I came to so far as to be able to ride one of their horses, but was not fully in my right Senses . . . afterwards met Mr. Donnom with my own Chair, which went into with him & drove home, kept still coming more & more to my Senses. Met Mr. James Donnom & Mrs. Donnom at my own house, who had been much alarmed and were much pleased to see it was no worse, one side of my face about my right eye is much bruised, and grown very black, my whole right side feels hurt, but is in no part black, my right hand, on which I intended to break my fall, hurt me much at the wrist, but does not appear bruised, is stiff & swelled, I can use it very well under my hand, but cannot turn it, nor lift it to my head. Was immediately blooded, two supper plate fulls, as soon as I got home, I did not seem to come quite to my self till was blooded, when was perfectly Sensible, but remembered nothing that happened after I felt myself falling, Sat down at table but could not eat any thing but a little thin broth, after dinner Mr. James Donnom went home in his chair, and as had been informed my Dear children, were greatly alarmed when they Saw Bristol crying so much, heard him say I was dead, Susy cried very much, and both begged to come over & See me, but as I felt myself much better I walked over with Mr. Donnom, Mrs. Donnom going in my chair, and stayed with my children till near dark, when I rode home. Continued still better, took a cooling purge, and sat up transcribing into my Diary till twelve O Clock at night, when went to bed & tied a hard egg over the bruised place, which kept bathing with strong vinegar and some salt armeniac dissolved in it, thus the Lord has most graciously & miraculously preserved me, amidst a very threatening danger. . . .

[144 (225)] *Wednesday September 12:1770* . . . About the middle of the
forenoon set off for Campbells hill . . . Dctr. Wlply[51] was going up to the
same place & passing at this time, rode in company with him, found my
very good friend Mr. James Donnom well, found Mr. Jordan & young Mr.
Forester also there. Dined altogether, were very free & cheerful in our conversation, of the five in company four of us were widows, which afforded
some innocent mirth about our refusals & disappointments, only Mr. Jordans unhappy temper seemed hurt a little, by his being too serious & galled
with his late affair, for it seems his high very high expectations has turned
out a disappointment, which cannot well bear. . . .

[146 (221)] *Lords day September 16 1770* . . . Found but few people at meeting, the poor Indian Land being at present in the Condition I have often
seen it, most exceeding Sickly, but also many of the old Inhabitants being
dead & gone, Many of the new ones desire little of my company. Have not
known it so Sickly for Several years as it is at present. Preached all day with
the Divine assistance & Gods most comforting & refreshing presence, from
Psalm 23:4 a most pleasant and delightful subject. . . . The little congregation appeared Sickly & poorly, & severals in the forenoon were obliged to
go out, all sat sweating with the violent heat & seemed often quite fainting
& overcome with the Sulteryness thereof. The Sight of a whole Sickly auditory, though small to what is usual, & the repeated prayers put up both forenoon & afternoon for the many Sick & afflicted, made it very melancholy
& affecting. . . . Rode home in the chair with my very particular friend Mrs.
P[52] to her Fathers Captain Mcphersons. . . . Found old Mrs. McPherson still
low& poorly, having an intermitting fever every night, found the poor old
Captain very ill, he has been bad for about a week with a violent nervous
fever, caused chiefly by his own intemperance, he was this day blistered but
tore if off, was quite insensible all this evening, exceedingly low, and upon
the whole as melancholy & humbling a sight as I have Seen. . . .

Monday September 17 1770 . . . I rode back to the old Captain, found her
something better, but found him still very low, his fever seemed off, & he was
Something in his Senses, after sitting some time with her Sick in one room,
went into the other & sat with him, and had a good deal of serious conversation with him, afterwards asked him if I should go to prayer, which he very
readily agreed to, & afterwards thanked me very kindly for it. Endeavoured
to deal very faithfully with him, especially in the prayer & was well assisted

therein, I never saw him so good humoured. Afterwards his wife & such of his children, that were present, desired me to speak to him, about some alterations in his will, which I did, in the most prudent manner I could, he very readily agreed to have it done, & told me it was very right & necessary, and that he had thought of it himself, & would have it done directly when a friend near at hand could be sent. He continued still very thankful, I then rode to his youngest sons Mr. Ulysses Mcpherson who is married & lives where Mr. Postell lived, found him & his wife both very poorly, they have been very Sick with severe fevers, acquainted them how their Father was, they were most pleased he had admitted me to pray with him, as they were just going to ride out & see the old Gentleman, which I encouraged them to do. I proceeded, called at Mrs. Graves to visit her Sister Mrs. DeSaussure, who is at present at her house, with her children, their new house, not being quite finished, found Mrs. DeSaussure with a slow fever, she again looks [147 (219)] very poorly, the child is bad with the hooping Cough, stayed about half an hour with them, & promised to come back & Dine, rode to Doctor Bowers who has been Sick, but is getting better, let a little blood, as have still had something of a headache, Since my fall, though blooded then, stayed about three quarters of an hour & proceeded, to Mr. Peter Roberts, who is just returned from Santee, Sick & poorly. His oldest child has been very ill, his youngest child also sick and his wife very poorly, & very near her time, stayed about three quarters of an hour with them, directing & encouraging them, think they are truly pious especially Mr. Roberts, proceeded to Mr. F whose Grandchild McLd is very Sick and has been very ill, Just as I got there, Mrs. Nugent, formerly the widow Plmto, came there with a child to baptize, as the house was washing & in Some confusion, I promised to come back after Dinner & baptize the child, rode back to Mrs. Graves & dined with her, & her Sister DeSaussure, Mr. DeSaussure being at the plantation, where they are making a Settlement. Was very kindly entertained, stayed about an hour & a half, Mrs. Graves with her two children, seems to be very comfortably settled here, rode back to Mrs. F's & baptized Mrs. Nugents child about two months old, her husband a very vile worthless fellow, was religiously bred in Pennsylvania, left her a few months after her marriage, robbed & plundered her, her brother & her first husbands child, carrying off some of their Negroes & has left her very destitute with a child to work for. Poor unhappy woman she was deluded with his fair tongue, married him upon too short a Courtship for a stranger & now she suffers severely for her folly. . . .

Tuesday September 18 . . . When got up, was obliged to speak a good deal to my house Negroes, who are grown so lazy, and keep both the house, the furniture & every thing even my linnens so dirty, and in bad order, & their cooking for me is of late so disagreeable, that have no pleasure at all in being at home, nor any comfort when I am there, Mrs. B's weak, silly, foolish conduct, has put me out of all conceit of marrying, and given me something of a disgust to the Sex . . . This day expected the company of some Ladies my neighbours to cut out clothes for my negro children & wenches, which they did, & afterwards stayed & did Several little things for me, Mrs. Strain came first soon after breakfast then Mrs. Donnom & afterwards Mrs. F, they found my linnen exceedingly bad washed, & badly done up of, and other things much out of order, for which they talked much to the wench who has the charge of these things, who I hope may do some thing better, at least for some time, they Dined with me, and stayed till late in the afternoon. . . .

Wednesday September 19 . . . [148 (217)] Visited the work men at the meeting house, & was pleased to see them so forward, came round by the houses on the top of the red hill, was met by Turnbull the School Master who has lately thrown himself out of Doctor Days employ, where he was very well, he spoke to me about introducing him to a school on the Saltcatcher, but gave him very little encouragement, only promised to know of our School Master after my return from Beaufort, whether he continues after his first quarter, or not. Was asked by one Kenan a stranger with his family come last week into the house where Bmbzn lived, whose wife is turned out so wicked as to be the means of driving him from this place, where he was in a very thriving way of living, was earnestly asked by this man to go in & visit his wife, who is taken very ill since she came here, which I complied with, though I did not much like to go into a house of such fame, found her very bad, & hardly conversible, gave her some advices & asked if I should go to prayer, which she intreated me to do, was well assisted in prayer both for her recovery & salvation, she seemed much affected, & after prayer grasped my hand, and very affectionately thanked me, desiring I should visit her, which I promised to do after my return from Beaufort, drank a glass of wine at my going in and at my coming out, stayed but short, Several vile people were there, who seemed amazed & surprized. . . .

Thursday September 20 1770 . . . After an early Dinner got ready, though met with some obstacles, and set off [for Beaufort]. The roads are still exceeding bad, about four miles from home I turned off, and went to Mr. Elts about a mile and a quarter off the path, and Baptized his child according to appointment on Monday last, the child is bad with the hooping cough, his wife was a most affecting picture of distress & trouble, poverty & Sickness, as I know some things very Singular in her life, the Sight of her extreme misery was to me very affecting, poor man he looked poorly & dejected himself, he has a large family, and in bad Circumstances. Had Gods most gracious presence & assistance, while celebrating this ordinance, the poor parents, poor indeed I am afraid poor every way, were much affected & in tears, in about a quarter of an hour after concluding this Service, I proceeded in a humble heavenly Spiritual frame . . . Called at Mrs. Williamson to inquire if she had any commands for Beaufort, she had tea immediately ordered and with some earnestness insisted on my staying to drink Some with her which kept me till after Dark, she has almost always used me very well & with great respect, and for some months past with all the kindness & freedom when I waited upon her, worthy Dear Lady, she is very Sencible of the injury her Mistaken relations did her on a certain occasion, when they persuaded her to act so contrary to her own inclination, promise & Engagement, both her & they have acknowledged, and offered me every compensation in their power. She has also let me know that she was abundantly Sencible that she acted wrong to be swayed by them at that time, but it is all too late though I shall ever regard & esteem her, & be a friend to her & hers. After Drinking tea with her and free affectionate conversation, I proceeded to my good worthy friend Mrs. Hatcher, whom I generally call my Mother and my children have always been used, even them who are dead to call Grand mama Hatcher, did not get there till sometime after dark, and was received with such kindness, care, and tenderness, as could not be exceeded by my own Dear Mother if she was alive, had a pleasant comfortable evening, and was in a humble thankful frame of soul. . . .

Friday 21 . . . After breakfast I proceeded to the ferry, over the river, & to Mr. Bowmans, where got about one O Clock. . . . This night in Conversation heard of some of the horrid deceitfulness of Main & his wretched family in giving out that poor Mrs. Dupont, Mary Cater that was, died a quiet, easy, comfortable Death, which they know to be as false as hell, for her Death was the most horrid & terrible, almost, beyond anything on record in history, was also informed that old [149 (215)] Mrs. Cuthbert Mother to Threadcraft is so base & wicked as to suffer herself to be the tool of propagating this but was also informed, that the real truth is known, in spite of all the pains taken to hide it, and the ungrateful Mrs. Cuthbert is known to be & is publickly called, what she really is, a most artful, conniving deceitful selfish person always devoted to them, who can be most useful to her, paying little regard to any thing else but self interest, a most smooth fawning, hypocritical deceiful woman as lives, in their practice & conversation, a character, alas too too true. May the Lord pardon & forgive her, if she has any thing of the root of the matter in her, Doubleness, she is laying up Scourges for herself. . . .

Lords day September 23 1770 All this morning and forenoon it continued a cold Small rain, and every now and then pretty hard showers, which prevented people from the country though two or three came, and as most of the inhabitants of the place were sick, expected but few hearers, and especially as the Established Minister did not go over to St. Helena though it was the day he should have gone, but poor Creature he is glad of any excuse, to omit his duty. In general he preaches one Sermon a day fifteen & once twelve minutes long, affects to be called a buck & delights in no company but those, who are the great rakes & libertines in all the place, among a few of whom he reigns, about ten O Clock Mrs. Green was sent for to attend a Cousin of hers, by her Fathers Side, who had been thought a dying from last night, Mrs. Frchld,[53] about thirty six years of age leaving a disconsolate husband & two children behind her, about Eleven O Clock we went to meeting, the Congregation was but Small, but the Lord was with us, & made it a most sweet & comfortable time . . . was most particularly assisted in prayer, both before & after Sermon and with great enlargement & tender affections pled & wrestled with God for that poor Lady so long in the agonies of Death . . . Mrs. Green who had returned & attended the afternoon Service, told me, that though the house was at a good distance, they very distinctly heard the prayers, and had it not been for the confusion, that was in the house, & the noise the Negroes made, they could have joined in the prayers, & attended to the Sermon. . . . [150 (213)] About nine O Clock rode back to the Doctors, soon after which Mrs. Green was again sent for to the dying Lady, and to Sit up all night, and the horse & chair being got, about ten I rode down with Mrs. Green, was immediately asked to walk up stairs, where was a most Melancholy & humbling Spectacle indeed, few corpse I have ever seen looked so gastly as this poor dying woman, she has been a very moral person, an excellent wife, mother, neighbour, and indeed most excellent in every relation, and is greatly lamented. She appears to have been in the agonies

Since Sometime on Saturday, lies motionless & senseless, her eyes half shut, mostly fixed sometimes rolling gastly & frightful, her mouth open, her breast heaving, her body in a burning fever, and all covered over with great drops of sweat, every now & then giving the most grievous & heart breaking loud sighs. I Sat about half an hour & prayed with great & even uncommon fullness & fervency, for indeed was greatly moved and affected, as were all in the room, we were a weeping company, was enabled to wrestle for her Salvation & Eternal happiness, for her greatly afflicted relations, and for her Dear children, who are both young, hardly had ever more of the Spirit of prayer, grace & supplication, than at this time. . . .

[151 (211)] *Wednesday September 26:1770* . . . I set out again for Indian Land, sore & weary, as all my riding horses were quite worn out I took two off the plantation, young creatures I had never been used to, rode to Mrs. Fb where her son & McLd lives,[54] was surprized to find, it was not the child I visited about a fortnight ago but another who was then in perfect health & some years older than the child I then prayed for, She was his oldest child, his only daughter, she was [taken] that very night I was there, and died of a warm fever, was desired to Baptize a child for one Mr. Rice, married to a sister of Mrs. McLds. The women are all Anabaptists, I asked the mother if it was in the least against her will, to have the child baptized, she answered, no, it very much my desire that you should baptize it for I think it is very right, though I was brought up in a different way. Poor Creature she appeared to have no reason for Anabaptism, but that her parents were of that way of thinking, as she herself has never been baptized, I told her, she could not stand for the child & that no vows could be laid on her, she wept, afterwards I baptized the child, during the whole of the ordinance she stood, and was very much affected, I directed the whole Speech to the Father & took all the promises on him. Afterwards I signified to her that her general profession as a Christian, & her being the parent of the child, Obliged her to bring it up for God, even though she did not believe infant baptism, nor came under such express & explicit engagements, as the Father now had, mentioned her very particularly in the last prayer, she was much affected and behaved well. It was a very solemn time, the company which was larger than I expected were remarkably serious & attentive, and was myself well assisted in prayer, in exhortation, & every part of this ordinance, afterwards the funeral set out for the meeting house. It was after two O clock before we dismissed from the meeting house yard, though was but short, both in prayer and in the exhortation

. . . Proceeded up the Indian Land of the Saltcatcher river to old Mrs. Cuthberts, to visit her family which I heard has been very Sick. Found her son
Threadcraft, very much reduced with a fever which he has had about Eleven
days, but seems now to be getting better of it, her two sons Cuthbert, have
also been very ill, but are getting better, Stayed here better than two hours
& drank tea with them, they received me with great respect, pretended great
kindness & friendship, God only knows their heart, I received it all with
good manners, and acted to them as became a Minister & Christian, Drank
tea with them and eat very heartily of loaf bread & butter, which found very
refreshing for was very hungry. . . .

[152 (209)] *Friday September 28 1770* . . . Received a letter to go & Baptize a
young child of Mr. Hskns, at Coosawatchy. . . . They professed the church
of England and expected I would make use of the Service book, which they
brought to me, but I acquainted them of my design to baptize their child in
the presbyterian way which they agreed to. My Dear children have been with
me all this day, there being no school and Mrs. Donnom as very usual in this
Neighbourhood, visiting abroad, I never was so disappointed and never lived
among such a people in my life, the Men are the most idle careless creatures
that can be, always hunting or some others much worse employed, and the
women almost always Gadding abroad, am grieved & distressed on account
of my Dear Dear children, but cannot help myself. . . . Betsy is but poorly,
being about cutting Some of her backmost jaw teeth, her gums are much
Swelled & her mouth very Sore, poor Dear child I observed her to be very
low in flesh under the Clothes, very full of sores, and much neglected, greatly
does she need a parents care. . . .

Saturday September 29 1770 . . . In the morning Mrs. Donnom sent me word
she was come home from Mr. John Browns, but upon my Sending her word
I would keep the children till night, she went immediately abroad again to
visit Mr. Strains family. She had come about eight miles, in the morning &
to Mrs. Strains is about seven. Such pleasure have Some people, in going
abroad, but Sure I am a family can never thrive, when the heads act in such
a manner, Mrs. Donnom is one of the best women in these parts, and reckoned one of the best heads of a family. How miserable & unhappy should I
be, if I should be so unfortunate, as to marry a woman that went much
abroad. . . .

[153 (207)] *Lords day September 30* . . . At the dismission of the congregation, rode directly back to the hill where one Kenan now keeps tavern, and married a Couple whom I had published in the morning Wm Shepherd, a very youth, to the widow B[55] and immediately returned to the meeting . . . took leave of my friends & set off for Charlestown. It Continued a Small rain, rode fast, till I got to the Savannah & stopped at Mr. Jacksons where had my horses well fed, & Drank tea, with some other refreshment for my self, which Mrs. Jackson got ready for me, she also spoke to me alone & thanked me for continuing my friendship to the family & to her Sister B, notwithstanding what had happened. She told me, that her Sister Mrs. B, acquainted her of the friendly letter I wrote her, and of the friendship I had in some instance shown her, Since her publick declaration to marry Mr. Wilkins, she told me, all the Sisters, & their families, as well as Mr. John Hunt & their Brother young Mr. Joseph Hunt, had the greatest esteem & regard for me, and would still look upon me, as a friend & relation if I should allow them, and that poor unfortunate Mrs. B expressed the highest veneration for me, and had often said of late, that she would ever retain it, and that my forgiving & behaving friendly to her, had given her great happiness, and removed the distress that was preying on her mind, & much more to the Same purpose, I assured her of my friendship & great regard for them all, not even excepting Mrs. B, and that I would do her all the friendly actions in my power, & that she & they might depend on it . . . I proceeded over the river, about three miles further to Mr. Brandfords, where got at half an hour after nine O Clock. . . .

[154 (205)] *Monday first day of October one thousand Seven hundred & Seventy years* . . . I proceeded on my journey . . . got to Charlestown, about four O Clock. . . . Spent the Evening mostly with Mr. James Carson a worthy Country man a Merchant who is lately begun to do Some business for me,[56] we supped together at Mr. Mitchells, with Mrs. Mitchell & the family, Spent the evening very agreeably & at Mrs. Mitchells desire gave family worship, before any of the company broke up. . . .

Tuesday October 2 1770 . . . There was a great confusion in town, Occasioned by some merchants having imported goods & offering them to sale contrary to the very just, the very necessary publick resolutions to import only some Coarse absolutely necessary articles from Great Britain till the Parlement repeals some very Cruel & Oppressive acts for taxing us Contrary to all the principles of liberty and the Constitution, yet such is the avarice of Some, that rather than deny themselves the usual profits of trade, they will expose all our posterity to slavery, even though they have signed & solemnly engaged to Observe the publick resolutions, the General Committee at last prevailed with the delinquents to give up their goods to be stored, but not till the mob were just going to tar and feather them, and in that Condition cart them round the town, which has been with good success practised in Some of the Northward Colonies, was almost all day engaged in necessary business. In the forenoon went to the Council chamber, and with others had my petition read to the Governor & council which was granted,[57] there were about two hundred this day petitioning for land, a sure sign that the province is thriving. . . .

Wednesday October 3 . . . [155 (203)] Got home before twelve at night, would have been at home by Eleven, but stopped at the plantation Sometime, for instead of riding round by avenue up directly to my own house, I rode through the plantation by the Overseers house, where was surprized to find he was abroad, & the Negroes in a cold frosty night carrying rice out of the water, and assured by the Sencible ones, that they had some of them still two hours work to be done, that the overseer went away early, that the negroes in general had made fires to themselves all about the field & barn yard which I saw, and kept lying about these fires, instead of finishing their work, that if the Overseer had stayed with them, the very weakest & idlest, would have been done as usual before nine O Clock but now many of them would not be done by one or two O Clock, afterwards met others of them crying & roaring aloud for cold. I encouraged them & told them, there should be no more such late working, was grieved & concerned for them & determined to reprimand the Overseer. I suffered a great deal this night with the Cold myself, which no doubt made me more concerned for them. Concluded the day with praising & blessing the Lord, for his goodness & mercy to most unworthy me, had rode by calling at some different places near Seventy miles & felt neither weary nor fatigued, neither my strength nor Spirits failed me, after Some refreshment called my family together, & gave thanks unto the Lord for his lovingkindness to most unworthy me and mine having heard the children were well.

Thursday October 4 Got up pretty early, after breakfast Mr. Ferguson the taylor came to cut clothes for my fellows & boys. . . . Was informed this day that old Mrs. Mctier, who was prayed for last Sabbath but was not thought bad, & walked about on Monday, died on Tuesday morning & was buried early on Wednesday. This gave me considerable uneasiness knowing that all the family would be much concerned at my absence, would have rode over directly but it was too late before I heard the news this night. . . .

Friday October 5 1770 . . . In the afternoon after an Early Dinner, rode over to the Indian Land Side to visit the late Mrs. Mctiers family, found nobody at home, Mrs. Shaw having gone to her plantation in the morning, & Mrs. Melvin, having just rode to her brothers, I accordingly proceeded there, was received most kindly by Mr. John Mctier, & all his family, & very much so [156 (201)] by Mrs. M, they all very readily excused my absence, though they lamented it as a misfortune, for none of them apprehended their Mother in any danger, they were uncommonly kind, Stayed & drank tea here. . . .

Lords day October 7 . . . After service though much fatigued, rode directly to Mr. John Russells, whose wife is dangerously bad, in a very melancholy condition, Discoursed suitably with her & then prayed, with great fullness, freedom & melting concern, then proceeded to Doctor Bowers who had Sent for me, Dined with him, consulted about some of his patients, then rode to Mr. Peter Roberts whose family are all Sick, one child seems a dying, sat about half an hour, & prayed with them, with pleasant assistance from above, then rode to Mrs. Graves to see her Sister Mrs. Desaussure, who is still there, found the child poorly & the Mother very much so. Sat about twenty minutes here, & proceeded home, where did not get till sometime after dark. . . .

Monday October 8 . . . Have some Negro Carpenters come to make a house & a Machine for pounding of rice, which will be a great ease to the Negroes, and many ways a great benefit to the plantation, my domestick affairs, suffer much, by my being so much abroad, and indeed as I know so little about what belongs to a house, they are very little managed when I am at home, my plantations affairs also suffer, and there is great necessity to have it looked after, as I receive very little on account of my labours, either from the one Side or the other, and very rarely any pecuniary acknowledgement for all my extraordinary fatigues, for all the kind offices I am employed in and Jehovah knows I never look for, nor in the least expect any for my private labours, but I only mention it as a reason why should look after my plantation business if I could, as my chief support for myself & children comes therefrom, but it is perhaps my misfortune, and theirs also, that I have no talents for looking after any such concerns. . . .

Thursday October 9 . . . In the forenoon set out to visit some sick persons, but after was about two miles gone, was obliged to come back, being sent for. Found Mrs. John Brown at my house. She seemed in great trouble & came to borrow a little money to make up some sum for want of which her husband would be obliged to go to Jail. I had but very little in the house, however lent her a Small matter out of that little, & Mr. Jonathan Donnom lent her Some, was detained at home all the forenoon. After Dinner set out again, rode to Mr. Strains, found him very poorly with the fever, and his wife something better of a Severe vomiting and fever which was like to carry her off, was concerned for this very worthy family, was informed that a poor family about a mile further had a child dying, which I had formerly baptized, upon which I rode there, found the child just laid out, & the poor parents in great distress, Stayed about three quarters of an hour discoursing to, & praying with them, Mr. Strain was with me, returned to his house where drank tea, as was riding home was informed that Mr. Cully the black Smith was sick but as he was not thought dangerous & it was after dark before I passed his house, I thought I [157 (199)] would call upon him to morrow, when I returned to bury this child. . . .

Wednesday October 10 . . . After Dinner rode to the meeting house, but saw nobody come, nor the childs grave made, was driven by a heavy shower of rain, into Old Mcuens where was obliged to sit about an hour, here I was told that Mr. Cully the Smith died Suddenly this morning, I immediately rode to his house and found it so. He was at work last week till Fridays night, on Saturday had a fever and vomiting, on Sabbath was better. Rode to Mr. Strains, & spent the day there, which is about two miles from him, returned home in the Evening, that night his fever returned, he grew delirious, and was never again in his Senses, and although I rode past his house twice yesterday, & the man that was with him, a person of a very ordinary character, owns he saw me, yet he never called me, nor came out to tell me, how bad poor Mr. Cully was, for whom he knowed I had the greatest regard, his excuse was that Mr. Cully was out of his head, yet still I would have chosen to have seen him and prayed by him. He was an excellent person, I am persuaded, a very gracious, worthy good Christian, and has made I doubt not a very happy change, and that he will be my Crown of rejoicing to Eternity.

The Lord seems just to have brought him and his wife to live under Gospel, & prepare them for heaven, and then took these Happy Couple, they were pleasant in their lives and in their Deaths they have not been long Divided, It is something better than fourteen months since Dear Mrs. Cully went triumphing to glory, and the poor man, he was not in such tender hands, & was never fully in his Senses, yet I am persuaded he had an abundant Entrance into Eternal glory. Was grieved & distressed to see his house & small effects in the possession of such persons, of the most worthless characters . . . As had met the Negroes going to making the childs grave, and afterwards, met the poor Father conducting the corpse alone, two of his Neighbours had called in at Mr. Cullys, I returned to the burying yard with them with me, and discoursed at the grave, the few that were present were melancholy & affected with the times. . . .

Thursday October 11 . . . About the middle of the day, prepared to Discourse at the [funeral] of good Mr. Cully, and in the afternoon delivered it from these words, It is appointed for all men once to die, with Gods most gracious & remarkable assistance, it was a solemn time, the auditory were very Serious & justly affected. I was hardly better helped on such an Occasion. Observed here & all who were present saw & talked of it, a very [telling] & affecting sight, the grave opened was about five feet deep, near the side of another, a little of a rising ground above & out of the grave not opened, there run about five feet from the Surface a strong Spring of the purest like yellow oyl I ever saw into the open grave, it appeared plainly to come from a corpse deposited about a year or eighteen months ago, to the look it was exceeding pure, rich & fine, but to the smell the most fetid, putrified & disagreeable that possibly could be, what poor creatures are we! . . .

[158 (197)] *Friday October 12 1770* . . . This evening heard, that Betsy had the fever at school, and after came home with the rest not a white person to take notice of her, they being abroad visiting as usual, without any call. Was grieved & distressed about my child, on many accounts, had Several thoughts of heart, about a serious trial for marriage, & reconciling myself to Some Circumstances that have hitherto been disgusting. All my trials indeed about marriage hitherto have rather on my Side been trifling amusements, than any thing else, a Single state I would upon all accounts prefer as for myself, but my Dear children lie heavy upon me, on their account, to bring them home, I would willingly marry and submit almost to any connection, yet perhaps they might be more unhappy at home, under a Mother in law, than abroad, and made most miserable. Lord council & direct me. . . .

Saturday October 13 1770 . . . About the middle of the day, fell into Something of a trifling silly disposition, taking my time with a bird (a parrot) & other such trifles, that have been keeping for my Dear children, was at first inwardly giving way to various thoughts about my children and afterwards for Some time Spent my time in a very childish manner, was Soon sencible of it and saw the hand of Joab (my own wicked heart or Satan, or rather both) in it, and was humbled for such exceedingly trifling conduct, and recovered, the concern of my Mind about the great important truths was ruminating upon . . . In the afternoon received a letter from Mr. Perry, acquainting me, that their only child was very ill, and intreating me to come there, I immediately set off, found the child betwext three and four years old, with the most violent fever, I ever remember to have seen so young a child have, never I think felt the like of it, in a child, every Symptom seemed mortal, it seemed hardly possible, the child could live till to morrow, found the poor parents very much distressed, and preparing blisters, Discoursed with & comforted them, then prayed for the child with great fulness & fervency and having sat about an hour, rode back, called at Mrs. Donnoms to see my Dear children being very much concerned about them, as the Sickness increases and is very mortal among children, stayed about a quarter of an hour & rode home after dark. . . .

[159 (195)] *Monday October 15 1770* . . . After breakfast and family [prayers] was over, and Mr. Donnom had left me, I set out to visit several Sick families. . . . Called on Mrs. Clark, who was prayed for yesterday & found her Something better, gave her Some directions both for body & soul, proceeded up the other Side of the river to Mrs. Melvins, found her Sister Mrs. Shaw very bad, she has had several severe fevers, & seems in a bad [way], exceedingly low Spirited, Endeavoured at first to rally her out of that then pressed her to make use of Medicine, which she is very averse to. Afterwards spoke suitably to her souls case & prayed with her. Was well assisted with great fullness, freedom & faithfulness. She was exceedingly affected, and wept much, especially the time of the prayer, after prayer her Sister & niece Mrs. Griffith, left the room. I again spoke very particularly to her, was much affected to see her so distressed both in body & mind, & having a great many visits before me, took a very tender & affectionate leave of her, it was very much so especially on her part and affected me, for a considerable time after I left her, they were all very much pleased with the visit, May the Lord make it useful to them, they are as far as the virtues of Society go, a very worthy family and exceedingly kind to me, returned again down the river . . . Was obliged to light & change horses twice before got half a mile past my parsonage, and at last turned one of the horses I depend most upon into the woods, proceeded with the other two to Combahee, where got a little before three O Clock, was informed that Mrs. M Died yesterday about four O Clock in the afternoon very Sensible, & also comfortable, that she herself and all present were well pleased with my letter, that the funeral was to be this afternoon, and that they had some hopes of my being there, which would be exceedingly acceptable to many. I stayed about three quarters of an hour with Mr. Johnson at ferry, and got some refreshment being in great need both of meat & drink, then proceeded over the ferry, to Mr. M's near Chehaw, found a good company who were much pleased with my arrival, found poor Mr. M in great trouble for which He has great reason, [& Saving] the Divine will to which I hope he will be resigned, As there was a good Company, and this is a place, one of the wildest & most profligate in the province, and a place where I never performed any Ministerial Service whatsoever, and the people seemed to have large expectations, I resolved to give the discourse I intended in the form of a Sermon. Accordingly began with prayer, omitted the first psalm, preached about three quarters of an hour or more from Job 14:1 then prayed & baptized [160 (193)] the infant of the deceased eight days old, and another child about an year old, prayed, Sang the hymn of the —— book, & pronounced the blessing by which time it was quite dark . . . after the Service, the Corpse was carried out to the burying ground of the plantation & laid in the grave, covered with boards, as she according to her desire, is to be carried to morrow morning down to the Round O, where she was born, to be buried along with her Father & Mother, the Company were much pleased & expressed great desire, that some way should be contrived, to have me preach in that barren wild corner upon Some other occasions,[58] to which I delivered a hearty willingness if they could contrive any place & opportunity, for the Gospel is here greatly despised and no doubt will be opposed. . . .

Tuesday October 16 . . . Betwixt three and four O Clock we dispatched the Negroes with the Corpse and in about an hour afterwards, we rode after them, very poor afflicted Mr. M, half brother of the deceased, another young man and myself. . . . As they were to pass Mr. Lambert at the Round O, I

left them and went to his house, where breakfasted . . . Did some business
and returned back to Mr. Isaac Haynes,[59] where dined and baptized their
child, having been desired to call there for that purpose. It was a solemn
comfortable time, was pleased to have the children of such gracious parents
before me on such an occasion, Mrs. Hayne being the Second daughter of
the Late Reverend & very worthy Mr. Huttson, and Mr. Haynes Father, having been one of the most Eminent Christians in his day, both their Mothers
were also good Christians, Mrs. Haynes Mother greatly excelled, was well
helped in the prayers for them and theirs. As Mr. Lambert had met me here,
rode back to his house, Got my own horse and proceeded about nine miles
farther to my old acquaintance Mrs. Cliffords at the horseshoe where did not
get till near eight O Clock at night having rode more than fourty miles. Was
very kindly received as have always been here, Spent the Evening mostly in
Conversation with Mr. Wayne,[60] husband to Mrs. Cliffords youngest daughter, and has for Sometime been obliged to be confined to the house, on
account of Some Embarassment in his affairs, being bred a Merchant. He is
a well behaved Sensible young man, whether misfortune or otherways, I cannot say. . . .

Wednesday October 17 . . . Set out for home, my horses in so poor a condition as hardly fit for traveling . . . visited some Sick children at one Mr. H's
on Mcgivens plantation, their Father brother to this Mr. H & Mother came
here from Ireland last Spring, both the parents are dead and have left five or
Six children who have been very ill, stayed about half an hour, called at Mr.
Jacksons who is very poorly, Mrs. Jackson told me her sister B is to be married tomorrow, and had expected me to visit her last night or this day according to my promise on Sabbath, stayed here about a quarter of an hour or
more, & proceeded and as was to ride past Mrs. B's, I according to my promise called on her, found Mr. Wilkins with her, his good old Mother, and his
Sister Mrs. Threadcraft, come down to the wedding, stayed & drank tea here,
and privately advised Mrs. B to invite her Cousin Mr. Hunt, who although
he was sick and could not come, yet after what [161 (191)] I had said to him,
was sure, that he would take it well, and advised her, to invite by letter her
brother Mr. Joseph Hunt who had told me, he would come, if invited, notwithstanding what he had formerly said, she promised me, that she would,
she received me in a very friendly manner but I behaved with great reserve,
lest should have given any offense, or should have caused any Ungrounded
Suspicions, in Mrs. Wilkins or her daughter, whom I looked upon to be more

observing than Mr. Wilkins himself, I had intended to have given Mrs. B, some other hints & advices, but thought it not proper, when such company was there, I neither Saluted her at going in nor coming away, and took no more notice of her than was barely necessary as the Mistress of the house, excepting just the above hint, Mrs. Wilkins & her Daughter, seemed Surprized to see me come there, which I observed & made an excuse for my calling on Mrs. B who has been very Sick, in my passing by, as was to sleep in the Neighbourhood, her little son had a hot fever on him, Mr. Wilkins carried it very well, I drank tea with them & stayed about an hour & a quarter. As it was almost dark, and a cold drisling night, Mrs. B repeatedly asked me to stay all night but had engaged to be at Mr. Donnoms nor would it been proper for me to be there on any account, Mr. Wilkins walked out with me when I took my leave, & asked me to favour them with my company to morrow at Dinner, I excused myself by having been so long from home, he then pressed me, to be no stranger to that house, & that I would look on them among my friends, which I promised him I would, and shall do so, while they appear to deserve it. . . .

Thursday October 18 . . . As I was afraid, my Dear little Betsy was going to have the quarten, or as it is commonly called, the third day fever & ague, I rode to Mr. Donnoms, and my poor Dear child, lying in a cold dark room by herself with a very hot fever, Sobbing and in tears, but very Silent and I thought much neglected, which I took notice of to both Mr. & Mrs. Donnom. They seemed much Surprized at my return, said they did not think her fever so bad, and they could not believe, it was any thing of the third day fever, & hinted, I made myself too uneasy, but I put them in mind, that this was the third regular return according to the nature of that fever, and that they might depend on it, she would have it worse next Sabbath afternoon, they were silent, but seemed displeased. The child had the fever most of the day at school and the School Master had sent home word for the Second time, that on the fever day she ought not to be sent, this they acknowledged, when they saw me so positive, as the childs fever was abating, I stayed till between eight and nine O Clock, her fever went intirely off, & before the childrens Supper came in, as the fever left her hungry she came & told me so, which was immediately taken amiss, & it was said, she could not be hungry, as they had all Coffy & bread with a little butter, when they came from school, and that she was apt to over eat herself if let alone, I said I was sorry to hear it, as they knew, she was naturally very moderate, and it showed she had worms, the child herself said, she had drank Coffy, but could not eat any, she was so sick, which the rest of the children confirmed, upon which I called for some of the cold bread, & stayed till I saw the children get their Supper, heard them Say their prayers & saw them get to bed, upon which I went home. I am this particular, not with the least reflection upon this good family, who I believe are as kind to my children as it is possible for people to be, to children who are not their own, but I do it, that if my Dear children live to read these writtings, they may see what a tender parent they had, what constant concern, & how much distress I went through on their account. I went home without staying Supper . . . was melancholy in mind & full of various distressing thoughts, on many accounts, and most exceedingly fatigued & worn out in body. Supper not being ready, I sat down to write, but being so overcome with labour I could not continue at it, lay down with a book in my hand, but instead of reading, gave way to various corrupt carnal affections, which Satan & my own desperately wicked heart fomented, in this evil plight of mind fell asleep, and about Eleven at night wakened in a worse frame of mind, then [162 (189)] gave way to murmuring unbelieving suggestions, was fretful & uneasy at myself & all about me, my carnal lusts & affections, indwelling Sin & various corruptions prevailed much, hurried my soul along with them, so that became very guilty & defiled, before I was aware, by Entertaining these evils of carnal sensual desires after Creature comforts & enjoyments . . . Saw that Satan had been busy with me for Sometime especially since Sabbath afternoon, that the great thing in view was by Spiritual pride, & other mental corruptions, to take me off my guard then to harry me into indulging in carnal affections, Sensual lusts, and so to plunge me either into actual guilt with all its terrible consequences, or by irritating my carnal affections to pollute, defile & distress my soul and so plunge me into such dark & perplexing exercise of mind, as would take me off from the active, lively useful labours I am now Employed. It is a time of great & general distress, universal Sickness, many Deaths, great & heavy afflictions, Ministers are very Scarce, and especially active Zealous ones, the Lord has for a long time, & especially at present, blessed me, with a great share of health, and with respect to Ministerial graces & abilities, they are more increased than ever, especially in publick, as all think whom I am conversant with, Now should Satan or my own desperately wicked heart, plunge me into guilt, or by plying my corruptions & lusts, passions & appetites, keep me in dark exercise opposing & striving against these, so as to take me off, or unfit me for my work, it would at this time, & in this place, be a great point gained,

this I saw to be Satans view & design, in working so much on my corruptions as of late, particularly endeavouring to blow me up in Spiritual pride,
or to sink me either by an unsuitable marriage, or by Indulging carnal affections in a worse way, and so spoil my usefulness, Either by rendering me
unacceptable abroad, (for all the abuses I have met with have not in the least
affected that) or uncomfortable at home, but glory, glory, Everlasting glory &
praise who has again, as often before, broken this Snare, disappointed Satan,
and caused my soul to gain new experience, & new strength, and to mount
up by faith, as on Eagles wings. . . .

[165 (183)] *Friday October 26 1770* . . . Received a note from James Donnom,
informing us, that the Reverend, the great & famous Mr. Whitefield, died
suddenly, of an astmatic fit the last day of September at Portsmouth in New
England, He has been a very great & burning, a most Eminent & shining
light, in the church of God, and most Eminently useful, O how greatly God
has blessed him to souls, and O how graciously Jehovah has dealt with him,
graciously through his whole life, & most graciously at his Death, in not letting him long outlive his usefulness. It had been observed that for some
years, though still very active, yet not so well blessed as formerly, and in
many things [strongly discovering] the weakness & imperfections, which
run through his whole publick life, but now God has taken him to heavenly
glory, where I doubt not but he met with numbers of precious souls, he had
been the happy instrument of bringing there, O happy thrice happy Servant
of God, It led me seriously to think upon the approaching time of my own
departure and made me earnestly, though humbly, beg & plead, with God,
that might not outlive my usefulness, nor be left to die like the Snuff of
a Candle leaving a stench behind me, If it was Gods holy will, I would
earnestly desire, to depart before I am a burthen to the world. The Great Mr.
Whitefield died on Sabbath on which he no doubt was to have preached, O
that God would grant me the Same favour. . . . Mr. James Jordan called
on me, & stayed till late in the afternoon. His business was, to Engage
me to marry him on Sabbath to Miss Susy Chrsty, a young Lady, who lives
at present in Doctor Days family about eight miles from this, her Father I
was acquainted with, a Gentleman of good living, & great abilities as a
physician, but had the misfortune of a very bad, worthless drunken wife,
who ruined his affairs. He died Eight or Nine years ago & left Several Children, well grown up but in low Circumstances, this his Second or third
Daughter is about twenty two years of age, a very comely person, but have

no acquaintance with her. Doctor Day where she lives is near Mr. Jordans, and Since his late disappointment with Miss B Oswald he in a few visits has made it up with Miss Susy C and I believe has greatly bettered himself, she being much more aimiable & desirable in my opinion, both in person, temper, & education. He carried himself more moderately than the last time he came on the Same occasion, yet his conversation was so seemingly tinctured with what he had in view, that it was not so very agreeable to me, whose mind, thoughts & affections were quite otherwise engaged. . . .

[166 (181)] *Lords day October 28 1770* . . . Published Mr. James Jordan & Miss Susy Christy, he was present all day & stayed till the banns were concluded. I have for several years, published three times at once as it is called, those whom I am well acquainted with, or have letters from their parents if young persons, and it has become a very general custom, and brings many more to be married by the Dissenting ministers, than formerly used to be. After publick worship was finished I set out immediately, & rode very fast to Doctor Days, where married the Couple above mentioned & stayed Dinner with them, which was obliged to be with Candle light, her behaviour was very becoming, & such as must command respect & esteem from every Sensible sober minded person. After dinner returned homewards, went to Mr. Donnoms where his Brother Mrs. James Donnom had Dined & was waiting for me, We stayed here till after midnight in different discourse all useful & edifying, yet it grieved & troubled me to be so much in company. Mr. Jonathan Donnom was gone with Some other Neighbours to the Sea Side a fishing or rather a frolicking, which Occasioned his Brother & me staying so long with his wife & family. . . .

Monday October 29 1770 . . . In the forenoon rode over to the plantation with Mr. Donnom and heard him give directions both about gleaning in the harvest, and about the machine that is near finished for pounding rice with oxen or horses . . . afterwards when his Chair & horses were ready, we sent them before us & walked together, when poor unhappy I mean misfortunate Gentleman, he gave me some letters to read full of some very affecting & distressing accounts, about his Daughter Mrs. Martin in Georgia, & about his youngest Son William, at the Jersies or the school in Princetown Colledge, which is like to turn out bad, poor Gentleman, was greatly [concerned] for him, & gave him my best advice in such trying circumstances, was about an hour with him, walked back & drank tea with Mrs. Donnom & the children, while he proceeded home to his own dwelling, this afternoon I received a very Genteel & Christian letter from a stranger Gentleman in Virginia Northfolk County, town of Portsmouth, giving me an account, that my brother Thomas who had married Some years ago and had two Sons born by his wife, a very worthy woman, had the misfortune about five years ago to lose his wife & Eldest Son by the small pox, that he left his youngest Son a child to board with an Elderly woman of a good character, and went to sea, as usual for He was Captain of a merchant Ship for several years, that no account of him, the ship nor any of the Crew, had been heard of Since, so that it was concluded, that they had all foundered at Sea, that his child was heir by his Mothers Father to some small interest, that a brother of the childs Mother, after the Death of the childs Grandfather, had claimed the child as its proper Guardian, had taken him from the good old Lady who had the care of him, and in order to make the childs interest his own, had used the poor orphan his own Sisters child, in the most cruel barbarous manner, that can be imagined, & brought him up in the most wicked & abandoned manner, keeping him as naked as one of his Negroe slaves, & bringing up in the Same manner as they are, being himself a most vile, wicked, profligate, villainous person, studying by indirect means to destroy his poor Nephew, for the sake of what small interest belonged to him, that some more distant [167 (179)] relations had taken the poor unhappy orphan from his most wicked & cruel Uncle, & placed him again with the good old Lady who has the charge of him from his Father, & having heard of me had wrote to know if I was Brother to Captain Thomas Simpson late of that place & intreating me to take the child & his interest into my own hands, this letter gave me great concern, consulted with Mr. James Donnom & determined to write immediately that I would take the child, and his interest if any left into my hands & would reward the good old Lady & all others who had been friends to him, and that by all means they should send me the poor child what ever they did with his interest, & that if I did not get him peaceably I would take some step at law to recover him from the power of such a barbarous villain his Uncle. . . .

Tuesday October 30 1770 . . . About ten O Clock set out for the Indian Land having received a letter from Mr. Charles Brown informing me that his Dear wife died betwext Sabbath & Monday morning, & desiring me to attend the funeral, she was a person much & deservedly believed, a very particular friend & well wisher of mine, of a remarkably quiet peaceable behaviour, friendly

& Neighbourly disposition, I accordingly went there, met with severals both my friends & otherways. Sometime after twelve O Clock we set out in the slow gate of a solemn funeral procession for the family burying place at the church, where I read the funeral Service of the church of England, with great seriousness, solemnity and tender melting affections, the company who although not numerous yet were of the Genteel & fashionable people, both of this place & some from a distance, behaved exceedingly well, were very serious & attentive. Just as finished the Service I heard some of the Ladies mentioning that Mr. DeSaussures child was this morning thought a dying, I had observed none of that family nor Mrs. Graves at the funeral but knowing of the child being thought so near his End, I immediately had my horses brought, & making an apology to the principal mourners, set off at full Gallop & ran the horse all the way back to Mrs. Graves near about four miles, when I got to the house, I found the Father & Mother crying & weeping most grievously, Mrs. Graves sitting with the child on her knee just a dying, Immediately kneeled down by her knee where the dying infant was, & begging the parents to join me, went to prayer for his precious soul, offering him up to the Father of Mercies through the Lord Jesus Christ. Was most graciously helped to plead & wrestle with great enlargement for this precious young immortal, for about a quarter of an hour, when he departed amidst prayer & praise, then pled for grace, comfort & support to the distressed parents for more than five or ten minutes longer, with great fullness, freedom, & most tender affections, this was a most precious time to my soul and seemed so remarkable a time to the parents & good Mrs. Graves, none of whom expected me, that they were filled with wonder & praise, & greatly composed beyond what they expected, stayed about half an hour longer with the disconsolate Father, while the distressed Mother & Aunt were laying out the Dear Corpse, & then proceeded home, where did not get till after dark. . . .

[168 (177)] *Thursday first day of November 1770* . . . Set out for the Indian Land, to bury Mr. DeSaussures child. Found Mrs. Graves children, both bad with the fever. Betwixt twelve & one O clock the Corpse was moved, & we went to the Meeting house, where I prayed twice & discoursed a full hour, on the advantages to be got by afflictions, and the great comfort that believing parents may have when meeting with the Death of their infant children, the Company was but Small but very Serious. I prepared this discourse on purpose for direction and comfort to the many mourners in this Neighbourhood

& hope the Lord blessed his word. Was in a very tender frame myself, delivered felt known truths, spoke from the heart & hope to the hearts of severals who were melted into tears, Endeavoured to comfort them, with the Consolations by which God has often comforted my soul. . . .

[170 (173)] *Wednesday November 7* . . . About ten O Clock forenoon, rode out in order to Dine with Mr. Jordan & his Spouse. . . . Was very kindly & affectionately received, Spent the afterpart of the day very agreeably here, believe he has got a very worthy Sencible Genteel well behaved young woman, & will be very happy in an excellent wife, retired with him after Dinner & advised him as Soon as possible to Send all his daughters clothes to her in Georgia where she lives, & also her Mothers clothes to her & to write her a letter, all which he promised me very faithfully to do, & declared himself very thankful for the advice. . . .

[171 (171)] *Friday November 9* . . . I received a letter from Doctor Bower at the Indian Land, letting me know, that there was a traveler a perishing very ill at his house, & begged earnestly to See some Minister, upon which the Doctor had Sent for me, as the Only one in these parts, this troubled & confused me, as was backward in preparatory work, & the more so as had not improved the beginning of the week as I ought to have done, yet could not refuse to go. Accordingly set out as Soon as my horses could be got. Was Melancholy & thoughtful by the way, & helped to offer up some ejaculations for my self and for the many Sick & afflicted, when got there found a very likely well looked man about Six or Seven and twenty years of age, born in New England, but has been wandering about in different parts of the world for Some years, & the last three in this province & Georgia, extremely ill & very dangerous, and seemingly in great uneasiness of Mind, the Doctor very prudently left us alone. Soon found he had been a very vile Creature, his education had been Sober, though not the most religious, but Since his rambling abroad, he has been very wicked & prophane, an open curser & Swearer, abounding in all manner of wickedness, living with a vile woman in drunkenness & idleness, & had left Georgia for debt being betrayed by his whore, His name is Meers a house Carpenter, worked a good deal for Mr. Zubly, Spent Several hours with him, and he had no right convictions though he was very afraid & unwilling to think of Death & kept making many promises, of what he would be & do if God would spare him this once. I laboured much to show him, the horrid evil of Sin, & quoted

many Scriptures which denounce the wrath of God, against such vile &
abominable livers as him, he seemed much terrified, yet not affected as he
ought to had been, I endeavoured to convince him of the corruption of [172
(169)] his nature, his need of a Saviour, the vanity of his promises of amendment without converting grace, but with most things, he seemed but little
affected, his great Concern seemed to be, that I should pray for him, which
I at last did with great earnestness, fulness & freedom, he seemed very much
affected & in great earnestness, during the prayer, I then left him to Dine
with the Doctor, afterwards visited him different times, Observed as his disorder, a fever & a flux seemed threatening or flattening, his sorrow for his
wicked life seemed to rise & fall, the third time of waiting on him, he made
some acknowledgements of more particulars, & with more seeming ingenuity than before. I gave him many instructions & directions, and at last took
my leave with the comfortable reflection of having done my duty but I am
afraid, to little purpose, he appeared before I left him not to be in such a
dangerous way as the Doctor thought him in the morning . . . Rode to Mr.
Donnoms to see my children, found them just come from school, but neither Mr. nor Mrs. Donnom at home, the children hungry & weary, and
roasting potatoes for themselves. My poor Dear Lambs complained much to
me, & asked why I did not send for them home, I was much affected & very
uneasy on their account, was also much fatigued & indisposed, stayed with
them, & in about half an hour or more Mrs. Donnom came home, I was so
melancholy, & ailing that could not be much company, and sat only about
half an hour, acquainted Mrs. Donnom I would not allow the children to go
any more to School till the Carriage wheels were mended, she seemed displeased however I repeated it, that they should not go any more to walk it.
This brought on some talk about my chair, the use of which, they have had
for near two years, & have taken so little care of it that the lining is all tore
off, the harness, & the wheels are intirely gone, and it needs a repair which
will cost near as much as the price of it at first. It has for Some time grieved
me, to see myself so put upon, Mrs. Donnom told me that she was going to
purchase a second handed chair from one of the neighbours, I told her I was
glad to hear that Mr. Donnom was come to that resolution, for I was going
to send mine aboard of a Schooner to Charlestown, to be repaired, upon
which she told me, that she always expected to have had my chair, for Mr.
James Donnom her Brother in law, told them they would have it at last at
Some low price, I told her it was very Surprizing to me, for I never intended

to part with it, & that I would by no means do it, and further, that not one of the Mr. Donnoms had ever asked me, if I would part with it, on any condition, and that I could not afford to make such a complement, she then said that she was Sorry she had used so much but that it was to carry my own children in, and that she had not used it a great deal but when they were with her, this speech, which I knew to be very wrong, not only surprized but shocked me very much, as my poor children have never been once over at the Indian Land, Since they were brought to this side, and very seldom carried any where, being mostly at school through the week & many Sabbaths not carried to publick worship, I made no answer, she considered better, & softened what she had said, still I made no answer, & turned the discourse another way. I saw plainly that they have expected the chair as a gift, which much Surprizes me, as what I give for the childrens board is by all the Neighbours, & all who know it, thought to be very high, and besides Since they moved down to this Neighbourhood, they are often getting things from me which I neither charge, nor have the One half returned. I took my leave very melancholy & much affected. . . .

Saturday November 10 . . . About four O Clock I rode over to Mr. Donnoms, he appeared not in a very good humour, for which I knew there were different causes, he had been up settling with Mr. Ingls a Gentleman of fortune in Charlestown,[61] who has a large plantation about two miles from Campbells [173 (167)] hill, which Mr. Donnom had the management of, but in such a manner, that Mr. Ingles was obliged to take it from him, & upon their Settling, he had very little to receive from Mr. Ingles, who is reckoned one of the most reasonable, humane & worthy Gentlemen in this province, this and his disappointment of my chair, besides my having lately complained, that I could not be always lending & giving away, that I was very desirous to be neighbourly & even generous, but that they who borrow, should sometimes repay, but on the other hand, Mrs. Donnom was exceedingly complaisant & told me, that Mr. Ingles was to be at meeting tomorrow, was to Dine there together with Mr. James Donnom & both to sleep at my house, & after some apologies, she asked me for the lent of two bottles of wine, as they had none, & for some rum a case bottle full as theirs was of a very bad quality, which I very freely told her, they should have, & any thing else, which they wanted, and I was really pleased, very much pleased, I had it in my power to serve them on such an occasion. . . .

Lords day November 11 1770 . . . In the forenoon before Sermon was applied to by Mr. Bmbzn to baptize his infant child, but as had some objections against it, put him off till the afternoon, betwixt Sermons, called the officers together & consulted with them, who all approved of my refusing it, till had further conversation with them, which Intimated to Bmbzn & he acquiesced in it, He owned himself to be a Roman Catholick, & yet that was not the chief objection, than his reputed a most vile adulterer. . . .

Monday 12 . . . About twelve O Clock Mr. Ingles returned, being on his way up to his own plantation, it came on a heavy rain, which drove him in here to avoid it, he stayed & Dined with me, and the rain still Continuing, he was obliged to stay all night, Mr. Donnom came back & stayed all night also, found their company very agreeable, Spent the day with Mr. Ingles a very worthy Gentleman & found his conversation [174 (165)] Manly, Genteel, Christian & useful, & have reason to hope, he will be of Service to our Congregation, yet I was uneasy to be so much in company, and to have little opportunity for study. . . .

Tuesday November 13 Another night of very constant rain. . . . About Seven went over to see my children, Stayed about half an hour with good Mrs. Donnom, with whom had some very tender & affecting conversation about the behaviour of Some of the Gentlemen when down at the Sea Side, in which both her Brother Mr. Ferguson & her husband joined & were very faulty, I was informed of it in the morning by Mr. James Donnom, who was much concerned about it & especially for his Brother, it also gave me great concern, & more particularly what Mrs. Donnom told me weeping, which occasioned my speaking about what I been informed of, however begged her not to take any notice of it, to her husband, and promised her, that at a proper time, both his Brother & I would speak to him, which might answer a much better purpose. She repeatedly promised to take my advice. . . .

Wednesday 14 Another very cold rainy night. . . . Last night received a message desiring me to attend the funeral of Mr. [Flgd] an Overseer for Mr. Mitchell, at the Indian land, who died on Monday evening after a short illness which was the reason of not being sent for in his Sickness, accordingly set out before Eleven O Clock, found the roads in a very bad condition, all overflowed with water, in many places deep & very dangerous traveling, the river rising very fast, still dark & cloudy, and a very bitter cold wind so that it was like the stormy weather we have at home. Was obliged to ride slow, found a very poor distressed family who depended for their support under God upon the life & labour of the deceased, who was a very sober careful industrious person but had a large Sickly family, and a help mate of little or no assistance, very few people attended. As had more than Six miles to carry the Corpse & rode very slow, we were like to be chilled with the cold, the wind blowing very bleak a good part of the way being very open, so that before we got to the meeting house yard some left us, had the corpse carried into the meeting house, and discoursed from the pulpit, prayed before & after, was very comfortably assisted, after this melancholy Service, I returned, called at Mrs. Graves where drank tea, which found refreshing for had tasted nothing Since the morning, & had taken but a very slight breakfast, had some talk with an old Negro wench, who wants to be baptized, & also with Mrs. Graves her Mistress about her consenting to it, which she very readily did, and had some very Serious experimental conversation with her about admitting both white & black to sealing ordinances. Was much pleased with her remarks and also with Mrs. DeSaussures. . . .

[175 (163)] *Lords day November 18* . . . Set off rather earlier than usual as expected to find the greatest part of the way upwards of eight miles under water, and found it to be so mostly to the horses breast, and the river near two miles over, the Small bridges all gone & the plank Swimming about in the ditches so that it was very dangerous to get past them, the water was up to the Saddle Skirts, & not withstanding all my care, it was far above the top of my boots, which were quite filled with water, so that after being about an hour and a half riding in water, I was obliged at the first rising ground on the other Side, now called Wilkens place, to sit down and have my boots drawn, to pour out the water. Pulled off my stockings, wrung the water out of them, and put them on again, afterwards proceeded, found a Congregation, though they thought it hardly possible I could come to them, Just before I went in was applied to by Mr. Hzl at Port Royal ferry to baptize his child as soon as possible after Sermon, for it was thought a dying, this determined me to deliver both Sermons at once without any Intermiss and to Acquaint the people of reason for so doing, which was the more necessary as it was much later, than our usual time of going in, preached from Jhn 6:27 with Gods most gracious presence and assistance. . . . [176 (161)] After having dismissed the people, baptized Mr. Grimballs infant child in the retiring or study house, with freedom & enlargement . . . proceeded with Mr. H down to his house, rode fast & was ahead of him, overtook two of the Miss Klsy, who had been at meeting, had some conversation with these very Sensible young Ladies which was useful in itself & might have been truely so, both to them & me, but alas, on my part, was spoke with too little Seriousness and in too trifling a manner. At Mr. H's found his child visibly a dying, baptized this Dear little babe with Gods most comfortable presence in the prayers, in the exhortation and every part of duty. . . . Proceeded to Mrs. Graves where stayed all night, as durst not venture to cross the river, when it was So very dark, the Moon having changed yesterday morning. Besides Mrs. Graves there was present Mr. DeSaussure & his wife, not yet going home to their own house, and Mrs. P C widow daughter to Mrs. Clifford at the horseshoe.[62] The conversation was mostly such as might have been very useful & improving on another night, but not so suitable to a Sabbath evening, and on my part, was generally too loose, free & careless, nor was I much Sensible of it till after Supper & prayers, when had retired, & was reflecting on the frame & temper of my mind. . . .

Monday November 19 1770 . . . Had some serious & useful conversation with a very old Negro wench who was here and has for some time been applying for baptism, she seems to be very Serious & desirous of Salvation through Jesus Christ, but is very ignorant. She seems to look upon herself as a very Sinful creature, as lost forever if not saved by Jesus Christ, but her Ideas are very confused, her knowledge very much circumscribed and hardly able to receive more, she is an African by birth, and though long in this province, yet has always lived in the grossest ignorance, and been very loose & wicked in her time. She speaks much of a religious mistress she had in her young days, who used in her widowhood to keep up family prayer, & took much pains to instruct her Servants, and laments she was so careless & wicked at that time, as to hate instruction, yet I hope this poor old Creature, who has lived in this parish these several years, and has for two or three years past attended very carefully on publick worship, has really got the root of the matter in her & such a knowledge of Jesus Christ as I doubt not will prove Saving which appears, by a very Sober, quiet, good life she lives, by a constant tending on ordinances, a great desire for [177 (159)] sealing ordinances & appears to have the highest reverence & esteem for God & Jesus Christ, gave her many directions and repeated instructions, about the corruption of nature, about Christ the Saviour, the nature & use of religious duties, & Gospel ordinances of faith & trust in Jesus Christ as a Redeemer. Afterwards had some talk with Mrs. Graves about her, who has taken some pains with her, but seems to think her almost too ignorant for the Ordinances, I think otherwise, for her Small knowledge appears to me, to be of the best sort, and to whom little is given, little will be required. Was well helped in family prayer, after breakfast left this agreeable company, and proceeded homewards in a humble penitent frame of soul, very earnest in prayer, for assisting, strengthening, receiving, directing grace, perceived my single state to be a great Snare, by leading into a freer and more trifling conversation, with Single Ladies, than would otherwise have, and that familiarity with them, that is expected & cannot be avoided, without giving offense, weakens my weight as a minister, and lessens my influence in that Sacred character, If reserved in such company, or speak only on serious subjects, they think themselves slighted & take disgust, this has really been the rise of many of the abuses I have met with, & the ill natured things that some of that Sex have thrown out against me, as being proud, self conceited because of my station, and circumstances being easier, on the other hand, the married Ladies are disgusted and think it unbecoming ministerial gravity to take notice of & discourse with the others in that free & familiar way, that is allowed to Single people, this makes the Condition of a Single minister, very undesirable, it is hard & difficult to walk in the golden mean, my easiness of temper & willingness to recommend religion, by a free, easy, complaisant, familiar behaviour, too often drives me into what is Silly & trifling, had many useful reflections through this day, & was well helped in ejaculations & watchfulness. . . .

Tuesday 20 . . . [178 (157)] Having been informed, that old Mr. William Wilkins, was thought a dying, I rode down that way to visit him . . . found him very low, but Something better than he had been two days ago, yet Seemingly not long for this world, his daughter & her husband were with him, he was much in his old way of flattering himself with the hopes of living, & not at all pleased to hear of his being so very ill, yet I took the liberty to let him know he really was in a very dangerous condition, and although he thought his state safe enough as to Eternity yet he ought by no means to put off the thoughts of Death, he has been many years a professor & very friendly to the Support of religion, yet giving no great evidences of much of a Christian temper & behaviour. I proposed prayer, he said nothing, however I went to prayer, & pleaded for him with great plainness, earnestness and fervency, he seemed to join with me, and thanked me when done, I was about an hour with him, then returned & called upon Mr. Browns family, who has been Sick and poorly Since his wifes Death & his children poorly, was affected at the Sight of so many destitute children in one family, two his Motherless, the youngest about Six weeks old, two of the late Millers, his wifes Sisters children, both Fatherless & Motherless, two of Mrs. Gdbys fatherless, had some serious affecting conversation with Mrs. Gdby, a very worthy Lady who being aunt to Mrs. Brown & left in straitened Circumstances, has had her home here for several years, and Drank tea & set out for home, it being about Sun down. . . .

[179 (155)] *Friday November 23 1770* . . . Am deeply Sensible, that my being so much abroad & in Company gives very great injury to the Spiritual concerns of my own soul . . . [180 (153)] being so much and Constantly abroad, my studies suffer as a Minister, my soul Suffers as a Christian, my children suffer & are losers by it, & my temporal concerns also suffer, yet it is the Lords holy will to call me to it, by the Melancholy providences of the time, when Sickness, & distress abounds, I rejoice to be employed for God, it is my desire & delight to be useful to mankind, but such is my weakness & proneness to folly, that the above disadvantages flow from that which is otherwise my duty & my happiness. . . .

Lords day 25 . . . Preached both parts of the day from Zechry 9:12. . . . Towards the close observed Some persons come into Meeting in a Condition very unsuitable, which grieved & distressed me, this seemed a good day to Several of the hearers, who seemed very earnestly engaged, when hearing the great truths of the Gospel, especially during the pressing call & solemn offers made in the afternoon. After Sermon I acquainted them, that the Lords supper was put off till this day fortnight, & gave suitable directions, expressed my displeasure, at the persons who had appeared in such an unworthy condition, and expressed my Concern to them. Before I left the pulpit received an account of Mr. William Wilkins Death this forenoon at ten O Clock and invited to attend his funeral tomorrow at four in the afternoon. . . .

Monday November 26 1770 . . . Proceeded to Mr. Wilkins plantation found a good company gathered, but much confusion among the first relations, & was witness to much [181 (151)] simple foolish & unbecoming behaviour, was obliged to take the chief management upon myself, the Coffin did not come till Dusk when most of the Company were gone, as it would have been very late, to carried it round to the Meeting house by land, we put it aboard of a boat & sent it up by water, & rode round by land to meet it at the bridge. Rode all very fast, so that it was liker a wedding than a funeral. At the house where the late Mr. McLeod lived, which is now a tavern, we stopped till the corpse arrived, and in the mean time, I ordered a dozen of Candles, & necessary liquor for the Company both before and after the internment, had the Corpse carried into the Meeting house, where began with prayer, delivered a discourse suitable to the occasion, and concluded with prayer, pronouncing the blessing, after the Corpse were in the ground as usual, thus was buried between eight & nine O Clock of a very dark night Mr. William Wilkins a Gentleman of a large fortune acquired by his own industry & frugality, the largest donor by much of any that ever gave to the funds who now Support the Gospel at this Meeting house which I took proper notice of in the discourse, and upon the whole showed all the respect to his remains in my power. . . .

[184 (145)] *Monday December 3 1770* . . . Early in the forenoon, was sent for to plantation to see some Sick Negroes, Observed one of Mrs. Holmes fellows, I thought Death struck as the expression is though he was up & walking about, he was very well on Saturday, but I am persuaded is now a dying, used some means with him, and Sent for the Doctor, who when he came thought as I did. . . .

Wednesday 5 This morning exceeding poorly, felt as if it was impossible for me to go through with the duties of this week, was informed by Overseer that the fellow I saw on Monday died this morning, & others both Mrs. Holmes & mine Sick with the same complaint. . . .

Thursday 6 . . . Did not begin service till twelve O Clock, had a good Congregation for a week day, and enjoyed Gods most gracious & comfortable presence while preached with great enlargement, fullness & freedom from last Sabbaths text, Jhn 6:51 middle clause. Was showing what it is to eat this bread spoken of in the text or to feed upon Jesus Christ [185 (143)] and also in Considering the nature of that life which this bread communicates to all them that eat thereof . . . Had several strangers from Beaufort, after Sermon gave the tokens, gave notice of Mrs. Blairs funeral to morrow, which will oblige me to come over again to morrow which gives me great concern, both as am very much indisposed, & have no time to spare, was very much employed both before and after Sermon in discoursing with several persons distressed in their families & distressed in their minds, admitted as new communicants Mrs. Grimball Daughter to old Mr. Roberts and the old Gentleman himself. The grace of God in this family is most amazing & remarkable, rode to Doctor Bowers who not being at home I wrote & left a letter for him about the Negroes Sick at the plantation, then rode to Mrs. G's & dined, afterwards rode to Mr. Roberts & admitted his Daughter a young woman Miss Sally Roberts, and also poor Mr. Grimball, discoursed largely & prayed with them. . . .

Friday December 7 1770 . . . About twelve O Clock set out for the Indian Land Meeting house, being to meet the funeral there as gave publick notice & not at Mrs. Palmers house some miles beyond the meeting for want of time, as was otherways Engaged, also after Sermon informed both of Mrs. Palmers Sons in law, Mr. David Toomer, & Mr. Archibald Cldr,[63] of the Same. . . . Rode to Mr. Charles Browns & borrowed a prayer book, as expected to be desired to read the publick Service, which I was willing to do, when got to the Meeting yard found they were not come, proceeded about a mile further, and met the funeral, a good decent company, considering the unchristian & indecent custom that now prevails through this province of very few coming out to funerals. Was desired to read the funeral Service & did so, then discoursed, prayed & pronounced the blessing extemporary as it is commonly called, or according to the Dissenters Method of burying which I was afterwards told gave great Satisfaction. It is my firm determination at all funerals in my own meeting yard when I am desired to read the Service of the church of England to add to it our own Service, and also to join the two Services together, in the church yard or other places as I may see proper, afterwards returned home . . . As have for sometime been growing gross & fatter, than I ever used to be, have felt some Symptoms of an inflammation in my eyes, for which took a very large quantity of blood last week & have taken frequent cooling purges. Two days ago I urged the Doctor when here to bleed me again but he refused it, thinking it improper, yesterday I felt something of a disagreeable burning heat in a Small spot high up on my left thigh not [186 (141)] larger than a point, felt Something of the same kind also down below my Ancle of the same leg, yesterday it was not constant but hurt me only at times, this day it seemed larger, about the breadth of my finger & felt also a kernel in the groin of the Same Side, was at times Surprized & uneasy at what it might be. Today found it increase very fast below my Ancle, and after the Standing at the Service it seemed to be wholly about my ancle, & spread fast with an intense burning heat, so that I began to fear an Eresypolas, or St. Anthonys fire as it is commonly called, having had it once very bad in the Same leg about nine years ago, this gave me great Concern, lest I should be prevented from the publick Service of Sabbath, and was also so busy in preparatory duties, that could not use any means for dispelling it, this Sent me repeatedly & earnestly to the throne of grace. . . .

[187 (139)] *Lords day December Ninth 1770* . . . When lighted off my horse, felt my leg exceeding painful & was very lame, but soon forgot it. Was very busy among the Communicants supplying some with tokens & discoursing with others before I went in, was truely in the Spirit on the Lords day & enabled to worship & Serve God in Spirit & in truth. Preached the action Sermon from Dan: 9:26. . . . Never saw a more serious, attentive & melted auditory. There was a great and general weeping till it was even heard as it were from every corner of the house. . . . When the Communicants came to the table, I observed there would not be room for all both white & black, without severals sitting back from the table, upon which I desired the Negroes to stay off, and we should contrary to the Custom of this place have a Second Service for them, which was accordingly done . . . [188 (137)] At the second table, which consisted of nine or ten Negroe slaves, discoursed in a free familiar way suited to their capacity, gave many necessary advices & exhortations, both to them & the rest of their colour & station who were spectators, this discourse, gave great satisfaction both to white & black who all begged me & particularly the Negroe communicants to continue this custom of Serving them at a table by themselves, as the discourse was much more suitable both to their capacity & station. This I resolved to comply with, as it was this day providentially begun without any fore design, & not in the least to gratify the pride of any and the Negroes themselves most earnestly solicited that it might be continued in both meeting houses, was well assisted after returned to the pulpit in discoursing to the spectators who were numerous, hardly any going away, that bad custom which prevailed so much in this place, seems to be going out . . . This was in several respects one of the most remarkable Sacraments ever given in this place, never so many members of the church of England joined before nor was there ever two Services in this house, most others of the church of England members lamented after we came out, that they had not applied to me for liberty to join, It was truely most amazing & wonderful to see such a great & glorious day, in this house, after the violent efforts of my Enemies against me, but the greatest wonder of all was to see old Mr. Roberts & so many of his family at the Lords holy table, a family once so remarkably wicked. . . . Was most remarkably strengthened & assisted through the whole Service which was about five hours, my voice & strength continued as well at last as at the beginning, had nothing of that excessively fatigued appearance which have in the summer. . . .

[189 (135)] *Tuesday December 11 1770* . . . Had many thoughts about making some proposals to Mrs. P C. She is daughter to Mrs. Clifford & the disceased Mr. Thomas Clifford[64] at the horseshoe, Father of my ever Dear & valuable friend that was, & who I believe is now in glory where she will be my everlasting crown of rejoicing Mrs. Sacheverell, who was so long my kind hostess. Mr. Cliffords family was one of the first I was acquainted with, and have always remained my very steady friends, they have always been looked on as a family of good character, among the principal Supporters of the dissenting interest in that part of the Country, a very sober industrious family always friendly disposed to religion in General, & the Presbyterian Interest in particular, regular attenders on publick worship, when they have a minister, yet the family no ways remarkable for religion, Mr. Clifford though an excellent member of Society and a constant attender on publick worship, yet never made any profession by being a communicant, Mrs. Clifford has been a communicant these many years and is a good kind of woman, I believe a really Sincere Christian but no ways remarkable for much Christian exercise, but very regular in all the externals of religion, and remarkable for Industry & thriving in the world, the children have so far been religiously bred, as that they have had good education abroad at Schools, been bred to regard publick worship, to Consider themselves as dissenters, and have had an example of Sobriety & industry at home, Mrs. Sacheverell & her full sister Mrs. [Yng] were both most excellent Christians before they died. Mr. Clifford himself died with a good character, the Eldest Son of the family, who had turned out very wild & extravagant, died this time four years I believe & on good grounds a remarkable Instance of Death bed repentance, and of the power and riches of Divine grace at the last hour. The family at present consists of Mrs. Clifford herself, two daughters & one son, about Seventeen or Eighteen years of age, they are in good, plentiful & thriving circumstances, & Since the Death of the old Gentleman the young people have lived in a gay fashionable manner. The Daughters have not shown any regard to religion in their marriages, and have both been unfortunate, much in the same way the youngest daughter, Miss Betsy that was, married about two years ago Mr. Wayne a young merchant English man, who broke last Spring and is at present confined at Mrs. Cliffords & likely to continue so for Some months, till he can settle with his Creditors, many hard things are said against him as to his prudence when in trade, his wifes fortune was made over to her by a trust deed as it is called before marriage, so that is Safe, the very Same thing happened to the now widow P C Miss Jenny Clifford that was, her husband Mr. P broke soon after marriage, and was confined at his Mother in laws near two years, where he died about two years ago & left one child still living. Mrs. P is sufficiently personable, seems Sensible, is good natured, but has a love for gaity, & might think my family too confined for her, shows such a regard for religion as the family have always done, but no more. Many of my friends have laid her out for me, ever Since she was Single, and have often persuaded to visit her, but had no inclination to it, as the imprudent marriages of both sisters was some thing disgusting, as none of their husbands were men of Character, and both loose in their morals & religious Sentiments, though poor Mr. P C appeared very penitent when dying, and Mrs. P's conduct as a widow has been very unexceptable, indeed much more solid than many others, who have made a great profession of religion, My good friend Mr. Lambert, who is very intimate in the family, who knows the preference they have generally given to me as a Minister, has been much at me to visit her, and as she has lately spent a fortnight at Mrs. Graves in the Indian Land whose families are related, I have been a good deal in her company, and now have Some Serious thoughts of addressing her, though have hardly any expectation, that I will be acceptable to one of her turn, I believe it would be very agreeable to Mrs. Clifford if her daughter would fancy to live & spend her life with me, of this I have had frequent hints, from good hands, this much I thought necessary to write, if I should make an offer of myself, as am more & more convinced it is an absolute duty, both to myself & my children, to marry prudently, and the thoughts of a second [190 (133)] marriage are distressing & still disagreeable, the Idea of my Dear Dear ever Dear Jeany Muir being still & ever will be present with me. . . .

Wednesday December 12 1770 . . . Late in the afternoon was able to draw on my boots, & rode out about three miles & back again, had a good deal of talk with a young man Christopher Langley, who acknowledged to me, that he

believed himself to be the Father of the child Miss Nancy Fletcher, was lately
delivered of, but seems something unwilling to marry her, I said a great deal
to him, he seemed to take it very well, but would say nothing positive as to
marrying her. The good old Mother is in great distress about it. He promised to call on me soon. . . .

Friday December 14 . . . Having occasion yesterday to write to Mr. Wayne
about a tract of land which Mr. James Donnom has to sell & which Mrs.
Clifford wants to buy, & give to him & his wife, I mentioned my design to
visit them on Monday next, but did not mention my business. This day I
received an answer, and a very kind invitation from the whole family to visit
them according to promise, May the Lord Jehovah be my Counselor &
Director, and if ever I should change my Circumstances, grant me a prudent
pious [illegible word] Suitable hand maid, & help meet for me & mine. . . .

[191 (131)] *Monday December 17 1770* . . . On my way to Mrs. Cliffords at the
horseshoe . . . got there betwext twelve & One O Clock, was very kindly &
heartily received by Mrs. Clifford & the other branches of the family. Mrs.
P was not there. This Seemed to relieve me, for as she knew I was coming
was resolved if she stayed out all night, never to think any more of such an
affair, and accordingly, though was alone with Mrs. Clifford at different
times, yet did not mention my errand & indeed had so little heart for it, that
if had not had business to do for my friend Mr. Donnom about the land
should hardly had desire enough to have gone there, yet determined if she
did not come home, not to mention to any one I had such a design, about
three O Clock she came home, having been at the place where her negroes
work. This again filled me with thoughtfulness, especially as what Conversation I heard & observed was not very engaging being mostly about some
frolicks & merry making they were to have about Christmas, & a dance in
which her & Mrs. S just come down from Sacrament had last week, with
another young widow in the neighbourhood of great fortune, and a perfect
stranger to every form of religion, this & other such things made me very
careless & indifferent, yet as they expected me & Mrs. Clifford wished for it
to take place, and as it has been said that I am unconstant & irresolute on
these occasions, proceeding from my little regard for any woman, & knowing had I returned without speaking it would have been said by my friends,
what they have often said, that I did not know my own mind, was too nice,
too critical & hard to please, I chose rather to take up with a refusal, than

have the blame of giving a slight. Accordingly about an hour after Mrs. P came, I was again left with her mama, when I mentioned my design to her, upon which she gave me a very hearty reception, but mentioned she always left her children to choose for themselves which poor Lady has been too true, to their great hurt, she wished me success, and spoke about my Circumstances which she doubted not were as good as they appeared to be, which I assured her they were & better than they appeared to be with which she seemed very well pleased, poor good Lady the predominate in her temper discovered itself on this Occasion and yet she has been most wretchedly mistaken & imposed upon, her great weakness & that of her daughters is their being dazzled with show, & bold impudent assertions. Afterwards hinted to Mrs. P what I had mentioned to her Mother. She seemed not at all Surprized & consented at once to give me her company in the evening, when the rest retired, Mr. Wallace an old Single Gentleman of a pretty publick character was here on Some business, about assisting Mr. Wayne to settle his affairs, he stayed all night, which made me the more reserved. The company were very merry & cheerful, but somehow I could not be much so, was thoughtful & almost melancholy. Mrs. P & I walked out in the dusk & often behaved to each other as people on these occasions but said nothing very particular to her till after Supper & prayers being over, for although Mr. Clifford never gave prayers himself in his time, yet it was his custom to require it both morning & evening not only of Ministers when lodging there, but of [192 (129)] private Gentleman, whom he knew to do it in their own houses, so that his Son in law Mr. Sacheverell was often to give prayers, this Same custom has been kept up ever Since, so that my friend Mr. Lambert is always called upon to give prayers when he is here, after prayers & the Company having sat some time, they all retired, & we were left together, I then proposed my Suit, which she answered in the usual way, but chiefly in these words, that she was sure she could never fancy me for a husband, which I could not help really believing to be true, however we continued together for betwext two & three hours, talking over many matters, she denied that it was my office of being a minister, & the manner of my family & housekeeping that made her she could not fancy me, but in so faint a manner, that shewed she was not much used to disguising her Sentiments, & that it was really the fear of being too seriously & strictly kept in her family that made her say she could not fancy me for her husband. She repeatedly expressed her dislike to be a mother in law, but as she has a child of her own, about three years of age, she had not much to say about being a mother in law, soon

found that my person, circumstances & character were agreeable, but my
being a minister, she was afraid of being too much confined, and would not
have the liberty of such company & dressing as she delighted in, her great
fondness for these follies she could not hide, she owned that my wife dressed
equal to any in her station and seemed one of the happiest of women, but it
was agreeable to her temper to be plain & serious, when she so repeatedly
mentioned her certainty that she could not fancy me (her own words), I insisted she had prepared her answer before hand, but she would not own it,
& immediately declared she would take time to consider of it, after which
we had a great deal of conversation on different matters, she appeared to be
of a very plain, open honest disposition, her natural parts good, but very little cultivated for conversation, and her Sentiments in general poor & very
wrong turned, her knowledge of the world & of mankind very contracted &
almost in every thing a very wrong biass, she is reckoned to be as industrious, I may call eager in pursuit of the world as her mother, & at the same
time is fond of show, dress, company, and expensive appearances, & yet in
other things very hard, and worldly minded, keen & sharp in looking after
her affairs, after her Negroes & making the world, & yet profuse, & incon-
siderate in expenses. Thought she did but answer my expectation, so well in
private conversation as in publick, having something smart, & what some call
witty in company, very cheerful & lively, but seems lost in private conversation which would make me very unhappy, should I have a wife, that was not
a Sensible, conversable companion, she was very free, easy & complaisant in
her behaviour & is I believe very good natured, & appears much more so
in private than in publick, being rather too forward there, not having that
soft, delicate, polite conversation so agreeable in well bred Ladies, but it is I
believe owing to her wrong education. In private conversation what is natural to her, appears & predominates, but in publick conversation, the wrong
biass of her education, and the company she has been most used to, appears
very evidently. In a word, she appears to have much more of good nature,
than good breeding, and had her education for breeding & politeness been
equal to her natural good parts and her good naturedness, & what her fortune could well have afforded, she would have made a figure. Sometime after
twelve at night we parted, very affectionately, I promising to return on Wednesday week if I can, & am not engaged in duties of my office, on the Tuesday week which is Christmas I am God willing to preach at Indian Land, if
there should be no Sermon in the church there, and on that day there is I
believe, to be a Supper & a private dance as it is called at this house, perhaps

not above two or three of the Neighbours. Some hints of it dropped now & then from Mr. Wayne. I mention this, as a reason for my not being more earnest in this matter, & which will save me from the charge of lukewarmness & indifference when my friend Mr. Lambert comes to hear of it, for know he & others of my good friends will rally me on my indifference and making my visits so short. After I retired committed this & all my concerns to God by prayer, & went to rest without any care or concern about the matter. . . .

194 [116] *Tuesday December 25 1770* . . . [195 (114)] After Sermon, rode off very fast with Mr. Starling to baptize his child, about a fortnight old, Grand Son to the late Mr. Wilkins, whose name I persuaded them to give to the child which was very agreeable to the Mother, rode hard as it was several miles out of my way & wanted to have got home before dark to have Sent for my Dear children as expected Mr. Donnoms family would be abroad as usual at this Season, before I got to Mr. Strlings house, I was overtaken by an express messenger desiring me to visit Mr. Charles Palmer,[65] who is extremely ill which I was obliged to put off complying with till the morning. Found a very mixed & disagreeable company at Mr. Strlngs, dined with them which I could not avoid, afterwards baptized the child, was uneasy & disturbed to have such company witness to so solemn an occasion. Mr. Strlng & his wife behaved very well. Was somewhat particular in the laying engagements, to bring her more to publick worship if possible, was helped to faithfulness. . . .

Wednesday December 26 1770 . . . Proceeded to the Late Mrs. Palmers to visit Charles, found him extremely bad of a pleurisy, brought on by riding after midnight when overheated at a merry making, his life despaired of, & in great distress both of body & mind, he was very anxious & desirous to see me, I was greatly affected to see him in such a condition. Dealt very plainly & faithfully with him. Endeavoured to open up to him his lost Sinful miserable wretched state by nature & by practise, then endeavoured to open up in the most plain and familiar manner the nature of Christs Mediation & the necessity of being born again, of receiving the Lord Jesus Christ by faith, in order to Eternal Salvation, he was very serious & attentive, and seemed to receive these Gospel instructions with great earnestness. Afterwards prayed with him, with great fulness, freedom, and the most tender affection, interceeded earnestly for his life but most especially for his soul, in all which he appeared to join with strong affections. . . .

Thursday December 27 1770 . . . Rode to old Mrs. Jeffreys & married her daughter Miss Nancy Fletcher who was some weeks ago delivered of a child to Christopher Langley the young man to whom she laid the child, he at first refused to own the child, & absolutely declared against marrying her, but after I dealt very seriously with him at different times, I got him first to acknowledge that the child was his and afterwards to agree to marrying her. I took an opportunity to have Some conversation with her alone before the marriage and talked very closely & sharply to her, especially for her vile prevaricating, and coming to the Lords table last Summer when she knew she was with child of a bastard, and had been by her distressed Mother very solemnly discharged from going there if she knew herself guilty. She cried very much & seemed penitent, may the Lord make her really so. Was called upon to baptize a child for one Mrs. Evans Sister of young Mr. Jeffreys, her husband Evans, was not present. I married them about two years ago. I was not very willing to baptize the child in the Fathers absence, and would for several reasons declined it altogether & endeavoured to put it off for although the child is born in lawful wedlock, yet was far from being Satisfied with the Conduct either of the Father or Mother, the Grand Mother was also present, and earnestly Solicited me, poor woman she has been a communicant [196 (112)] many years, and for the greatest part of them, appeared to be a serious Christian, but a long train of exceeding bad usage from a very worthless husband, has produced very Melancholy effects. I for sometime refused for reasons which I thought were too visible yet after walking out & considering the affair over & over, as there was a child then present not born in wedlock, which I expected to be soon offered to baptism, the parents having both acknowledged their fault & this day Married, It had some weight with me that there should be an encouragement given to marriage, by preferring this child, besides after examining the conduct of the Mother saw more reason for pity and compassion, than for resentment, and considered that at least I would make a solemn dedication of the child to God, & be very earnest for it in prayer, upon which and several other reasons, I agreed & accordingly baptized the poor infant with great seriousness & concern, having instances of drunkenness before my eyes, as had at another place very lately, which has greatly grieved & distressed me. Dined here purely out of regard to the good old woman the Brides Mother, & to put some respect on the family, after Dinner returned, called and drank tea with my children and here again was distressed with the Sight of drunkenness, in another professor, who alas is too often guilty thereof. . . .

Friday December 28 1770 . . . After morning duties set out for the Indian Land, to visit Mr. Palmer, found him considerably better, and now thought to be in a hopeful way, stayed several hours here in agreeable useful conversation with him, his Sister Calder, and Mrs. Devaux, who was here, was pleased to hear him speak so sencibly of the Lords goodness, & of his resolve to live a more regular life, after Dinner, prayed with him, he seemed very fervently to join with me, he was very humble, teachable, and thankful. In the afternoon returned homewards, rode some miles with Mrs. Devaux daughter, by her first husband, Miss Mlsy Splt a girle about fourteen years of age, she was going by her mama approbation to spend the evening at Mr. Ben Ganlkes,[66] Mains brother in law, where I rode with her in the chair, was pleased with her young. innocent, Simple conversation. . . .

Saturday December 29 1770 . . . Early this morning before daybreak a messenger arrived from Captain Joseph Miles, Ashepoo, acquainting me that He was very bad, thought a dying and was very earnestly desirous to see me. . . . Set off about Sunup, rode very hard, his house is about thirteen miles from this, got there before nine O Clock, found him very ill, with a most violent pleurisy, and though several physicians had been called, yet all appeared to be of no use, he was taken about nine days ago, was not thought dangerous till last night, when he took leave of his wife and children, Sent off for me, and gave some very particular directions about his funeral, I found him very Sensible, very much affected with the thoughts of Death, Judgment & Eternity, very desirous of my discoursing with him & praying, very desirous of instruction, which I endeavoured to give him, in the plainest manner, as concerning our naturally lost state, his Sinfulness by nature & practise, his short-comings of duty, his need of a Saviour, & offered up the Gospel Method of Salvation, the nature of faith & repentance, the nature & necessity of regeneration, and every thing else I thought needful, he seemed to drink it in with greediness and was greatly affected with what was spoken & in the prayer, in which I was uncommonly assisted, was helped to plead & wrestle for him, with the greatest fervency, he thanked me with great affection, and begged me to give him as much of my time [197 (110)] as possible, excused himself for calling out on Saturday, begged me to speak to & pray for him, as I thought proper. . . .

Lords day December 30 1770 . . . Preached from Deuter: 32:29 a very solemn & awful discourse, Soon after we had begun Service, it began to rain and continued for between two & three hours to pour down the most heavy and violent rain, which occasioned me to enlarge upon almost every particular, especially when was giving the reasons, why Sinners should immediately & without delay consider their latter End, or Enter into the Service of God & true religion through the Lord Jesus Christ. I enlarged particularly on shewing the hardening nature of Sin, & the dreadful state of those whose evil habits are rooted, strengthened and long continued in, I described the degrees by which young people especially, & those of them in particular who have had a religious education, & make some profession, advance in wickedness till at last the conscience becomes Seared as with a hot iron, and insisted repeatedly on the hardening tendency of evil Company, of drunkenness, and uncleanness, of Sinning contrary to principle, to light & conscience, afterwards expatiated upon Satans activity & diligence in destroying souls, his great experience & knowledge of human nature, the many ways & strategems by which he betrays & ruins the unwary, and particularly insisted on his betraying young people into with the hopes of Secrecy, while at the Same time having once initiated them into these evil habits & wicked practises, he soon discovered them to the world, and by persuading them their characters were gone, made them more bold, hardened and callous in Sin & wickedness, afterwards shewed the unreasonableness, the Sinfulness, the hurtfulness, and extreme danger of delaying in a matter of such infinite importance as entering into the Divine Service, & securing Eternal Salvation through the Lord Jesus Christ. . . . There appeared a very lively & visible concern on some, a pleasedness & Satisfaction in Severals especially the most serious hearers, to see vice in every shape so earnestly attacked, & Satan as it were so close pursued to all his lurking places, so that it appeared to be a remarkable time. . . . Before I got out of the meeting house severals expressed their great Satisfaction, with being so entertained during the long & heavy rain, but Just as I stepped out of the door Mr. Huttson, the Eldest Son of my Dear & Reverend predecessor at the Indian Land, came up to me, and with a faultering speech asked me, if I had any books or Sermons of his Fathers to return them directly, for I had used him very ill, I was very much Surprized at his Speech, & when looked up at his Countenance, Saw [198 (108) him in the most violent & outrageous passion I ever beheld, indeed there seemed a Mixture of passions, of rage, madness, fury, despair, & horror, all colours, seemed also in his face, red, purple & pale, seemed all working together, a high red prevailed first, then a deep purple, & at last a dark dirty pale, I took him by the hand, and asked what was the matter, and what had put him in such a condition, he pulled his hand from me, & said I had reflected on him in the Sermon, and that I had deprived him of great pleasure for he was determined never to hear me again, I told him, and assured him, he was absolutely mistaken, for I had no thoughts of him more than of others, that I abhorred making personal reflections, that it was Sin I had described and not persons. I took again by the sleeve, & begged him to walk to the retiring house and I would satisfy him, I had not the least of him, and that I was most perfectly innocent of the charge but he turned violently from me, I asked him then, what he thought was personal, he said I described him when I spoke of those, who had been religiously Educated & strictly bred, of whom better things might be expected, I assured him I had no such intention, and was amazed at his vanity in thinking he was the only one there who had a religious education. He insisted upon it he was. I then told him there were severals there had as religious an Education, as ever he could pretend, for although they were not a ministers children, yet some of them had even a stricter Education than him self. He then said It was him, he had been some times drunk, that he had lately had several drunken frolicks at his house, and had been drunk at such times, and he supposed I had heard it, but that he was no whoremaster, that he defied me to charge him with it, and as to drinking I might have told him of it in private, and he would not have been angry but that now, he would never forgive it, I then assured him, I never had heard of his having drunken frolicks at his own house or of his being Drunk at such times, that it was conscience and not me, that had made the application, and that if he had kept his own council I would not have known it & proceeded to look upon it as from another hand, but he turned more enraged, he asked if I could lay my hand on my heart, and declare I had not heard the above, that I did not mean his Conduct at such times. I assured I could, and if it would Satisfy him, I would do in the most solemn manner. He then cried, he could not be Satisfied and would never hear me again. I then told him, to do as He pleased, Severals began to take notice of us, and then I believe began to make some applications to him, which before they did not think of, he mounted his horse & rode off in a most furious manner, His brother in law Peronneau & his Brother a young man just of age were with him,[67] & Observed him & me together. I turned from him to severals of the people who were waiting to speak to me, and took no notice of what had happened, almost every body Spoke of the Service, and how remarkable it was that God should send a rain which confined all the young and wild part of the auditory, to hear what was so necessary and Suitable for them, I heard all & said but little, Others observed how well timed the Sermon was, to the Season of the year, to the Sickly & alarming times, and how much they were favoured by providence, in getting a fair morning to come to Service, & now getting it fair above head to return home, almost every body was making some remarks of this kind. After I had mounted my horse, to proceed downwards to Captain Miles, Mr. Jordan & another Gentleman riding down that way, came & asked me to eat in Mr. Jordans & take Dinner, for they were sure I had much need of it, and that though they had never heard me with greater pleasure, yet they could not help being Sorry for me, as I seemed greatly spent & looked much more fatigued than usual. Among other things Mr. Jordan said I wonder that you made so many apologies about the length of the Sermon, and that you so often told us you would stop as Soon as it gave over raining, for my part says he I was Sorry when it began to clear for I really thought you exceeded yourself, and could have Sat with great pleasure to have heard you three times longer, I made no other answer, than that I was very glad it was so much to his Satisfaction, the other person spoke much the Same as Mr. Jordan, who concluded with saying, he was sure every body must have been highly pleased & edified, I only Smiled, & wished that it might be so, for I was really so fatigued that I could not talk, so different was the effect of this Sermon, indeed a very remarkable one, I should not have taken notice of the great Satisfaction, almost all the hearers expressed on this occasion, was not for the treatment I met with from the unhappy youth above mentioned, poor young man my heart bled for him. A great degree of insanity has been hereditary in the family he is descended from by the Mothers Side, he once gave some Symptoms of it, when at the Colledge of New Jersey for his education, which occasioned his being brought back when he had made but little progress, though it was apprehended, by his friends & his Fathers executors that he feigned a good part of it [199 (106)] to get clear of the trouble of a Colledge Education, at least it is well known to them all, that He feigned an indisposition in his eyes, which was said to prevent his application to reading, for although of remarkable weak parts, yet he has a great degree of low cunning & very violent passions, being very hasty and at the same time, very Obstinate & unrelenting, taking up with imaginary affronts, in common life, & then valuing himself that he never forgives, his most excellent & pious Mother herself had the misfortune in her younger days, before she partook of Divine grace, to be Confined in her Mothers house for a year or two. His Eldest Sister Mrs. Peronneau, upon an imaginary slight from her husband, soon after their marriage, was for about one year confined, sometimes raving mad & at other times Simply foolish to the greatest degree, this poor unhappy young man, looked today to be under some such unhappy influence. He has a very large Estate & lives upon it, his friends were much pleased that he seemed to have a regard for me, and were in hopes I would be of use to him, but Satan seems resolved that I should not. This unhappy prejudice gave me Considerable concern, lest it should have any influence upon others, but whatever effect it may have, the allseeing God, the Searcher of hearts knows my innocence of what he imagines. As I was in a hurry to get to the poor dying Gentleman, and had been long detained by the rain, I declined going into Mr. Jordans for any refreshment, and proceeded on . . . Got to Mr. Miles about four O clock. Found him very ill, was informed that after I left him, his reason failed him more & more, yet he often spoke of me, and at times expressed his longing desire to see me, I immediately waited on him, and he knowed me for Some time, but would soon begin to wander, Death was working hard with him, however I kept very close by him, and took every opportunity to drop a few Sentences to him, which he always understood, I also often offered up short petitions with him & for him, and about Seven at night I proposed prayer. It was earnestly desired by all present, especially by his truly valuable & much affected wife, I spoke of it to himself, in such a way as to humour his delirium, but he appeared all at once perfectly Sensible of his sickness & great danger, I spoke pretty largely to him, then went to prayer, was greatly affected, all present were so, all were in tears, I was never more affected nor moved in any prayer, than when I had finished praying for him as a dying person. I came to pray for his wife and three small children, the room echoed, with groans & tears, sobs and cries, was greatly enlarged, helped, & assisted, an extraordinary influence seemed present amongst. Was helped to plead & wrestle for him, with the greatest fervency, especially for his Salvation, he lay still all the time, seemed very earnestly to join with me, was himself greatly moved & affected, & when I concluded, he took hold of my hand with both his and in the most affectionate manner thanked me again & again, then spoke a few sensible sentences, took some nourishment & immediately fell into the same raving way as before, this was the last and most remarkable interval of Senses he had from yesterday afternoon. Some time after this, I got some Supper which I had great need of and found myself remarkably refreshed by it, Gods creatures are not only necessary but most good and comfortable in their place. I continued mostly with him, dropping now and then a word to him, & often offering up short ejaculatory requests for and with him, for which he was often thankful but mostly intirely out of his Senses, and at times very Ungovernable, I was much pleased with the Company about him, who not only showed great concern for his life, but especially for his soul, in such a manner as far exceeded my expectations, especially his dear & valuable wife, one of the foremost women both in person and parts I ever met with in this province, and whose behaviour as a wife waiting on a dying husband, the husband of her youth, the husband of her choice, far excelled almost every thing I have met with or seen in this part of the world, often & often did she call to my mind, my Dear ever Dear Jenny Muir, when she thought I was dying.

[200 (104)] *Monday December 31 1770* Last night I did not cast off my clothes, but sat up the whole night by this dying Gentleman, excepting about two hours, that I lay down with my clothes, I continued taking all opportunity to drop some sentences to him when in his Senses, concerning his condition, and offering up short prayers & ejaculations for & with him, had a great deal of conversation with Mrs. Miles, whose concern was very great, for the approaching loss of so dear & valuable, for the loss her Dear children would sustain, and the confusion & trouble, they would be thrown into by Mr. Miles being cut off, so suddenly in the midst of his days, and in the midst of many schemes to advance their fortune, which although considerable in itself, yet will very probably be greatly hurted, by so sudden a death, but above all her great & chief concern was about his immortal soul, & Eternal Salvation, with many tears, did she earnestly plead for his being restored to his Senses, her whole conduct was very worthy of the fine woman of great sense, & well improved parts, of the very affectionate & tender wife, and becoming the good Christian, she discovered a knowledge of the Christian mysteries & of the nature & necessity of the Gospel Salvation, far above what I expected. It was a very tender scene, especially when at times he raved exceedingly & was quite ungovernable, often he forgot & lost knowledge of his Dear wife, and of all about him, he always perfectly knowed me, and behaved with that decorum he thought my presence required, which kept me, the closer by him, as at times no body could do any thing with him, but myself. . . . Late in the forenoon . . . took my leave, promising to return on Wednesday or in the morning if I heard no accounts from Indian Land, where I had been told before I left home Mr. Samuel Wilkins was taken in fits, and that his son in law Mr. Hill Samways was bad . . . Was very desirous also to spend this night and to morrow morning at home, that might conclude the old and begin the new in prayer and covenanting according the manner I have used to do when not engaged in publick Service. When I rode through my plantation, one of my fellows told me that both Mr. Wilkins and his Son in law, were dead, last night, and that there was a letter, over at my house, desiring me to attend their funeral to morrow, this affected me much, a very awful and Solemn providence, poor Mr. Wilkins was present when I discoursed at his brothers funeral, he had for some years given himself up to liquor, & given over coming to publick worship. That night I discoursed in great faithfulness, and especially insisted upon the presence of the Gospel, and the advantage of enjoying it, as well as the obligation all were under to attend upon it, my subject naturally led to do so, as Mr. William Wilkins was the greatest donor to these funds which now Support the Gospel at Indian land, Mr. Samuel Wilkins was also a very considerable donor to the funds and always professed and shewed a great respect and regard for me, even after he had left off all attendance on publick worship. His excuse was his being subject to fits, blessed be God that I was helped to deal faithfully with him the last opportunity I had. . . . Wrote a letter to poor Mr. Hutson desiring a conference with him, when & where he would appoint, & in the presence of any person he would name, that I might if possible remove his groundless prejudice, this I thought was my duty to propose, and if he refused it, I then left my cause to the Searcher of hearts my Eternal Judge & his. . . .

1771

[201 (102)] *Tuesday first day of January one thousand Seven hundred and Seventy one years* . . . After some refreshment set out the Indian Land, to the house near Pocotaligo from whence the Corpse were to be carried to the grave at the Meeting house, was in a most humble [202 (100)] heavenly spiritual cheerful frame of soul, yet deeply affected with the solemn scene I was now to bear a part, and a very affecting scene it was, two large Corpses, in one house, Mr. Wilkins about fifty years of age & Mr. Samways, about twenty four, had both corpses taken into the Meeting house and according to the late custom begun with a short prayer, discoursed about half an hour, from Ecles: 12:7 then prayed more largely, Sung a psalm was well assisted, had a very decent serious auditory, all were greatly affected, a Solemn awe sat upon every Countenance, was myself deeply affected, it was an awful Sight

January 2, 1771

to see two such large Coffins on the communion table, and both laid in one grave, the divine presence & power Seemed remarkably with us, at the grave, the large wide grave, I spoke a few words of its being the house appointed for all living and pronounced the blessing, it was near Sun down before this awful Solemnity was concluded . . . Continued much and seriously affected with the awful beginning of this year in my Congregations especially at poor Indian Land.

Wednesday January 2 1771 . . . Set out for Ashepoo to visit Captain Miles if in life, rode fast as usual hoping to find him alive, but when was about four miles from his plantation, met a young Gentleman Billy Dry, who informed me, he died in the night still unsensible, after a very long & hard struggle, and some violent convulsions before he expired. He has really been a dying since Saturday, and very hard, however as was so near, I proceeded, found he had spoke of me to the very last, found his family in great confusion, his Dear, dutiful & most affectionate wife in great distress, she thanked me for all my care & kindness, and begged to attend to morrow, & do the last kind office, by reading the Service of the church of England, and adding a discourse and prayer as usual among the dissenters, which I promised to do. . . . Rode homewards in a chaise of the deceased with Doctor William Day, where called and sat about half an hour, & rode home just before Dark. . . . Was much concerned this night on the following account, received letters this day from Mr. James Donnom at present in Charlestown, containing a letter directed for his brother Mr. Jonathan Donnom, where my children board, but left open for my perusal, informing him that there was an offer made him Mr. Jonathan Donnom, to go & Overlook three plantations belonging to a Gentleman of fortune, Mr. Shubrick,[68] at the distance of about thirty five or fourty miles from this more to the Southward, where he would receive five hundred a year currency with other Emoluments, and at the Same time his own plantation might go on here, and advising him for many reasons by claims to engage in it, for though it would in a great measure remove them for two or three years from the Gospel yet it might put it in their power to return afterwards and be more useful, as Mr. Donnom is in straitened circumstances, and very considerably in debt and a Spanish war expected any day which always greatly distresses this province,[69] he will certainly accept of it, and may indeed look upon it as a very kind providence, and yet perhaps for some reasons, it may not answer so well as he expected, but should I try to persuade them of it, I would be thought selfish, and indeed if this does not help his family & him, there is no prospect he will ever get out of debt, into which chiefly misfortune has brought him and his good family, Mrs. Donnom will be very uneasy to leave the Gospel, but necessity will make her submit, what troubled me was, what to do with my children, for cannot Send them at so great a distance, and especially away from all ordinances, as they are now capable [203 (98)] of receiving some instruction, to take them home is not in my power, & to Send them to Charlestown they are much too young, this affair gave me great Concern, and Sent me to prayer, to plead that God might direct me & provide for them.

Thursday January 3:1771 This morning still much concerned about my poor Dear children, was in a humble frame of soul, my heart & affections with God, yet also thoughtful about altering my Condition, which now there is more than ever a necessity for, and that very urgent, so that I am afraid I may be at last precipitated to act imprudently in this most important step, it is very easy to alter my condition, but to do it prudently, & discreetly, to get a Mother for my children, & not to hurt and prejudice them, is a very difficult matter, my circumstances makes it vey difficult to marry, It is hard to get a good Mother in law, difficult to get a woman prudent & Suitable for a ministers wife especially for one in so publick, & noted a Situation as mine. This morning Mr. Donnom came over and informed of his determination to accept of the offer made him, if he liked it upon viewing the place, & further information, and that good Mrs. Donnom had after a nights consideration agreed to go. I told him I could by no means advise him other wise, though I was Sensible it would at present be a disadvantage to me, as I did not know what to do with my children besides the loss of so good a Neighbour, whom I will miss on many accounts, especially good Mrs. Donnom, in case of Sickness I would be very destitute, yet I could not but advise them to accept of it . . . Set off in the rain . . . found a considerably good company at the house of the diseased, Several almost all people of fortune & fashion, Several relations from a distance. As the rain continued, waited till between three & four O clock before began the Service, and when we did it rained so very hard, that was obliged to perform the Service in the porch of the house, the people standing in the hall & rooms, besides what were in the porche or piazza, I read the publick Service of the Established church, having some earth brought from the grave, for the ceremony of throwing it on the Coffin, at the words dust to dust, ashes to ashes, Earth to Earth.

Afterwards I spoke a little, to the improvement that should made of the providence. Could not enlarge, as it was growing near Sun set, and many had to ride away in the rain, the auditory were exceedingly attentive and mostly in tears, while I was discoursing of the melancholy & affecting providence, and of the diseased . . . poor Mrs. Miles was within hearing but could not appear. There was much weeping in the time of the last prayer, afterwards we walked through the rain to the burying ground, deposited the Corpse, then spoke a few words as usual & pronounced the blessing, never was witness to a more decent funeral, hardly ever saw a company, friends, neighbours, and acquaintances so much affected. . . .

Friday January 4 1771 . . . Went over and drank tea with my Dear children, here learned from good Mrs. Donnom, their determined resolution to go to the place providence has thrown in their way, they repeatedly advised me to marry soon and not to be too niece in my choice, acknowledged it would be quite improper to carry the children with them, advised me strongly against getting a house keeper, because of the worlds censoriousness and advised me rather to board out the children, than to do so, & mentioned a particular [204 (96)] family who are soon to move, to the place where good old Mr. Lambright died, they are a sober family, but do not preserve so much as the form of family religion, the Mrs. of the family is a very good sort of woman, has for some time been a Communicant, I shall like much to have the children at School with her, who is very capable of instructing young Girles but should not much chuse them to board in the family. . . .

Lords day January 6 . . . It continued a drisling rain, and the roads being so unpassable, was obliged to begin late, had a good Congregation notwithstanding all the discouragements. Preached largely, fully & with great freedom from Job 14:1. After a large, suitable introduction, and very fully explaining the text, insisted at this time chiefly on mans days being few, not only few compared to the days of the antedeluvian Fathers, few compared to Jobs & the other patriarchs, but absolutely few, short & uncertain in themselves, and few very few considering the great & important work we have to do in them, few very few considering what depends upon the right improvement of them, and considering a following Eternity. . . . It was a solemn time, the late Deaths amongst us seemed to Cooperate with the word. . . . Rode over to Mr. Donnoms, being uneasy about Betsys Cold there being at this time

in Charlestown, & in many places in the country a most Malignant fever &
sore throat, which proves very mortal & generally comes on by a Cold,
found her still very much indisposed with the cough but rather better than
otherwise. . . .

[205 (94)] *Thursday January 10:1771* . . . [206 (92)] As I rode through the
plantation the Overseer stopped me, and told me, that John Splat, Mrs.
Devaux Son by her first husband was dead, & that there was a letter for me,
desiring me to attend his funeral to morrow, this very much Surprized me,
as the young man, a youth about Sixteen or Seventeen years of Age, was at
Meeting last Sabbath, and I had not heard of his being Sick, It seems he was
taken last Sabbath night, but was not thought dangerous till yesterday, when
he died Suddenly to the great distress and grief of his much afflicted Mother,
to whom he was always a very dutiful child, and was now capable of being
very useful to her, in her widowed state. Poor good Lady, her afflictions are
many & great. I believe she is a truely gracious person, and I hope & believe
gets a Sanctifying use of her various troubles. Sincerely Sympathized with
her and was helped to remember her in prayer. . . .

Friday January 11 . . . About twelve O Clock, set off for the Indian Land.
. . . The company were late in gathering, so that did not move the Corpse
till after three O Clock, and by the time we got to the meeting house, had
not time to discourse so largely as Intended but was well assisted in discoursing as long as the time would permit, to a very weeping auditory, there was
a very decent company, a good many young persons. I mentioned & discoursed chiefly from these three Scriptures, Man that is born of a woman, is
of few days & full of trouble. O that they were wise, that they Understood
this that they would consider their latter End, and remember your Creator
in the days of your youth, particularly directed to the young people, there
was a great weeping. It was just dusk before we concluded, had spoken in
the house to the afflicted Mother, from the Shunamites answer to Elisha Servant, when he was sent to inquire, If it was well with her, well with her husband & well with her child, though the child was dead, which was the cause
of her Errand to the prophet, yet she answered It is well, a noble answer,
worthy of the best of Christians. Also promised the Congregation, to make
a further improvement of this as well as the late providence, Some Sabbath
Soon . . . [207 (90)] Got safely home, after nine O Clock at night, found my

Dear child, with a most violent fever, which had increased from the time I left her, She had a great flushing in her countenance, great starting & twitching in her nerves, a great anxiety & pressure upon her Spirits. She had fretted and cried much, but was much appeased & satisfied, when she Saw me. I had been much concerned about her all day, but was now greatly alarmed, remembering how suddenly my other dear children had been carried off, Endeavoured to do for her what I could, and to God my Father & Friend, and poured out my soul before him . . . It was a comfortable & yet a troubled night to me, saw my Sins in my Judgment, Saw Gods Fatherly anger against me, yet was helped to cleave to his Smitting hand, to kiss the approaching rod, however severely I may Smart under it, this was indeed a good night to my troubled soul.

Saturday January 12 1771 Greatest part of last night I was awake, with my Dear afflicted child, who was greatly distressed. Her great & severe sickness put me much in mind of my Dear Sacheverell, all this day her fever Continued with a raging violence, attended with every mortal like Symptom, I apprehended it to be a dangerous worm fever and so did the Doctor Mr. Bowers whom I sent for, poor Dear child, she wavered & wandered very much especially when dosing & sleeping, was often very stupid and insensible, I was very much distressed & afflicted, it renewed my former griefs, and seemed to set my every wound fresh a bleeding . . . In the afternoon I received a letter from good old Mr. Atkins informing me that his Son Thomas died last night & desiring me to attend & discourse, at his funeral to morrow afternoon, which I promised to do if my poor Dear Motherless child could be left. Every Symptom seemed very fatal. The Doctor apprehended a violent nervous fever, which seemed to have its rise from worms & he gave Medicines accordingly, to me this was a day of self searching, I saw Sin, my Sins, my prevailing Sins to be the cause of all my afflictions and Sorrows, and mourned before the Lord, as still continuing to Sin away my pleasant & lovely comforts. Oh what a backslider, what an abuser of mercies, & what a misimprover of afflictions am I, hence my crosses are so often repeated, was filled with self convictions, & self Condemnation, and at the Same time with wonder and astonishment at sparing mercy, that had any comforts at all. . . . This evening the child complained much of her left Side, and it appeared plainly, although worms may be a great cause of her disorder, yet it is a violent pleurisy & fever with very nervous Symptoms, the Doctor had suspected this and had given directions accordingly. . . .

Lords day January 13 1771 Another watching night, with my Dear child, who was all pain in her left side, which I had often rubbed with Campherated Spirits. . . . As it began very early, a cold drisling rain, was very cloudy, & great appearances of bad weather, I did not expect there would be an opportunity to preach, as the roads are so broke up, & the whole earth, I mean our part of it, deludged with water. Was informed that Mrs. Donnom was so indisposed, that she could not come over, this gave me great concern, as could not think of leaving the child, though her fever was somewhat abated, and she was Sensible, which was the case with her yesterday morning, for an hour or two. The old Christian wench is very Sensible & careful having all her life been used to attend children, the child also Consenting to my going, & sending some white person to stay with her till I returned, which I resolved to have done if I had gone out, & left the child among the Negroes, but about ten O Clock, Mrs. Donnom came over & brought her children with her, Betsys fever and dangerous Symptoms began to increase fast, at Eleven O Clock I set out for [208 (88)] meeting, though the weather still very threatening, found but a few people come, among others met with my friend Mr. James Donnom from Charlestown, who had come to Mr. Jordans last night, & was to Spend this night at my house. He introduced me to a young Gentleman from the Northward, come to receive & close the Subscriptions which the Reverend Mr. Caldwell was last Spring making for the New Jersey Colledge. I was Surprized to see Mr. Huttson with him. I spoke to him as usual. He at first seemed reserved, but was evidently more from Confusion & something like shame than from resentment. We then spoke freely together. The Occasion of his being here contrary to his verbal & written declaration was, He had been at Colledge with this young Gentleman who was particularly recommended to me & therefore had come to meeting out of Complaisance to him, this Mr. Donnom informed me of. However, whatever was his motive, I thought it my duty to take no notice of what was past, and perhaps there may be a providence in it to keep him to his duty, which poor youth he very carelessly observed, for he never used to attend above once in four or six weeks, nor so often, and not once in Six months went over the river. As it was near twelve O Clock before any thing like a Congregation was collected, I acquainted them with the Obligation of my performing Service at old Mr. Atkins, & of the Circumstances of my family, which Obliged me to return this night, so that I proposed only to give prayers. Was well assisted in a large prayer suitable to the Sicklyness & Mortality of the times. Was helped to plead with God for the Congregations, for the Neighbourhood and for the Country in general, which is at present in great distress by Sickness & Deaths both in Town & Country, afterwards Sung a psalm as usual then read the text I designed to have preached on Psl: 119:125. The chief thing I had in view, was to press my Dear hearers to begin the year by setting apart some time for solemnly, expressly & explicitly entering into Gods Service. . . . Acquainted them, of the many Instances of mortality we have had among us Since this present year began, of the Malignant disorder that prevails in Town, the Ulcerated Sore throat, which prevails like a pestilence especially among children, great numbers of whom it carries off, & is also very mortal among adults, especially the young and the Middle aged, and from these & other considerations pressed them to avouch the Lord for their God. . . . I then proceeded downwards riding as fast as the roads would permit. Had received a line to pray for & and wait on old Mr. Pge, my former overseer who lies very ill. Accordingly called upon & visited him, found him very low, and in great Measure uncapable of instruction, they had Sent for me on Friday but missed me, sat sometime with him, & got him made Sensible who I was, he was much affected, and appeared in a humble, pious frame of mind, desiring rather to be gone to Jesus Christ than to Continue longer in this world. He has been a very great & open Sinner in his time but for three or four years has professed a great change, and has upon the whole given good evidences thereof, and appeared to me at this time, to be in a humble, penitent, believing, Spiritual frame of soul, after discoursing with him, exhorting and directing him, I went to prayer, he appeared to join me with great fervency & melting affections. I then proceeded to Mr. Atkins, got along with great difficulty, found a larger company than was at meeting. Discoursed about three quarters of an hour or more, from Ecles: 12:7, prayed twice, Sung a hymn, proceeded just as usual when bury at the Meeting house, the auditory were attentive, serious, and well behaved, not the least appearance of drunkenness among any, which I was afraid of, the family were greatly affected. . . . Did not get home till near eight at night, a very dark cold drisly night. Found Mrs. Donnom & Mr. James Donnom with my child, and learned that a good many friends had called, found her still very bad, & learned she had been exceedingly so through the day, and that all my friends had but very little hopes of her, as for myself I had none, was in a humble, resigned frame of soul, Satisfied of her Eternal happiness and willing if the Lord my God required it, to part with her to the blessed regions of glory, where I shall soon follow her if so be that the Lord at this time takes her off. After got some refreshment, walked home with Mrs.

Donnom & after returning Mr. James Donnom sat up with me till midnight, when he retired. I gave her a dose four grains of calomel, or sweet mercury, which I have found of the greatest benefit in Childrens obstinate fevers, whether proceeding from worms or other causes. . . .

Monday January 14:1771 Last night slept very little, for soon after I began to dose a little, the childs physick began to work, both by vomiting and stool. She was greatly oppressed with Sickness, before the operation began, and greatly distressed before it was over, being often up & down so that she was quite spent, I was early in the morning to have given her a purge to carry off the [209 (86)] mercury, but as it had worked well itself I delayed it for some hours, her fever abated more than it has yet done, & after the purge had operated twice or thrice, she looked something more lively, & my friends thought much better, than yesterday. This forenoon the doctor called & gave further directions, he thought her still in a dangerous way. About the middle of the Day, my old house keeper came, she has been earnestly Soliciting some friends to interceed with me, to take her back, and no doubt, she will endeavour to improve this as a favourable opportunity, Could hardly bear to see her go near the children, yet have always used her civilly, & perhaps may have more need of her at this time, than I expect. In the forenoon Mr. Huttson and his Brother, with the Gentleman from the Northward Mr. Ogden, came, and would have dined with me, had not the child been so bad here, however I had assisted in having Dinner provided at Mr. Donnoms, and the child being easy and the old house keeper with her, I went over with Mr. James Donnom & them & Dined with Mrs. Donnom. Mr. Huttson and I were very free, and as much intimate as ever, and thought it most proper, to take no manner of notice of his behaviour nor of his foolish letter. Soon after dinner Mr. Donnom came home from visiting the place at the Southward, but poor man was sorry to see that he had not been more careful of himself. His wife, his brother & I were all very much concerned, his brother set off immediately for his own house, the young Gentlemen going up with him, I stayed but a few minutes after. Mrs. Donnom followed me to the Door & observed to me, with concern, that she could not possibly come over this night, I returned very melancholy, much affected with the thoughts of my Dear childs illness, my desolate circumstances with respect to having her taken care of, was distressed to think of her Death if the Lord designs that and almost no less so to think what I shall do with her & her Sister, as to providing for them, with a kind, tender, careful hand, Lord pity, guide &

direct me. Towards the Evening, her fever began much to abate, so that we began to have some hopes of her life. . . .

Wednesday January 16:1771 . . . Betsy had a restless uneasy night . . . about the middle of the day, it abated, and in the afternoon went intirely off, all her complaints abated and she got up, had her clothes on, and was cheerful. . . . About the middle of the day, received some certain, but general intelligence of an affair of which I have had some hints formerly. Bull of Sheldon,[70] & Main have long been insinuating to such of the people of Indian Land as would give them the hearing that I neglect them, & wanted to give them up, that the parsonage Negroes which were hired to me three years ago were of more value, than their part of my Salary came to. They have also insinuated that with the work of the Negroes & a subscription set on foot, they would be able to maintain a Minister for themselves. Bull who also pretends to be a Trustee, has been offering to hire the Negroes, and pretends, that he will now insist on having them, about four months ago one of the parsonage Negroes had some falling out with the Overseer, and absented himself and it seems is kept out by the connivance of the above Enemies, I was this day informed that their design is, at the time the Negroes use to be hired out, that Bull shall demand them, in the mean time they are endeavouring to permit a subscription among some of their own kidney, under the pretense of assisting the Meeting people to have a Minister wholly to themselves, and are at the Same time persuading the people, who they know are excessively fond of me, that I slight, neglect & even despise them, Since I got as they call it, into good & Independent Circumstances, and that I want an opportunity to drop them altogether, this Scheme, which is not really levelled at me but at the Dissenting Interest itself, to which Bull is a great Enemy, and against which he is enraged by seeing the serious church people daily joining me, has been carrying on for some time. Satan is greatly enraged against the Gospel and the Success thereof, & it is the Gospel itself and the good of souls, that He stricks at, Main is greatly enraged to see me prosper in my circumstance, credit, & usefulness, and it is me he strikes at, whom to hurt and ruin he would very willingly Sink not only the Dissenting interest, but even the Gospel itself, Bull, who is the head [210 (84)] in this black design, aims at nothing so much as destroying the Dissenting interest. The Information I got this day is from a person of certain and undoubted Credit, and knew nothing of one of the parsonage Negroes being run away till he learned it from them. He is also one whom they can never Suspect. I was a good deal Surprized, for although I had heard some hints of such a thing designed, yet I did not think it possible that Bull could be concerned in any such thing and as for Main, he could have no influence without Bull, I looked upon it only as a Surmise of my friends, the wickedness of these men, in endeavouring to Overthrow the Gospel truely shocked & amazed me, and their baseness to keep up a Slave, a strong able fellow, since August past, the property of whose work belongs to me, I could not have believed, without such assurance as I this day had, it gave me great Concern for Some hours, I am very willing to give up Indian Land, were they well provided for, in a faithful Gospel Minister, but to leave them destitute, is what I cannot think of, and will never do, while I am near enough to preach to them. After asking Council & direction from God, and committing the cause and inter-est of the poor people of Indian Land unto Him, I was quite composed & resigned to his holy will, being firmly resolved by his grace helping me, nei-ther meanly to desert my office at Indian Land, nor to accept of any terms from those Enemies of the Gospel but will through Gods assistance dispute every inch of that Sacred ground where God has so greatly blessed my La-bours against Satan and all his Emissaries, Main, Bull, and all the confeder-acy, My God will be with me, his grace I hope, I believe, I trust will be made even in this affair, Sufficient for me and his strength perfect in my weakness.

Thursday January 17:1771 . . . Mr. James Donnom came & spent the night with me. I acquainted him with the wicked Scheme of my Enemies. He much applauded my design to stand by the Serious people there and neither to desert them because of my Enemies nor to be tempted to leave them by any offers that can be made me, from other places, for at this very pres-ent time Ponpon, who are very rich & powerful, would give much greater worldly advantages to have the half of my time. . . .

[211 (82)] *Lords day January 20 1771* . . . I had some thoughts of acquainting the Congregation after Sermon of the design of the Enemies of the Gospel in this place, of their design to get the Negroes into their own hands under the pretence of getting the whole of a ministers time to them alone, but before I went into Service was informed that Main was Sick, & his wife very ill, which made me think, that perhaps God was working for the Congrega-tion in his own way, that I need not alarm & distress the Serious part of the Congregation with any publick intimation of it, and therefore omitted it intirely at this time . . . In about a quarter of an hour after I got home, I was

called upon by the Reverend Mr. Ellington,[71] who came to stay all night
with me. He is a very worthy Clergyman of the church of England, who
came in about three or four years ago for Augusta on the Georgia Side of
Savannah river, where by his great zeal, and diligence, he was thought to be
useful, and was much more acceptable, than ever any Minister before, had
been to them, but at the Same time, he had Considerable discouragement,
It being a very wild back out of the [way] place, built & inhabited chiefly
for carrying on trade for the Creek Indians. In England, he was what they
call a Methodist, and was mostly Connected with Mr. Whitefield. He was
not Educated for the Ministry nor had he what is called a learned or liberal
Education but had I believe what may be called a genteel good Education.
What He was first bred to, whether as a teacher of English reading as I have
heard, or a Mechanick, I know not, but after He was grown up, and awak-
ened under Mr. Romain,[72] he was employed, as I have been told, as a Reader
of prayers & homilies, and being found truely religious and Industrious to
improve himself, he was by the interest of the Misters Romain, Whitefield
& others received into orders, in order to come out to America, and for
Augusta in particular. Soon after Mr. Whitefield came last into this province,
he left his perish at Augusta, and went to live at the Orphan house, to teach
English retorick or to teach English Grammatically, preside as Chaplain in
the Orphan house Academy and to preach Occasionally at Savannah, but
Mr. Whitefield dying Suddenly in New England before the Academy was
properly founded, He has been obliged to look out for a perish. The people
of Augusta would receive him, but he has declined it, and came into this
province Some time ago, and being invited by the church wardens of this
perish, or at Ponpon as it is called, has accepted their invitation, and is now
the Established Minister of the perish. I had the opportunity of Seeing him
about three years ago at Mr. Zublys in Savannah, and when at the horseshoe about a month ago I had recommended him very earnestly, which he
had heard of, and called to Intimate his design to Cultivate a good correspondence with me. He is I believe a very particularly excellent & very zealous Minister, He does not pretend to study or Compose much, but honestly
owns that he preaches other mens works chiefly Misters Romains, Henrys,
Jones,[73] Whitefield [212 (80)] & others of the same stamp, so that He is
truely an Evangelical preacher, He is said to excel in reading the publick Service, and his Sermons, which makes him very acceptable, even to them who
dislike his Subjects & the matter of his preaching. He is I am persuaded a
Sincere experimental Christian, & truely Gospel Minister. The Dissenters at

Ponpon especially my friends are much taken with him. His natural abilities seem far from great, but He is very zealous to advance the glory of God, the Dear Redeemers kingdom, & the good of precious souls. He professes himself, and really appears to be, very Catholic, so as to have a very good opinion of the Dissenters in general, and I believe pays no great regard to the outward forms of religion, nor to the ceremonies and habits of the Established church and yet appears to have very high notions of the Hierarchy. His knowledge appears to me, to be very Contracted, He seems to have little Ministerial experience, for at present He is so full of himself as to think, hell must fall before him. He repeatedly expressed his expectation, that there would be no longer any dissenters about Ponpon but all will follow him to the church. He wanted much to know if I had any thoughts of preaching that way, and could not help signifying there was no need for it, He expressed his expectation of Jacksonburgh soon being a very Christian place, poor Gentleman, I often looked at him with pity, He put me in mind of Philip Melancton,[74] who imagined before he began to preach that he should convert all his hearers, and that none will be able to withstand him, but afterwards he owned his mistake, & found that old Adam, was too strong for young Philip. Something of the Same I remember to have experienced in myself. Poor Mr. Ellington, if he preaches Christ, yet I am afraid he does not preach the cross, I doubt much, that too like my self, in my younger days, he has flattered himself as to his usefulness, and it is my opinion, that without being more exercised, with self denying providences, he never will be very useful, and am persuaded, that if God designs him for usefulness, He will humble & empty him of himself. This is what very zealous preachers often fall into imagining, that their zeal can effect that which only grace can do, and what grace often does effect, by unlikely Instruments. Found him very fond to preach often, & in different places, which it is easy for him to do. I mentioned to him, that his preaching at both his churches, i.e., Ponpon & Ashepooh in one day would not be accepted, but that he had better preach twice a day, at each place, but with some warmth he declared, against it, and exclaimed against two Sermons on the Sabbath in one place as absolutely useless, which Surprized me much, & discovered much vanity & self conceit not to say self seeking, I found him very impatient of any Sentiments contrary to his own, and I said very little on these points wherein I differed from him as thinking it most proper to appear yielding at our first meeting, I just mentioned that the preaching both forenoon and afternoon was both necessary and useful for the greater Sanctification of the Sabbath, and

especially in this Country where so few pay any regard to the Sabbath except
at publick worship, which He acknowledged as what he had not thought of.
I also Signified that running about, as is common with the Curates in England, performing Service in different places on the same day, rather tended
to the prophanation of the Sabbath, and that the Methodist manner of
running from place to place to give sermons, with crowds attending them
or waiting for them, was no better, and that in general, when no particular
providence called a minister to preach & perform Service in different places
that He might do more real good, & answer the Ends of his ministry to much
better purpose, by Spending the whole day in one place, and that whatever
Itinerants might do, that fixed Ministers who had the pastoral charge, were
more in the way of their duty to Spend the day in one place, than in different places in ordinary cases, he said but little in answer to it, yet on the whole
this was a comfortable evening and on the Doctrines of grace our Sentiments
Seemed much to agree. He would I believe preach in the Meeting house if
allowed to read the publick Service, but not to perform worship according
to the Dissenting Method of worship, the first I hope will never be allowed
him, His Catholickism is far from being so extensive as he imagines it, He
in this matter I believe, deceives himself as well as others. When speaking of
my reading the funeral Service on some Occasions he seemed to think it was
an honour for any dissenter to do so, but that it would be greatly the reverse
for a church Minister or a Clergy man as he expressed it, to omit any part of
the publick Service, his expressions frequently were, that a Dissenter, a Dissenting teacher, might very well use any part of the publick Service or prayer
book, but that a clergy man, could not with any propriety omit it nor perform Service without it, we conversed on many things, at least I heard him
speak of many things about himself & his Ministry, and upon the whole I
found that while I keep away from Ponpon [213 (78)] & in general give place
to him, that we may agree very well but no longer, however I resolved just
to go on as usual, doing nothing designedly to offend him, nor in the least
refusing to perform every Ministerial Service there when called to it. . . .

Monday January 21 1771 This morning got up early on Mr. Ellingtons
account, who wanted to get forward on his Journey for Augusta to settle
some business he has there, which is upwards of an hundred miles from this,
& then he goes down as far to Savannah, & is to be absent about three weeks.
At my desire he went to prayer, and had a very excellent prayer, but appeared
to be at some difficulty for expression, as if not much used to prayer without

book. As the River is so very deep & even dangerous to a stranger, I rode with him. . . . It drisled in the morning before we set out, and afterwards rained most of the time I was with him. He was exceedingly well provided for the weather, for besides what is usual, He had a large Silk Cloak, & hat case dressed with oyl & wax, the whole did not weigh a pound weight and yet keeps out rain for any number of hours. He has in general Something very particular about him. He is of appearance delicate like, a very smooth face which makes him look very young like, though about thirty or upwards, a weakness in his Sight, obliges him constantly to wear spectacles, fastened on his head for that purpose, so that He eats, drinks & converses with them at all times, and I am told even sleeps with them, which makes an odd appearance, in a person so young like, his boots are of a very particular kind, fastened to his Saddle, and Serve for boots, stirrups, & stirrup Irons all in one, and at the Same time like the step of a Stair, to mount his horse from, He is very niece in his eating & drinking, generally carries victuals and all necessaries with him, and as he cannot swim, he carries, what is called the marine belt with him, which will Support a person in any depth of water, in any position for any length of time even if dead, he is very careful of his health in every respect, which is certainly his duty, yet such care may be carried to an extreme, and such extreme niceness & concern, does not seem to be very apostolical nor much like an Evangelist, yet how happy should I be, were such things as these my only weaknesses, after a very kind and affectionate parting, I turned off and went to visit Mr. Jordan, who has for several months given up attending on publick worship, or appearing at any publick place at all. Found him very fat, fresh, and hearty, not the lest appearance of his being under any concern of mind or of his undergoing any Mortifications, but all appeared to be the reverse, after the common civilities & first Salutations were over, I let him know my design was either to prevail on him to attend on publick worship as usual, and to act like a Man and a Christian, or that from this day I broke off all connection with him as a Minister, would have no longer any Charge of his soul, and renounced the pastoral relation to him. I said a great deal to him, both in a mild & in a very solemn manner, Endeavoured to lay before him, the Sin & danger of his conduct, and to allure, persuade & Engage him to his duty, both by encouraging promises from the word of God and awful denunciations of wrath, threatened in the same Sacred Oracles, he at first made trifling excuses which I severely animadverted on, as being false and disingenuous as a mocking of God and even a dealing deceitfully with the Most high and little less than lying to the Holy Ghost. He was for some time hardened & sullen, but I continued to deal very faithfully with him, & to discharge my own soul, he then began to soften and burst out in many tears, cried & bitterly lamented himself, complaining of his misery and wretchedness, promising to be directed by me, begging me to be his Spiritual guide, & to pray for him. I then dealt mildly with him & explained the obligations he was under to live as a Christian and to wait upon the Gospel, however desperate he [214 (76)] might think his own case, I frequently omitted discoursing to him, about this particular business and conversed very freely and friendly about other matters, walked out with him, Stayed Dinner, conversed with his wife about her Baptism, but still kept in view the business I came upon, at last got him repeatedly to promise, and engage, to his duty, and to be over at the Saltcatcher next Sabbath, if the river and the weather permits, after set out for home, I found Satisfaction in this Service, I had been engaged in. . . .

[216 (72)] *Monday January 28 1771* . . . Mr. James Donnom, went over to the plantation to see how the business went on, I went over with him to visit the Sick Negroes, whom we found very much neglected, a Sensible wench was ordered, from the barn to Nurse & attend the rest, & Mr. Donnom gave the Overseer a strict charge, to see that she did her duty, and at the Same time reprimanded him for his Neglect, one of Mrs. Holmes wenches being dangerously ill, and intirely neglected. The Overseer was affronted with the reprimand, and answered Mr. Donnom very indiscreetly, upon which some words passed, the Overseer giving Mr. Donnom more than ten words for one, and expressed himself very unbecomingly, upon which Mr. Donnom told him, if he would not do his duty, to leave the Employ, upon which the Overseer expressed himself very indiscreetly, I said nothing, but desired Mr. Donnom to come away. We accordingly walked back to my house. In a little time the Overseer came and made several acknowledgements repeatedly begging pardon of Mr. Donnom, Mr. Donnom & him had some discourse together, & matters seemed made up, only Mr. Donnom referred him to me, & privately desired me to give some advice, which I accordingly did & he seemed thankful and repeatedly begged me to write a letter to Mr. Donnom in his favour, who had gone home, as he was just Setting out when the quarrel happened, which I promised to do after I returned from Mr. Perrys funeral where I was to give Service, this affair had given me Considerable uneasiness, but now I thought it all over, accordingly with great composure of mind made preparation for the Service before me. About three O Clock,

as I rode through the plantation, I observed the Overseer looking very angry
and passionate like, he called to me & said I have been thinking on Mr.
Donnoms usage of me, & I have changed my mind, I believe I will leave
your Employ. I answered, he was at liberty to do as he pleased, & passed
him. Afterwards I turned back and asked him when he intended to leave us,
He answered I am not quite determined, but if I leave you, it will be tomorrow morning, I am going abroad this afternoon, I will return at night &
then I will know, I made him no answer. I supposed he was going to consult
Mr. Hamilton who is his Uncle & did not doubt but He would advise him
to go back to his business, or at least would not encourage him to go away,
till he saw Mr. Donnom or me to inform him, how the difference was, and
where the fault lay . . . As I returned with moonlight, I called at the plantation and found the Overseer was not returned, and was Informed by a person who met him, that he talked of Mr. Donnom very indiscreetly. I rode
home and between nine & ten at night, received a line from him, that he
would leave us very early in the morning, & repeatedly desiring me, to be
sure to come over early & take charge of what was under his care. I wrote
him that he had his charge from Mr. Donnom & was to return it to him,
that I would not go over early, & would look to him, if any thing was miss-
ing from my plantation. This very Ungrateful & injurious behaviour of the
Overseers to whom I have been as a Father, to go & leave my Interest, in the
hands of the slaves whom he very well knows will make great destruction,
[217 (70)] besides four or five of them, are dangerously ill, and he knows very
well that I can do nothing as to looking after the Servants & am so often
abroad that I cannot even attend to the Sick as I otherwise would, his Un-
faithful, Unjust, Unkind, Ungrateful & injurious conduct, gave me great
concern. I dispatched a boy up to Mr. Donnom with a letter, though it was
late, this affair disturbed, & troubled me, but endeavoured to look unto the
Lord, to put my trust & dependence in his holy & blessed name.

Tuesday January 29 . . . In the morning Engaged in preparing Some Medicines for the Sick Negroes, went over in the rain, as passed the Overseers
house, Saw him getting ready to move his things and Observed Mr. Hamiltons horses, boys & cart, waiting to move him. Mr. Hamiltons behaviour in
this affair surprized & shocked me exceedingly, that He should not give such
a friend as Mr. Donnom has been to both him & his Nephew, so much as
a hearing, but should believe whatever his rash, foolish, illbehaved, and I am
afraid, worthless relation, should say to him. I just gave him the common

compliments and passed to the Negro house, where found six of the people bad, administered medicines humbly supplicating for the Divine blessing. Gave the nurse directions, then went to the barn, gave some directions to the most trusty fellow, & put the plantation under his charge, then returned to the Overseers house, asked him what had made him change his mind after he had repeatedly begged pardon, he began some invectives against Mr. Donnom. I stopped him short, & asked him how he could use me so basely and ungratefully, who last winter, so often visited his few Negroes when so very ill at his Mothers & with my own hands so often prepared & administered medicines to them, & now in return, he was going to leave mine in distress & expose my interest to the greatest injury, without giving me time to provide myself, he had little to say, I then as a friend made him an offer to stay & advised him to take another days time to think of it, before he throwed himself out of so good a place, when he was well assured he would not meet with the like of it, for his wages and priviledges are great. He answered he was sure what he did was right, & he would think no more about it. I turned about & went home. Lord, what is man, what poor Creatures are the best of us, how little to be trusted and fided in, the baseness & ungratitude of this foolish young man, to me, put me in mind of my own baseness & ingratitude to an infinitely better friend, my glorious God & Saviour. . . . I set out although still raining, in Company with Mr. F to a vendue of household furniture, some miles over on the Indian Land where I had some business & expected to see some friends, & designed to inquire after an Overseer. . . . The Overseer, his Uncle, Brother, & Brother in law, Mr. Roberts were all at the Vendue. The Overseer was inquiring for a place, I heard of Some Overseers to be got, but none that I liked. . . . Was somewhat melancholy, concerned about my sick Negroes and about my interest so much exposed, but far more concerned about the awful providences with which this Sinful land is at present visited, the dreadful rains, being not only very destructive in many respects, but so unhealthy that there is a very great & general Mortality both among black and white, was helped in prayer and intercession. . . .

Wednesday January 30 . . . [218 (68)] Went over to the plantation, found several of the Negroes still very bad, gave Medicines and applied blisters, and after Spending about two hours among them and the workers at the barn and Machine, I proceeded to go to Mr. Jordans, having heard Some time ago that a relation of his wants a place, but it was with the greatest difficulty I could proceed, though well mounted, the whole land both in the woods and the publick roads are deep under water, all small water courses are Swelled into large rivers, all bridges gone, fences carried away, great trees and logs every where brought from the woods and Scattered through the roads, the whole face of the Country is the picture of devastation for there has been the most violent winds, and highest tydes (it being this day full moon) ever known in the memory of men, every where it looks, as if some great cataract, or water spouts accompanied with a violent hurricane, had fallen from the Clouds at once, with great difficulty riding up to the Saddle Skirts in mud & water, and often obliged to stop, I got along till I came within Sight of Mr. Jordans, but could get no further, the bridges all the way through the Swamp, that leads to the knowle where the house stands, were all washed away, so that there was no getting nearer than about half a mile or more, not even by Swimming on horseback. . . . In the afternoon rode home through the woods, when came to the plantation, was told, that the Overseer had been there, and at my house, wanting very much to see me, this made me think, he was beginning to see his folly, I think I may say wickedness, and although he has behaved in such a manner, as he ought never to be received, yet the distress and necessity of the times which prevents our getting any other, will oblige us to accept of him. . . . Was informed this evening of great destruction by the waters every where, vast quantities of clean rice, lost at landing places, by being overflowed, and that the large bridge over the river, was in the utmost danger of being carried away, the Gentlemen had Sent & moved off the planks to preserve them, Mr. Clarks house like to be carried away, the water being two foot high in the hall, was fatigued & distressed both in body & mind but found prayer my best exercise.

Thursday January 31 1771 Very poorly & indisposed, found most of the Sick Negroes rather something better, was informed of great destruction at the publick landing belonging to this Neighbourhood, most of the Neighbours having ten, fifteen or twenty barrels of rice there, I indeed had none, yet was greatly concerned for the general distress & calamity. My friends Mr. James Donnom & Mr. H had five hundred bushels of Salt lately come up & thought to be well Secured in their Store houses, but is every ounce of it, washed away. I had about Seventy Bushels, in barrels considerably damaged, & so had Several others, after having visited the plantation, I rode up to Mr. Donnoms at Campbells hill, to persuade him to come down to my house, as he would be near to the landing & to the bridge to give necessary directions, as all hands were employed in giving assistance, but wanted some Judicious head to direct. I also desired [219 (66)] him to consent to take back the Overseer, if he appeared sensible of his faults & was desirous to come. Mr. Donnom was something averse to it, but at last at my Intreaty, he consented to overlook his behaviour and receive him back, if he would promise amendment and Engaged heartily in the business. I then applied myself to Mr. Hamilton, who was present, and desired him to deal faithfully with his Nephew, & to bring him to a Sense of his duty, I also told Mr. Hamilton how much I thought He himself was to blame in hearkening to his Nephews story & accommodating him with his horse & carts for his removal, before he saw Mr. Donnom or me, Mr. Hamilton took it amiss & some sharp words passed but it was Soon over and he began to hearken to reason. Dined and Spent the afternoon together. Mr. Hamilton engaged to do his part for bringing his Nephew to his Duty, & to be down at my house in the morning. Mr. Donnom rode home with me, we called & spent the Evening at his brothers, where several of Neighbours came, for refreshment, who had been working among the store houses at the landing, and among others our Overseer. We behaved very friendly to him but took no particular notice of what we had been talking with his Uncle. . . .

Friday first day of February 1771 . . . After breakfast & morning duties, Mr. Jonathan Donnom came over from his house, and we went altogether the two Mr. Donnoms & myself to the plantation. We were soon afterwards joined by the Overseer & in about half an hour more by Mr. Hamilton. The Overseer soon Signified his desire to return, & Mr. Donnom his willingness to receive him, upon such & such Conditions to which the Overseer very expressly promised and engaged, I was intirely Silent, only in one thing, I proposed that Mr. Donnom and the Overseer, should have their agreement in writting, and that if the Overseer left us, he should give us a months warning, and if either Mr. Donnom or I discharged the Overseer, we should give him a months warning or a months wages, which was very readily agreed to by all parties, we then went back to my house, where the agreement was concluded, we drank a Glass of wine together, and they all went over to Mr. Jonathan Donnoms . . . I returned home by myself, much easier in my mind, than I have been since this Seperation took place, for was not only concerned about the number of Sick negroes left by themselves in so desperate a Season, about the Crop & interest left to the will of slaves, was not only Uneasy & distressed, by being obliged to be so much among the slaves, & looking after these worldly concerns, for which I am altogether unfit, but my great concern was least any difference, should take place between Mr. Donnom, myself, and this neighbourhood, most of whom are Some way or another related to the Overseer & his family, who are of such a stamp as I should not chuse to quarrel with upon any account. . . .

[220 (64)] *Lords day February 3 1771* A dark cloudy damp morning and Sometimes a drisling rain. . . . Heard last night of the Death & burial of a worthy good Christian widow Lady one of my Charge, high up the Salt-catcher on the Indian Land Side, Mrs. Styls, a great loss to the Orphan children of her disceased Brother whom she had the charge of, she was taken with a pleurisy & died in a few days, they did not Send for me, thinking it impossible to get to me, or that I could go there, Yesterday I sent to Mr. Blakes plantations down the river, to inquire for a boat or Canoe to go over that way but there was none to be found, last evening received notice that Mrs. Clark, who had left her house, & gone off in a Canoe, to Mr. Murrys on the other Side who lives on a hill as high as where I live, was returned to her house. I sent her word to keep that Canoe, at her house for my getting over today. Accordingly after morning duties and breakfast, having committed myself to God & my family to his care, set out, One thing affected me much, was my Dear little Children had heard a great deal of talk about the waters, & the danger of going over, they had also heard me often intreated by the Gentlemen who were here through the week not to venture over. I did not imagine, they had taken much notice of it, but last night they often asked if I intended to go, & this morning, when they saw me getting ready, they were both very uneasy especially my Eldest daughter, Several times, mentioned I might be drounded & shed tears, it affected me much and put me in mind of what a distressed condition their Dear Dear ever Dear Mama would have been in this morning, her tender Conscience would not have desired me to stay, and her tender affections would have been greatly alarmed, Could not but look on them, with some Concern when I set off . . . at Mrs. Clarks I went into the Cannoe, with an acquaintance going part of the Same way, a poor white man a foot traveler paddled us down to the river, over it, & as far on the other side as we thought necessary. My Servants partly Swam the horses & brought them safe, where we got upon them. Gave the poor traveler the horse to ride my Negro fellow had come on & made him carry back the Canoe to Mrs. Clarks with orders to meet me at the Same place about Sun down. We then proceeded through the water about

two miles further, often times very deep. Was near about two hours in going
from Mrs. Clarks to Mr. Murrys, who immediately got a horse, and piloted
me, through the woods & over very small & dangerous dams to what is now
called Mitchells place [221 (62)] from which we Crossed into the church path,
& turned into the woods, & rode through Cusins place, now possessed by
his Son in law Mr. Prkns. Here was kindly invited to light, till he Sent a boy
& horse to carry over his Dams the water having broke them down, & overflowed the Causeways, which brought me into the direct road to the Meeting about a mile & a half from it. Before I could get there, though I rode
fast where the way would allow, it was twelve O Clock. This round about
way I was obliged to take, as the water Occasioned by the rain had rendered
the causeways on the publick path unpassable and the same reason had prevented people from getting out, and besides hardly any thought it possible
I could be there. Found only two women, Mrs. Williamson & Miss Betsy
DeSaussure, who at present lives with her, that end of the parish not being
liable to the tydes & the ground higher, was not so much under water. There
were about five or Six men, after waiting Some time and no more coming I
prayed larger than usual . . . for grace to improve such awful providences,
that the Lord would bind up the clouds, grant fair weather, & give opportunities to wait upon his Ordinances. After this free & fervent prayer Sung
the 91 Psalm long Metre then gave an Exhortation, read the texts I intended
to have preached on, put them in mind of the awful Judgments of God now
prevailing in our land, in the long continued deluging rains, in the violent
storms of wind, the great Sickness & Mortality which still prevails. Mentioned the names of Eight grown persons who have died belonging to the
two Congregations during the Month of January, Six of whom have left families. Mentioned three others, in the Saltcatcher parish but not belonging
to the parish. Gave suitable exhortations as to the improvement we should
endeavour to make, and concluded with the Apostolical blessing, then returned the Same way, in which I came, stopped & took a little refreshment
with Mr. Prkns. It was just dusk before I got to the place where I had ordered
my Negro fellow to meet me with the Canoe, but found him fast asleep &
when wakened so drunk that I durst not venture in the Canoe with him &
was afraid he could not paddle himself back, however ordered him to go back
without me, and thought it safer to ride or Swim on horse back than go with
him so that after dark I had to ride about three quarters of a mile often above
the middle of my thighs in water when sitting high on the horseback, however got safe through it all & led over the bridge, where the greatest danger

seemed to be, as two of the strong pieces were broke, got safe home about two hours after dark. . . . When I came to examine my fellow how he came to be in such a Condition, I found he & some others had been employed most of the day to cut fire wood for Mrs. Clark who was in great need of it, and as they worked deep in water, she had been too kind to them in giving them liquor, upon his acknowledging his fault I admonished & forgave him. . . .

Monday February 4 1771 . . . [222 (60)] Mr. James Donnom & I went over to the plantation, & spent about an hour & a half there, found the Sick negroes all much better . . . afterwards returned & spent about an hour with my Dear children, whom it greatly grieves me to have Constantly with the Negroes, and almost as black & dirty as the Negroes themselves. . . .

[224 (56)] *Monday February Eleventh 1771* . . . Late in the afternoon, rode to Mr. Wilkins where drank tea, had Some particular conversation with Mrs. Wilkins about her Brother & her Cousin Mr. Hunt still being offended with her. She thanked me for some favours I have endeavoured to do for her & her husband & repeatedly desired my kindness & friendship. I observed her frequently in tears when speaking with me, and Seemed anxious to hide them from her husband. Poor Lady, I understand she is Sensible of having met with great disappointments, she appears to be forward in her pregnancy. I repeatedly assured both her & her husband of my friendship, & when she strongly expressed her obligations to me I repeatedly assured her, she was under none to me, that I acted not from any particular regard but from the principal of doing all the good I could. I gently reproved her for having so much forsaken publick worship. She made many excuses & that with tears in her eyes, both Mr. Wilkins & her pressed me to stay all night, but for many reasons, I thought it best to refuse them though she was very urgent. . . .

Tuesday February 12 1771 . . . A very cold, rainy night pouring down as from Water Spouts . . . Went to Mrs. Miles the disconsolate Widow of Captain Joseph Miles, she was much affected at my first going in, and wept much, it affected me, after Some time, she recovered herself, I spent the afternoon here. Dined & drank tea with her, Spent the time in Serious useful and improving Conversation, Endeavouring to comfort, assist & direct her. She is one of the finest women as to natural parts and Education I have ever met with in this or any other part of the world, She is naturally of strong good

Sense, of great acquirements, adorned with every quality, that can be an ornament to her Sex and to human nature, and I think at the Same time, has a Sense of true religion, a high relish for the Doctrines of the Gospel, good knowledge of Divine [225 (54)] things, and I hope is truly religious, but at the Same time, has a very strong relish for high life, to which she has been much used, had much conversation with her, she is truly a very aimable and excellent person. . . .

Wednesday February 13 1771 . . . Visited old Mr. Pge, whom I heard was bad, and found him exceedingly so, had some discourse with him, not so much to my Satisfaction as I could have wished, though I think have good reason to hope he will get his soul for a prey, & will be Saved though as by fire, prayed with him with great freedom & earnestness, took again my leave of him, hardly expecting ever to see him again, he was so far recovered, as to be at Meeting last Sabbath, and was taken very ill that night, was reflecting in very harsh terms on himself for going to hear the word of God, was what I blamed in him. . . .

Thursday February 14 1771 This morning was surprized with the Sight of the parsonage fellow, who has been run away Since the Middle of Jully last, and who as I was lately very Creditably informed has been kept out by some of my Enemies on the other Side, He is come in just two days before they should all be carried over to the Trustees, to be hired out, the rest are in great trouble lest I should part with them. He looks very fat & hearty, is well clothed but will own nothing. I had him given a slight correction, and set him to work without putting any irons on him, leaving him intirely to his liberty, I suppose he is Sent home as a decoy for the rest but believe none of them will join him in this affair, examining him & visiting Sick negroes took up all the forepart of this day. . . .

[226 (52)] *Lords day 17* . . . [227 (50)] Had received a letter before Service began, to remember in prayer, young Mrs. Brailsford, Miss Betsy Mcpherson that was,[75] whose marriage last spring made much noise and bred much disturbance, as being in very low dangerous condition, & desired to visit her after Sermon . . . After Service set off immediately with the Messenger. Had about nine miles or more to ride, when got there found her in a very Melancholy distressed condition, indeed after her marriage she was soon with child and indulged herself exceedingly, of late months she has been very Sickly and on Tuesday last was as was then thought with labor pains, and has ever Since been in a lingering bad way, besides the Midwife she has had two Doctors, almost constantly with her, they were all much pleased at my coming especially herself, her Mother and husband. After having got some refreshment, which I stood much in need of, I was acquainted very particularly with her case, and then desired to go to prayer for and with her, I and some other Gentlemen relations being in the hall, her & the women in a room adjoining, which I accordingly did with great earnestness & fervency, pleading and wrestling for her, in a Suitableness to her condition, which I apprehended to be a very dangerous one, was most graciously assisted and directed to Suitable requests & expressions, and all present seemed revived and encouraged. Stayed here till about dark, then proceeded between two & three miles further, to my good friend Mr. Postells, his wife was with her neice, found Mr. Postell very seriously employed in reading the Scriptures, Spent the evening here, in Serious useful Conversation, was considerably fatigued, was much Concerned for this poor young Lady, and her tender affectionate husband, who poor young Gentleman is in great distress. My chief concern was upon her souls account, poor young Creature, both She & her Mother were greatly pleased and lifted up with the Match, so as both to forget themselves very much, the poor young woman appeared to have little sense of religion, though religiously Educated, and even Mrs. Mcpherson has lately seemed greatly to fall off, from her former profession which had been very grieving & afflicting to me, and now, the Condition is such, that though Death I am afraid will be the Issue yet little can be done for her precious soul, had some uneasy reflections, about the little opportunity I have of being useful to the Lambs of the flock, I mean of Catachising & instructing children. My constant employment in visiting the sick & afflicted, in discoursing with & praying for & with the dying, preaching at funerals, preaching abroad, & other duties of that nature, puts it out of my power to be employed among the young ones, as I would desire, besides when I used to Catachise the children, parents were in general so backward in bringing them out that I had no encouragement, yet the Omission of it gives me uneasiness. O to be faithful! O to be sensible of the charge & weight of souls.

Monday February 18 . . . [228 (48)] After breakfast & prayers I returned to Mr. Brailsfords, had some hopes of her having been delivered, but found myself disappointed. Discoursed with both the Doctors & the Midwife, and was confirmed in my fears of her Condition being very dangerous, though it was the opinion of them & all present, that she had still some chance for life & would very probably at least Continue Some days. I was desired to go into the room where she was & to discourse with her, advising her to patience & to observe directions, and to Submit to the management necessary for her, also to prepare her for being told, that in all probability her child was dead, to encourage & instruct her as I saw proper. I found her in very great distress, a very humbling & melancholy object, I endeavoured to comfort, to direct & instruct both with respect to her present condition, and what might be for the Issue of it, either in Death or life. She appeared very humble & teachable, but as might be expected, very desirous of life, I went to prayer with her, and was helped to plead & wrestle with the greatest earnestness, fullness, fervency and freedom, all were in tears, she herself was most exceedingly earnest, often repeating after me. I took particular pains in the prayer to intimate her great danger and repeatedly prayed for, very expressly, as very probably drawing towards Eternity. She was very thankful after prayer, I continued a considerable time with her, exhorting & Instructing her. During the time that I was in the room, her pains which during the night had left her, seemed to return, so that she was Six or Seven times seized with them very regularly, attended with some other promising Symptoms, which made it necessary for me to leave the room, and all of us, both Doctor & Midwife, began to have good hopes that all would be well. I acquainted her with my design to go home, and return to morrow, to which she, her husband and Mother very readily consented, about twelve O Clock I left this distressed family after having spent Some time with old Mrs. Mcpherson, who had come up to see her Grand daughter, in her distress, and was herself taken bad. I called on the old Captain, and found him also in a very bad condition. . . .

February 19 1771 . . . Early in the forenoon, I set off amidst a strong bitter froast & very deep, [229 (46)] found the River still increasing & flowing over the planks of the great Bridge . . . at Mrs. Clarks on this Side of the river I was informed, that poor young Mrs. Brailsford died about ten O Clock, last night, yet thought it my duty to go & visit her greatly distressed husband & Mother. Got there about one O Clock, found a very distressed family indeed. Poor Mrs. Mcpherson both grieved & afflicted me, as there was no getting her pacified, or to express herself as became a Christian, Mr. Brailsford was in deep silent reflection. I discoursed with, comforted & encouraged both to submission, and at last seemed to prevail. I was informed that for some hours, after I left them yesterday, that everything Seemed hopeful but unexpectedly her strength failed, the pains of labour seemed to work & pressed upward and it was evident that the patient was a dying, which was at last made known to her, and greatly shocked & affected her, she cried earnestly to God for mercy, lamented her family neglects, was in great agony & distress, but endeavoured to place her trust in the Redeemers Infinite righteousness & mercy. Continued very Sensible to the last moment. Parted with her Mother, who was almost distracted, and with her very tender & affectionate husband in the most moving, Melancholy & distressed manner, begging him to be kind to her Mother, & in the midst of these distressing circumstances, her breath growing shorter & shorter, she suddenly expired. Stayed here about an hour and a half. Saw the Corpse sent off, to be buried at her Fathers place where he lies and a half Sister, a daughter of her Mothers by a former husband, at both of whose funerals I discoursed Some years ago. . . .

Wednesday 20 . . . In the forenoon set forward for the late Captain John Mcphersons, who was my very good friend, Father to the young person to be now laid by his Side . . . Soon after I got there, a Messenger came for a young woman one of the [230 (44)] company, whose Father Mr. John Bty,[76] had died Suddenly, they lived the very next plantation to Mr. Brailsfords, He had been complaining a little for two or three days, but it appeared so very slight that his wife & his daughter, attended Mrs. Brailsford all the time of her Indisposition as Neighbours. I saw them both there on Sabbath & Monday nor did they mention any thing of Mr. Beatys being Sick, yesterday the daughter Miss Sally accompanied the corpse to this place, this forenoon Mr. Beaty, when they were going to bleed him, died very unexpectedly, this Message throwed into great Consternation, & the poor young woman into the greatest distress, I was obliged to spend Some time with her, and Some Christians friends rode home with her, to her very disconsolate Mother. This was indeed a very affecting incident. There was a good company gathered, I preached from Proverbs 8:4 with great fulness, freedom & flowing affections, to the most weeping auditory I ever Saw, all were melted down, Men & women into floods of tears, I was often much moved & was at times obliged to restrain myself, all were bathed in tears especially when I addressed the young & greatly afflicted husband, the old & greatly distressed Mother, putting her in mind of the two former Occasions on which I had discoursed in the Same place, and that God, who had been her Support in former troubles, would be her Support still, for he never leaves nor utterly forsakes, any that put their trust in him, and I truely believe, that she is one of real, children & people, notwithstanding her late remarkable decay & backsliding. The Lord was most graciously present with us . . . After the funeral was over, & having taken leave of these very afflicted mourners, I proceeded down the parish. . . . Rode to Mrs. Williamsons, whose youngest child has been very ill, found the child Some thing better, Spent this night very agreeably in serious useful free Conversation with Mrs. Williamson, & Miss Betsy DeSaussure, who at present lives with her, who having at Beaufort had the opportunity of reading many excellent books of what is called the Belle letters, of different hands, is greatly improved, and is indeed one of the most Sensible & conversible women I know in these parts. Good company and well chosen books, with a generous turn for improvement, is a great blessing. She at the Same time seems to retain all her regard for true experimental religion and even to grow therein, so that she is truely a most accomplished young woman. Most of her late improvements is owing to an honorable connection with a very worthy young Gentleman, with whom it is expected, She will be happily united as Soon as Some circumstances will permit, which at present cannot be accomplished.

Thursday February 21 1771 . . . I rode to Mr. W Russells having in the morning Sent for Mrs. Anderson to meet me here in order [231 (42)] to engage her to come & live with me, & take care of the children. She is some relation to the family of the Reverend Mr. Orr who was many years a liver & preacher on Port Royal,[77] the remains of his and his eminently Christian Brother are still on that Island, mostly in low circumstances but of good character, this woman was Some years ago Married to Mr. Bishop, who lived long on the Indian Land, with whom she lived very happily, after his Death, she was married to one Anderson a Taylor, who proved a very worthless fellow and above a year ago run away for debt and left her, having as is reported served other women in the Same manner, in other provinces, Since that time she has lived mostly at Mr. Russells & young Mr. Bowmans, and being of a middle aged person of a very sober, quiet behaviour, & religiously inclined, I have consulted with my friends and have come to the resolution of engaging her as a housekeeper. She is not capable of teaching my children much but my design is to put them all day with Mrs. Smiley, who has kept School and exceedingly well accomplished for teaching Girles. Accordingly I met with Mrs. Anderson and engaged her for a year, and am to send for her, next week if the roads will permit. . . .

Friday February 22 1771 . . . Was employed in meditating & preparing a discourse for Mr. Beatys funeral, received a letter last night informing me that he was to be buried this afternoon, in the Meeting house yard, & as his house was at a great distance the funeral was to be held at Mr. William Fergusons. That is the house of my most cruel Enemy & unrelenting persecutor the Unhappy Mrs. Broadbelt that was, who has often declared & vowed, with imprecations, that I should never come within her house, or if I did, she would abuse me, at first I doubted whether I should go or not, thinking it would be enough to meet the corpse at the Meeting house, but after the most mature deliberation I thought it best to go that way, if I should meet the corpse well & good, if not I would go up to the house, as I know, if I did not go, she would improve it to my disadvantage, by saying I carried my resentment so far, that I would not perform the duties of my office to the dead at her house though she was only accommodating a neighbour, & in so doing acted a Christian part, and if she should make any reflections on me for coming (as her resentment is rather frenzy & madness, than any thing else), that they would only fall on herself. The two friends with whom I spent the night also advised me to go. Accordingly after breakfast & prayers, I set forward, when came to the Meeting house, found the Negroes making the grave, but very backward, as it was a very strong froast, and at the same time the Earth so full of water, that they were obliged to keep one constantly throwing out water as they dug. I encouraged them to proceed and rode forward, about a mile beyond the Meeting house, I met Mr. Roberts, my neighbour who is lately about six miles further up to Mr. Ingles plantation, going to the funeral. I knew that the unhappy Mrs. Ferguson had some time ago used him & his wife very ill, and asked him to go back to the house, but he would not, I used many arguments with him but could not prevail, by Marriage he has Some connection with Mr. Beatys family, and had sat up with the corpse last night, but upon no account would be prevailed on to go where the funeral was kept. I proceeded alone, when got there [232 (40)] found a Considerable company, the Men Sitting as usual on chairs & benches out of doors, I went and joined myself with them, but immediately Mr. Ferguson who is my very good friend, came & insisted on my going into the house, and taking such refreshment as is common at funerals, while the

Gentlemen had it sent out to them, which I accordingly did, and very well used, Mr. Ferguson taking particular care, that I should be so, as for his wife I never Saw her, she being upstairs with Mr. Beatys daughter, and a few others, and as Mrs. Beaty herself had not come from home being greatly indisposed, I did not go where the mourners were, which I generally do, and always at the time, the Managers are nailing or skrewing down the Coffin, At the meeting house I discoursed from these words, Job 30:23 for I know, that thou wilt bring me to Death, & to the house appointed for all living, with freedom & fluency, but was shorter than usual & longer in the prayers, having observed to the people, that these repeated calamities, seemed to call more for our joining in earnest & fervent prayer to God, than being entertained with large discourses on Death & Judgement, improving time & preparing for Eternity, as these discourses of late turned very often, was well assisted in every part of duty. . . .

Lords day February 24:1771 . . . [233 (38)] We had Several Genteel strangers, some of them young people, who were traveling past, and came in after the Sermon was begun, but Soon appeared to be wonderfully Surprized & pleased & were in floods of tears, while was proclaiming the awful terrors of the Lord against all who were not the Servants of God, but the Servants of the World, the devil & their lusts, and while was exposing the many ways, by which many professors of religion deceive themselves by thinking they are Gods Servants, when they are really Servants of Sin. Have not had a more comfortable Season, nor been more Sensible of the Divine presence & assistance in publick worship for a long time. . . .

[234 (36)] *February 27 1771* . . . Set out to visit and Spend the night at Mr. Strains who have for a long time expected me, before I got to the Meeting house, I saw Mrs. Perry returning very much wet. She informed me that both horse and Chair were near about Swimming before she got to Mrs. Clarks, that she stopped there & Saw a boy on horseback Swim before he got to the large bridge, upon which, she returned, & in her way back was very grossly used by a drunk man who frequently attempted to get into the chair with her & the two children, her niece a girle of about Eleven years of age and her daughter about four years old, that upon being repulsed he cursed & abused her much besides beating her Negroe fellow whom she had taken with her besides a waiting boy. She was very much frightened. I encouraged her and saw her proceed till she was out of danger of any such abuse, I then [235 (34)] turned back to the tavern on the hill Kennans into which the insolent drunkard had gone, Saw him, learned his name, and left word with Kenan, what he had done, who he had abused, & what notice he might expect would be taken of his behaviour, then proceeded . . . Did not get to Mr. Strains till near dark. After had sat a little, Mr. James Pstl attorney for the Honourable Daniel & William Blks,[78] both in England, being at the plantation, came from the house built for him to stay at when up, & desired my Company, I accordingly went & Spent the evening with him, in Sencible & improving Conversation about publick affairs. Mr. Postell was an Early acquaintance of mine, when I first went to preach at Wilton. He was at that time held to a Lady who had the greatest esteem for my Ministry, and was himself always very friendly & respectful to me, and was this night exceedingly so. . . .

Thursday February 28 1771 . . . Spent about an hour & a half talking with my Children, greatly to my comfort & Satisfaction, was Surprized to find what great memories they have, especially Betsy, whose memory is extraordinary, & gives a most surprizing account of the New Testament History, & so Does Susy of every thing they have read, Betsy two or three days ago found the famous Doolittle on the Sacrament of the Lords supper among my books,[79] which she is most strongly taken with, and has for these two days past been asking me very Uncommon questions, about the Death & sufferings of the Lord Jesus Christ, May the Lord of his infinite Mercy Sanctify and bring them to the saving knowledge of himself. . . .

[236 (32)] *Lords day March 3* . . . [238 (28)] After Sermon, sent to Mr. R's for horses, having Sent back those I rode to meeting and went to Mr. Browns, where dined. Sat about an hour after Dinner, when it was about Sun down, then proceeded to Mrs. Mcphersons who had been at meeting, which I was glad to see, as it is too common after such an affliction as she so lately met with, to be several weeks before they come to publick worship. Got there about Dark, found her disconsolate Son in law Mr. Brailsford with her, he is exceeding kind to her, Spent this evening in serious useful and improving conversation, endeavouring to direct & comfort this disconsolate family. Was helped in prayer & conversation, after I had retired to the room where I was to sleep and had been near an hour reading, I stepped into the hall for Candle snuffers when I found poor Mrs. Mcpherson Sitting on the step of the door in a clear moon light looking on the tomb which is full in Sight where

her Dear Daughter was so lately laid and bathed in tears, upon which I
raised her up. Sat with her in the hall for more than half an hour, persuading her against such a conduct and at last prevailed with her to retire. Sat up
late myself as usual in reading and meditation. My heart was with God. . . .

[239 (26)] *Wednesday March 6* . . . Rode about five miles to Dine with Mr.
Griffith & his family he having insisted upon it yesterday. Spent the afternoon here in Company with Mr. Griffith, his wife & Miss S M.[80] Was
uneasy and concerned to have such evident proofs of a Growing and alas
Universally prevailing evil in Mr. Griffith. How amiable & desirable does the
Virtue of Sobriety appear, when viewed with & compared to the Contrary
vice . . . Spent the evening at home . . . Find it most pleasant and Comfortable to have my family joining with me, in morning & evening duties. My
house, Since the children and house keeper came home, has more the
appearance of a Christian family. May the Lord build us up and do us good.

Thursday March 7 . . . Received a letter, informing me that old Captain
Mcpherson, who had been indisposed on Sabbath & Monday, died unexpectedly on Tuesday & was this day to be buried at his own plantation &
desiring my attendance. This obliged me to alter my purpose and set about
preparing to discourse at the funeral as expected a good Company there,
Captain Mcpherson being naturally the oldest Gentleman in the parish, and
one of the first settlers, but exceedingly well respected as he deserved . . . As
the funeral was at the plantation the Service was performed in the house,
preached from Psl: 89:48. There was a good Company, which behaved most
Suitable to the Occasion, was well assisted both in prayers and the Sermon,
blessed be the Lord for all his goodness & mercy to a poor, weak, worthless
Creature. It was something remarkable that my Most cruel & inveterate
Enemy Main was there, and set the Psalm which was much taken notice of
by all present. All Captain Mcphersons children and family were on different [240 (24)] accounts present at this very unexpected event . . . Endeavoured to deal faithfully with this numerous family by calling & directing
them to improve the repeated breaches that have within these few weeks, first
Mr. Perry, whose widow was present, then Mrs. Brailsford whose husband
Mother & brother was present, and now the old Gentleman himself. There
was another family in the parish Mr. Benjamin Hskns[81] where I not long
ago baptized & buried a child, He kept a tavern and by the encouragement
had lately made a race ground or Course as it is called, on his own land, and

round his dwelling house, and had got large Subscriptions for a plate etc. to be run, for His whole life had been much spent about such affairs being a famous horse dealer. He generally professed himself a free thinker, yet had his Children baptized & took pains to have them educated, this race for which a great many horses were come, took up all his thoughts, and the Sabbaths were for Sometime most shamefully abused by using the horses to the ground, or running them over it. The great rains, which threatened to Spoil their sport, had occasioned his often expressing himself in a most blashphemous manner, he had for a long time been in a Sickly condition, and often expressed himself lately in most horrid language about his living to see the races. On Tuesday morning, the day on which the races were to begin, he expired in a very melancholy & affecting manner, notwithstanding which the races went on according to the first design, and his corpse was kept till this afternoon when one of the Neighbours was employed to read the funeral Service of the Established church over it. At the time of Interment races were run, many hundreds of pounds lost and won on every one of the three days, his wife and others who assisted Constantly employed in Serving the great crowds of people who were there with liquor, So that here was an house of feasting and mourning at the Same time. This has been one of the most shameful and scandalous affairs I have ever known or heard of, that notwithstanding the Death that was before them, and the Corpse of the principal manager, was in their Sight, yet the races should go on, yea and be carried on by some of the great men of the province, and of the parts, countenanced and encouraged by several professors of religion from all parts and severals of my hearers from the Saltcatcher as well as on the Indian Land Side where the ground lay, and many others professors of religion intended to have been there if the river, the loss of the bridge and the badness of the roads had not prevented them. This Setting up of a race Course, has given me great uneasiness & concern, as it introduces So much wickedness of every sort, into the parish and neighbourhood, on Monday last I bore my testimony against it, & chose the text preached on, that day for that very purpose, but the Circumstance of Carrying it on notwithstanding the hand of providence has appeared so evidently against them, in the general Calamity of the times, & the particular stroke of the family where it was carried on, has shocked and amazed me, has grieved & terrified many, and is such a daring piece of wickedness as cannot be sufficiently mourned for. Oh poor Indian Land how art thou fallen, thy assemblies and meetings used to be of another kind. After the Service of this day was over, I set out for Mr. Postells being some miles further, found him very bad, indeed he has long been sickly and ailing, has had something of a bad Cold & pleuratick symptoms which are removed, but has a constant fever, vomiting & purging . . . Spent the night here, endeavoured at times to talk with him, about Death, Judgment and Eternity, but he did not seem fond of conversation, though his wife pressed him much, and I repeatedly attempted it. He seemed little Sensible of his danger, or of his Condition in any respect. Was distressed for him and yet afraid of increasing his aversion. In family prayer endeavoured to make him Sensible of his very dangerous Condition by the requests I put up for him, but he dosed much and could take little notice. His wife was greatly afflicted on his souls account and often urged me to talk more & more to him when I had little heart to do it, O the folly, the extreme folly and madness of trusting to a Deathbed repentance, too rare a thing is it, for mercy either to be sought or found at a dying hour, this was a touching providence to me in many respects. . . .

[242 (20)] *Monday March 11 1771* . . . As had received a letter yesterday, acquainting me, that Mr. Postell continued still very ill, desiring the prayers of the Congregation, & that I would visit him this morning, I accordingly Set out after breakfast, and having with difficulty got over the waters, I proceeded to his Mother in laws old Mrs. Mcphersons. Found her very poorly and to all appearance, as if she would not be long after her husband. Staid & Dined with her and her lately widowed daughter Mrs. Perry. The hand of providence has lately been very heavy on this family, the two old people have had a great deal of Sickness, in the fall Mr. Perry a son in law, died, then Mrs. Brailsford their Grand daughter, then the old Gentleman, whom all in five weeks time, now Mr. Postell another Son in law thought to be dying, and the good old Gentlewoman herself labouring under the infirmities of old age and Sickness. Our conversation was suitable to the distress of the times. After Dinner I proceeded up Mr. Postells and found him very ill indeed, apparently so bad as if he would not live out the night. Both the Doctors intirely despair of his life, though while there is life, there is hope and all things are possible with God. What was very distressing to his friends, particularly his wife, was his being so much out of his Senses, that we seldom got any conversation. I took every opportunity to discourse with him, or to put in Something Suitable to his case, & after being about two hours with him, I went to prayer by him, but in a few minutes he was raving and insensible and was no way able to join with me, was very earnest and fervent in his behalf. All present were in tears. I spent the night here, taking every Occasion upon the least interval of reason to talk with him, but to very little purpose. . . .

Tuesday March 12 . . . After breakfast I left this afflicted family, and rode homewards . . . Rode to Mr. ThreadCrafts . . . his wife very bad in bed and Mrs. Wilkins, the late Mrs. B, just able to sit up, after a dangerous illness. On Saturday week Mrs. Wilkins and her husband ventured in their Chair the length of Mrs. Clarks and from there, crossed the river in a Canoe, to within half a mile or so of this place their brother in laws, and all this fatigue and danger was undertaken to be present at the races, where Hskn died, on Sabbath night, Mrs. Wilkins was taken out of order and it seems has miscarried and been dangerously ill, so that several times last week she was thought to be dying. I had but lately heard of it, poor Creature, she looks dismally, her accommodations very inconvenient. She was much affected when I came in and so were they all, for they have been in great affliction though I had not heard of it. Old Mrs. W is at present with them and old Mrs. Cuthbert [243 (18)] was just come to see them. After sitting about an hour I proposed to go to prayer and to offer up thanks, that no breech had been made among them, in which they most heartily joined. Was by Gods most gracious presence enlarged in prayer & praise, with them and Mrs. Threadcraft. Was greatly affected. Mr. Wilkins was also much affected, afterwards staid about an hour longer & took dinner with them, then went home. . . .

Wednesday March 13:1771 . . . This morning Mr. James Donnom acquainted me of some very base behaviour in some of my Saltcatcher neighbours, who having been offended at my plainness and freedom in finding fault with their Idleness and excessive fondness of vain Diversions, as the men spending so much of their time in hunting, fishing and in idling away their time at one anothers houses to the great prejudice of their family duties & concerns, the women perpetually visiting abroad, both men & women excessively fond of Card playing in their own houses, dancing and other such vanities to call them no worse, because at times I had made remarks on these parts of their general Conduct, that they were much offended & set against me, watching my every word, censuring and backbiting me, and whispering about themselves things to my disadvantage, as that I was proud, selfish, mercenary, fond of the rich & neglected the poor, partial in my respects to my people, censorious and the like, particularly that they envied my intimacy

with him & his brothers family and had endeavoured, by misrepresentations
& even gross falsehoods which they did not expressly affirm but insinuated,
to make a difference between his brothers family and me, and had lately been
very busy both with Mr. & Mrs. Donnom to promote a misunderstanding,
endeavouring to persuade them that I was not so much their friend as I
pretended, and that I had found great fault with their charges about my children, and other such things. This did not at all so much Surprize nor trouble me, as might have been expected, for I had above a twelve month ago
observed how very much I was deceived & disappointed in these people, and
have taken notice of their coolness & keeping at a distance from me and
have been very Sensible of their jealousy and envy because of my Intimacy
and friendship with the two Mr. Donnoms, but could hardly thought, they
would have proceeded to such wicked lengths, Considering the profession of
religion they make and the Consciousness they must have of their endeavouring to set me against the family where my children was boarded, & the
many ways they separately tried to have my children boarded with some or
other of themselves, and the offers that some of them made me to take them
at a much cheaper rate. I thanked Mr. Donnom for his kindness, in putting me on my guard and watch, and told him my own observations which
Corresponded exactly with his own and his brothers, and also with Mrs.
Donnoms. After some time his Brother came over, when we agreed not to
challenge any of the false, base insinuations they have been making to Mr.
Jonathan Donnom and his wife against me, nor what they had insinuated to
me, against them, but that we should all of us be on our guard against them,
that we should adhere more closely together in more Aimity and friendship
than ever as a proper [244 (16)] balance against them, otherways the neighbourhood would soon fall to pieces, & the most unhappy consequences
would probably follow. Afterwards Mrs. Donnom came over here, the baseness, the weak & mean behaviour of these families, her old neighbours &
most of them related to her, has often given her great uneasiness, and especially their Conduct to me. A good deal of this is Occasioned by the Overseer, the persons here alluded to are J R the first & chief of them married to
the Overseers Sister, T H his Uncle, T L his Brother[82] all religious professors
with their families and I hope good people, but the most self righteous, self
conceited, proud, weak, obstinate, mean, low lifed suspicious set of people I
ever knew, very idle, & much given to the diversions above mentioned yet
all communicants regular attenders on publick worship and worshippers of
God in their families though some of them obliged to use forms, to these

may be added the Overseer whose vanity & self righteousness is most ridiculous, D F may also be reckoned among them, but he never made any profession of religion at all, and never professed to have any regard for men of my cloth, and but little for me, and is I believe a Sincere honest hearted man but obstinate, & opinionated in many matters. In the forenoon parted with both the Mr. Donnoms, after they were gone this discovery, or rather confirmation of what I had Suspected, gave me many thoughts of heart, helped to humble & lay me low in the dust, lest should have given any cause of offense, though am not conscious of any, Made me see the great need of constant watchfulness, of being reserved, and on my guard before whom I speak, and not to be so ready to [take] every one for my friend who professes to be so. . . .

Thursday March 14 . . . The forenoon pleasantly employed in study & writting for Sabbath in hopes of preaching twice, about Eleven O Clock my neighbour & Clerk John Roberts called upon me & afterwards my neighbour Thomas Lambright both to do some business & ask some favours of me, which I very readily granted. They behaved with all the fawning complacence they have always treated me with, but I was on my guard, they stayed dinner with me, I used them with all the Sincere hearty friendship I ever used to do, but was not so open & free as usual. . . .

[245 (14)] *Friday March 15:1771* . . . Was engaged in Study & writting for Sabbath, and also in making some preparation to Discourse this afternoon at the funeral of old Mrs. Murrys Son Charles, a young man of about twenty Seven years of age, who had the misfortune to have little use of reason but always behaved very quietly, had learned to feed himself, to dress and undress himself and to do many things about the family. He was taken on Wednesday with a pain in his Stomach attended with a violent vomiting & purging and Died on Thursday morning. Late in the forenoon I rode to Mrs. Perrys to inquire of any accounts of Mr. Postell. Heard he continued still bad, then rode to Mr. Jordan, designing to have dined here but they were set off for Charlestown, which was a day Sooner than I expected. Afterwards rode to & visited old Mr. Pge, who is getting better, then proceeded to Mrs. Murrys where found very few people and the Coffin not being come, the Corpse was very offensive which obliged me to leave the house, and walk about the field for about an hour and a half. Afterwards, when the coffin & some company came, I discoursed in the house, as usual, read for a text Psl: 89:48 but

insisted mostly [on] the Sovereignty of God in dispensing gifts to his Creatures, and that where much was given much would be required. Mrs. Murry
I thought behaved exceeding well and seemed very Sensible of the goodness
of God in this dispensation, as the thoughts of leaving this poor young man
among strangers was often very distressing to her. . . .

Lords day March 17 . . . [246 (12)] Towards the close of the Sermon, I spoke
of the remarkable hand of God in discouraging the horse races in this place.
Took particular notice of the awful circumstances thereof and of the Shameful Conduct of being witness to & assisting in Carrying on these publick
diversions notwithstanding the Death of the principal person concerned,
and hope was helped honestly & faithfully to bear my Testimony against it
and against the Introduction of such Diversions into this parish. . . .

247 [10] *Wednesday March 20 1771* This morning poorly and very much
indisposed with a cold, something of a Soreness, and Swelling in my throat,
which gave me some uneasiness as I am So very subject to most distressing
disorder & inflammations in my throat and as for many months a most fatal
disorder, Called the throat distemper, has prevailed in Charlestown and in
some parts of the Country very Mortal & has lately made its appearance in
both these parishes.[83] The most able physicians both in this and the Neighbouring Colonies look upon it to be an intirely new disorder not known in
Europe or at least never so violent & fatal there as in America. They look
upon it also to be something of a plague or pestilence and as a Scourge raised
up by Divine providence to prevent the growth & increase of the American
British provinces . . . Received a line acquainting me that old Mrs. Murry
was taken last Friday night after the funeral was over and I had returned
home, with a violent Cold & Sore throat and was not thought to be in any
great danger though a physician was sent for on Monday, and that last night
she died Suddenly & unexpectedly of the throat distemper. This affected me
considerably and appeared very awful, as she seemed in perfect health when
I buried her Son on Friday afternoon. Lord prepare & make me ready. O
God deal mercifully with these congregations. . . .

[248 (8)] *Thursday March 21 1771* . . . After breakfast & morning duties, went
over with the children to Mr. Donnoms & saw him & his wife & family set
for the Southward where they are to live. Poor Mrs. Donnom was in tears.
He was very melancholy and so were we all . . . About the middle of the day

there was a very heavy rain for about two hours which prevented my getting
to the funeral so early as intended, knowing that the young Lady Miss Sally
Murry the only one now left of the whole family would want to have some
conversation with me, I found her a good deal concerned, yet not so much
so as I expected, she earnestly begged my direction and advice to assist her,
which I assured her of, she had at first thought of chusing a Gentleman this
way for her Guardian, her Mother having died without a will and she is now
left heiress of a good Estate without a relation in the world that she knows
of. I intended to have gone as soon as I heard of her Mothers death, but
upon Second thoughts I deferred it considering my Single state and the
world are so ready to talk, and she is not a person I would have any thoughts
of. After I went there I was informed that she had changed her first design,
through the persuasion of a person present who wanted to carry her home,
against which I advised her, which she agreed to, and told me, that she had
sent for her Intimate acquaintance and mine Mrs. Shaw, and that if she came
she would in a day or two go home with her, but if Mrs. Shaw did not come,
she would be directed by me till I could get her Sent there, which I approved
of. Sometime afterwards Mrs. Shaw came, and also a relation young Mr.
Mclchln, who has for some time been paying his respects to Miss Sally
Murry and I believe is to have her, I acquainted Mrs. Shaw with what had
passed, and that I gave up the Directing of Miss Murry intirely to her, but
advised that for Decencys sake, the young Gentleman should not stay after
the funeral but go on with the company, which was agreed to. At the funeral
I began with prayer & made a short discourse from Job 14:1 then prayed
again, and then for several reasons I concluded with reading the Service of
the church of England, in the way to, and at the grave, after the Service was
over & the company going off, I stayed with Mrs. Shaw & Miss Murry
at their desire till two hours after Dark, was sorry to Observe Miss Murrys
unconcern, and indeed, the time was but trifled away by us all . . . Miss
Murry asked me, whom I would advise her to chuse as Guardians and Managers of her interest. I mentioned Mr. John Mctier brother to Mrs. Shaw &
Mr. James Donnom whom her Mother had intended for her Guardian, she
approved much of them both & said if she chose any, it would be these
Gentlemen, but upon conversing with her found she was rather inclined to
Marry, which I advised her to by all means, and we had some free conversation about the young Gentleman above. Learned many useful lessons from
this evenings Conversation, particularly the great need of settling my affairs
so as to have my children in proper hands in case of my disease and of [249

(6)] their being properly educated while I am with them, & afterwards if necessary. Saw much of the necessity & advantage of formal Education in the best manner, as infinitely beyond leaving them an Estate without it, and of their being so treated as to reverence, to love and Esteem their parents, with many other useful Observations. . . .

[250 (4)] *Tuesday March 26* . . . In the evening, I received letters by an express, from Ponpon Congregation, letting me know, that at a meeting last week, they had Subscribed a very Unanimous call for me, to be their Minister, in conjuncture with my charge at Saltcatcher, pressing me to give up the Indian Land, as they may either join with Beaufort & Port Royal to get a Minister, or can if they please, enjoy my ministry at Saltcatcher, and using various arguments to give up half my time, to them, who have long been in most destitute circumstances, and the Congregation like to be intirely lost and broke up, and the great prospect of the most extensive usefulness, etc. I had received notice of this design several weeks ago in different letters, but for some time took [no] notice of it, and when at last much pressed to give some answer, I let my friends there know that I was determined to be intirely passive, and follow the call of providence, this matter has been much upon my Spirit, and the thoughts of giving up my Dear Indian Land has been very distressing to me, and made me often very melancholy, but if the Lord calls me to it, I must submit. Lord I am thine, wholly thine, Send me where thou pleases. . . . At last I wrote to them much the same I had wrote to my friends, that as it was a most weighty, & important matter, as I was afraid the charge would be too great for me, as I had very strong attachments to Indian land, and as the matter must rest ultimately with the Presbytery, that I was determined to be wholly passive, and to follow what should appear to be the voice of God, that if their call continued to be unanimous, was approved of by the Presbytery, and it appeared that I might be more extensively useful than at present, that I would cheerfully accept of it, and cast myself upon God for his Support & assistance, but if it appeared otherwise, I would refuse it, and hoped none would be offended. . . .

Wednesday March 27 . . . Went over to the plantation, visited a Wench (Aimy) belonging to Indian Land Congregation who has been these several years in a very Sickly declining way and is now thought to be a dying, had a good deal of talk with her, much more [251 (2)] to my Satisfaction than I expected, she being a poor African, who could neither learn to speak nor understand English, was always a very stupid & vicious Creature, yet she seemed to have Surprizing knowledge of Eternity, of heaven, & hell, of God & Jesus Christ, and often called upon God & Christ. I prayed by her, which she was much pleased with. . . .

Thursday March 28:1771 . . . Proceeded to Mr. Donnoms where Dined, Mr. Donnom took me apart and shewed me some letters from Ponpon, Mr. Hyns[84] letter I did not much like, and am apprehensive matters there are not so well as good Mr. Lambert imagines, yet I was Surprized at Mr. Donnoms behaviour about this affair, which in three letters from Charlestown, he encouraged me to think of as what might come to pass. The Congregation has demanded from him an account of the funds or of the Negroes for Supporting the Gospel there, which for some years have been in his hand, very hard things have been said & thought of him, I believe very unjustly, & Mr. H his quondam ward seeks an opportunity against him. Advised Mr. Donnom to give them the meeting they desire, and at once to remove their aspersions & calumnies, their fears and apprehensions, by laying open his whole management before them at the time requested, which he said, he would do, but complained of his Enemies. I showed him a copy of the answer I wrote, which he said he approved of. Some things appeared Mysterious, but I was Silent, and could not help being affected, & troubled. . . .

[255 (244)] *Tuesday April 9* . . . In the afternoon walked out & sat about an hour with Mrs. Smiley, had some talk with her, about my children going to school to [her] next Monday, which is to keep them to their reading, to teach sewing & other things necessary for their age & Sex, had also some talk with her about keeping school for other children, she told me, that some families whom she expected to Send their children refused to do it, as thinking her charge for boarding much too high, had some general talk with her about these things, and could not help thinking that by her charging so very high, that she did herself and family a real prejudice. . . . After [256 (250)] returned home, had many thoughts about this good woman, so well qualified for teaching, so capable to be useful to herself and others, and whose family so much needs her help & assistance, for their Support & [upkeep]. Thought it a great pity, she should prejudice herself by charging so very high, & concluded to write her on that account & let her know what had been the practise of Others in her circumstances, & wrote the first draught of a letter for that purpose, being very desirous to give no offense, & that it might be blessed to do good, in the way intended. . . .

Saturday April 13 . . . Got to Beaufort about twelve O Clock . . . Spent the night till very late as usual in preparative duties. . . .

[257 (252)] *Lords day April 14:1771* . . . As the church Minister is gone to Charlestown, had a large auditory both parts, their small meeting house could not hold the half of them, and though it blowed very hard, yet a great many sat without doors . . . After Service went to Mr. DeSaussures. Spent the evening in Serious religious conversation, laid before them the call & letters from Ponpon and the reasons of their offering it, had much said to me not to accept of it, told them I should not determine for myself, and that they & other friends in this place, might take what steps, they pleased to prevent the presbyterys offering it to me, for if the ministers give it as their opinion I might be more useful by giving one half of my time to Ponpon, I would certainly accept of it, whatever blame I might meet with from my Indian Land and Port Royal hearers. . . .

Monday April 15 . . . Spent the night at Dr. Cuthberts. . . . Sat up with the good Doctor, and his very pious Lady till near two O Clock in the morning, the first part of our conversation, was about the [258 (254)] call from Ponpon which this good family and all the religious people are very much against my accepting, the Doctor acquainted me, that there would be a letter Sent from Port Royal & another from the Indian Land Signed by numbers to the Presbytery requesting my being continued. Afterwards our conversation mostly about the trouble & concern of the Doctor & his truely pious Lady, about her two Oldest Daughters, Mrs. Green & Miss Nancy W, who though both remarkably reserved, serious, & submissive to their parents, yet do not show that value for religion, that their parents so earnestly desire, and seem to have some attachments, the very thoughts of which is worse than Death to their excellent Mother. . . .

Wednesday April 17 . . . [259 (256)] In the afternoon set homewards . . . As rode through the plantation was informed that the parsonage Aimy was dead, a wench that had for several years been a burden upon us, & whose Death is a real deliverance to us & I hope to herself, about an hour after Dark I got home & found my Dear children & other family well, blessed be the Lord therefore. . . .

Saturday April 20 . . . In the forenoon set off [for Ponpon] . . . Got to my friend Mr. Lamberts just before dark, he had been under some uneasiness lest I should have been prevented, learned that there is a good deal of Sickness in these parts, that people are very desirous of my coming among them, & that near Seventy persons have Subscribed the call, which is a most Surprizing number, and Seems Something of an extraordinary providence. He also acquainted me, that he has sold off his plantation & slaves, except two families, one of which he wanted me to purchase, as some of them are baptized, and the other family he intended to keep, with a design if I accepted of the Ponpon call to live at their parsonage, & keep a furnished room for me. His design in selling off, is that He may have a more retired life upon the Interest of his money, this is what he might very well expect [260 (259)] having now a large Sum at Interest, but it is not imagined that he will do so, being of an anxious temper, for this is not the first time he has sold off with the same view, and [returned] into business again. . . .

Monday 22 . . . Spent the forenoon in agreeable Conversation, with these old faithful and steady friends,[85] & their Son in law Mr. Abraham Hayne, who came with his wife & prevented my going to their house where I intended to spend an hour or two. Afterwards rode to Mr. J B's whose Lady is lying in. Here I met with the Reverend Mr. Maltby, who came there on purpose to have some conversation. Poor Gentleman he has been very Sickly and looks as if he would not be long in this world, his children are all sent off to their Mothers relations in Bermudas excepting one, who stays with an Uncle by the Mothers side in Charlestown. Dined here & stayed till about three O Clock & proceeded over the river. Stopped in Jacksonburgh and Drank Coffee at Doctor Spences who is lately married,[86] visited a Sick family and proceeded four miles further to the church parsonage, and Spent about an hour with the Reverend Mr. Ellington in religious conversation. He is a most excellent person. Just at Dark went to Mr. Isaac Haynes where spent the night. He was abroad and did not come home till near Supper time. Had useful & improving conversation with him, poor young Gentleman he as yet is very far from treading in his pious and excellent Fathers steps of whose eminent piety I have often heard. He is the first subscriber upon the call, but am afraid does not act with a Single view to the glory of God, seems not at all to be in earnest, but to have some else in design very different from obtaining the Gospel. Was melancholy & concerned to see so little of any thing like true religion or seriousness in the descendants of such eminently worthy parents, his Lady being a daughter of the Excellent & reverend Mr. Huttson my worthy predecessor at the Indian Land,[87] It gave me many distressing thoughts about my own dear children, and engaged me in humble supplications for them, that God might early Season their hearts by Divine grace. Was much grieved to hear of the wickedness, that prevails in this Neighbourhood of the little Town Jacksonburgh, which is a place of good trade being by all accounts the most profane place & most notorious for wickedness in the whole province. Great is the need for faithful ministers in this place, & very little is the prospect of usefulness, wickedness of all sorts, is at the greatest height, I almost ever heard of, every species of Debauchery is gloried in and boasted of, and that in a place where religion once prevailed much & by the posterity of many eminently godly ancestors, these things greatly discourage, grieve & distress me & make me tremble at the thoughts of coming among them as their minister.

[inside back cover]

Christ is all and in all.

[inserted page (126)][88]

My Dear Cheverill was at school on Thursday October 21 taken bad Friday 22 Died on Lords day October 24 about half an hour after four in the afternoon.

Epitaph on Sacheverill Simpson

adorned with knowledge grace and manly sense
meekness, humility love and Innocence
modest, Obedient to his parents will
given to prayer, affraid of doing ill
Swift was his race with many favours blest
Soft was his passage to the land of rest
His work concluded e'er the day was done
Sudden the Saviour stooped and caught him to his throne

a lover of Jesus, to Jesus he's resigned
to Jesus gone, his holy heaven born mind
His work was ended, his day was scarce begun,
when Jesus stooped and caught him to his throne.

Friday 22 he desired his Mama, & then me if he died of the Sickness to bury him beside his little brother Archie, Saturday I asked him if he loved God & Jesus Christ, & trusted that God would save him for Christs sake, Friday told him depend on God to make him well, Lords day morning I got that answer in prayer I have heard three in a time accepted etc., he was observed to spend extraordinary time in prayer while I was down, and it was found he was earnestly praying for my health & return. I strove with all my might, I never was so before. Last time at Meeting, he came home Singing these lines in the 17 Psalm. About 3 weeks before he died, was at the Meeting house yard with me, and Said he would die & be buried there, Said all the catachise on Tuesday on Wednesday read his chapter most distinctly.

VOLUME 8

April 23, 1771–January 9, 1772

[inside front cover]

Christ is all and in all

[1] pater omnipotens   alma Deus[1]

Christ is all and in all

Archibald Simpson his book

April 26 1771[2]

[2] This is a continuation of my Diary from Monday April twenty Second one thousand Seven hundred and Seventy one. Volume Eight—

Tuesday April 23 1771 Last night about ten O Clock it began to rain and continued the whole night and all this day, without any Intermission, which prevented a meeting of this Congregation,[3] which was to have been at the meeting house, about appointing Some to present the call to the Presbytery, fixing upon the Salary to be given me, if I should determine in their favour, and the way of raising and paying that Salary and some other matters, the Disappointment, gave me no manner of concern, rather a Satisfaction, for have not given them the least encouragement, to expect that I will accept of their call, and indeed if it would please God I would much rather continue in my present Station, and tarry at my Beloved Indian Land. Things here look dark and gloomy, and a pastoral charge in this place is very undesirable, the fatigue is terrible to flesh and blood, and great difficulties must be Surmounted to be faithful, all my feelings as a man are against it, yet there seem some strong reasons for it. I am not to determine for myself but am wholly at the Divine disposal, and whatever God by the mouth of his servants in Presbytery shall determine, that I am resolved to do, not that I would so far submit to the ministers and others in Presbytery as to act contrary to what I was convinced to be my duty, but in so doubtful a case as this, where I cannot determine for myself, their opinion and advice layed into the Scale with other reasons will help to determine me, and to clear my way . . . Was in a humble Spiritual frame of soul. About ten O Clock rode through the rain to Mr. Lamberts. About Eleven we Sent a boy to the meeting house, lest any of the Gentlemen should have ventured out. The boy stayed till after one O Clock, but none came, and none could be expected as it continued to pour down without intermission, tho Sometimes it abated a little. Dined and spent part of the afternoon here, had Some conversation, about purchasing the Six negroes he wanted me to have, but we could not agree, as his price was most extravagant. Late [3] in the afternoon I rode up to Mrs. Clifford at the horseshoe, where was very kindly received, tho I expected Some coolness, on account of my not taking a more formal leave of Mrs. P C or not waiting on her again according to promise, although for five or Six weeks it was absolutely out of my power, without violating my conscience and neglecting the important duties of my Sacred office. Mrs. P has been very Sick which I had not heard of, and is still confined. Had much conversation with Mrs. Clifford and her Son in law Mr. Wayne, about my coming to preach the half of my time, which they are all very desirous of, and have all Signed the call. In the evening was desired to walk into Mrs. P's room, found her very poorly and just able to sit up. Was received as by all the rest. Was better than two hours in her company, but as we were never alone, I took no particular notice of what had past. Had intended to have made an apology and offered to renew my Suite, but as either Mrs. Clifford or Mr. and Mrs. Wayne were constantly with us, and it seemed to me to be done on purpose, I made no apology, and behaved just as if such a thing had never happened, & believe shall never take any more notice of it. . . .

Wednesday April 24 Last night, it continued to pour down in the most violent manner, till after nine O Clock this morning, so that there has been the greatest fall of rain this way than can well be thought of in so much time, which of general must have done great damage to the planters, and affords a most melancholy prospect to all whose lands are any thing deep, was in a humble, spiritual thoughtful frame of soul, concerned to see Gods Judgements so evidently abroad on the Earth, and few laying to heart and improving them. . . . [4] Set off in the rain, which continued till after twelve O Clock. I found it very difficult traveling, as every where was Overflowed deep in water, and all the bridges Overflowed, and, for Six or Seven Miles saw great numbers of Negroes employed in cutting drains, or repairing dams, and great appearances of much destruction. At the fish ponds accidentally met a negroe coming over, & hired him to go back & pilot me, was obliged to swim in some places & got very wet, but met with no other misfortune than wetting Some papers in my Jacket pockets, though strove to save them. . . .

Thursday April 25:1771 . . . As was Informed that Mr. Donnom was returned from visiting his brother at the Southward, and having some important concerns to consult about with him, I rode up to his house in the forenoon and spent most part of the day there. He seems to think, that providence designs me for to go to Ponpon, and mentioned weighty reasons for his thinking it will be my duty to accept of the call if it is not stopped at Presbytery, who in general bear no good will to me. [5] There seems a cloud over Salcatcher Settlement, the great rains threatens to prevent their planting who live up the river and have deep lands, and the greatest part are in such circumstances that another short crop will greatly distress them. The loss of the bridge, the long continued freshets in the river, has given occasion to a very avaritious person to impose on people a very high charge for ferrying them over the narrow channel, for though the river has for several months been over its banks for near two miles, yet the boat goes no farther than the length which the bridge reached, this expense and danger in coming through the waters, has almost intirely prevented any coming from the Indian Land Side on Sabbath, and if the Bridge is not got up soon none will come from that side to take pews for another year, which will greatly hurt the Gentlemen, who have gone to the expense of pewing, and enlarging the Meetinghouse. The interest of religion is like to sink intirely at Ponpon & it is thought my going there might be a mean with the Divine blessing to revive it, & that their friends might support me in preaching the Gospel though I get but little from Salcatcher, but on the other hand there are weighty reasons for my staying at Indian Land which I have not time to mention in this place. May the Lord dispose of me as shall be most for his glory & the advancement of religion. . . .

Friday April 26 . . . In the afternoon was obliged to go over to Mr. Smileys, found my Dear little Betsy with a fever. Drank tea here, had a good deal of conversation with Mrs. Smiley about her keeping school, was concerned to find myself considerably disappointed in my expectations as to the improvement that my Children might make, but I have no choice and must do the best I can, since it is not in my power to do as I would, must also submit to every charge however high and unreasonable, there is nothing in this world but disappointment. [6] I am always disappointed in dealing with Creatures and no doubt so are others in dealing with me, may this make me always circumspect and careful to answer every reasonable expectation. . . .

Lords day April 28 1771 . . . When got to the river found it very high, almost as much so as ever, by the great rains in the beginning of the week, got safely through the waters without being so wet as usual. Found an uncommonly large Congregation and was informed that a report had been spread, nobody knew by whom, that I had absolutely accepted of the call from Ponpon and determined to leave this place, which together with my two weeks absence, gave very great uneasiness and concern. Some were very angry, others greatly discouraged, but all much pleased when I assured them it was an absolute falsehood, and all expressed great desire I should continue among them, & though all wished I had determined for myself and had determined in their favour, yet none could much blame me, when I told them I had left it to the Presbytery, and that they might represent their own cause to the Presbytery as they pleased . . . [7] Rode over to Doctor Cuthbert who was over from Beaufort, stayed near about an hour with him consulting about the congregation affairs, read the draught of a letter he has drawn up to be presented to the Presbytery in the name of the Dissenters on Indian Land and Port Royal Island, petitioning I may be continued. Was satisfied with the general tenor thereof, but could have wished some things had left out. . . .

Monday April 29 . . . The weather very sultry and threatening for more rain, a very Judgement like Season indeed, but alas how few observe the hand of God. In general religion is on the decay, the love of many waxes cold, iniquity abounds every where, profanity and vice of every kind boldly sets up its hydra head, prevails and triumphs through this whole land . . . [8] Proceeded to meeting where a considerable number were met, and others sent their friends to Subscribe for them. About twelve O Clock we went in, and began with prayer, in which enlarged considerably and plead earnestly for the Divine blessing, presence, and direction. Afterwards Sung some verses of the 132 psalm, Watts version long Metre, then acquainted them of the business to be done, put them in mind how Trustees had always been Elected, and that we proceed now exactly in the Same Method. Told them Doctor Cuthbert, one of the now oldest members and the only survivor of the Trustees Elected and ingrossed on the Trust deed, drawn up some years ago at the Subscribing for the present funds, & the last settlement of this church, had drawn up an Instrument of writting expressing their empowering such Gentlemen as should be unanimously chosen, to act as Trustees for this Congregation, and had also drawn up a letter and petition to the Presbytery for my being continued, both of which if approved of was to be signed by them. After being read and considered I then offered to withdraw that they might deliberate and speak their minds with greater freedom, but they all desired me to stay. I was then desired to read the above writtings, both of which were very cordially approved of, though for my own part Some things in the Instrument appointing the Trustees I did not like as it seemed to connect us too much with the Presbytery, but as it referred to a large Trust deed, to be drawn up afterwards, I said nothing, because can have it then properly altered.[4] The Gentlemen, named to the Congregation, and very Unanimously chosen for Trustees are Doctor James Cuthbert, James Donnom Esquire, Mr. William Russel, Mr. George Threadcraft, Mr. Thomas Bowman Junior. The letter to the Presbytery was also signed with great cheerfulness by a great number of persons of the church as well as the Dissenters. It appeared that it will be signed if time is allowed for it, by [9] the Inhabitants except Bull of Sheldon, Main and the unhappy Mrs. Fergusons family who got her husband kept at home both yesterday and today, being indisposed, as he frequently is, being very sickly. The business was transacted with great harmony & cheerfulness, many applications were made to me to determine for myself & refuse the Ponpon call, but I adhered to my first resolution. I never on no former Occasion saw a better Spirit prevail in this place than to day. Blessed be the Lord God, that there is still such an appearance of love to & regard for the Gospel. . . .

[10] *Wednesday first day of May one thousand Seven hundred Seventy one years* This morning felt it Sweet and comfortable to spend the night in my own bed . . . Continued raining all last night, & all this day till about the middle of the afternoon, so that there is again a great deal of water upon the Earth & planting put to a stop every where, great quantities of Seed rotting

in the ground, and many have not the least prospect of planting any rice at all, So that the Lords hand lies very heavy on the province, His judgements are evidently abroad on our part of the Earth, and yet few very few laying it to heart. . . . [11] About the middle of the afternoon my good friend Mr. Donnom called on his way from Ponpon, where he went on Monday last about Some business . . . He informed me of our friend Mr. Lamberts great Uneasyness, about settling with the persons to whom he has sold his plantation and negroes, which is just what I expected. He also informed me, of Some slanders of the Enemies of the Gospel and of religion about Ponpon against me, as if I had refused to pay to Doctor Reeds Widow, a demand which she has made against me from the Doctors books, which many years ago I had repeatedly offered him payment of, and which He refused as making a complement of his Services to me and my family while I lived in those parts, which is a matter publickly & well known, yet I have not refused to pay it, but only desired Mrs. Reed, a Lady of great fortune, but also of great avarice, to let me know if she ever heard the Doctor say, He intended to charge me, and if she did not know that He received the thanks of all my friends and a great addition to his practise by his kindness to me. I have also informed her that though the law cannot Oblige me to pay it, yet I was resolved to do so, and would have paid it before now, had she repeated her demand, or informed me either by word or writting that she believed it a just debt, poor Lady, she is to be pitied, it was surely bad enough to demand an unjust payment, to expose her husbands memory, but it is still much worse to endeavour to hurt my character, my usefulness, and the interest of the glorious Mediator who I serve with all my might, but blessed forever blessed be God, it is out of her power, may the Lord forgive her and all her abettors. May the Lord restrain their wickedness, Sin and folley. Was glad to find that some friends stood up for me & for the truth and shall as soon as leisure will permit, pay her what she demands and has no manner of right to nor no way to obtain, but from my tender concern for religion, which might suffer by misrepresentations. I esteem nothing too Dear to part with, other than be the innocent cause of that Holy name by which I am called as a Christian and a Minister should be evil Spoken of on my account, where I can do any thing to prevent it. Lord I am thine, I commit my cause unto thee. . . .

[12] *Friday May 3* This day began preparatory dutys for Sabbath, and was comfortably assisted in them till interrupted by various necessary Concerns and by Company, young John Cuthbert[5] Some months ago returned from

Jamaica, a very great Bearing, sober and well behaved, to what the generality of young people are, has a good deal of the traveler about him, found him Conversable, yet not so much improved in general knowledge, as might have been expected from his parts, had he employed himself, though I believe his improvement in the knowledge of trade and business is considerable. . . .

[13] *Lords day May 5* . . . Had a meeting after Service with the Trustees of the Congregation, who appointed to meet next Wednesday, to think of Some way of getting the payment of former Subscriptions. There was Some company went home with me, which too too often introduces conversation not so Suitable for a Sabbath, yet was helped carefully to avoid it and to be retired. Mr. Donnom and Mr. Lambert from Ponpon stayed all night, poor Mr. Lambert is in the greatest trouble and distress. Wayne, Son in law to Mrs. Clifford, seems evidently to have taken Some advantages. He intends to have a resettlement if possible to be obtained either by law or otherwise. His extreme melancholy and great uneasiness, made it a work both of necessity and mercy [14] to discourse with him about his affairs, in Order to encourage and direct him, and yet it introduced a great deal of conversation about such worldly matters, that I would much rather it had been done Some other day, although as He is in great trouble both Mr. Donnom & I were much concerned and seriously affected for him, which brought the conversation to be mixed with many observations on the mysterious Conduct of providence, and also in discoursing over parts of the Sermon which was without being designed exceedingly Suitable to what we were conversing of. . . .

[15] *Tuesday May 7:1771* Last night the heavy deluging rains returned, and continued all this day, this I know must be very distressing to many. The Judgements of God are evidently gone out against us. O that we might learn righteousness, but alas iniquity prevails daily and seems even to grow more rampant than ever was known in this part of the world. . . . As the Negroes could not work out in the field, they were brought over to do up the new addition to the house with clay and Sand, which is of so white a colour that it resembles free stone and lime and seems to be Something of the Same kind, with the artificial stone of the ancients, for at a little time it grows almost as hard as stone, and I believe might be improved to the hardness of Marble. . . .

Wednesday May 8 . . . After morning duties, set out to meet the Trustees of this the Salcatcher congregation, at a Small house in the woods, where the

Neighbourhood used to have a hunting club, about [16] Seven Miles from my house, stopped Some time at Mr. David Fergusons till such of the Gentlemen came up as were to come from the Salcatcher, proceeded and got to the place appointed after Eleven O Clock, all did not attend, Stayed better than two hours, and though had a sufficient Majority yet little or nothing was done. There is near one half of the Salary promised for the first four years not paid, and no prospect of getting a fourth part of what is due, so careless are people to Support the Gospel or to pay to a minister what they have Subscribed. I acquainted the Gentlemen with my straits and difficulties by being so kept out of my Salary, they promised to write letters & take Some pains to endeavour to collect at least Some part of what is due, they asked me if they should get warrants for the deficiencies, I answered by no means that I would rather lose it all. . . .

[18] *Lords day May 12:1771* . . . Preached from [19] Math: 6:19:20:21 with great fulness & freedom, liveliness & fervency . . . Went home with Mrs. Dxn, who lives with Mrs. Graves[6], they keep house together. Mrs. Graves told me, in the morning, she was to go to see her sister Mrs. Henry DeSaussure, after Sermon & Spend the night there. I had some thoughts of going directly home after meeting, without calling anywhere, but upon Mrs. Graves telling me the above, I resolved to go home, with Mrs. Dixon. As some people had imagined I went there more on Mrs. Graves account than for refreshment I thought this would be an opportunity of showing the contrary, which was very vain & foolish for me to give myself any concern about but the same vanity of heart which prevailed by this idle and specious pretense, continued to prevail & led me into a great deal of conversation, which might have been useful & improving on a week day, but not suitable to the Sabbath because, not all necessary, had a great many ill natured reflections & suspicions about the call from Ponpon & letter wrote to Presbytery for my continuance here, as if Dr. Cuthbert & I wanted to put this congregation under the jurisdiction of the Presbytery or I had encouraged it only to alarm the people here, & to have the world see what a number of friends I have to the Southward, notwithstanding all that has been done by my enemies to prejudice the world against me with many of their mean unworthy reflections, of which I am altogether most innocent of, and these made by some of whom better things might have been expected, which made me almost hope the Presbytery would determine Ponpon, my heart & affections have been at the Indian Land, & had the Presbytery determined for Ponpon, I had designed to endeavour to

have put it off till the fall and encouraged the Indian Land people to have
made another application against it, but the vile Suspicions that have been
propagated among them of the calls only being made a tool of, to introduce
their Subjection to Presbytery, etc. etc., has made me almost desire that I may
be removed, & resolve to follow the Presbyterys determination cheerfully and
readily, if it should even be to leave my beloved Indian Land. . . .

[22] *Wednesday May 15:1771* . . . After morning duties, in my family & private, with some comfort and freedom set out for Indian Land expecting to
hear the Reverend Mr. Ellington, who is this day to have preached at the
church there, a weekdays sermon. Both he & I are Sensible that they who
pretend to encourage him among the heads of that parish have no real liking to him, but endeavour by his means to draw the church people from the
meeting or from following me there on the Sabbaths, yet both he and I have
thought it best for him to come as often on the weekdays as they will send
for him. Last Sabbath I gave notice from the pulpit, that he was to preach
on this day & strongly exhorted both church people & Dissenters to attend
as they would hear pure Christianity & the Gospel faithfully preached, for
his design is to draw sinners to Christ & to nothing else, & to encourage
them I told I would attend myself, & always gave notice from my pulpit,
whenever I knowed he was to preach at church. Accordingly I set out hoping to hear him, & being late before I got up my horses from the woods, I
rode very hard, & was very uneasy lest I should not get there till after the
Service was begun, which I thought would be a bad example. When I got
there a quarter after Eleven O Clock I found a number of people mostly my
own people in the churchyard but no minister nor any of the heads of the
parish, and was informed, that he had not been sent for. What might be the
reason of this, I shall not say. Mr. Bull of Sheldon was expected to have sent
for him, but did not, & the reason he gives is, that Some others should have
done it, & that the people had no reason to depend on him, & that he would
not be put upon by the parish, the people in general seemed a good deal displeased, & seemed all to think it was designed, and that some people had no
real liking to Mr. Ellington as being too much of my stamp. After I mentioned among the people, especially those belonging to the church, that the
only way not to be disappointed, was to join & buy a horse or two, to be
given as a present to Mr. Ellington, to come up & give a week days sermon,
as often as he can till they get a minister of their own, which hint was well
received, & I believe may be put in practice. It was also hinted to me, by [23]

Severals of the church people that a Sermon from me would be very accept-able, but I waved it though I have good reason to believe the greatest part would very willing have attended me to the meeting house though more than four miles distance and would most gladly have heard it, either in the church or in the yard. It was observed, that the keys of the church, which are lodged at Sheldon, were not sent, and it seemed as if the disappointment was known by the principals of the church as well as at Sheldon for none of them attended. After spending near half than hour among the people, we all broke up. I proceeded some miles further to Mr. Henry DeSaussures, whose child being in a poor low condition, I appointed to baptize at his own house after Service. Stayed Dinner here, & in the afternoon, baptized the child a Daughter (Jean, my favorite name). Besides Mr. & Mrs. DeSaussure, there were present his two sisters Mrs. Dixon & Miss Betsy DeSaussure, her sister Mrs. Graves, and my old neighbour Mrs. Williamson. Never had more of the Divine presence & assistance in administering any gospel ordinance in all my life, than at this time, for the Lord was truly with us. . . .

[26] *Monday 20th of May 1771* Though slept much last night, yet got up earlier than usual in a very humble penitent frame of soul, deeply sensible of my manifold backslidings and evil departures from God. Was helped in prayer to confession of sin of all my degeneracy & decays and to earnest wrestling with the Lord my God not only for pardon, peace & the light of his countenance, but especially for the healing of my backslidings & the return of the Holy Spirit to my soul in his gifts, graces, operations, and in-dwelling. The greatest part of this forenoon was spent in prayer, searching my soul, & in the correct exercise of faith & repentance. Among other dis-coveries I found that the numberless evils, backslidings and decays which for some time have prevailed against me, proceed from this greatest of all evils, my forgetfulness of God. This indeed is the Source of all my degeneracy, and therefore my firm resolution is to guard against this great evil as the Spring of all the rest and to endeavour at all times, and in all places, to consider myself as in the Divine presence. I also discovered that another great evil is my not correcting faults in my practice when discovered, and acting agree-able to my resolutions, especially my resolutions about the beginning of this present year. In order to correct this evil I am determined, by Divine assis-tance, to read at the end of every month, what is wrote in my Diary, that I may discover what has been my temper & conduct during that time. Oh how am I fallen from my first love & my first works. Well do I remember when

my first and last thoughts were with God & glorious Christ, when it was almost as natural & habitual for me to have my thoughts fixed & centered on God, and my Dear Redeemer, as ever they went out after any favourite creatures, but alas how dead, how lifeless, how vain & wandering are all my thoughts & affections. About Eleven O Clock set out to visit as a minister & neighbour up the Saltcatcher. Called upon & spent about half an hour with Mr. Thomas Forster, who is [27] in a deep consumption, & is come from Charlestown to live with his brother for the benefit of the country air, had serious conversation with him, but nothing particular as to his own case. Proceeded upwards to Mr. Jonathan Lambrights where Dined & Spent the afternoon. Our conversation was serious & improving. All the neighborhood this way are of a sober, serious & religious turn, but self righteous & conceited, and far from being teachable. In the Evening rode about [three] Miles further to Mr. Roberts, who lives for Mr. Ingles. This is the highest place up this way where I have any charge or Connection. Spent the evening agreeably in conversation becoming men & Christians. Was all day in a very humble, Spiritual self denied frame of soul, almost ashamed to receive the kindness and respect shown by these good people. Was something melancholy on my own account both of body & mind, so that had not much Spirits for conversation, and was also very much on the reserve, as know the likeness of these people, which to me has bordered on insincerity, yet it is my duty to bear with such weaknesses, who have so many faults & shortcomings of my own which deserve a much worse name. . . .

Tuesday May 21:1771 . . . About Eleven O Clock left this good family pleased with my visit and turned homewards. Went to Mr. Hamiltons, who is now moved to Campbells Hill, the house where Mr. Donnom lived, & Mr. Donnom is removed over to his house. The reason is, Mr. Donnom & Hamilton have joined hands to plant together, & Mr. Hamilton is to have so many shares for taking care of the whole business, they plant on Mr. Donnoms land and & Mr. Hamilton whose circumstances oblige him to it, is his overseer, & upon that account they have changed houses, that Mr. Hamilton may be more convenient to the business, was kindly received by Mr. Hamilton & his family, but not with that apparent openness and freedom that used to be, nor could [28] I be so free & open myself. Dined and spent the afternoon here, as was not quite so well as I felt myself yesterday, and being also much exercised in mind, & having many prudential reasons to be reserved, had no Spirits for any lively conversation, what was said amongst us, was only on things indifferent, & all in a very serious and improving way. Was melancholy on many accounts, and this among the rest, that I should be obliged to change my friendly sentiments of any whom I really believe have the root of the matter in them, & who on different accounts are really dear to me, but am Satisfied that they are incapable of that friendship I once thought they had for me, & which my free sincere temper & disposition requires in all whom I would call friends. Endeavoured in every part of my converse, to be useful without appearing to take anything of the teacher or the Superiour upon me. As have suffered so much by being out after night, took my leave, rather sooner than usual on account of my indisposition. Rode home slowly, had satisfaction in reflecting upon all that has passed these two days, only these visits were to me rather too formal & ceremonious but openness is my great failing & a great disadvantage to me, therefore reservedness is my great duty, and I am sensible I would soon find it greatly for my advantage. . . .

[29] *Thursday 23 May 1771* . . . [30] I was surprized with a visit from the Reverend Mr. Zubly, my worthy good Brother in his way from Georgia to Charlestown, had called to spend the forenoon & take Dinner with me. His company was exceedingly welcome, yet would have been glad to have been alone this day. Had sweet fellowship with this worthy minister of Christ, whose conversation full of piety & learning is always most useful & improving to me. Soon after he came I received a letter from Mr. Donnom in Charlestown letting me know that the Presbytery had continued me at Indian Land, but at the same time some of the Brethren Mr. Huet of Charlestown & Mr. Henderson of Edisto,7 had made very free in railing against & abusing me, because of my great popularity as they expressed it, saying I grasped at nothing less than a Bishops diocese, that I certainly deceived the people, & was actuated by bad principles. Mr. Donnoms words are, "It is looked upon here that the Presbytery did the great honour. Henderson was the spokesman, Huet heartily accorded to him. They cried out much against your popularity & Influence, provoked to the last degree that so many at Ponpon should subscribe for you, and a still greater number from Indian Land, etc. Henderson suggested that you only waited for Mr. Maltbys Death, and his charge would be added to you, that it might be the same case should Mr. Huet Die or go away, that it was amazing, had Christ no minister here but Simpson etc. etc. etc. etc. Mr. Martin arose to defend an absent brother, but could not be heard. Mr. Lambert, who presented the Ponpon call, when you

see him will be more particular when you see him." Thus am I used by them who call themselves ministers and my Brethren, who are convinced in their consciences that my popularity as they call it, for which they so much envy & affect to despise me, is the effect only of my unwearied diligence, zeal, activity & faithful in every part of my ministry. It is true, if this is the way to popularity, they will never be popular. If my plain, faithful, frequent preaching, my constant visiting, praying with, comforting & exhorting the Sick & afflicted, the dying & distressed renders me accepted & believed by the people of all ranks, I esteem it as a blessing. If I acted from the mean & despicable principle of merely gaining the applause of the vulgar & ignorant, they might justly complain, but they are very Sensible that the reverse is true. As for the two Gentlemen who so liberally traduced & abused me, they both set up for what the [31] world calls fine Gentlemen, or rather the late comer, from his Chaplainship in a marching regement of foot at Augustine, sets up for what the looser part of the world, call a good fellow, or approaches near to what some call a Buck, the One, (& both, when opportunity serves) attends all the Balls, assembly, plays & dances in Charlestown, and plays a good fiddle at all the consorts, the other has attached himself to one particular Gentleman, the principal of his Congregation, with whom he almost constantly hunts, rides, afrequents billiard rooms, etc. etc. These I acknowledge are accomplishments I have no claim to but to pass it over it is just what I expected. My continuance at Indian Land is much to my satisfaction, and if my popularity & influence acquired as above, makes me vile in the eyes of a majority in the presbytery, I hope I shall be more vile still, and if my attempts towards faithfulness & usefulness, if my zeal, diligence and laboriousness, activity, & constant fatigues in my ministerial duties, endeavours to do good, hurts them, I cannot help. I hope still to give them more cause to complain, & while life & health permits to be more & more laborious. Alas my grief & burden is I can do so little good, & at present, can hardly attempt it. This abuse and ill usage from these time serving Brethren, will I hope make me increase diligence, & has engaged me to resolve it. . . .

[33] *Lords Day May 26:1771* Soon after midnight, the rain returned again, and has continued all this day without any intermission, so that poor Indian Land has again had another Silent Sabbath . . . After 10 O Clock gave up all hopes of going over & thought to send my boy, lest any should be at meeting, but it poured down so violently that I could not even send him, this increased my trouble & concern lest God had again been provoked, by my

many backslidings, and especially by my not being more serious & earnest
in the pulpit this day fortnight, & not being more watchful this day week,
to reject my offered Service, this at times much distressed & troubled me, &
helped me to great humility & self denial, to lowliness of mind & self abase-
ment before God. Had before I gave up all hopes of preaching, gone through
family duties with Mrs. Anderson & the children, & such servants as were
at hand, with greater enlargement than I usually have time for on a Sabbath
morning, and as soon as was Satisfied I could not go out, humbly & earnestly
begged of God, to assist me in spending this day with my family in the Constant exercises of Secret & family worship that might have a Sabbaths frame
& a Sabbaths blessing on the private exercises of religion, and blessed forever
blessed be his holy & glorious name, who graciously heard, & assisted a poor
creature, and made this a day of comfort & profit to my soul. Called my
family together at three different times for solemn prayer, reading the Scriptures & instruction suited to their capacities. Would have had the Negroes
over from the plantation, but could not on account of the constant rain, indeed the greatest part of the house was wet, appointed the children what to
get in their Catechisms, & repeatedly heard them, also heard them read the
Scriptures, Dr. Watts hymns, some parts of the token for Children[8] & other
Small pieces suited to their age. Susy who is very tenderhearted was often in
tears, when I was speaking to them. Spent my own time much in prayer, in
examining into the state of my soul, & in different Spiritual exercises, such
as writting, reading the Scriptures, the memoirs of the life of the Eminent
Doctor Doddridge,[9] a book greatly useful to me, and which I never read but
with profit & advantage, while it fills me with shame, to think what an useless [34] creature I am, and how unworthy the name of a Christian minister
compared to that great Divine, that excellent Servant of God. . . .

[35] *Wednesday May 29* This day not so well as the two days past, much troubled with my cough, my hoarseness much increased & the disorders in my
breast more distressing, yet was obliged to Spend all this day in writting letters to the northward, Reverend Mr. Potter in New England, Reverend Caldwell in New Jersey, Reverend Dr. Rogers New York,[10] to my sister & husband
and to my Dear Mother in law in Glasgow Scotland, to Virginia about my
Brothers Son, which took up the whole day, the constant writting was very
distressing to me. . . . In the evening began study and preparing for Sabbaths
delightful work, helped to look unto God & to lift up my soul in humble
supplications and found it pleasant to draw near to the throne of grace.

Thursday May 30 Still poorly and indisposed, still maintaining an honest warfare against corruption, and longing for deliverance from all iniquity. The river which has for several days been rising has this day got as high as it has been all this winter, came to the foot of the hill where I live, filled all the rice field with water especially a piece which had given to Mr. Jonathan Donnom to plant. After breakfast went out to encourage the Negroes by going among them, which poor creatures have all this day been employed in water very deep, in some places making dams to keep it out, other places making ditches to drain it off. Was detained longer than I expected encouraging both them and the Overseer. Saw destruction and distress everywhere. . . .

[36] *Friday May 31:1771* This morning, troubled, uneasy and concerned on various accounts, chiefly that I can really do so little for God, am so ailing, & indisposed, while my Enemies, especially my Brethren in the ministry, are abusing & despising me as a madman, an Enthusiast, or as a Designing person & a deceiver for striving to do so much. Would heartily rejoice in all their abuses was I but sensible of doing good, was I but able to exert myself in that degree of diligence, that any way deserved to be so singled out, it would be some satisfaction, but to be at home, groaning under weakness, infirmities, prevailing lusts and corruptions, deadness, decays, slothfulness & many backslidings, and to be abroad run down and abused for the opposite of all these seems indeed a dark strange providence. Applied to God by prayer & found comfort in pouring out of my soul at the throne of grace. . . .

[42] *Monday June 10:1771* . . . [43] Rode up to Mrs. Graves who is at present in Charlestown, and baptized a very old Negro wench called Mary who belonged to the late Mr. Prioleau, there was no white person present which gave me an opportunity of discoursing to this poor old slave, & to others present, in a most plain & suitable manner, in a most familiar strain. Spent about a full hour, it was a good & comfortable time for had Gods most gracious presence and assistance, both in praying & instructing. The Lord Jehovah was in this place, this poor old creature, applied to me about eight months ago and has often been privately instructed, & given me good Satisfaction as well as others whose concern in her made them inquire into her knowledge. I hope & believe that this poor Ethiopian brought many years ago from Africa has really stretched out her hand to the Lord Jesus, and that He has most graciously taken her into the ark of his covenant. May she &

others in this land, be as the first fruits of their Land and & colour joining themselves unto the Lord. . . .

Tuesday June 11 1771 . . . [44] Mr. & Mrs. Donnom called to spend the day with me, which they did. Learned by him that he is much taken with living to the Southward, is much pleased with his Employer, who he thinks is no less so with him. I wish indeed, that it may continue, on both sides, and that my friends may not deceive themselves, but if things continue, as they expect, I suppose they will remove their Interest to the Southward against another year. Learned also that they are much dissatisfied both with Mr. and Mrs. Smiley who lives at their place especially with him and am afraid they have Some reason. Am heartily sorry for poor Mrs. Smiley who is a very worthy deserving woman, and would very willingly do her part, but is far from living equally yoaked. He is of a very soft Indolent disposition & too fond of company. She is most exceedingly careful, diligent & industrious at her needle, but much too sedentary. Was she more stirring, it might turn out much more to her advantage, and the familys, and might in part counterbalance his inactivity. Learned several useful & important lessons, and among other things to look a little more into my worldly concerns, as am fully satisfied that more of my professed friends, are endeavouring to provide for themselves, & will leave me to Sink or Swim as I can. . . .

Wednesday June 12:1771 . . . This forenoon I rode out to wait upon Mr. Hamilton at Godfreys Savannah. . . . Wanted to have settled some business with Mr. Hamilton of considerable importance. He was one of the first who joined to invite me to this side, though he had always been bred to the church. He has the largest possessions in these parts, or among the largest, but has been remarked as very dilatory in making the payment, and in general too negligent, about his affairs, too much of the Idle Gentleman. He has for this year or two suspected to be in a bad situation. He has been an annual Subscriber to my Salary but never paid anything excepting once a Small matter. Last fall I had some Cattle from him for the use of my plantation. The stock belonged to him & two others, one of whom, was also indebted to me. I acquainted Mr. Hamilton I will discount what they owed to me, & pay the balance when he should let me know, what price they set upon the cattle, as I had them by order, and [45] the price to be fixed afterwards. I found him very melancholy, & making many complaints about the hardness of the times. After Dinner, he took me out, and hinted repeatedly at my becoming

security for a considerable Sum of money, for which he is like to be immediately distressed if not paid by the first of next month. This I would by no
means agree to do, but at last consented upon his earnest entreaties to write
to Mr. Donnom & Mr. Mitchell, who are both intimately acquainted with
the Merchants who are threatening to distress him, to interceed with these
Gentlemen, to be patient, till the winter, when if he does not raise the money,
he will sell off as many of his Negroes as will clear him from all incumbrances.
I then acquainted him with my business but could get nothing down, he
pretending he had not the books, and that he could not do anything in it,
till he saw another of the company, when the price should be fixed, and he
would give me Credit, for what he owed me & would get Mr. Holman,
another of the company who owes me, to do the same. Upon the whole I
found to be too true what has often been charged upon Mr. Hamilton, that
he is not so much to be depended on, as could be wished, that he is very
much involved, that I am like to be obliged to pay an exhorbitant price for
the Cattle to his Creditors & lose what is owing to me. I saw that I could do
nothing more at present, and must get my friend Mr. Donnom if possible
to settle this affair for me. I put him in mind of his agreement & mine, &
of my expectations from his honour, and professed friendship, did not chuse
to express my fears. Had promises from him as usual and great professions
of friendship & esteem. . . . Have this day had yesterdays lesson, of being a
little more careful about my worldly concerns, repeated & confirmed, things
at present bear a most melancholy aspect, with respect to the Gospel interest in this Neighborhood, the great rains, which have continued for above a
year, has prevented people from the other side of the river from attending on
publick worship, & the great appearance of the Wet Season continuing,
makes them give up all thoughts of taking pews in this meeting, especially
as there is no prospect of getting the Bridge repaired. The same cause, the
almost unpassableness of the roads, has the same effect on Several families,
who live at a considerable distance from the meeting on this Side of the river.
Another great cause of this evil disposition is the little prospect, that great
numbers have, of their making any Crop of rice for the ensuing year, which
discourages people from doing anything for the Support of the Gospel, so
that although, there is a great expense accumulated by the additions to the
meeting House, yet we have not any prospect of one half of the pews being
rented out next week, which is the time when it should be done, notwithstanding these melancholy thoughts both concerning my own [46] private

affairs, in which I am much straitened, & like to be more so, and concerning the publick interest I am connected with. . . .

[47] *Lords day June 16:1771* . . . After pleasant intercourse in morning duties I went forth to public service trusting & rejoicing in the Lord my God. Found a large congregation, & yet many absent, preached in the forenoon, from 2 Corinth: 5:19 last clause, with great freedom, clearness, and tender elevated affections . . . My soul was on the mount of God, the pulpit was to me a Mount Tabor, cannot tell nor express what I enjoyed, it was heaven upon Earth. Was filled with the most melting compassions for poor souls, this was as a time spent in heaven, for was filled with joy unspeakable & full of glory. The power & glory of God, seemed also amongst the auditory very remarkably, they appeared charmed & overawed into a most close & reverential attention. In the afternoon preached from Proverbs 8:17. Was showing the Special & Singular encouragements, that young people have to Serve the Lord, who most graciously helped & assisted a poor creature, to plead his cause with poor thoughtless youth, of whom a good number were before me. As some of the youth under my particular care & charge had been guilty this day fortnight of a very gross profanation of the Lords day, in a private family after publick Service, & afterwards going to different taverns, and getting very drunk, I took occasion in the application to [48] reprove for the same, and was helped to do it, with the greatest awe & solemnity, with the deepest concern, and at the Same time with the most affectionate tenderness & compassion, I remember ever to have obtained to, had been very earnest with God for direction & assistance in this most difficult part of duty, and was most graciously heard & answered. Had the comfort to see it well exceedingly well received, & have a present & happy effect, received repeated thanks for my faithfulness as soon as I came out, for which I praise the Lord & give glory to his name, which made this a glorious & most comfortable day of the Son of Man. . . .

Monday June 17:1771 . . . After Breakfast rode out about two miles and baptized two children, one for Mr. Christopher Langely, and one for the Widow Hill daughter to old Mcuen, whose husband died a few months ago, had reason to bless the Lord for his wonderful presence in this ordinance. . . . I returned up to Mr. Hamiltons at Campbells hill, to visit the widow Beatys child, a boy about Seven years of age, who has for two or three days been bad with the malignant sore throat, found the child in the most melancholy condition, evidently a dying with that most terrible distemper, which begins to Spread in the neighbourhood, he was a most melancholy and very humbling Spectacle, his poor mother who lately lost her husband overwhelmed with Sorrow, not so much with the approaching loss of her Dear child, as to the great distress and misery he was in, and may suffer much more before he expires. Spent the day here comforting & encouraging this afflicted family, for all are very melancholy & distressed on the account of this very fateful & distressing disease being among them. Two of Mr. Hamiltons children are getting over it, three more have not yet had, Several of the Negroes down with it, the whole neighbourhood trembles because of this visitation. My fears are many on account of my Dear children, & also on account of my Servants. . . .

[51] *Thursday June 20:1771* . . . After morning duties was engaged in study for Sabbath, & in making some preparation to discourse at the funeral of the child I visited on Monday, who held out till yesterday morning, & suffered such distress before he expired as was most grievous & afflicting to all present, and made all even the Dear Mother thankful to see him delivered from his extreme misery. He was buried this forenoon at the meeting, there was considerably more people present than I expected, & some entire strangers, who never had been there before, who had come to have some business done, with Mr. Hamilton, as a Magistrate. I discoursed near about half an hour, upon the improvement of afflictions, the good to be got thereby & chiefly on submission to the Divine will. Poor Mrs. Beatty herself was there and was much affected, as the greatest part of the very attentive auditory were. Discoursed from the pulpit, began with a short prayer, then Discoursed, beginning with these words, man that is born of a woman is full of trouble. Afterwards prayed at a great length, then sung a hymn the 5 of the first book Dr. Watts, then came down from the pulpit & walked before the company to the grave, where the corpse had been deposited about an hour before, not being thought proper to be taken into the meeting house, spoke a Sentence or two at the grave, & pronounced the apostolical blessing. I mention these particulars, because in this form I propose to give the funeral service in general, whether at meeting or in private families. It was a Solemn serious Season. . . .

[52] *Lords day June 23* . . . After service rode [53] home, with Mr. Brown, being to Certify a Citation, which I had published for him. Stayed & took

Some Dinner, and then proceeded back over the river, having a funeral to attend at the new meetinghouse, to which was invited this morning very early. It is the funeral of Mrs. Gold, Sister to my old housekeeper. She has often been in a poor Sickly way, but has for Some months been much better than usual, was last Monday better than usual, and continued very well till last Thursday afternoon, when she seemed to be taken with a cold & Died yesterday. She has been all her life a well disposed person, I believe a very serious Christian, has had a life of great trouble & affliction many ways, and doubt not but now she has entered into the rest, that remains for the people of God, and for which she often longed. Found a good congregation waiting for me. Began with prayer, and proceeded as usual. Discoursed about three quarters of an hour upon the shortness & uncertainty of life, the difficulty & importance of preparing for Death, Judgment & Eternity, and the absolute necessity both of a relative, & subjective change, of our being regenerated, renewed & Sanctified, as well as pardoned & Justified. Was very pressing and earnest, the husband of the deceased came in about the middle of the Discourse. I took the opportunity of a very close and particular address to him, who is very loose liver, a prophane wicked creature, dealt faithfully with him which I may never have the opportunity to do again. Was well assisted in every part of this service, both in preaching and in the prayers. . . .

[56] *Saturday June 29:1771* This has been a busy day with me, my heart was in my duty, my soul was lifted up to God and often poured out before him, felt divine truths and was deeply affected therewith, was mercifully preserved from wandering melancholy discouraging thoughts, though expected to have been troubled with them, for yesterday received from Mr. Lambert whom I found at my house when I came home, a very particular account of the abuse that I received for my popularity, as it is called, from the two Brethren previously mentioned, in the presbytery, this gave me a little uneasiness & concern, to be so basely treated & so vilely misrepresented, and I expected it would have given me more, that it would have troubled & confused me this day, as Satan often makes use of such things, on the Saturdays, as grounds for his Suggestions, but the Lord mercifully freed me from all concern about it, for when it was once like to be a little troublesome, went to prayer for my Enemies, and for the Divine restraint to be laid on them, and was no more troubled with it, prayer I still find to be the best lever at a dead lift. Was helped in prayer & pleading for the Divine presence, help & assistance tomorrow, and found it always good to be drawing near unto God.

Lords day June 30:1771 . . . Went forth to meeting in a very humble, serious frame, somewhat melancholy, which was increased when saw so many absent, severals of whom I have good reason to believe, have just stayed away, that they may not be called upon to continue their support to the Gospel, by taking pews next Wednesday, and these such as two & three years ago made a very blazing profession, but alas many deceive themselves as well as ministers & others, and where are many real conversions, there will be several Counterfeits. Preached all day from 2 Corinth: 5:19 and finished this great & to me a very instructive & a very delightful subject it has been. Delivered the forenoons Sermon under a considerable degree of melancholy to see the word of reconciliation So little regarded & Esteemed, so much neglected & despised, was very deeply affected therewith, my concern was visible, was all day showing the way & manner in which the Holy Ghost applies purchased redemption & brings sinners into a state of actual reconciliation with God, was very closs & experimental, was enabled to handle it in a very searching & trying manner. Often called the hearers to make the application to themselves and to examine the state of their souls. At the close of the account of the different Steps of the Spirits working in the soul, turned it into interrogations, & direct addresses to every hearer. The power of God [57] was very remarkably among us, and the word preached seemed accompanied by the Holy Ghost especially in the afternoon. Towards the close of these very searching sermons, when came to address myself to such as have had actual reconciliation wrought in their souls by the Holy Spirit & to those who are still in a state of rebellion against God, the Spirit seemed to move on the waters of the Sanctuary, there was a very great concern, & much weeping among the hearers, especially among some young people of fortune & fashion, who were greatly affected. This may be only a moving of the passions, as I believe often is the case, under lively, close, affectionate preaching, and as often ends without any real change, yet it is desirable to see people, especially young ones so serious, attentive & affected, and very often the Spirit of God begins with these short transitory operations, which increase, & take a deeper & deeper hold, till at last they prove effectual. . . .

[58] *Wednesday Jully 3:1771* . . . Went to meeting at the ordinary time, where saw but few people at first which was discouraging though afterwards had a good Congregation, yet still severals absented themselves, the very families hinted at last Sabbath in my Diary. As the people were late in coming & the

Trustees had business to do in altering the roles of the old, & fixing the roles of the new pews, we did not begin till twelve O Clock. Preached with great comfort from 2 Corinth 5:14 first Clause, For the love of Christ Constraineth us, was obliged to omit much of what I designed to have said on the doctrinal part, that I might have time for an improvement Suited to the Occasion, and yet exceeded much my time, preaching near an hour. Was most graciously assisted in both prayers. Was enlarged in pleading with God for his church in this place & the old congregation, & in blessing Jehovah for all his former goodness to us. As this was one of the hottest days ever remembered and I was elevated both in preaching and in prayer, I suffered greatly from the heat, was in such floods of Sweat that it run down on the floor round the pulpit, against I was done, was ready to drop, & was for some time after I went out obliged to sit down & be fanned, & frequently heaved & [59] reached to vomit, this remarkable weakness was not only owing to the most extreme heat, but to my fatigue in the night, & my not having tasted any Sort of victuals, however after Some refreshing Drink, I was Soon better. The Congregation did not break up till late in the afternoon, when all the pews were taken except Six Small ones, two of which are designed for common pews, if they are not taken up. Some absent we have reason to think will take up what remains. The new additions to the meeting house, at the one End is fitted up with seats for the Negroes, & at the other End, besides a thoroughfare has Six double pews, so that there is already a greater number taken pews than was last year, & it is not doubled, but the rest will be taken up. So good & gracious is Jehovah, beyond our fears, yet could not but observe that the poorer or middling sort, shewed the greatest desire to accommodate themselves for hearing the Gospel by mostly taking a pew for each of their families while others of fortune & wealth joined generally five families in taking one pew. Had much kindness & respect shown me by all, great peace & Harmony prevailed, so that this has been a much more comfortable day. . . .

[60] *Friday Jully 5 1771* This day still very poorly & much indisposed . . . Have a disagreeable Cough, great pains & a weakness in my breast, & am far from being so hearty as last Summer. Think to begin soon on a Course of peruvian bark, camomile flowers & Snake root, which I generally take through the summer, & fall, and indeed in every Season, though have omitted it for some months, that might by the Divine blessing find it more effectual in the Summer & Sickly months. . . .

[61] *Monday Jully 8 1771* . . . Rode out to Mr. Strbls, who lives on Mr. Gibbs place, overlooks & manages his business, by the way called & sat about half an hour or more at Mr. Strains, whose family grows Sickly, Dined & spent the afternoon at Mr. S's, he and his family are Germans [62] or Swiss, the Genteelest people, I ever knowed, from these parts, very Sensible, polite & good Christians, they are in plentiful circumstances, and have hearts both to enjoy the comforts of life & to do good with their substance. Spent the day very agreeably in Christian, useful & improving conversation, this visit was both necessary, & useful. . . .

Tuesday Jully 9 . . . Was soon alarmed with an account that the malignant sore throat prevailed much up the Saltcatcher, & came nearer to this place, also received a line from Mr. Donnom, that he was much indisposed, & afraid of the distemper, upon which I made ready to ride up that way, when an old acquaintance, once in good thriving circumstances, but now much reduced through various misfortunes especially by a lawless gang, who live in the North east parts of this province, his coming detained me, till about dark, when left him with my the family and proceeded. Spent the Evening with Mr. Donnom, in serious conversation. Was in a humble frame of soul, & my heart lifted up above a vain, deceitful, perishing world.

Wednesday Jully 10:1771 . . . After breakfast & morning duties with freedom & comfort, proceeded about four miles further to Mr. Roberts whose two oldest children, have been very ill with the Scarlet fever & Sore throat, stayed about two hours & more here, the parents very disconsolate. Discoursed of the vanity of all creature comforts, gave some medical directions and prayed. Afterwards rode back & went to Mr. Hamilton. Was overtaken in a most violent thunderstorm, & got socking wet. Found Mr. Hamiltons two Children better than I expected. Stayed about an hour & a half, & when the rain abated a little rode back to Mr. Donnoms, where Dined & spent the afternoon. After it cleared up Mr. Hamilton came over, who is in a very poor state of health, & thinks himself going into a consumption, endeavoured to encourage him, to buy some means, to which he is very much averse. . . .

[63] *Thursday Jully 11:1771* . . . Busied in making up some medicines for Some Sick Negro children, who have fevers, and complain of their throats, though blessed be God, nothing of the malignant sort, as yet appears. After giving directions, set out to visit Some families at a distance, rode to Mrs. Perrys,

who had Sent last night, to let me know severals of her people had the worst sort of Sore throat & desired my advice. Made up a water for washing the throat, & a mixture of oyl & camphor, to be applied outwardly, called & delivered them with directions. . . .

Friday Jully 12 . . . [64] Mr. Donnom & I received Some letters, about Mr. Hamiltons affairs which greatly Surprized & troubled us both, & made me see what a snare I have escaped, & the great wisdom of Solomons advice not to strike hands suddenly with any man. I also saw how graciously, and mercifully Divine providence has been working for me, when I thought little of it. We were both much concerned, & yet resolved to give all the help, we safely could. In the afternoon was employed in getting out summer clothes to the Negroes, my own & Mrs. Holmes. . . .

Lords day Jully 14 1771 . . . When went to meeting it was so excessively Sultry, that we could scarcely breathe. All were employed in fanning themselves, it was even fatiguing to do that, all expressed much concern to think how I should go through the duties of the day. I almost trembled at the very thoughts of it, but cast myself upon the Lord. There was a good congregation, yet not so numerous, as it often is, preached both parts of the day from Jhn 6:51 middle clause, If any man eat of this bread he shall live forever, with great freedom & Enlargement . . . yet the Extreme heat seemed to overpower the auditory so that we were all ready to faint & sink under it, yet there was great attention and the power of God seemed evidently amongst us, both parts of the day, Betwixt sermons, I was not able to stand nor sit up for some time, was entirely overcome with the violent heat & exercise, & urged much to vomit, though had nothing on my stomach, and was Sometime before I could keep down any drink I took. In the afternoon, we had the most violent thunder, and sharp lightning, which so alarmed & distressed many of the hearers, that I was [65] obliged to make several digressions & spoke to them, not to be frightened. This lengthened out the service, much beyond what I intended, it was a very solemn awful time, and a great season of the Son of Man, against I concluded, was hardly able to get on my horse & when got home, was obliged to lie down immediately & was quite lifeless & stupid with fatigue, for some hours, Indeed could not sit up till late, was much pleased with the kind offices of my Dear children, who kept drying the sweat off me, fanning me, cooling my hands & feet with vinegar, and doing all they could about me. . . .

Tuesday Jully 16 Last night it began to grow surprizingly cold, so that the night was very agreeable, slept well & got up early, but was most exceedingly amazed to find it as cold as a day in beginning of winter, the Mercury Sunk about 30 degrees Since Sabbath, so that we were obliged to cloath for some hours as in winter. Was much concerned as expected this if it continued a day or two would bring on an unusual Sickness among the Negroes, who are in general such stupid careless creatures, as intirely to neglect themselves on such occasions, felt the sudden & amazing change very Sensibly, yet was careful to provide against it, both for myself & children, & directed the servants about the house to clothe warm. Was in a humble, serious frame of soul, after morning duties, rode over to the plantation to see how it was there. Found one Negro boy belonging to the parsonage with greater Symptoms of the Sore throat than has yet appeared among us here, gave directions, and proceeded over [66] about ten miles on the Indian Land Side and married a young couple, of very decent but poor people, was about three quarters of an hour in the house, then rode to Mr. Calders, where visited a young Lady a niece of Dr. Bowers from Scotland extremely bad with a nervous fever, & seemingly a dying, she was sensible & knowed me, but nowise able to converse, yet appeared to understand what I said, was much affected with her melancholy condition, gave her Suitable exhortations, and prayed with great freedom, was well assisted, all present were much affected, she appeared to be affected also & thanked me for the duty. . . .

Wednesday July 17:1771 In a very serious thoughtful frame of soul, uneasy for want of more retirement, occasioned by tradesmen at present about the house, this want, or the Neglect of retired duties, always brings me much deadness & formality, yet it is some comfort that I am Sensible thereof, and that I cannot live without conversing with God in the Special duties of devotion, I cannot conceive what sort of religion that is which many have who go nothing further than a fair behaviour with respect to the world, doing as they would be done by, which is indeed a golden rule, but then they know nothing at all of the love of God & of Secret Spiritual duties, or at most, they think these belong only to young Christians, and to persons at their first conversion & setting out in religion. Many I see or observe, who seem to rest here, even those who once made a noise in the world, & of such as I can have no doubt, but are real Christians, yet to me, there seems to be great decay & backsliding, and whither it be so or not, Lord keep me from falling out that way. Have since Sabbath had great uneasiness & concern, about Some whom I expect to join in communion with me, Some whom have been former communicants in a well constituted church, it might perhaps be proper, & useful to keep them off, but in the circumstances of this congregation, it would very probably be far otherwise. Have also had great concern about a young (Married) Lady of a very aimiable behaviour often much moved & affected into tears while hearing the Gospel, of a tender heart & what is generally called very good dispositions, one of those of whom, we generally say that if in good hands, they would make a figure, she is naturally of a very gay open cheerful disposition, her Education hardly deserving the name [67] of religious, & her husband affording no help, though not any remarkable hindrance, she has been often under my ministry, and constantly so, for more than this twelvemonth. She let me know her design last Sabbath, which much surprized me, desired some assistance from me, by books & conversation and appears to be promising, yet I am in a strait what to do, am afraid to discourage her, as would not limit the holy one of Israel, and am afraid to give encouragement, though after viewing it in all lights am more inclined to the latter as my duty, with the resolution, as much as possible to labour for her Spiritual advantage, by improving for that purpose, the great interest I seem at present to have in her esteem. . . .

Thursday July 18:1771 . . . [68] About twelve O Clock rode out according to an appointment, to visit Mr. Jordan, who is poorly, & to Dine there with some company, rode through by Mrs. Perrys whose Negroes are still much afflicted with the distempered throat but none die of it, & they who had it very bad are getting better. Then proceeded to Mr. Jordans, the company had near finished Dinner before I got there. Mr. Jordan very poorly indeed, after Dinner had some opportunity of talking with Mrs. Griffith according to her desire, & gave her Willisons Small Sacramental Catechism, or instructor for young Communicants,[11] promised to spend some time with her next week at her own house . . . was pleased to find Miss Sally Murry still serious and impressed with her early profession, as was afraid of her losing all such concerns, since her being wholly her own Mistress, and now in a family, not the most friendly to such matters, was Surprized that was not applied to about Mrs. Jordan, as I expected it. In returning rode with Mr. Griffith, his wife & Miss Murry, being in the Chair, acquainted Mr. Griffith, of his wifes applying to be a communicant & that I had desired her to consult him, which he told me she had & that he was very well pleased with it, afterwards had a good deal of very serious conversation with him, till we came to the road by my house, when we parted, this was more than I expected. O that the Lord might bless the Gospel and who knows, but he may, & will, make it a blessing to the most careless, thoughtless & unconcerned. . . .

[69] *Lords Day Jully 21:1771* . . . Preached all day with the Divine presence & most comfortable assistance. . . . Just as closed the exhortation [70] & was pronouncing the blessing, I was seized with a kind of moving stitch, or fly-ing pain in my left breast, arising as it were from my heart, which pierced through to my shoulder & kept moving upwards, so very extremely violent, that with difficulty I pronounced the blessing & sat down, it seemed as if in a minute or two it would have killed me. I never felt anything like it, and was never so bad, but it soon went off, though some remains of it continued after I went out. It is not possible to describe what I felt, I could not but look upon it, as a forerunner, perhaps some such Messenger will carry me off. Lord grant I may be ready, & if it is a lawful request, I would also add, Grant Lord it may be in the pulpit, while I am engaged in thy service. I felt something of it, for more than half an hour after. Rode to Dr. Bowers where Dined, and then, went along with him & another relation, to Mr. Calders & visited the Doctors niece, the young Lady I visited last Tuesday, who is still alive, found her quite insensible and having taken some opiates on account of her vari-ous disorders, that she could not be kept awake. I discoursed at times to the company present of a Suitable improvement of such a melancholy & very affecting providence, and stayed about an hour & a half, but she still remained insensible. . . .

Tuesday Jully 23 . . . [71] Received a letter from Dr. Bower, informing me of his nieces Death early this morning, and desiring me to attend at her funeral tomorrow nine O Clock, this gave me some concern, as Mr. Ellington is to preach at the church there tomorrow forenoon, lest it might be thought I took the opportunity of keeping people from going to church, and was the more concerned, because had been informed by Reverend Mr. Zubly that when Mr. Ellington lived in Savannah, he at different times entertained such Suspicions of him, without a cause, which made some coolness between them, I wrote to Dr. Bower, that if he wanted the church service read, it would be most proper to get Mr. Ellington to do it, but if the Dissenting Service I begged them to move early, that such as desired to hear Mr. Elling-ton might have an opportunity of doing it, as he knew some Enemies would make false reports upon such an occasion. . . .

Wednesday Jully 24:1771 . . . Went over after breakfast to the Indian Land to attend the funeral, having heard nothing further from them. Stopped about nine O Clock at Mr. Browns hoping to meet them but did not & proceeded, Overtook Ben Ganolke Brother in law to Main going he said to the funeral, though he went no further than the store. He told me, if we did not make haste, Mr. Ellington would be very much disappointed, if the people did not get to church. I told him, I was desirous they should go, & would do what I could to hurry the [72] funeral. This B G is general looked as a spy upon me for his Brother in law Main, who is a great encourager of Mr. Ellington at the church, in opposition as he thinks to me. I proceeded to Mr. Calders where the corpse was, but could not get them to move till about Eleven of the Clock so late was the company in coming, so that before we got to the meeting it was past twelve, I proceeded as usual, and was about half an hour or more in the Service, Discoursed with great freedom & clearness from Psl: 39:4. Made an apology for being short, that some might still go to church, if they desired it but none went, B G attended all the time, what report he might make I know not. I intended to have gone to church myself but before we left the grave, it was one O Clock & was desired to go back to Mr. Calders which did. Spent the afternoon there in company with the Doctor who was much affected with the Death of his niece, & another relation, with whom had serious & useful conversation. . . .

Thursday Jully 25 1771 This day Engaged in study and writting for Sabbath & also in study for the preparation & action Sermons. . . . About four O Clock the extreme heat being abated, I rode to Mr. Griffiths in order to converse with his wife, about admitting her to the Lords supper. Have had many thoughts about it & think it my duty, not to refuse her. She & Miss Sally Murry attended last Sabbath at Indian Land, & seemed much affected there, was very kindly & respectfully received by Mr. Griffith, but alas poor Gentleman, I was sorry to see him, he hurts himself with [73] what he thinks an antidote against the fever & ague in the Country, & does so almost every afternoon. After had sat about half an hour, retired with Mrs. Griffith into a Room, & after having just sat down I asked if she would not choose Miss Sally Murry present, which she agreed to, and I thought most proper for several reasons. Conversed about three quarters of an hour with Mrs. Griffith and had much more satisfaction than I expected, she wept much & was greatly affected, was very free and ingenuous, told me freely of the religious impressions made on her mind at different times, her knowledge yet if but slender, she seems very teachable & desirous to improve, she answered the questions put to her with great freedom and I hope has not only seen her lost state by nature & practice, seen her need of Christ & got some knowledge of the way of Salvation, but has had something of the drawing power of grace on her heart, inclining her to close with the Redeemer, after giving her what advices & instructions necessary, I agreed to receive her, and then called in Mr. Griffith & the family and went to prayer, it was a Solemn & Serious, and I hope a good & comfortable time. As it was just Dusk and fine moon light, they pressed me much to stay Supper which I did, had conversation with Mr. Griffith about indifferent things, and sometime before Supper had conversation alone with Ms. Sally Murry, which she desired, poor young Lady, she is now uneasy for having put herself so much in the power of Mr. Griffith, whom she finds to be altogether unfit for taking care of her affairs, and little to be learned in the family, though Mrs. Griffith is of a most aimiable disposition, and had a fine Education, yet is about a year younger than Miss Murry, and has not all the influence in the family she desires. I gave Miss Murry some general advices, for was afraid to say much in such a nice affair lest I should make myself enemies, and lest she should have other views than I have, but promised to advise her more particularly after the Sacrament. . . .

[74] *Friday Jully 26:1771* This morning wakened very early and had many thoughts about Miss Sally Murrys conversation to me last evening, was afraid lest had gone too far, in promising to direct her, about an administration on her parents Estate, she applied to me very early, but I avoided any concern, because of the censoriousness of the world, & thought she was very well in being with Mrs. Shaw, & the McTier family, but it appeared soon that there was a design to marry her to a relation of that family of some interest but otherwise very worthless whom she could not fancy, this made her quit Mrs. Shaw & her sisters, & come to Mr. Griffiths, whose wife is of the Same family, & now she is not Satisfied with him, & blames me for being so reserved, as her Mother had always consulted me, about their affairs, all this & more, she has informed me, yet I am afraid of meddling in her concerns, as she applied to me formerly at Mr. Smileys, when her & Mrs. Griffith sent for me there about two weeks ago & last night spoke with great freedom, yet I am afraid of some collusion, & know not what to think, got up & begged the Divine direction, pleaded with earnestness for my people and congregations in general & for blessings to her & Mrs. Griffith in particular & other young communicants. . . .

[76]

Tuesday Jully 30 1771 . . . Should have mentioned yesterday, that in the morning I received a large letter signed by the Reverend Mr. Thomas minister of the Independent Congregation,[12] or as it is called of the White Meeting but wrote in the name of the whole church, informing me, that their pastor Mr. Thomas being in a very bad state of health, they had by an unanimous vote made choice of me, with two other ministers near Charlestown, to Supply them once a month or as often as I could, in their ministers absence, who is obliged for some time to go off to the Northward for his health, this Surprized me, as have never preached there, though have been invited, Saw a Divine hand in it & hope the Lord will make it for the good of souls. . . .

Wednesday Jully 31 1771 . . . [77] This evening discoursed with & agreed to admit as a communicant Mrs. Anderson, the housekeeper. She is a very serious person, and a real good liver. Was afterwards engaged in prayer & other preparatory duties, till after midnight with good comfort & pleasant to my soul.

Thursday First day of August 1771 . . . All the morning was every now & then very heavy showers, & it seemed as if it would be a very rainy day, however it cleared up about the time of going to meeting, went out trusting in the Lord & hoping in his name, found a large company. Just as I lighted, was sent for to Mrs. Jaudon, who with tears acquainted of her being detained at home, when she thought to have waited on me to receive baptism, & with many tears begged me to wait upon her at her husbands tomorrow, I told her I could not do it, and proposed that she should go home with me, but she gave me reasons, why it would be very improper & that she could not go, upon which & her urging me I promised to ride up tomorrow though it will greatly straiten me for time, was afterwards, desired to admit Mrs. Ppr,[13] who has often communicated in church of England which I readily agreed to, she being a very worthy person, afterwards discoursed with and agreed to admit John Hunt, Esq., his desiring it Surprized me, however dealt very faithfully with him, & was well satisfied, also admitted Mrs. Jackson both for the first time of communicating, then called the Elders as a kind of Session, acquainted them with the persons to be admitted, all of whom they approved, Inquired if they had objections against any old communicants, they desired me to serve them all, but to reprove & exhort four or five, who were named, which after the Sermon I accordingly did, and it was exceedingly well taken, preached from 1 Corinth:11:24 these words in the middle clause, this is my body broken for [78] you. Was most comfortably assisted in delivering, an experimental Searching Sermon which the Lord seemed to accompany with his power and I hope with a gracious blessing. . . . This evening heard several things of my neighbour Mr. Hamilton which for some time much affected me. Poor Gentleman, his conduct for some time past has been such, as I could never have expected, and makes it almost doubtful, whether he has any real experimental religion or not, yet I would fain hope he has really the root of the matter, poor man, It is not the falling into what is commonly called failings and miscarriages of life, from these he is in general very free, as much so as almost any person whatsoever, but great self righteousness, and a fixed habitual opposition to the experimental, Spiritual and even practical parts of religion. Have been greatly concerned for him, was helped to mourning and prayer upon his account & others, especially that religion seems to thrive so little in my own neighborhood, among professors who were brought up in a family of religion from their infancy, but alas are I am afraid settled on their lees or built on a very false foundation. Yet it is my comfort and support that religion thrives and flourishes in other parts of the parish, especially among them who never heard the Gospel till within these few years. Thus a Sovereign God dispenses his grace & mercy. The wind of Spirit bloweth where it listeth.

Friday August 2:1771 . . . About twelve O Clock set out though it was raining to go up to Mr. Jaudans. Crossed the river in a canoe at the free Negroes. Was about an hour & a half riding ten miles, found it very difficult in getting through the river Swamp which made near three miles of the way, it continued raining all the time, found some of the relations, I mean his relations gathered together upon this occasion, which by the Divine presence with us, was I think before it was finished one [79] of the most solemn, serious, & comfortable I have ever been concerned in dispensing in a private family. Spent near about an hour with Mrs. Jaudon in private, who seems I think one of the most pious young Ladies I have been acquainted with, and I hope will make a great & Eminent Christian. Her husbands bad behaviour to her, and the preaching of the Gospel in these two congregations, has been the greatest mercy to her, God has blessed the Cross and the word together to effect I hope a great, a glorious and Saving change upon her. I have had frequent conversations with her for these twelve months past, always with pleasure, but this day had great comfort & satisfaction. Poor Dear young Creature, her discouragements and difficulties have been very great, & are still many, but glorious powerful grace has I hope done great things for her, but have not time to be particular, Was myself filled with praise wonder & gratitude, that God would make use of such a poor worthless creature to bring souls to himself, and that he should give me such comfortable Instances thereof. Afterwards in the publick Hall I proceeded and baptized her, began with Demanding of her, if it was from a conviction of her duty, etc., she desired this ordinance, or if her husband had by any means strove to influence her to it, to which she gave a most clear & Satisfying answer, that it was wholly from a sense of her duty, and that no manner of influence, had ever been used with her. I then demanded her to declare, if it was also from real conviction of mind, that she believed Infant baptism, & submitted to this ordinance by the mode of Sprinkling. To which she also declared, her firm belief of infants right to baptism, that as for the Mode she looked upon it as indifferent whether dipped or Sprinkled, but that she chose the ordinance from me, as having been most blessed to her soul. I then proceeded to take her confession of faith and her solemn personal covenanting, she was in floods of tears, spoke with a clear audible voice, was greatly affected, and appeared in the most serious solemn Spiritual frame I ever saw, nothing could exceed it, was myself greatly affected, was much enlarged, had the Divine presence with my own soul, all present were in tears, the least affected, was her Sister several years older than herself. The power and glory of the Lord Jehovah, was most evidently amongst us. It was a great & glorious Season, the Lord Jesus & his Spirit was with us. It was such a time as I think I hardly ever saw the like, and shall never forget. Was greatly enlarged in leading to avouch the Lord for her God, & devoting herself through Jesus Christ, in laying on the vow & engagements, in exhorting her and all present in prayer & every part of this Solemn duty, this most precious Sacrament. Poor Mr. Jaudon himself was greatly affected, & behaved exceedingly well, had a close conversation with him alone after the ordinance & have some hopes, he will return to his duty, and attend publick [80] ordinances as usual. . . .

Lords Day August 4:1771 This has been an high communion Sabbath to my soul, a day of heavenly pleasure, joy & delight, a day of heavenly glory . . . [81] Went forth to publick worship, rejoicing in the Lord, and found it most transportingly delightful to go from the Mount of communion with God, to the mount of Gospel ordinances, where mounted up as on Eagles wings and soared aloft by Faith & love. Had severals to speak & discourse with before Service began, & was helped to speak to their several cases, admitted Mr. Strains & daughter, a young person about Sixteen years of age, preached the action sermon from Proverbs:18:24: and there is a friend that sticketh closer than a Brother. My heart & soul was in the subject and O cannot tell what enjoyed, while preaching & delivering it, the house was Crowded with the most attentive, Serious auditory I ever saw . . . the Divine presence was most gloriously, remarkably with us through the whole of the Service and there was the most general universal weeping I ever saw, all ranks seemed to be bowed under the almighty hand of God, even those who never appeared to be touched with religion before, especially towards the close of the Sermon, when had been making the most full & free offers of Christ, the friend of souls, when was taking witnesses to the offer, & discharging my own soul, it seemed as if the Holy Ghost had come down amongst, & the whole assembly bowed under his influences, the place was made a Bachim, a place of weeping,[14] not a mourning through fear & terror but the most kindly affectionate weeping such as I never was witness to . . . [82] We had three Services, were greatly favoured in the weather, which was fair, & although very hot yet Moderate for the Season, and was most amazingly supported, so that was upwards of Seven hours in the Service yet felt much more comfortable than often after the ordinary duties of Sabbath, was enlarged in the prayers, the praises and exhortation. After communicant [sic], served the Negroe Communicants at a table by themselves, as last time at the Indian Land, for the sake of addressing them, in such language as they could best understand, the service continued till after six O Clock till about half an hour before sun down yet there was not the least appearance of wearying among the hearers but a great eagerness of attention, and tender weeping to the very last, thus this day which I was afraid to venture upon because of the Season of the year, has been one of the greatest & most glorious days of the Son of Man I have seen upon Earth. O the goodness, the faithfulness & truth, the rich grace, the undeserved mercy & infinite condescension of Jehovah. . . .

[85] *Thursday August 8:1771* . . . Was this night informed that Dr. Green upon the Indian Land was taken sick last Saturday, died on Tuesday morning and was buried on Wednesday, this affected me much as he was a young Gentleman I had a singular regard for, and would have been very desirous to have seen him on his dying bed, and he also would have been most desirous of it but was Informed of my being at such a distance from the parish,[15] and

soon lost his senses, resolved to make some [86] improvement of this affecting providence on Sabbath, & also of the Death of the young Lady I buried
about a fortnight ago, both of them young Europeans. How many such find
their grave in this place & yet I am spared, O the wonderful providences of
Jehovah.

Friday August 9 Early this morning Mr. Donnom went over the plantation
& found that the rice is suffering greatly for want of water, and that if there
is not a great fall of rain soon we would make little or nothing at all. This
put him on viewing some ground between it & a river through which it has
been thought, a canal or drain could be brought, that brung water from the
river, which would be of the greatest service to me, if it could be effected,
after breakfast he asked me to ride into the woods with him & the Overseer,
to view the ground up the river side to see if it was practicable, this suited me
very ill, but I could not refuse it as he was putting himself to so great fatigue
upon my account, so that was obliged to go with him, we were out about
five hours in the thickest part of the woods where we often could not pass
till the way was cleared before us, this fatigued me most excessively beyond
any labour of preaching or riding, my very bowels seemed melted within me,
for after got home, was much indisposed with a violent purging, & sick all
night. . . .

Lords day August 11:1771 . . . [87] In the afternoon preached from Ecles: 12:1
with a view to improving the Death of the two young people mentioned
above, and blessed be the Lord was most graciously helped & assisted in
delivering this Sermon, which seemed accompanied with divine power, was
enabled to deal most faithfully with precious immortals, & especially with
the young & thoughtless, indeed the greatest part of the auditory were but
young or scarcely middle aged, there was a very great & affectionate weeping especially when called for them to recollect the many Deaths that has
been among them, the many the very many breaches both they & I have had
in our families, Since we lived together, for there was not one person in the
whole auditory, that I could observe come to the years of Discretion, but I
had buried some of their nearest relations & Dearest connection, which I put
them in mind of very particularly. Took occasion also to mention, the great
breaches in my own family, and the bereavements they had seen me meet
with, particularly the breach I met with tomorrow five years, in the Death
of my Dear little Jeany, and the still greater breach made upon me, last

Wednesday, Six years ago, in the Death of my Dear ever Dear Wife, this was a good & comfortable time, young & old were much melted & affected. . . .

[88] *Monday August 12:1771* . . . In the afternoon rode to Mr. Griffiths who was not at home, when I went there, but came about an hour afterwards, was much pleased to find Mrs. Griffith & Miss Murry with the Bible they had been reading in, and a small religious book of Burkets which I had never seen before, but a very useful and instructive one.[16] Had some very serious and Satisfying conversation with Mrs. Griffith about religion, and the profession she has made, which gave me great pleasure & satisfaction. There is at present strong appearances of a great & remarkable work of grace upon her soul. Afterwards had some very serious, intimate & Satisfying conversation about Miss Murrys affairs, the particulars of which I may take notice of afterwards. Mr. Griffith came & behaved with his usual good nature to appearance & complacence, but poor man continued through the evening to be too kind to himself, though much more on his guard than the last time I was here, Indeed everything was decent & becoming, he opened his mind very freely to me in several respects (as about some ill usage he met with last Monday from Bull of Sheldon when petitioning the commissioners at the church for a road to the place, he is going to move to over the river, about some ill usage from his partner in trade having charged him, to their correspondent in England with some neglects, and about some demands made upon him, by their merchants in England etc.) all of which I gave the hearing & gave my best advice about. . . .

[89] *Tuesday August 13:1771* As there is very great appearances of an obstinate drougth by which my crop of rice among others, will be mostly lost, for by the most extreme heat, there blows continually the most drying westerly winds, and air filled every night with the greatest number of fiery Meteors I ever saw, all which are reckoned Signs of a distressing drougth, Mr. James Donnom, being much concerned not only for me, but for his Sister in law Mrs. Holmes & the share he himself has in the crop here, was out this morning by daylight, with my overseer, and several of the Negroes, laying out the way for the drain to be brought if practicable & found to be absolutely necessary. . . .

Wednesday August 14:1771 This morning alarmed with some noise and disturbance among the Negroes from the plantation, which took some time to inquire into, the disturbance, was with one of Mrs. Holmes Negroes who stole several things of value from her Mistress in Charlestown, and was lately sent here, after breakfast rode out with Mr. Donnom to old Mrs. Jeffreys[17] to get leave to cut the drain, through some part of her land, which she very readily granted. Stayed after Mr. Donnom rode home to give some advice about her Son in law Mr. Langleys affairs, which are like to go wrong. . . .

[90] *Saturday August 17:1771* . . . About twelve O Clock rode out to the meeting house, to attend the funeral of the child of Mr. Thomas Timmons. Discoursed as usual from the pulpit, about half an hour upon the benefit of affliction, the duty of patience & submission under the rod, was well assisted. The parents, young people, were in great distress, the Lord seemed to bless his word to them, as they appeared more calmed & composed afterwards. There was a considerable number present, and all were much affected, the Death of young children is a very trying circumstance to young unexperienced people, and yet a Small, a very Small trial to what they may meet with afterwards. . . .

[91] *Monday August 19:1771* . . . Early in the forenoon went down to the river Side with the boy who carried breakfast for Mr. Donnom & the other Gentlemen who were gone down to direct the Negroes who this morning begun the drain, a very great & laborious work, but will in all probability be of the greatest Service & advantage both to Mr. Jonathan Donnoms Land & mine, and will if it answers as is expected more than double the value of our plantations, returned soon, and rode to Mr. Griffiths, where had agreed to Dine. . . . Dined & spent the afternoon here very agreeably. Had little opportunity of private conversation with the aimiable and excellent Mrs. Griffith, had about three quarters of an hours close conversation with Miss Murry, which ended most agreeably, though we were much interrupted by Mr. Griffith, the continuance of the rain confined us all within doors, & the house being very Small & incommodious, it was Somewhat inconvenient. Had much talk with Miss Murry about her particular concerns, and matters of a very interesting nature. [92] As Mr. Donnom was to be all night at my house, I proposed to go home about Sun down, but as it rained & lightened much, the Ladies, were very anxious I should stay, till after Supper, as it might clear up, which I was very willing to do but at first it appeared not so acceptable to Mr. Griffith as usual, though I had acquainted him with my design in conversing with Miss Murry, as he seemed somewhat reserved, but afterwards

was more free, & turned very facatious & pressed me repeatedly, had prayers before Supper as usual in which was most comfortably enlarged & assisted, it was a pleasant season. Sat a little after supper and was obliged at last to set out in a dark drisling rain. . . . Was in some anxious concern about what had passed & helped to look up to God, to commit all my concerns to him, the Father of Mercies. . . .

[93] *Wednesday August 21:1771* . . . Was myself poorly and sick at my stomach, feverish and very much disordered, yet busy and diligent in getting ready for Charlestown. . . . Was something melancholy and low spirited and most things appeared to me in a dark gloomy light without any particular known cause of distress. This is what I am very rarely subject to, and when it does happen have almost always found that the soul has some kind of secret, unaccountable Sympathy with some distant but approaching trouble, this evening I took a vomit of hermes mercury which I ought to have taken Some time ago, I took about three grains as usual but by the great quantity of bile, & the otherways bad habit of my body, it operated in the most violent manner, so that have not been so worked for many years, was greatly reduced and kept in the greatest distress till about two hours after midnight. . . .

Thursday August 22:1771 . . . About half an hour after Eleven O Clock [94] set out for Charlestown . . . got to Mr. Brandfords on the other side of Ponpon, about six O Clock at night. . . .

Friday August 23:1771 . . . As the weather is most excessively hot, & the roads bad, the whole Country down this way, and the Sea coast under a deluge of water, though appearances are bleak where I live, both the parishes very much burnt up for want of rain, and our crops greatly hurted, was obliged to ride slow, rested about two hours or more in a Jews house at Ashley ferry, chiefly to refresh my horses, the Jew pretending to respect as having known me formerly at Wiltown and yet made me pay at a most extravagant rate for everything I called for. Stopped a little at Mr. Burns as going into Charlestown and did not go till about half an hour after six. . . .

Lords Day August 25:1771 This has been one of the most comfortable Sabbaths I have had for many years . . . [95] Preached in the forenoon from Math: 28:5 with Gods most gracious presence & assistance, delivered the most experimental heart felt truths with life & power, with great fullness & freedom.

Was entirely free of that fearfulness & timid disposition which I am a still liable to when preaching in strange Congregations before such numbers of the polite who in many respects are much my Superiors. The Lord was with me, and gave me an entire command of myself and of my subject. This is reckoned to be one of the richest & most polite Congregations in all America, and reckoned the best Judges of preaching & very Critical. Their very worthy pastor the Reverend Mr. Smith was present & took a particular care in the Evening to declare his approbation.[18] He before his parlytick disorder was reckoned one of the best and at the same time one of the politest preachers that ever was in America. The Congregation was very large & very attentive, all attention. There was great weeping, and the power of God was evidently present with us. As the afternoon service Does not begin here in Summer till four O Clock, I had a long interval, but was helped to improve it well. Was most excessively fatigued with the forenoons service, was about an hour & two or three minutes in the Sermon, but they were all Surprized to find it so short as they have heard so much of my loud & long preaching and were highly pleased, blessed be the Lord God Jehovah for all his goodness. In the afternoon preached from Psl: 48:14 with great comfort & Elevation of soul. The power & glory of God was among us, this though a much deeper Sermon yet was not so popular as the forenoons, though through the goodness of God was highly acceptable & accompanied with gracious influences from on high. As there was a most extraordinary Congregation, not only in the house but the yard & opposite street full of people, as it clouded up & thundered much, I imagined from the darkness that had preached too long, so that stopped some what abruptly after had preached about an hour & twelve or thirteen minutes, after giving an use of information and exhortation to the happy persons who have a Covenant interest in the God of Zion as their God, but omitted the address to them who have no interest in God, which gave me Some concern when I came out and found I had not been so long as I thought. Severals of the congregation observed it and desired me not to straiten myself for time. Was much pressed to preach in the Evening, but declined it, though promised next time I return to preach three times. Was earnestly Solicited to stay till next Sabbath, but gave them Satisfying reasons why I could not, nor return so soon as they desired. Had several invitations to spend the evening abroad but went first to my lodgings and afterwards went with Mr. & Mrs. Mitchell to Mr. Daniel Legares where was a considerable company met, and among others the Reverend Mr. Hugh Allison the Presbyterian [96] Minister of James Island was there.[19] He had dispatched Service at his own meeting house early and come over time enough to hear the afternoon Sermon. I saw him come in during the first prayer. Had some conversation with him about the Presbytery. Afterwards the conversation was more immediately religious and experimental, and more agreeable to the rest of the company. It was a very pleasant & comfortable evening. . . .

Monday August 26:1771 . . . Was all the forenoon busied about various affairs, had Some improving conversation with young Mr. Sct, an attorney at Law,[20] who has a great deal of Sound Orthodox head knowledge, has something very honest and Ingenuous, but is very wild as it is called. Dined with Mr. Ingles, who has a plantation up above my neighborhood. Mr. James Carson, was with us, Mr. Ingles had been much surprized that I did not preach in the Scots Meeting as usual in former years, and thinking it might be owing to some coolness between Mr. Huet & me, about presbyterial affairs, he contrived to have us together, at Dinner, the conversation was all general, had nothing at all about presbytery affairs nor about any of our concerns as Ministers. Spent the afternoon very agreeably, afterwards was about some business, and spent the evening in my lodgings. Should have noticed, that spent an hour or more, this morning in conversation with Mrs. Peronneau, Miss Polly Huttson, that was, & her Sister Miss Hetty,[21] who has for some time been in a very melancholy way, some trouble of mind, but whether a religious concern or not, is not very certain. Was much pleased with Mrs. Peronneaus conversation, she is a person very much like her Mother and I hope is a solid Christian, the circumstances of the women of this Dear family, is most melancholy, Mrs. Hayne, Miss Betsy Huttson, that was, has for some time been greatly disordered in her mind, Mrs. Peronneau was so some years ago, Miss Hetty was in much the same way. It is thought to be a family distemper. On Friday night when I came to Town was informed by report of the Death of my Dear friend and Comerade the Reverend Mr. Richardson, and this day had it confirmed. This has afflicted me much, and in many respects, the loudest call I have ever met with to prepare for the Eternal world, O that I may be found ready and may give up my accounts with joy. His Death is a very great loss, to that part of the Country where he lived. He was a burning and a shining light, and a Star of the first Magnitude, a [97] great Christian, a most Eminent minister of Jesus Christ. He has left a Disconsolate Widow behind but no children. His Death was something remarkable. He was of a strong robust make, & in general healthy, but of a heavy melancholy disposition, subject from his very youth to vapory disorders. His labours for some years were very great, about three or years ago He began to decline, his vapory disorders increased, his Intellects seemed to fail, He turned very Deaf, and lost much of his Spirits & liveliness in preaching, but was still very useful to his own people, about three months ago He turned Sickly, but his people & family thought he fancied himself to be worse, than he was, as he did not keep his bed, and appeared as usual, only kept his house. Sometime in June one of his Elders was visiting him, and in order to Divert him, had entered into some argument with him, in which Mr. Richardson talked with a good deal of Spirit, and afterwards went upstairs to his room, but was to be down to Dinner, as usual. Accordingly when Dinner had waited some time they went upstairs and found him Dead on his knees, one hand holding the back of a Chair and the other lifted up as in prayer, so that he seemed to have expired in the act of devotion, and to all appearance had been dead some time. A most desirable Death indeed, O Lord God let me die the Death of the righteous and let my latter End be like his! Have been much affected with this great loss to the Church of Christ, have this day been particularly melancholy to think I am still in this wilderness of Sin & Sorrow groaning under daily prevailing corruptions and increasing troubles . . . The above is such an account of my Dear Comrades and Reverend Brother Mr. Richardsons Death as I could learn by report, having not received any letter about it.[22]

Tuesday August 27:1771 At the forepart of this day very busy about different concerns. Acquainted Mrs. Holmes of what had passed between Miss Murry & me at Mr. Griffiths & of my fears that Mr. Griffith was against me, & would Serve me as Main had done, she thought otherwise and I went to Some expense though expected nothing but disappointment. Visited Mrs. Strbl who is lying in, at one of her own houses in Charlestown, and has got a fine child, she was much pleased with my short visit, & it was nothing but my duty. Mr. Strbl is up in the Country at the plantation he takes care of. I am told they have some thoughts of leaving the Country altogether, which will be a very considerable loss to [98] me, & the Saltcatcher Congregation. Took a short Dinner with my good friends Mr. and Mrs. Mitchell & was kept so busy, that did not set off till after four O Clock. . . .

Thursday August 29:1771 . . . After Dinner I rode up to Mr. Griffiths where was informed, that he, Mrs. Griffith, & Miss Murry were gone to spend the day at Miss Murrys plantation. This I thought did not look well, as they must

have expected me, and it seemed on purpose to avoid me, however, left word
I would call in the evening. Accordingly I rode up to Mr. Donnoms, from
there to Mr. Hamiltons, and stayed with them till near Dark, then returned
to Mr. Griffith, who received me very Coldly. I saw a storm a gathering. Miss
Murry was in the hall, Mrs. Griffith kept out of sight, I applied myself to
Miss Murry & insisted on an explanation of her change of behaviour, which
she at first refused. I insisted on it, & to have it publicly, as all the family
knowed what had passed. She said Mr. Griffith would give it to me, & went
to him, when he began very rudely, and said Miss Murry had been too pre-
cipitate & had next morning changed her mind, that I had over persuaded
her, and had used him ill in speaking ill of him to her and making observations to his disadvantage, on his conduct in his family. I earnestly applied
myself to her, and asked if she had not promised so and so to me, which she
owned, I then asked if she had changed [99] her mind, & wanted to be off
from her own free voluntary promises, she said yes. I then told her she was
free, absolutely free. She cried very much and Seemed in great agony. I then
applied myself to him, and asked what she had said of me, and what it was
I should have said of him, for I had never used him ill, never spoke ill of him
nor to his disadvantage, that I was ready to appeal to herself in his presence.
His wife, who I hope has the root of the matter in her, came in about this
time, crying and Swimming in tears, she went immediately into the room, I
found Miss Murry had by some means or other told him every advice I gave
her and not only so, but either she or I believe he himself had added innuendos, which I never thought of and which the words would not bear without designedly torturing them, and two most gross falsehoods. I owned all I
had said, and appealed to her if I did not express myself so and so, which she
sobbing and crying owned, and owned also that I spoke well of him and the
whole family connections. He flew in a passion and said she durst not or
could not express herself freely before me. I called upon her again & again to
say nothing but truth. One of the falsehoods, she said she thought I meant
so, but owned I did not say so, it was about her dying Mother, whom I never
saw on her Deathbed, and made it plain to Mr. & Mrs. Griffith that I could
not be understood to say so, as both her & I lamented I had not been with
her Mother when in her last Sickness. As to the other gross lie, when I
repeatedly appealed to her that I neither said nor could have said anything
like it, she made no answer and at last got up and went out, and would not
return though repeatedly Sent for. Mr. Griffith used me, with many very
harsh expressions, and ungenteel threatenings. I answered him with the

utmost Spiritedness, firmness and resolution, yet with calmness, for had a clear breast and a good Conscience, his wife behaved in such a manner, as gave me the highest respect and regard for, and Indeed my greatest concern was about her, lest this should prove such a stumbling block to her, as she might never get over it, and if she should still be desirous of keeping up to her late profession, yet it is a thousand to one if he will allow her to attend on that Gospel by which she has been so greatly Edified, for he would not suffer her to take Doddridges Rise and Progress of religion in the soul, which I had brought up from Charlestown for her, but insisted I should take it away with me, though she once got [100] up and stretched out her hand to take it from me, which He strongly forbid. It has been remarked that he has never been at Meeting since she showed any concern about religion, and now in all probability he will forbid her ever coming there, this was a great trouble to me, that I should be the innocent cause of so great an evil to her. It troubles me much more, than to be put in the mouths of the world, as for Miss Murry, I was pushed upon to make the proposal I did, by the advice of others & particularly encouraged by one who suffers more than I do from the disappointment, and thought she was Serving me, when she encouraged me to it, when I had not the least thought that way. Mr. Griffith once or twice, cast up Main & the disceased Miss Cater to me, which galled me much, yet I bore it with patience, only repeatedly told him, he durst take no such liberties with me, but in his own house, which was unmanly. After much altercation on both sides & Miss Murry refusing to appear, and Mrs. Griffith weeping much, and the Negroes wondering to hear me & their Master so loud, I took my leave, by very heartily wishing that God might bless them all, that is to say Miss Murry, Mr. & Mrs. Griffith, naming each of them expressly and that He might forgive them who had wronged & abused me, and came away. Mrs. Griffith expressed herself with great respect and kindness. Mr. Griffith lighted me with a candle in his hand to the door, and wished me well home. Miss Murry did not appear. As the night was very dark, I rode home leisurely, filled with wonder and amazement at this most surprizing providence. What most of all surprized and astonished me, was the Conduct of Divine providence, in bringing such things in my way, unsought for, unlooked for, undesired and as it were pressing upon me, and then causing such disappointments. Clouds and darkness are round about Jehovah, the footsteps of His infinitely holy & wise providence with respect to me, are in the deep and his goings in the great waters, unsearchable are His Judgments, and his ways past finding out. Who can find out God? Who can by all their searching know the almighty to perfection. His thoughts are very deep, too profound for our short line to fathom, yet He suffers his poor creatures to talk with him of his Judgments, and expects that we consider the operations of his hand, though with the Modesty that becomes creatures, poor beings of yesterday, who know nothing. I have experienced more than once, that God my heavenly Father has dealt with me, in this strange and Surprizing manner, both in Spirituals and temporals, and it has always turned out and Ended greatly to my advantage. My Dear wife now in heaven, was also very sensible of this way of Divine Providence towards us both. I shall mention one of both kinds, with respect to the purchase of Land & a settlement for my family, I had long been anxious about it, and frequently there was put in my way as it were, advantageous bargains as they seemed, and when just in my grasp, something unforeseen fell out to disappoint me, and yet at last, providence in a very unexpected manner, gave me a tract of Land & settlement incomparably more comfortable & advantageous than any or all that [101] I ever thought of, this I call an Instance of a kind providence in a temporal affair. The other is, I had often very advantageous offers to all appearance of removing from Indian Land to great & flourishing Congregations, where there was the greatest prospects of usefulness, while that poor Congregation was daily diminishing by Death and no prospect of there being any people left, & yet still some disappointing providence intervened, and at last in the most unexpected manner my settlement at Saltcatcher took place, where the usefulness of my ministry far exceeded all that could have been hoped for in any old settled congregation whatsoever, and so I am firmly persuaded, if ever it shall please God, that I marry and alter my condition, that it will be in rich mercy and for Gods glory and my good [and] far very far exceed all the prospects I ever had. . . .

Friday August 30:1771 Last night slept very comfortably, and found that a good conscience is a continual feast. Got up in a humble frame of soul, Sensible of my weakness & imperfections, of my blindness, ignorance, propensity to evil and absolute unfitness to guide and conduct myself. Was still full of wonder and amazement. Was melancholy & distressed to think of being put again so undeservedly in the mouths of the profane, to be at the mercy as it were of a most worthless fellow and one of no capacity yet a designing crafty subtle [sic], of being perhaps the most innocent cause of the misery of a very worthy excellent young Lady, I mean his wife Mrs. Griffith, who was never thought to be happy in him but the contrary, & will be more so now, and of being more than probably a great hurt to another not undeserving young Lady were she in safe hands, these and a thousand other melancholy thoughts crowded upon me, yet as know Idleness to be a great Enemy got up rather early and after morning duties in the family and in the closet, was engaged in preparing for Sabbath. Afterwards rode down to the new drain where was informed Mr. Donnom was with my Overseer, among my other troubles & disappointments since I returned from Charlestown, where the Lord gave me so great fair with his people, I find that the drain a most laborious piece of work does not answer, without a great deal of more work both on the old one and for a mile and a half to make a new one, however am convinced that the Gentlemen who direct the work, have my Interest [102] at heart, and they are enlarging the first, & making one from another place to join it. After had been about an hour there acquainted my good friend Mr. Donnom with my ill treatment. He told me, He had his fears about it from Griffiths general Character, & particularly from his altering his behaviour to me, that afternoon, when he saw I was on such good terms with Miss Murry, and that he was persuaded, that whatever change was in her, she was brought to it, by Griffiths persuasions, and that the saying I had spoke against him, was chiefly contrived by himself, by putting other constructions upon the hints & advices I had given her than I ever intended, or she at first understood, but having by her Simplicity having let him know them from her, he now put his own Sense on them to have some excuse for breaking with me, and keeping me at a Distance from his wife, as well as from Miss Murry whom he most certainly designs for Some relation of his own, which has been talked of, or designs to keep the management of her fortune, longer in his hands. These were just my own Sentiments and what I am persuaded is the case. My friend then encouraged me, against my fears & melancholy apprehensions from the talk that may be made about it, and as for Mrs. Griffith in whom there is such hopeful appearances of a good work begun, if it is really such, God would undoubtedly find means of carrying it on. . . .

Saturday 31 1771 This morning when reflecting on my bed, on the dark steps of providence through which I have passed, & putting up ejaculations, that the Lord would show me, why He contendeth with me, the particular grounds of His controversy, and enable me by his grace to improve by all his dealings with me, it pleased the Lord in infinite goodness, to shine in upon my soul, and showed me very particularly my great need of such a disappointment & of such a humbling providence, as this may turn out to be, in some heart evils that were again beginning to prevail, notwithstanding the blow they had got by some such former providence, as an inordinate desire to be placed in Independent Circumstances beyond what I am at present. Worldly mindedness has never been my particular failing, nor usual predominate but rather, a carelessness and neglect of my worldly concerns and interest, but the temptation which has very Secretly & too much prevailed to the producing of this evil in my carnal unrenewed mind, of late years, has been a persuasion that the more Independent I was, & the less I required from people for the Support of myself & family as a minister, the more acceptable my ministry was to them. This I know and have experienced to be in a great measure very true, but Satan & my own wicked heart, has pushed it too far, so that it has become a snare to me. It is true the easier I have been in my circumstances, the more abundant I have been in labours and ministerial work, as is evident to all and often acknowledged by my greatest Enemies. Yet perhaps was my condition in life absolutely independent or rich & affluent then my conduct might be otherways. Spiritual pride, because of my gifts, popularity, unceasing labors & usefulness is undoubtedly another cause, of the Lords exercising me, with this mortifying providence. My being much in publick duties, & my great fatigues, has caused [103] too much carelessness about, neglect of & formality in Secret duties as a Christian, these & several other evils the Lord discovered to my soul with such a sweet convincing influence, as deeply humbled me before him, filled me with wonder, love, & gratitude for his wonderful mercy & goodness, in bearing with such a creature & taking so much pains with such a repeated backslider, was melted into penitence, love & praise, right for prayer & adoration & got Sweet access to God. . . .

Lords Day first day of September 1771 . . . After service went home with Mr. Henry DeSaussure, and had a very pleasant evening in conference & prayer with these I hope truly religious young people, was much pleased, with their great seriousness, their sober, retired Christian life, and also to find that the Lord so blesses them in their temporal Interest, the Season having suited them, & their little crop of Corn & Indigo likely to turn out much better than was expected in the Spring of the year. The Seasons, this Summer, are very unequal, Some parts of the Country have continued to be deluged with rain, other parts very much burnt up for want of rain, as the Indian Land in general, my plantation and some others in my neighbourhood, the Lords will be done. I rejoice to see any of my Dear people thriving, whatever the Lord should do with me, and indeed I have great cause to bless and praise his holy name for his great & Singular goodness to me in providing so richly and bountifully for me & mine. . . .

[105] *Wednesday September 4:1771* This morning able to be up early. Employed in writting & study for Sabbath, have at this time many writtings to do, & among others, am to send down to a Lady in Charlestown, a Copy of the sermon I preached there on the Sabbath forenoon. Her case, was something very extraordinary. Mrs. Scott, wife of Captain John Scott, in rich & plentiful circumstances, his children married, has all or the greatest part of her life, been a very Serious professor of religion, I believe a real but melancholy Christian. She has for these some years, been in great darkness, full of fears & doubts, which had increased so, as to render her almost incapable of her family affairs, and was worn to a mere Skeleton, was often on the borders of Despair, and often giving over all duty & again applying to them, Sometime ago she seemed to have some comfort from some promises when reading the Bible & also brought into her mind at prayer of an approaching deliverance, her husband a good worthy Gentleman & her family knew her great distress, her intimate acquaintance suspected it was at a great height, and dreaded the Consequence to all this, as well as to herself. I was an entire stranger, only I had known her by Sight, & in former years had spoken to her but not these several years that I remember. It seems the Lord directed the forenoon sermon, to be the means of her comfort & deliverance, in a very glorious and wonderful manner. I observed her during the Sermon to weep most excessively, as many others did, I saw her husband, often to look at me in such a manner that surprized me, Sometimes he seemed to frown, I took notice of it while preaching. After the evening sermon, she spoke to me & begged me to call on her before I left Town, & told me where they lived, I promised to do so. On Monday she sent me a note, to the place where I dined & late in the afternoon I waited on her, when with many tears she told me her case & wonderful deliverance. Her husband observed her, to be greatly affected & to retire, as soon as she came home, but knew not how it was, yet his concern was so great, that he desired her company for a few minutes, and immediately asked her, if she had not wrote to me, nor sent me any message, she assured him, that she never had, upon which he asked her, if she did not think it was from the Lord, & that if she did not receive it as such it would certainly [106] be exceedingly Sinful to give way to Satan any longer, when all her fears & doubts were so exactly & fully spoken to & her

exercise for so many years laid all open at once. She then told him with tears of joy, what great things the Lord had done for her, so that they wept & praised the Lord together. Her very children took notice of the change, one of her Sons a very serious youth mentioned the Sermon to her, another of them the young Lawyer whom I was with on Monday forenoon at Mrs. Holmes was also at the meeting but not in her Sight. He had heard my voice was so loud, that he sat out of doors. In about an hour after the forenoons sermon, he wrote the heads of the sermon and sent them to his Mother. All this account, much larger than I have time to write, I heard with humble wonder & praise, and thanksgiving. She begged me for a Copy of the sermon as soon as I could. I promised to send it her, then gave her several suitable advices, as to put the Crown on Christs head, and give God alone the glory, to continue humble watchful & thankful, to lay her account [to] returns of Clouds more or less and to be earnest in prayer for me, and took my leave, but alas my troubles, concerns & hurry since I returned home put it almost out of my power to make good my promise. . . . Was busily employed in study and writting when two Gentlemen Mr. Archibald Calder & young Mr. John Cuthbert, came to Dine with me, after Dinner they sat about an hour & a half & desired me to ride a part of the way with them to Mr. Jonathan Wilkins, where they were to sleep, which I agreed to do, and continued riding with them till we got there, found both Mr. & Mrs. Wilkins bad with fevers, he has been sick for some time, sat about an hour & drank tea with them, and there being a good deal of company, though I was much pressed, yet I chose to return though just dusk when I left them, rode slow as it was very dark and did not get home till about Nine O Clock. Found a heavy dew & the night more damp than I expected. Mr. Calder is a very friendly young Gentleman of influence & fortune, and never was here before so that I could not well avoid this ride, yet would have much rather been at home. . . .

[108] *Tuesday September 10* . . . [109] Late in the afternoon got a letter from Mr. Donnom about some affairs of importance, in our temporal concerns, & acquainting me, that an old acquaintance was at his house who would be glad to see me, accordingly rode up in the Evening & spent the night there with Mr. Donnom, & old Mr. John Cuthbert, who is a general Director to many Gentlemen through the province about Indigo planting, which turns out to the greatest advantage of anything ever cultivated in this part of the world, and as I have a great quantity of Land, down upon the river Side, of

the most excellent quality for it, my friend was projecting to make Some preparation for planting Indigo as well as Rice for another year. Spent the evening agreeably in useful conversation but still feverish. . . .

Wednesday September 11:1771 . . . After breakfast & prayers Mr. Cuthbert & his Son, went over to Mr. Donnoms place, where Mr. H now lives, to be present at the boiling a vat of indigo. Mr. Donnom came down with me, to look at my old field lands upon the riverside, when we got to my house, & he had sent for some of the Negroes to go & lay out some part of it, for being immediately turned up, he asked me, to ride down with him. I told him I could not do it as being very busy & but poorly, yet he again & again repeated his request, and I consented to go, for I could not refuse it, as he is so great a friend to me, in my temporal affairs, and puts himself to so much trouble & fatigue on my account, yet I was very desirous to be alone. Accordingly we rode down to the old field which he was very much taken with, and laid out part of it. Afterwards rode up the riverside, & turned off to the drain, going up all the way to the place, where it is cut into Black Creek. I would just mention it here, that the drain answers and will be of the greatest value and advantage to my plantation, also to Mr. Jonathan Donnoms, who is above mine, & at old Mr. Jefferys plantation who is above his, & through a part of whose land Black Creek runs, the water is now running plentifully into all our fields, which will be of great advantage to us, if it please God that the cold weather keeps off a few weeks, though a great deal of our rice is already past recovery, and our present crops will be very short, the Lords holy will be done, blessed be his holy name for his goodness to most unworthy me [110] & mine in the two last years, especially the kindness of providence last year was remarkable for what Mrs. Holmes & I made has sold at a very great price. From the head of the drain Mr. Donnom and I rode home, about three O Clock, we had been out upwards of four hours. I was exceedingly Indisposed all the time. We found Mr. Cuthbert & his son, at my house, waiting for us to dine, I sat down with the company, but could not eat any excepting a little broth, after about two hours found myself something refreshed with resting. Mr. Donnom went home, and when I expected Mr. Cuthbert & his Son were going over the river the old Gentleman expressed his inclination to stay all night, this quite disconcerted me, as I intended to have gone directly to bed, but I could not do less, than invite him to stay, with the Son the same who was here lately with Mr. Calder, old Mr. Cuthbert well knew that he deserved no entertainment from me for many

particular reasons which may be seen in different parts of my Diary of former
years, as well as for his general behaviour to me, when he used to be about
the Indian Land, but for these very reasons I thought myself obliged not only
to invite him to stay all night but to exert myself through the whole evening,
that he might not think I received him coolly or showed any resentment. As
he expressed great desire to see more of the land, than can be seen from the
hill where the house stands, and as perhaps my friend Dr. Cuthbert on Port
Royal, with whom he at present lives, had desired him to see what sort of a
plantation I had got, I carried him over to the plantation, showed him the
barn, the Machine house, & all the buildings there, through the Cornfield
& part of the rice field, with all which, he either really was, or pretended to
be exceedingly much taken, through the evening I entertained him in the
handsomest manner I could, and after Supper and prayers we retired. . . .

Thursday September 12:1771 . . . I stopped at Mrs. Clarks, one McDougal a
tradesman who works about, and generally pretends a respect for me, as being his Countryman, [111] he desired to speak with me alone, and though
my fever was increased and was very hot, yet I walked out into the woods
with him, when he told me that he had been at Griffiths who abused me in
the most violent manner, telling him all the abominable lies and falsehoods
with which he had charged me, in presence of his wife & the poor betrayed
Miss Murry who said nothing. This did not surprize me much as I had
expected to hear of it before now, and wondered I had not considering Griffiths great enmity to the gospel even when he carried it fair to me. Yet it gave
me concern, as it affords a fresh triumph to the wicked and to my most cruel
and inveterate Enemies. I told McDougal the truth of the matter & easily
let him see the baseness & falsehood of the Innuendos Griffith had put into
Miss Murrys mouth, and left him to guess his End and design in doing so,
which was very easy to be done. McDougal expressed his Satisfaction with
the account I gave him and his concern for me, yet paid little regard to what
he said as he is a poor drunken creature for which I am often obliged to reprove & frown upon him but he is generally very acceptable to Griffith. . . .

[112] *Lords Day October 13 1771* At my good, my worthy and very kind friends
old Mrs. Hatchers. It is utterly impossible for me to give any account of
the sore and grievous distress I have undergone, since the last time I wrote
in this my Diary[23] . . . [115] On Sabbath 29 had some company from the Indian Land a poor Negro wench (Simons Priscilla) who is I believe a serious

experienced Christian of many years standing before I was in this province, that when she reportedly heard I was given over and was very earnest in prayer for my life as many of the poor praying Negroes were, that the Lord comforted her with that Scripture which for some days, was much carried up on her mind John:11:4, this Sickness is not unto Death, but for the glory of God. Was pleased to see her care & concern about the Gospel being continued, & that she had such a spiritual understanding. The poor [116] slaves in these two parishes will arise & take the kingdom of heaven when many very many of their masters will be shut out of it, Mr. Murry from the other side of the River, spent a good part of the day with me, and gave me a large account of the abuses, calumnies & reproaches that Griffith & his friends are throwing upon me, how active & busy my old Enemy Main & the unhappy Mrs. Ferguson & others are in doing me all the mischief they can, and of the great advantage they have all taken of my Sickness, and unability to speak for myself, this I partly expected & so was in some measure prepared for it, yet I did not think that so many at the Indian Land who made some show of friendship, were so false & base, as this affair has discovered them to be, and were really waiting for my halting, and so ready to rejoice when they thought they had got something against me. It is true there are very few of the old Settlers, or their Children left at Indian Land, and there are a great many new settlers from different parts of the Country, the most of whom are very wicked and profane, yet as they generally showed me a good deal of respect, and sometimes came to publick worship where they behaved with Decency, I could not have expected such insults and abuse from them or that they would made me their Song over their cups & laughing stock at their hunting & racing clubs, yet so it has been, while those who professed themselves my friends would either smile or joined in the ridicule. These aspersions & abuses though false as hell, are a trouble & cross to me so far as they cause the name of the Lord Jesus Christ to be blasphemed, and greatly would I rejoice to be kept from or delivered from such crosses, yet blessed forever blessed be God who enables me to bear these things with a Christian temper & disposition, who enables me to pray for my slanderers, and abusers, and most conscientiously to abstain from saying many things which I could with great truth to their hurt & disadvantage. These things help to keep me humble amidst great popularity and great applauses I sometimes meet with. I believe God will in time wipe them off, and that thereby I shall be made more cautious & watchful & more diligent in seeking wisdom from above to cut off occasion from some who spitefully seek it . . . [117] Was very much concerned about future usefulness, and had many thoughts of making a visit to Scotland, where perhaps my days of usefulness will be lengthened out beyond what they can probably be in this land. My work seemed to be ended at Indian Land and my affections were much weaned from them. Began to think that I opposed the will of providence in so obstinately staying at that place when there were so few serious people left in it. On Wednesday October 2, I heard that Mr. Griffiths child, their only child, was dangerously ill and [118] having still some reason to have a regard & concern for the Mother, I sent a boy on Thursday the 3 day to inquire how the child was. He himself spoke to the boy & sent me a civil message, that the child was extremely ill. On the 4 day I heard the child was rather better but still in danger, on Saturday 5 I sent again to inquire for the child when he sent back a very insulting abusive message, that it was brave, & I was told he abused me very much before severals of his friends and Creatures. His wife said nothing but one of his aunts, Mrs. M, told the boy the child was in a hopeful way. Mrs. Shaw the other aunt was also at breakfast but said nothing, though I am told they both rail against me, though him & them had lately great differences, I resolved to send no more, but Continued to pray for the poor Infant & also for my Enemies. On Sabbath 6 had a visit from my good friend Mr. Donnom, who spent the afternoon with me, as it was fair and the weather moderate, we rode out together, I inquired at him about the abuse Griffith was so basely and undeservedly casting upon me, and the Countenance he had met with, Mr. Donnom confirmed all I had been told this day week & more, that Patterson, the School Master, who lives at Mr. McTiers, had carried Griffiths lies & falsehoods from Mr. McTiers to Main, who immediately spread them all about with many additions of his own, that Main had Sent all his letters & papers of lies to McTiers & did all he could to spirit up Griffith to abuse & reproach me, that Charles Brown a pretended friend to me, had been very active in spreading it both in Town & Country, that the hunting Club at Indian Land, had used me most vilely, that Mr. Hamilton in this neighbourhood & Mr. David Ferguson, seemed to join with Griffith, and acted as if at last they wished all his lies were true & that they were really my Enemies, that notwithstanding all the abuse, Insults and opposition made against me and the glorious work in my hand, I had still many friends, that it was plain to the truly good and religious, that it was wholly owing to my faithfulness in the Gospel, that I had so many Enemies, for the corruptions of Main could not bear such close searching preaching, and that I had no reason to be discouraged, I told him, how much my heart was weaned from

Indian Land, and how glad I would be to be loosed from all connection with the place, how strongly I was impressed to go home, & acquainted him what great prospect I had of acceptableness and usefulness, I had from the many Invitations [119] I had received. He insisted much on my not thinking of any such thing, and that I ought by no means to yield to Satan, and entreated me to take no step that way till I waited some months & observed what providence should bring out of this very dark & trying affair, which I agreed to, I also agreed to clear myself by giving a true account of the affair to all or any who should desire it, but never to mention or take any notice of it at any other time. . . . On Monday the 6 instant about Eleven O Clock I set out in my chair for Mrs. Hatchers, proceeded very slowly, being exceedingly weak, called at Mrs. Graves to whom my first visit, was most justly due, she having not only visited me in my Sickness & often sent to inquire after me, but showed very great concern, found her bad with a fever, which she has had for Some days, & in bed. Sat about an hour with her in Serious, improving conversation, though could not speak much through weakness, which was the case with her. After sitting about an hour & being refreshed, proceeded & called at Mrs. Williamsons, whose behaviour during my Sickness did not deserve it, but heard that one of Mrs. Dixons children was very sick there, found that Child better. Mrs. Williamson made some excuses for herself, saying her children had been sick & she did not know that the bridge was passable, was Informed here, that the Reverend Mr. Ellington, who is a very indifferent friend to any Dissenting Minister, was to preach at the church here on Sabbath See night the 20th Instant, which made me alter my resolve to not preach in Indian Land meeting that same day, for as both places have been so long without publick worship, thought it a pity that we should be both in one place at the same time, and especially on that Side of the river, where both auditories are so very small, therefore resolved to preach on that day at Saltcatcher, gave notice accordingly. After sitting about half an hour I again set out, & did not get to my worthy friends till after Sun down. Was received with the greatest kindness & tenderness, as a Son by a Mother and as one restored from the dead . . . [120] On Tuesday October 8 my Dear friend Mrs. Hatcher, let me know her concern because of the new abuse cast upon me, & the ungenerous conduct of severals at Indian Land, who pretended a regard for me. This led me, in the afternoon when the family were altogether, to give her a true & exact account of the whole matter, which to unprejudiced minds carried its own evidence along with it, and convinced all present of my absolute innocence, & filled them with wonder at

the malice of my Enemies as well as their horrid wickedness, in endeavouring to ruin a Gospel interest. My good friend was with me filled with wonder, at the permission of Divine providence and that such an affair was so
strangely brought in my way, she spoke much to comfort & encourage me,
repeatedly acknowledged that I had great reason to be disgusted with Indian
Land, but earnestly entreated me, not to leave the Country, but rather to
extend my pastoral care to Port Royal & also to preach sometimes on St.
Helena, and acquainted me with what she herself could do to promote such
a matter, & used many arguments to persuade me to think of residing a
good part of my time on the Salts and by no means to leave these parts. I
promised her as I had done to Mr. Donnom, to Mr. Strain & others, that I
would observe the conduct of providence & if I lived till the Spring, I would
determine according to the light I then should have. . . . Had a very distressed night after went to bed, a very high fever, my head much affected,
great pains in my back & loins, lay all night in the most violent sweats, and
was very melancholy through the night and strongly resolved if I recovered
any strength to go off in the Spring either to the Northward provinces or to
Scotland. . . .

[123] *Wednesday October 16* This morning I set out for home, being resolved
to venture to the pulpit once more, and through the Divine help to preach at
least once on Sabbath next at Saltcatcher. My Dear good friend Mrs. Hatcher
had said much to persuade me, not to continue, but I was convinced it was
my duty and my heart was set upon it, and she could not prevail, accompanied me with many prayers that I might be strengthened & spared for a
blessing. Her kindness to me, has been such as I think and hope I can never
forget, she not only took the most tender care of my weak sickly body, but
made it her study to comfort & encourage my troubled mind. H has been
a most kind & affectionate mother to me. Last night after earnest entreaties
I would not think of leaving the Country, that I would be more careful, sparing and indulgent of myself, that I would preach oftener at Port Royal and
spend more time with her, she made me a handsome present, & this morning filled my Chair with everything she thought would be acceptable & useful to me. After expressing my grateful acknowledgments & fervent prayers
with this Dear family, I took an affectionate leave, & proceeded very slowly,
being still exceeding weak and poorly. Called at Mrs. Prscts, sat about three
quarters of an hour with her discoursing mostly of Dr. Green, lately deceased,
who lived with her and has left her Executrix & sole heir to all he was worth,

thought to be about Six or Seven thousand pounds Currency, it looks dark, God only knows [124] how things have been, He alone knows the Secrets of all hearts. . . .

Monday October 21:1771 This morning in Something a lively, more cheerful yet Serious frame of mind. Was helped to bless & praise the Lord for his goodness & mercy to me yesterday in his house of prayer, rode up to Mr. Donnoms, Spent the forenoon with him & Mr. Lambert in Serious conversation, contriving for the good of this neighbourhood, if they will [125] permit us to serve & assist them. Mr. Lambert has some thoughts of purchasing a Small place amongst us chiefly with a view to strengthen Mr. Donnoms hands and mine in Carrying on a Gospel Interest. . . .

[126] *Lords Day 27 1771* This morning in something of a Sabbaths frame . . . Rode over to my once much beloved Indian Land full of concern and many anxious thoughts. . . . After service married a Couple at a small tavern, not far from the Meeting house. Met with much kindness & respect from all ranks among my auditory, who expressed great Satisfaction at seeing me once more in that place. Was detained near half an hour after Sermon by the kind enquiries of my hearers. Just when I came out, I was invited to Dine at Dr. Bowmans, but refused it, thinking to have gone somewhere else, but after being detained for so long I sent my boy to let him know, I would, which I did after marrying the people, found some company, I did not at all expect or would not have gone there, Dr. Bowman, has behaved very ungratefully to me who had the chief hand in Setting him up in that place, by his base Conduct to me, in this late affair, resolved that this should be the last time of my calling on him, except when business required it, could not avoid some conversation with one whom I know is my avowed Enemy and I knew would be ready to take every advantage. . . .

[127] *Monday October 28:1771* . . . In the forenoon rode to Mr. Job McPhersons where my friend Mr. Postell also came, all very hearty friends. In the afternoon rode to Mr. Russels, was stopped by Charles Brown at his door, who insisted on my lighting & coming in, which on Mr. Postells account, who had Some business I did, & drank a glass of wine, though knew that Mr. Brown has acted very basely by me in this late affair & very industriously published about, what he thought might render me ridiculous and be hurtful to me, though he himself did not believe it, or that I was capable of

any such unworthy conduct. Was about ten minutes here, spent about two hours at Mr. Russels & drank tea, afterwards visited Mrs. Devaux who has been very ill and is getting better. Then went to Mrs. G, where spent the night. She has been very kind during my Sickness, and acted with the utmost friendship, during this matter of Calumny & abuse, and so has Mrs. Devaux, told the whole affair to them, and spent the evening very agreeable till very late in serious improving conversation, upon past providences which we had all been witnesses of & also experienced.

Tuesday 29 . . . Just as I was setting off my Reverend Dear Brother Mr. Zubly called to stay all night, in his way home. He has been sick in Charlestown, but is better. After a little refreshment, I got my chair, & He went up with me to Mr. Donnoms, whom we found very poorly indeed, Spent the night here in Serious useful [128] conversation.

Wednesday October 30:1771 . . . Mr. Zubly returned to my house, after a bit of early Dinner with me, and set off for home. I rode over to Pocatiligo with him. He took no notice whether he had heard of my late troubles and abuses but related many of his own to me, & some very late ones, his troubles, abuses and opposition from the world, has been great, exceeding great, and much oftener repeated than mine has yet been. Was much comforted & refreshed by his conversation as I knew, that he had heard of my base use, and gross abuse, of the vile Calumnies and reproaches cast on me. I took this way of encouraging me, exceeding kindly. . . .

[129] *Monday November 4 1771.* Slept but little last night, got up early, as found the bed uncomfortable. We had a very sharp froast, the first that has been this year, which has been one of the most favourable harvests that could be wished for, a great deal of late rice has been brought to maturity, and with respect to the fruits of the Earth, the Lord has dealt most mercifully with the Land in general, though otherwise his Judgments have been many in the great sickness & many Deaths especially of Ministers. O to be humble and thankful and to have my life so wonderfully spared, wholly employed for God. . . .

Tuesday November 5 . . . Mr. Lambert my old pious friend has bought the place where Mr. Roberts lived about two miles from me, and is soon to come and live there. . . . Rode to Mr. Jonathan Wilkins, was very kindly received both by him, & my old Intimate . . . [130] After dinner Mrs. Wilkins, who has acted & continues to act a most friendly part towards me in this troublesome affair, introduced Some confusion about it which gave me an opportunity to give them a fair & true account of it, which they were much pleased with, and expressed great friendship, & hearty good will. My old Intimate expressed the tender affection and concern for me, stayed with them, till Dusk, when rode over to Mr. Dunlaps, where spent the night, in conversing about & narrating the same affair, to Mr. & Mrs. Dunlap & her Sister Miss Polly F, than whom, have no heartier friends. They expressed great satisfaction, and repeatedly declared their Esteem & regard to be heightened & increased, by the courage and resolution the Lord helped me still to show in the work & Service of the Gospel. . . .

[131] *Thursday November 7.* . . . Prepared to study & write for Sabbath, when was informed that one of the plantation Negroes who belongs to Mr. J D & had been lent out to work at a Neighbours, had fallen off a tar kiln & was thought to be almost killed. The Overseer rode immediately & bled him, Sent some Furlington to give him Inwardly & followed as soon after as I could, he was about two mile off, found badly hurt but not so dangerous as was afraid of, Sent for the Doctor & had him examined, one of his ribs are broke & another much bruised, shattered & drove inwards so that his case may be very dangerous if a fever follows. This confused me for some time, & soon after my return home I met with an accidental stroke with the Small End of a horse whip in my own hand on my right eye, which cut quite across the eye but very providentially missed the Sight, though the Small veins, in the white of the eye were so cut, as made the blood pour [132] down my face & gave me great pain, yea the most exquisite pain. I concluded for Some time, that I had lost my eye, but in about ten minutes I took Courage & examined it before a Glass, and found although it was badly hurt, & might be of dangerous consequence, yet there was no immediate danger, had it bathed & washed with warm milk & water, and bound up, it continued to bleed from the white of the eye for some time. . . .

Friday November 8:1771. Found great relief last night from the white of an egg beat up to a very fine froath, applied to my eye, and repeatedly keeping my head dipped under cold water, which greatly allayed the pain & inflammation, & entirely stopped the bleeding, while continued long still to weep from it. Was in a very humble, thankful, admiring frame of soul. . . .

[133] *Lords Day November 10:1771* . . . After service which was late by the peoples being late of coming in the forenoon, a very cold frosty morning, I was
detained for some time, by Elias Roberts and his Sister [134] in law, the wife
of Peter Robert, bred an Anabaptist. She was lately dipped by Mr. Pelote,
who is putting books among several of this people to turn them that way.
The Roberts family were for several years in this place very irreligious, about
two years ago there appeared a great change among them, when they were
mostly admitted to the Lords table. They have for some months been swerv-
ing towards some erroneous notions about the Trinity & especially this Elias
has showed a desire to exhort & take preaching on him, which has naturally
led both him & Peter, to incline towards the Anabaptists or Baptists as they
call themselves, who are a Sect that encourage lay preaching. Was detained for
Some time talking with them, which afterwards I was sorry to have yielded
unto, as found them both very ignorant of the grounds of the Controversy
and very uncapable of reasoning about it, and her I thought very ignorant
of more important matters. . . .

[136] *Friday November 15* . . . Got up early, and prepared to set off for Beaufort & Port Royal where am to preach next Sabbath, if the Lord shall enable.
. . . Just as I got out from my plantation, I came up with Miss Sally Murry
alone in a chair and a Negro boy riding before her, she had Seen me first,
and attempted to get off, so as not to be seen by me, for I was Surprized to
see a Lady in a Chair alone, and the horse drove at a Gallop, and thinking
some accident had happened I rode up after the chair not knowing who it
was. When I came up so as to perceive who it was, she pulled her hat over
her face, while I passed and seemed as much as I could observe to be in the
utmost confusion. I galloped along without taking the least notice of her,
not so much as moving my hat or putting my hand to my head. Just as I
passed her I came up with my Neighbour Mr. Forster riding the Same way,
and kept him company till we got near the Bridge, where He turned into the
Blacksmiths. I have reason for being so particular in mentioning this affair,
was glad to meet or overtake Mr. Forster, as it [137] relieved me from a multitude of affecting thoughts that were crowding in upon me, poor creature,
she might well endeavour to avoid the Sight of me whom she has so basely
betrayed, and that in the grossest manner. No wonder, she was ashamed &
confounded, but poor creature, unhappy immortal, she must meet me where
there will be no covering, no hiding her face, no flying from her Eternal Judge
and mine. . . .

[140] *Thursday November 21 1771* . . . Got up in a very humble Spiritual watchful frame of Spirit, for was this day to venture into Company I had never been used with, to Dine at the Hunting club, which I had promised to do Several months ago, if they would change it from Saturday, to any other day in the week. They fixed upon Thursday in compliance to my request, and engaged me to Dine sometimes with them. They some time ago used me very unhandsomely about my late affair, but most of them made great concessions and acknowledgments Since, and as my good friend Mr. Postell was to fund the dinner, I chose the day when proceeded to Dine with them. Mr. Postell went soon after breakfast, I spent the forenoon at his house and went there at twelve O Clock. There were twelve Gentlemen present, who behaved with great decency and much respect (my good friend Mr. Job McPherson was a little too free). I dined & stayed till three O Clock. They expressed great Satisfaction, and gave me no reason to be in the least uneasy. . . . [141] When got home met with some trying circumstances, where I expected no temptation, a fellow in whom I had put great confidence had been complaining, I suspected something bad, and sent him this morning to the Doctor who wrote me he was infected with a vile disease and very bad with it. This obliged me to talk to him very sharply and to threaten him with severity. Soon after two runaways, one belonging to the Indian Land Congregation & one of Mrs. Holmes who have been out about two months came here. After talking to them delivered them up to the Overseer for some correction but very moderately. At the same time, had several strangers come for lodging, a Lady belonging to Georgia, who had known me when at Altamaha some years ago, and a white man waiting upon her, the Reverend Mr. Zublys two sons young men, and my friend Mr. Lambert, all which confused me somewhat, and prevented my Spending the Evening and night as I desired. Every finished room was full and had Mr. Lambert sleep with myself, was in a confused carnal disposition and vanity in various shapes prevailed in my foolish, desperately wicked & deceitful heart. . . .

[142] *Lords day November 24:1771* . . . [143] After Service received Some letters from my good friend Mr. James Donnom present in Charlestown, about my preaching and giving the Sacrament of the Lords Supper there next Sabbath, which gave me much concern, as doubting for Several reasons whether it was proper for me at this time to join with that Congregation in giving them that holy ordinance, as it might give offense unto and Stir me up more Enemies in the Scots Congregation, whose minister is far from being friendly

to me, besides my Enemies & opposers are abusing me much, about my late trouble and abuse from Griffith, that it might be more prudent only to preach and as that is their Sacrament day, to put off my going down a Sabbath longer. Was much perplexed about this affair, and consulted with my friend Mr. Lambert, who was much for my going down, according to my first appointment, and to embrace the opportunity of being useful without any regard to the hints above, upon the whole as I understood they had some dependence on me and I had no opportunity to inform them of the Contrary, I was inclined to go down, and to be employed as the Congregation shall see fit, as I knew nothing of its being their Sacrament when I [144] proposed to preach to them on the first Sabbath of December, so that no just exception could be taken against me, by the Presbyterians for Serving the Independent Congregation accidentally on such a solemn occasion. Mr. Donnom also Informed me of the Death of the Reverend Mr. Maltby who died in New England his native land where He had gone for his health, the Reverend Mr. Thomas is also dead in the city of New York since he went off, both very gracious men and worthy Ministers of Christ. Continued through this evening in a humble thankful heavenly frame of mind, my heart & affections with God.

Monday November 25 1771 . . . About half an hour before Sun down I rode over to Mrs. Perrys, to call upon her and her Sister Mrs. Postell from the Indian Land, was repeatedly asked to stay Supper, which did. Our conversation was Serious and improving, after Supper gave prayers, and rode home with good moon light, in a humble thankful frame of mind blessing God. I have yet Some real friends, of every station of life, perhaps no man living, for the number of Inhabitants in this and some of the Neighbouring provinces, has more friends, and Enemies, than what I have. May the Lord be my Everlasting friend. . . .

[146] *Friday November 29:1771* . . . Proceeded for Charlestown. As was most part of the way alone, had the most pleasant Meditations on the glory and excellency of the Lord Jesus Christ, was helped to pour out my soul to God, in the most earnest Supplications, praise and adoration, So that this was one of the most comfortable Seasons, I have for Some years enjoyed on horseback . . .[147] Did not get to Town, till two hours or more after Dark, which made it very dangerous riding, as the night was cloudy, & neither moon, nor star light . . . Learned that as I had not come down early in the week, that

no Sermon was expected, but that it would be necessary to consult with good old Mr. Smith, whose infirmities in a great measure have laid him aside from Sanctuary work. Learned also that the people expressed great uneasiness & concern lest I should not be down to preach to them at all, and that the Congregation continued very desirous of my poor, weak, worthless labours, for which was helped to be humbly thankful to the Lord my God, and earnest, very earnest, for his grace & Spirit, to be faithful, acceptable and Successful.

Saturday November 30:1771 . . . Soon after breakfast, I went to the Reverend Mr. Smiths, & with some difficulty His son and I prevailed with him, to consent that the Lords supper should be omitted tomorrow as there had been no preparation Sermon through the week & no notice given last Sabbath, so that the people did not expect it, and besides that there was so great an appearance of bad weather, that there was great reason to expect few people out, the old Gentleman at last consented upon condition I would engage to come down on the next Sacrament day, the first Sabbath of February, and administer the ordinance among them, to which I agreed if in the mean time the Minister whom they have sent for to Pennsylvania, to settle among them, did not come in. . . . 24

[148] *Lords day first day of December 1771* . . . Preached in the forenoon from Heb: 12:5, and in the afternoon from Psl 27:13 to large, full and very attentive auditories, Some of whom were much affected, and in many tears, the power and blessing of God, seemed evidently to attend us. . . . Spent the Evening at Mr. Daniel Legares a good religious family, in Serious, and Spiritual conversation, was well assisted in family prayer, though hoarse and much affected with the cold. Mr. Mitchell, spent the evening here also. . . .

Monday December 2:1771 . . . Was most of this day busy about my temporal affairs, and concerns, In the forenoon, visited good, pious [149] Mrs. S, who was greatly affected with the yesterdays discourses, both parts of the day, to whom I hope the Lord has blessed them, & also to several others, that heard of. Had some very experimental discourse with her, she appears to be a deeply exercised Christian, much in the dark for the most part. Dined together with Mr. Legare with the Reverend Mr. Smith, who lives with his Son, a very pious worthy Gentleman, a Merchant in this place, rich and thriving, has a fine family of Children and is exceedingly dutiful, to his worthy Father. The good old Gentleman received me as a Son, with great kindness and respect, but could not have much conversation with him, as I could not understand him, by reason of his Infirmity, his speech being greatly impaired, and not easily understood, by those who are not used to him, was much pleased with his Sons family and conversation, promised to cultivate the acquaintance. Late in the afternoon, visited Mrs. M, a woman who has a year or two, been under very dark exercise. She has in general been a professor of religion, and for the greatest part of her life, rested on the form, Some years ago, she seemed driven from that false refuge, and to have tasted of the powers of the world to come, but afterwards became a backslider in her life conversation, but again fell under awakening and has for a long time, been in the most despairing, dark melancholy way, I almost ever heard of, so as to have attempted her own life, but thankfully prevented and is often quite useless in her family, she has heard me, these two Sabbaths I preached in Charlestown and had expressed great desire of conversing with me. My friend Mr. Daniel Legare carried me to her this evening, found her in a much better way than I expected, very free and conversible. Stayed about an hour and a half, in Spiritual experimental conversation. Acquainted her with some of my own exercise in my younger days. She was much pleased to find that any have ever experienced anything of the same with herself, gave her some necessary directions, was also well pleased with her husbands conversation, who seems a good serious Christian, concluded this visit with prayer. Both Mr. & Mrs. M expressed great satisfaction, and I promised not to be a Stranger. Returned and Spent the Evening, with the good family where I lodge.

Tuesday December 3 1771 . . . [150] Was a good deal busy, about various concerns. On Saturday last, I got a large packet of letters from my friends & relations in Scotland, the only letters I have received for Some years, many having miscarried. By these I find my Dear Mother in law is still alive, labouring under the Infirmities of old age & other Distresses, God has exercised my Dear Sister & family with a lot much like my own, they have buried four Children boys, and have three daughters alive, the Death of these children, especially of the two last Sons, has been a heavy stroke to my most pious Sister, who is also blessed with a very pious husband, their Circumstances otherwise are very thriving and flourishing. My aunts circumstances & her family are also good and so are the circumstances of an old Intimate acquaintance who wrote me, all joined in earnestly entreating me to come home, at least to bring the Children, and stay myself one Season, which I am much inclined to do, have consulted Some friends here, and although all are very unwilling to consent to my going home next Summer, lest I should be prevailed on to stay, yet all own, that they think it my duty to carry home the children, as the best of Education is to be got there, young people are brought up in a much more sober & religious way, and there they would be with their relations, which would be much better than leaving them here in case the Lord should take me off, so that last night I wrote and this day delivered a letter to a friend to be sent off by the first Ship, my desire & Intention to bring home the children next Summer if nothing prevents and I see my way clear. May the Lord direct me, in this important concern. . . .

[153] *Friday December 6:1771* . . . Late in the afternoon rode over to Mr. Smileys who together with Several of Neighbours, have been out at the Seaside a fishing since Monday was a week, their wives are at present greatly distressed about them. Such is the foolish conduct of old heads of families in misspending time & exposing themselves to needless dangers. I observed Mrs. Smiley who works for all the Ladies in those parts making up some Silks, she told me they were for Miss Sally Murry, who is to be married in a few days, to a very profligate young man, a friend of Mr. Griffiths recommending who had waited on her in her Mothers time, but was turned off, as having no character, friends, nor Interest.[25] It seemed to be told to me with a Sneer, but I took no notice of it, was not in the least moved nor affected by it, but expressed my sincere and most hearty wishes for their welfare and happiness, poor young Lady I Sincerely forgive her and all her abettors. Her repeatedly throwing herself in my way, by sending for me, and Insisting for my advice in her affairs, and her using every means consisting with modesty, to acquaint me, that she would put herself and [154] all her concerns into my hand, in the nearest connection, her telling a young lady of great veracity & honour, at my own house one day in July last, that if I would ask her she would immediately accept of me, her acting & behaving so, I had good reason to believe was in Simplicity & Sincerity, from her own desire and inclination and also by Mrs. Griffiths desire, but how she came to change so suddenly and act so base a part I believe would be no difficult matter to discover, Mr. Griffith undoubtedly influenced both his wife & her, for reasons of his own, and yet I believe he is in a great measure disappointed, the Noise the world has made about his behaviour to several others, as well as to me, has obliged him to give her up to a friend here, when his design was to have carried her off to England next Spring for a relation, the design of

persuading her to go to England he has owned & acknowledged but denied the other part, though the Secret has been whispered about. I returned in the evening and made some preparation for Sabbath, was somewhat taken up in admiring the deeps of providence, the Invitation of myself and children to go home, & the Strong appearance of its being my duty to carry the children to their numerous relations, seems to clear up the dark providence of the late strange disappointment, and perhaps to make me more Sensible of growing Earthly mindedness, was the design of permitting it to take place, all which was in a great measure not only contrary to my seeking but even against my Inclination. . . .

[156] *Tuesday December 10:1771* This has been a good and comfortable day to my soul . . . The forepart of the day was employed in writting on religious subjects, in communing with my own heart, and looking into the state of my soul. About noon rode to Mr. Strains, who had a Child about three years old died, when I was in Charlestown, in two days illness, their Eldest Son about fourteen years of age died about two months ago. They are worthy good people, very kind & friendly, have still four Children left, they have also met with Some other trials, & difficulties this fall, Dined and Spent the afternoon with them, there was a good deal of Company present, so that I got not talking so much with these afflicted mourning parents as I wanted, they appeared both very melancholy. . . .

Wednesday December 11 . . . After an Early Dinner, rode over the river, to visit old Mr. Grney, who is almost quite worn out with old age, & is very lame. It began to rain, before I set off and Continued most part of the afternoon. [157] Found both these good old people, much bowed down with age & infirmities, Especially the good old Gentleman, so very low as not able to carry on any conversation, hardly able to speak at all so that had little discourse with him, the good old Lady, has still something of her natural flow of Spirits, but very weak in body. He appears as if he could not hold it any time. Several of my friends were there, so that spent about two hours very agreeable, the old people being much pleased with my visit, a little before Sunset began to clear up, when I took my leave and got home in about an hour after dark, had a comfortable evening only was Somewhat fretted with the house wench, whose behaviour is often very bad, & makes home disagreeable to me, she being lazy, careless & sluttish, to the last degree. Was afterwards uneasy with myself for being fretted and vexed with her conduct, as it is to so little purpose. . . .

[158] *Lords Day December 15* . . . The Day was most excessively cold, a strong froast, and a violent cold wind, by which the hearers seemed much incommoded, and Severals went away betwixt Sermons, this evil practice, begins to take place at the Saltcatcher, as I have observed for Some time past and gives me great concern. It was always in Mr. Huttsons time too much the practice at the Indian Land even from the first settling of the Gospel there, and prevails much through the province, but has not appeared at Saltcatcher, among the sober sort of people till within this Six months . . . Was a good deal persuaded to preach only once a day, for every Sabbath during the winter, but would by no means agree to it, but determined to Continue the Same practice, I have always observed, to preach twice a day for ordinary, and Sometimes to put both [159] Sermons into one, as I may see it necessary, and circumstances may require, for should the Cold in the winter be admitted, as an excuse for preaching only once, the heat would be made an excuse in Summer, and so on, till we entirely dropped the afternoons service, as is the practice of the church of England in all Country places both in England and America and is for two or three years past the prevailing custom in this province, so that since Mr. Richardson died I know not another dissenting minister in the province, that preaches twice every Sabbath, besides my self except it may be Mr. Edmunds and Some of the Baptist lay exhorters in the back parts, had several arguments used with me this evening, by Some whom I did not expect to have engaged in any such cause, but was helped to stand firm, and hope the Lord will Support, strengthen, and bless me in it.

Monday December 16 . . . After morning duties, set out early in the forenoon, for Mr. Jonathan Donnoms, with my friend Mr. Lambert about a quarter before one O Clock, we called at Mr. Samuel Wilkins that was, where I had some business, about a niece of Mr. Donnoms whom her uncle Mr. James Donnom was to carry to her parents in Georgia, for which place, he sets out tomorrow, we sat about an hour and a half with the widows Wilkins & Sameways, whose husbands I buried on the first day of this year, they can hardly be called widows indeed, we then proceeded in agreeable conversation, but did not get to Mr. Donnoms till after dark, found them all in health and good Mrs. Donnom as well as could be expected, having been about three weeks ago delivered of a daughter, a fine child, and the Mother though still weakened yet most Surprizingly well considering her advanced years, and infirm state of health. Had a cheerful, comfortable evening with these good friends. . . .

Tuesday December 17: Having been informed, that the Reverend Mr. Ellington, the church of England Minister, was to preach in a Gentlemans [160]
house about ten miles from this place, & to baptize some children, and as
Mr. Donnom had designed to go there & hear Sermon, and also good Mrs.
Pepper, who although a young woman or hardly middle aged, may well be
called a widow indeed, I agreed to go with them, as it would be convenient
enough for the children I was to baptize to be brought in the afternoon.
. . . Heard Mr. Ellington preach or rather read an excellent good sermon
from 2 Corinth: 4:5, after sermon I waited on the baptism, but no more
approve of their form than of their prayers & thanks. After Service was over,
I received a great deal of respect from all the Gentlemen present and was
much pressed to dine, where the Service was performed, or to Dine with
some of them at their own houses, but was obliged to decline it. Was also invited to preach at this Gentlemans house, if I should at any time preach in
this neighbourhood, we returned immediately, and as I rode in the Chaise,
with Mrs. Pepper, had a great deal of the most serious conversation with her,
and found her to be a most pious Lady, & not only truly religious but one
of the best educated & most sensible women I have met with any where, she
has had great afflictions, & they have been greatly blessed to her. . . .

Wednesday December 18:1771 . . . This morning when was just going to set
off, was detained by good Mrs. Donnom, for near an hour, acquainting me,
with her troubles and distresses of different [161] kinds, some of which I
plainly observed the very first night I came, to my great concern to find old
evils still remaining and prevailing, poor good woman, she shed many tears.
I expressed my Sympathy, gave my best advice, and assured her that neither
her nor her family should be forgot. About Eleven O Clock, after many persuasions to stay because of a thick drisling Cold rain, Mr. Lambert & I set
homewards, the rain Soon increased much and the roads being very bad in
many places, we were upwards of two hours in a heavy rain before we got to
Mr. Pelotes, the Anabaptist Minister, my old acquaintance, a most worthy
pious good man in affluent Circumstances, were most kindly received, and as
the rain continued till after midnight, we were obliged to stay here, though
I wanted much to get home. Spent the afternoon and evening in improving
and agreeable conversation. Mr. Pelote & his wife a Sensible good Motherly
woman, hinted once and again about infant baptism, and dropped some
words disrespectfully of it, but I very carefully avoided taking any notice of
it, any more, than once Saying, Well well, let that pass at present, I have

repeatedly offered to Dispute, or debate the point with him, or any of their Ministers in publick, but thought it not proper to take any notice of this ungenerous behaviour, as in everything else they acted most friendly. . . .

[163] *Monday December 23* . . . In the afternoon rode to Mr. Jordans, found him very ill, and a good measure insensible except when roused and not at all capable of conversation, for any time, yet endeavoured to have some discourse with him, but to little Satisfaction, only found that his mind run on Spiritual & Divine things by Some broken Sentences of Scripture & hymns, he was now & then repeating, was well helped in prayer for & with him, but observed he could not be much attentive to it, was a good deal affected when I took my leave, and so was he, fearing it might be the last time but both expressing our expectation of a happy meeting in heaven. . . . Observed that Mr. Jordan is very closely attended or rather strictly watched by Dr. Day & his wife, relations of the present Mrs. Jordans, whose Conduct I very much disliked, but whether proceeding from want of experience, or from Indifference, I know not, perhaps from both, methinks it a teaching lesson to me, never to attempt to marry a person of too great a disproportion of years. . . .

[164] *Wednesday December 25 1771* A good & comfortable day to my soul . . . Preached upon Luke 19:37:38 with so much of the Divine presence & assistance as made my soul rejoice indeed. . . . Prayed publicly for Mr. Jordan, as had done last Sabbath, and immediately after service set off for his house, found him still very low, though I thought not quite so stupid & insensible as on Monday, but no grounds to expect recovery. Had Some conversation with him, but not very satisfactory, though still spiritual things seemed to be uppermost with him, prayed by him with most melting affections & gracious assistance, was much concerned that so great a professor of religion should not bear a greater testimony to it on his dying bed, should appear so attached to a present life, so much taken up with his worldly concerns. Spoke close & home, was about two hours in the house. Was much troubled to observe several things in the persons about him, his wife acting as above hinted, his Eldest son, a thoughtless youth, much caressed, by a Designing person and simple enough to be imposed on, the person above hinted at Doctor William Day a relation of Mrs. Jordans told me that Mr. Jordan had desired him to be an executor, but would not suffer his will to be opened upon any account and therefore made his Son James, wrote this addition as they called it, on the paper which enclosed the will, witnessed by the young

man [165] himself & Mrs. Donnom, there appeared to me, to be so much baseness & design in this, & so much Simplicity in the young man, that I was greatly troubled & made my visit the shorter, for saw plainly a Combination, between the wife & her relations, and the Eldest Son about eighteen or nineteen years of age, foolish enough to be drawn into it. The youngest son is about thirteen or fourteen, of a Soft turn, both bound to merchants in Charlestown, and the poor man himself fallen into a Snare. Was much concerned that our common friend Mr. James Donnom was absent, being at present in Georgia. Took my leave with a sorrowful heart on several accounts, did not get home till after dark, Continued melancholy and Concerned all the night and endeavouring to make some useful improvement of what I had seen & heard. . . .

Friday December 27:1771 This morning in a humble Spiritual frame of soul, got up early & took a small vomit Hippocacuana, to clear my breast of phlegm, having a most violent Cold. It worked me much more than I expected, and brought up a great deal of bile & turned downwards, but before it was quite worked off I received a letter acquainting me, that Mr. Jordan died last night at Six O Clock in the evening and desiring Mr. Lambert & me to come & see the Will opened, at first I refused to go but afterwards upon Mr. Lamberts urging the consideration of the hints above, that my going might be of real Service, I went, imagining that so Simple a vomit, would not hurt, after so well worked off. Soon after got there the last Will sealed up, with the writting above mentioned in the outside of the Cover was delivered me, and in the presence of all concerned, Mrs. Jordan being in a room within hearing, I opened & read it, and found myself, Mr. Hamilton [166] & Mr. Donnom, left executors, & his Eldest Son. My being mentioned was very unexpected, was sorry to Observe so large a part of Estate given away from his children to his young wife, to whom he had been about fourteen months married, and received little very little with her, but has given her two Negroes more, than the third of all his personal & movable estate with his riding Chair & best chair horse, his daughter his firstborn, who disobliged him in marriage, with whom he seemed to have made all up, & who is in great want, he has cut off, with one Negro girl, this greatly shocked & amazed me that so unrelenting & unforgiving a temper should prevail to the last. Lord, what is man! The rest of his Estate, that is to say, his lands, and two thirds of his slaves & movables to be equally divided between his two sons, which will amount to about nine or ten slaves a piece, and some good lands, from the moment I read it, & also when saw what means a Christian Gentleman was using to be an executor, I determined not to act, as the children had finished their Education, but as none of the other executors mentioned in the body of the Will, were present excepting the young man who is entirely devoted to Dr. Day I thought it proper to keep the will in my Custody for some days. Mr. Lambert and I returned Soon after the Opening of this will, Dr. Day declared his design to act if possible. . . . Had many melancholy reflections upon what I had been witness to, within these few days, the young widow is to live upon his Settled plantation, at the expense of the Estate while his widow, which I think is very proper, but to me it appears extremely affecting to see what a worthy good woman had for many years been gathering amidst great difficulties for her children, given away by their own Father, to one who may be called a stranger, and an only daughter, left to poverty, for the imprudence of making [167] a love marriage with a young man every way deserving of her. . . .

Saturday December 28:1771 . . . In the afternoon attended on Mr. Jordans funeral and discoursed from It is appointed for all men once to die, was much enlarged beyond my first design, took particular notice of our losing a worthy good member & officer of this church, notwithstanding his failings and Infirmities, which were particularly in his temper, took very Special notice of his being present on Sabbath See night, and his leading in that most desireable part of publick worship, Singing the Divine praises, which He was always very ready to do, when the stated Clerk was absent, which was the case that day, addressed myself particularly to his children, the Company was but small, but very Serious & attentive. Good Mr. Strain, was obliged to return home before service began, very ill, and seeming as if he would soon follow his friend and neighbour. This made it a very affecting Scene, as both he & Mr. Jordan, were most serious good men & the most ready to foreword & promote every good work in these parts, was very busy through the Evening till late, in preparatory duties & had the Lords comfortable presence with my soul.

Lords day December 29:1771 . . . Preached from Eph: 4:24, Put on the new man, was well assisted, and enlarged [168] above my purpose. There were a good many gay young strangers, but was enabled to deal most faithfully, with Sinners, to deliver my own soul, and to declare the truth as it is in [illegible word], the power and presence of God was with us, and though an application which was very close, & particularly suited to the follies, frolics, & Diversions of the time & season, did not seem so acceptable to some of the gay young Gentlemen who showed tokens of growing weary, and indeed the service, was long, yet they gave me the hearing. Others were much and greatly affected, and the word preached seemed accompanied with a rich & powerful blessing, was myself in a very Serious affectionate frame of mind, filled with pity to my poor fellow Sinners, and very anxiously desirous to be the means of pulling to them as brands out of burning. . . .

Monday December 30 1771 . . . In the forenoon, had a good deal of company and among others young Mr. Jordan, Dr. Day & Mr. Hamilton, to whom I read the late Mr. Jordans will, Mr. Hamilton being named an executor. I delivered the will to him, but by general consent it was given back to me, & desired I would keep it till Mr. Donnom returns. I made an apology to young Mr. Jordan, for not choosing to act, & gave my reasons, which were accepted of, poor youth he was none to act, but Dr. Day who has no right and is every way very improper, Mr. Hamilton did not Signify, what he would do, I plead much with him, out of pity and compassion to a misguided youth as well as for the younger one, to act, Dr. Day although a Witness to the Will, & only Mentioned, on the back of the paper which enclosed the Will, still insisted to act as an Executor, which seems contrary to law and reason, however to make all easy, I proposed that advice of Council at law, should be taken upon it, and that the Estate should be at the expense of a fee to a Lawyer, which all parties [169] agreed to. We all dined together, with my friend Mr. Lambert who is still here, & Some other of the Neighbours. After Dark, Dr. Day & young Mr. Jordan went away. The Neighbours stayed about an hour longer, during which time, was much Surprized with Some behaviour in Mr. Lambert, was troubled & concerned on his account, for had observed something of it twice before. Lord what is man! Lord keep me poor me always humble & watchful, always depending on thee. . . .

1772

[174] *Thursday January 9:1772* Was up early, my heart & affections with God . . . Dined at Mrs. Graves where baptized a Negro of Dr. Cuthberts, who has been these three years under religious impressions & has attained considerably good knowledge, & lives a good life, but soon after I had Sprinkled him, & was in the last prayer, he tumbled down and rolled about on the floor, as

if overcome Somehow or another. I disliked his behaviour, shortened the prayer, and rebuked him, with some sharpness, he said, that He could not help it, he was so affected, to think of his arriving at such a priviledge, yet I discharged him from the like again, and told him I would not suffer [175] him to be a communicant at this time, but would observe his future Conduct and if nothing appeared amiss, he might be admitted the next Sacrament at Saltcatcher, was a good deal fatigued, & stayed about an hour or more after the Baptism, heard Some strange abuses of the Enemies of the Gospel but was easy and cheerful. Dr. Cuthbert rode from meeting with me, and talked much against my going off with the Children, So did the two Ladies I dined with, all the people in both parishes, are much against my going least I should be prevailed on to stay in Scotland or not spend much time here afterwards, and yet all own it as a duty to take care of my Children, and excepting the danger of the Seas think what I propose the best thing I can do for them. It gives me much thought & concern, what to do, I have made it so publick on purpose that I might know the Sentiments of my friends and by means of its being talked of I might receive Some light. Am afraid least I should run unsent, or desert my work and duty here, and yet there are many very pressing reasons, that something should be done with my Dear children, as to getting them a proper and suitable education, and no place seems so proper, as to carry them home, among their relations, where the best of Education for them is to be got, and incomparably greater advantages with respect to religion, piety and good examples. Yet my Station is so Singular and remarkable, the Lord having so wonderfully Supported me, as a very uncommon Instrument in his hand, of labouring in his vineyard in this part of the world, that I am afraid least I should be acting out of my proper sphere, & what providence has fitted me for. O to be guided & directed by that wisdom that is from above. It was after dark before I got home, was a good deal fatigued, and was not so active, and diligent as I ought to have been. Alas I am a poor carnal creature, always backsliding, Lord pity & compassionate, a wretched Sinful creature, and help to adore & bless, thy glorious name for all thy mercies & goodness to most unworthy me. Here Ends, the Eighth volume of my Diary, the keeping of which I find most useful & advantageous to the spiritual life in my soul, Lord keep me lively.

VOLUME II

September 8, 1783–March 25, 1784

1783

[254] *Monday September 8* . . .[1][255] At five O Clock, several Gentlemen came aboard of us, Mr. Cunningham[2] & I went ashore, in the ships boat, and were Safely Landed before Six, for which, I Silently gave thanks to God. Before we proceeded up the wharf, Each of us gave the Sailors a shilling. Went up to Stewarts Tavern, Mr. Cunningham and I treated the pilote, & Some other Gentlemen, & spent 2/ Each. Charleston very much altered, by the desolations of the war, whole Lanes & streets in ruins, heard of Some of my old friends being alive, and lately returned to Town, from Philedelphia where most of them had been Sent. Was put to some difficulty after Dark, before I could find out my good friend Mr. Daniel DeSaussures.[3] Got a most hearty welcome from him & his pious wife, who though still frail & tender, has been most wonderfully supported under all the hardships she has been exposed to, in the late horrid & most barbarous war. Was in a truly humble & most thankful frame of soul, and at the Same time somewhat melancholy & dejected.

Tuesday September 9: Had a very comfortable nights rest, though slept on a mattress on the floor, this worthy family after being greatly plundered were Sent off by the British to Philedelphia, from whence, they returned Some months ago, and have not yet, got their house properly furnished. Was this forenoon, waited upon, by a very well Dressed Gentleman, a Doctor Ramsay,[4] who is one of the first physicians of this place. He said, that he had often heard of me, & was well acquainted with the Character I bore when formerly in Carolina, that he was a native of Pensylvania and had come to this place Some years after I went to Britain. Gave me an Invitation to Dine with him, which I promised to accept of at another time, as for Some days I would be very busy. He then Earnestly Intreated me to stay in Town & preach next Sabbath, which I agreed to do, if agreeable to the Governor, and if I was properly applied to by the Managers of any of the Dissenting Congregations, that he assured me would be done, and that he now applied to me in the name of the Independent Church. All this passed in Stewarts Tavern, after he was gone, I was Informed, that He was one of the principal Citizens, had been very lately a member of the Continental Congress, was married to a Daughter of the Reverend Doctor Witherspoon,[5] was one of the Managers of the Independent church, and was a Gentleman of strict honour, Integrity & real Religion . . . [256] Waited on his Excellency the Governor, Benjamin Guerard Esquire,[6] with whom I had formerly been well acquainted, & who was often a hearer of mine, at the Indian Land, he gave me a most kind & hearty welcome, and told me, that I had been a very great Sufferer by the war, yet, that it was with great pleasure he could Inform me, that I was neither Confiscated nor amerced, which many other Innocent absentees were, through the Confusion of the times. He treated me as an Intimate friend, and all who were with me, Misters Cunningham, Oliphant, & Scot, my friend Mr. DeSaussure, Introduced us. Afterwards called on Misters James & Edward Penman my attorneys,[7] who were exceedingly happy to See me, & to whom I am under great obligations, here, I learned that, although my losses at the plantation, in Crops, Slaves & stock of all kinds, were very great, yet that my affairs, were on the whole, in a much better way than I expected. In the afternoon, wrote to my Dear family by Captain Stead, who sails tomorrow for London. It being by this time publickly known, that I am returned, was visited by many of my old friends & acquaintances, and called upon Some others, was earnestly Solicited to preach next Sabbath, which I have Engaged to do, the place of worship, formerly called the White, or New England Meeting house, belonging to what was then called the Independent Congregation, but now, the Independent Church, is almost in ruins. It is the people of this Church, who have Invited me, the Scotch Meeting house, has the pulpit Standing, and Some pews left, and though otherwise much abused, yet may be preached in, with Some decency. The

Presbyterian Congregation who usually worshiped in this place, are quite broken & Scattered, the most of that Congregation having Joined the British & gone off, with them when they Evacuated this Town, the Independents have applied to such of the Congregation as remain, & got the use of their meeting house for me, while I stay in the place, which is to be cleaned out, & God willing I am to preach there next Lords day. Have been in a truly humble, lively & Spiritual frame of Soul, blessing & praising the Lord, Filled with wonder & admiration, at the Divine goodness, to poor unworthy me, yet at the Same time, Melancholy, and much affected, at the Sight of the many & great dissolutions in every street, and much more, at the great Change, which I already See, in the manners of the people, very much to the worse, in every respect, as for Instance, I have already heard more prophane Cursing & Swearing, the most horrid oaths on the publick Streets, than was to be heard for months together, in former times. Drank tea with my old friend Mr. Mitchell, one of the managers on my Estate. Spent part of the evening with Mrs. Edwards, & was in a large Company of the Children, of my former friends, and now in families of their own.[8]

Wednesday September 10: A refreshing nights rest, filled with praise and gratitude, to the Lord my God, & Father, helped in prayer for myself & family. Much pressed by the friendly Dr. Ramsay, and by my former friends in this place, to Stay Some weeks, in town, as the Country at present [257] is very Sickly, as it always is at this Season of the year, and Besides, the whole Country, at any distance from the Seat of Government is still in a very unhappy Situation. Robberies are almost daily Committed, & many murders very lately perpetrated by an armed Banditi, who generally call themselves British Refugees or Loyalists, and Sometimes call themselves Americans, taking revenge for the Evil treatment they have met with, and yet further, the Saltcatcher where my plantation lies is Reckoned the most dangerous place in the whole state, and several Gentlemen have very lately been Robbed & Murdered on the high Road, very near my house, so that I think, I shall stay till next month, and am the more Inclined to do so, for the following reasons — Mr. Gourlay,[9] who with much political art, acted as a private Tutor, to Some Gentlemens children during the late unhappy war, is again preaching at Indian Land, where, as I am told, he has a very few hearers, the Settlement, on the Saltcatcher, & on in that Neighbourhood, is almost wholly broke up. Mr. Henderson, who went out as a Soldier against the British, & afterwards took their protection is again preaching at Wiltown. My Design is to preach wherever, the Lord Shall call me, while I stay in this Country, which does not appear to me to be the Same that it was, nor, can I as yet, have that desire to live in it which I formerly had. . . .

Thursday September 11: Though Slept well last night, yet this morning felt Somewhat Indisposed, with a cold, and chilliness, which obliged me, to apply to Mrs. DeSaussure, for more Covering on my bed in the nights. Stayed in my Room all this forenoon. Instructed & Comforted in Reading the Scriptures, particularly the 34 chapter of Ezekiel. Yesterday morning the 103 Psalm, was my ordinary & Expressed the very Language of my soul, have been Engaged in study & writting some alterations in the Sermons designed [258] for Sabbath & had the Lords most gracious presence, for which I bless His holy name, yet Cannot help being much grieved, to See so little religion in this place, which I knew formerly to be very famous for it. All are busy, very busy about their own things, few, very few, or none, seem to care, for the things of Christ & Eternity. They, who formerly had the profession of Religion, have in a great measure, or rather wholly cast it off, and Even those, who I hope & believe are truly religious, are greatly declined, & woefully backslidden. The very awful Judgments, and heavy afflictions, they have gone through, do not appear to have been blessed to the Inhabitants of this place, which most certainly is the heaviest Judgment of all. I have before observed, It is the people of what is now Called, the Independent Church of Charleston, who have applied to me for Sermon. Their place of worship, was made first an hospital, and then a stable of when the British possessed Charleston. The Scotch church was made a place for the Loyalists from the Country to live in, and is in Some better order. The members of the Presbyterian church are very few, and as yet give themselves no concern about publick worship. The Independents have got the use of their church, till their own is repaired, which they are determined Soon to Set about. Infidelity & Deism prevails in the most open and avowed manner I ever read or heard of, in any Country, and that not only here, but more so, through all the Northern states, and alas the vilest profanity & grossest wickedness abounds Everywhere. Have been in a humble, serious, thankful frame of mind, helped in prayer & praise, in devoting myself, & family to God. . . .

Friday September 12 . . . This forenoon wrote to Misters Lambert, Dr. Cuthbert, old Mrs. Hatcher, & the Reverend Mr. Gourlay, but do not yet know of any opportunity to forward these letters. Dined with Dr. Ramsay formerly mentioned as one of the Trustees for the Independent Church. He is a Gentleman of fine parts, of good Learning, very Conversable, well acquainted with men & books, and what is the beauty & ornament of all, a man of true piety and real Godliness, was happy in his company. [259] Was much pressed by him, & others, to stay here, till a minister, whom they expect from Philedelphia arrives, or, if he does not come, that I would accept of their Church, gave them no Encouragement to expect either the one, or the other. In the afternoon visited some old acquaintances. Drank tea with good old Mrs. Ohear, who lives with her Son James,[10] a most excellent young man, who has for Several years been an Inhabitant of this town, and at present has an office, under the Government of the state, and is in good credit, has been twice married, & has two children by his first wife, his present wife, a young Lady, whom I baptized at Wilton, his mother keeps a School for young Children, and both are in a very good way. Spent the Evening at my lodgings, in preparatory duties, was up very late, had the Lords most comfortable presence, and was well assisted in Secret duties. . . .[11]

[264] *Friday October 17* Have spent this day mostly in my Room, in study, writting & preparatory duties for Sabbath, with the Lords most gracious & comfortable presence. Wrote another letter to Mr. Lambert, & delivered it, to Mr. Joseph Donnom. Dined at home. Mr. DeSaussure sat at table with us, but is still very poorly. Two more of the family are sick, one of his own Daughters, the other a Daughter of his deceased Brother Henrys, both girls about thirteen years of age. It gives me uneasiness to be taking up a room in their family, when so many are sick in it, yet at present cannot help myself as it would affront them should I change my lodgings, while I stay in town, and they Insist I shall not leave him till I set out for my own plantation. . . .

Monday October 20 . . . [265] The weather continues very cold, and as there is no fireplace in my room I am obliged to sit with my surtout, or great on, and though have on Socks, yet find that the cold pinches my feet, and that if the cold continues I shall be obliged to go to my own plantation sooner than I Intended. . . . Dined at Mr. Halls an attorney at Law, there is a Captain & a Major Mitchell Brothers, living in the Same family, Lately officers in the Continental Army. The Major is married to a Daughter of Mrs. Halls by a former husband. Mrs. Hall knows me very well when I used formerly to preach in Charleston. My friend Mr. John Mitchell carried me in his Chair to this family. The Major was obliged to be in the Country, and did not get returning so soon as he expected, the Captain is a Batchelor and appears to be a very Sensible man. Both Brothers I am told behaved with great bravery & good conduct during the war, and are much respected. Both families appear somewhat attached to the Presbyterian church. Spent the afternoon here in agreeable conversation yet it always troubles me to sit near two hours at Dinner which is very much the Custom in this place. Surely it is a great loss of time, and what I very much dislike. . . .

[266] *Thursday October 23* A very cold night, but blessed be God, that through the care of my Dear and affectionate Mrs. Simpson,[12] am well provided to be kept comfortably warm in the night . . . Dined at Mr. Broadies, married to an old acquaintance of mine. He appears to be a very Sensible good man, and is a zealous friend to the Presbyterian church. Spent part of this afternoon, with Mr. James Hamilton & his wife from Saltcatcher, my old friends, received some letters from Mr. Lambert, and have reason of thankfulness that matters at my plantation are so well as they are. . . .

[267] *Friday October 24* . . . Have all this day suffered very much with the cold, was distressed in body & grieved in mind, troubled & confused, clothed myself in the warmest manner, yet was shivering with cold, and could not help myself. The house is so very much out of repair, having been plundered & ravaged by the British army, and for Several months uninhabited before the family returned from Philedelphia, my bed on the floor, much glass broke in the windows, both on the Stair case, & in my room, and no fireplace. I cannot describe my painful feelings from the cold nor my concern, least I should not be able to preach twice next Sabbath, was through the greatest part of the day Employed in preparatory duties as much as I could but made very little progress. . . .

Saturday October 25 . . . About Eleven O Clock was most agreeably Surprized, with good Mr. Edmonds a most worthy Reverend Minister calling upon me. He had formerly been a Colleague with Mr. Hutson, in the Independent church here, and has been long in this state, a very pious good man, of no regular Education, nor of much pulpit ability but of a most Excellent Character, and had acquired an Easy fortune by marriage, has no family, and is now a widower. He was obliged to leave the Country, while the British troops were here, and has [268] been traveling & preaching through the Northward states. He has been some time in this state, and came to this City yesterday.

After Common compliments & Some general conversation, I Invited him to Divide the day with me tomorrow, which he consented to do, choosing to preach in the afternoon, this was very agreeable to me, and made me very easy, in my mind on Several accounts. I afterwards saw Mr. Josiah Smith[13] with whom Mr. Edmonds lodges, & some other Gentlemen principal Supporters of the Independent church, & told them, what I had done, with which they appeared very much pleased. Afterwards visited old Dr. Skirvine,[14] and was received by him, in the most friendly manner. . . . Spent the remaining part of the afternoon chiefly in writting, Drank tea at Mr. Mitchells who has this afternoon been Settling Some affairs of mine with Mr. Edwards Estate and am Informed that things are much in my favour though my losses are very great, yet that I have the greatest reason to bless the Lord for his mercy & goodness to me & mine, in preserving what I have left, for which my friends had Some struggle, though even by Some of them, I have been a great loser. . . . Am very happy at the thoughts that I may get up to my own place next week, and that good Mr. Edmonds is now here, so that neither the Independent, nor the Presbyterian church will be destitute.

Lords day October 26 . . . This forenoon preached to a very numerous Congregation, both within & without doors, with freedom & fullness from Isaiah 30:21, this is the way walk ye in it. The auditory were most Serious & attentive, and I humbly think that the power & glory of God was remarkable in this our [269] Sanctuary. . . . About three O Clock, Mr. Edmonds came to my lodgings, and spent twenty minutes with me, conversing about the State of Religion in Scotland. Walked to Church together, where he preached from Psalm 64:9, a remarkable text. His method was, to point out the duties required of good people, in this text, which were First, to Consider Gods works & doings in his providential dispensations, to the States of America, & this state in particular during the Late war, 2dly that they were to fear & reverence God, for his Judgements on the Enemies of America, 3rdly that they were to declare the work of God, to own the Lords hand in all his providences of Judgment on their British Enemies and his mercies to themselves, and to thank God for the Same, with a particular application about the former Sufferings, & present temporal mercies of this City. I was very uneasy during most of the Sermon, and was very much disappointed. The Congregation was numerous. He was very Serious, & at times much affected. I know he is a pious worthy good man, and it would appear that his Sufferings from the British, his banishment from this Country, about two years or Eighteen months ago, during which time, one of his daughters a young woman died, and his now happy return to this Country, where he has still one daughter living, has so affected his mind, as to have turned all his thoughts, upon these things. Many good things were said, much, very much was wanting. He is just come from Philadelphia, and has been above these twelve months preaching in Pensylvania, Maryland, the back parts of Virginia & North Carolina. I would willingly hope that the Ministers in the Northern States are in general preaching in another strain, more Spiritual & Evangelical, or preaching the Gospel in its heavenly Doctrines, its simplicity & purity. . . .

[270] *Tuesday October 28* . . . Was Informed in the Evening that the members of the Scotch Congregation now called the Presbyterian church, had met for the third time, and subscribed very generously for repairing their Church, and Supporting the Gospel until a meeting of the assembly next January, when they expect to be Incorporated, according to the Laws of this state, and then have a legal power to Inquire into what funds are remaining & to apply them to the Support of the Gospel, as near, the original design of the Donors, as the truly Christian & Catholic Laws of this State will admit, where the Christian protestant reformed religion, is declared, to be the Established religion, and all Denominations of protestants are to be on an Equal footing.[15] The occasion of their two former meetings I shall mention afterwards. This afternoon they chose Trustees, to whom their Subscriptions are to be paid, & who are to take the management of their Church affairs. . . .

[271] *Wednesday October 29* . . . Was helped to improve time usefully in my room, the weather cold & disagreeable, had about an hour and a halfs conversation with a Captain William Atcheson, who is acquainted with Several families in Greenock & Port Glasgow. He appears to have been mostly connected with the Seceders, is lately come in here as a passenger from one of the French West Indie Islands. I have observed him in Church these two Sabbaths. He appears to be a Sober Serious man but rather talkative. About the middle of the day, or about noon went out and did Some necessary business. In the afternoon, dined with the Misters Penman, & Some other Company. They are very worthy Gentlemen, to whom I am under great obligations as my attornies, though according to my desire, they have always paid themselves, what the Law allows them. . . .

Thursday October 30 . . . In the forenoon began to prepare for Sabbath, & was proceeding very pleasantly, when Brown the Patroon of the galley called to let me know, that he would Set off tomorrow for Beaufort, upon which, I left off preparatory duties and Spent the day chiefly in purchasing articles for a present to my Negroes, for their faithfulness, near above a double allowance of their yearly allowance, and also in purchasing articles for my keeping house, at Saltcatcher, having nothing left of my very plentiful furnished house, and also, in purchasing several articles for Mr. Lambert. This was a work, I was altogether unfit for, and have been troubled these two days, how I should go about it, however took advice, & did the best I could, It was a loss to me, that Mr. DeSaussure is sick and is this day again taken with the fever, I have been [272] very busy & much hurried, yet can truly say that my heart was lifted up to God. . . .

Friday October 31 . . . At five O Clock, was called upon by the Patroon, Roger Brown, took my leave of the good family I have been so kindly Entertained in, and went along to the Galley, a boy with a wheel barrow, carrying Some Small parcels. At the head of one of the wharfs, the Patroon suddenly dropped us, going I believe into Some dram shop. After the boy & I had searched for him near an hour, we went back to Mr. DeSaussures, where the Patroon came to us. I thought this was very strange behaviour, but said nothing as he appeared to be touched with liquor. Went along with him, to the Landing place. As was stepping in to the Cannoe, it was so far overset, that I had my whole right side, from head to foot, plunged in the Sea or Salt water, however as my left arm & leg were in the Cannoe, I immediately recovered myself. Thought this a hard beginning of my going to the Country, but was Satisfied, that was in the way of my duty, and was Submissive to the divine will, trusting in the God of my Salvation. Got aboard of the Galley lying out in the Stream about seven O Clock. Pulled off my Coat & Jacket, had the water wrung out of them, & put them on. Young Mr. James Hatcher, and another young Gentleman go passengers. It is with difficulty that these two, the Patroon & myself, can press into what they call their Cabin, where we cannot Sit upright, but when we Sit on the floor of it, & have not room to stretch out our legs. This was an armed vessel during the late unhappy war, built in Charlestown by the British & called a Galley from her particular make, fifty three feet in Length, twelve in breadth, and Six foot deep, both ends exactly alike, though the one is called the head & the other the stern, where there is a rudder hung. She has two masts, one at the head, one in the

Middle, from which there is a boom goes over the stern, has what they called a foresail & a main Sail, had Eleven Oars on Each Side, time of the war. Her gunwales, or ledges are only one foot high above the deck, on the top of the Gunwales were high rails, with stuffed netting, a barricado for the Soldiers she carried, these rails are now taken away. She carried two large nine pounds, one at the head and the other at the Stern, [273] so fixed with a strong Swivel that they could be turned to either side, and usually carried fifty men with muskets, her Magazine was at the stern five feet in length, her Cabin the Same. The rest to the head is open, seven feet wide in the middle, where men stood & fired their muskets, on each side of the opening the deck is two foot & a half wide, for the men to walk upon from the head to the stern. We have five Negroes aboard, two of them & a boy belonging to the Patroon, & two fellows going to the Indian Land, who work for their passage, this Galley was taken from the British some before they evacuated Charlestown, and purchased by the present Patroon, who has Several Negroes and a Small plantation of his own. His two fellows & himself are sufficient to work her, with the help of the Sails, & his boy cooks, & otherwise assists them. I am to sleep in the Patroons Cabin, which is indeed a very ordinary one, my head when being down being within Eight Inches of the Deck, the Patroon & the two young Gentlemen sleep in the Magazine, which they Enter, from the Main Cabin, by an opening just large Enough, for one person at a time to creep into on his knees. Was in a humble, resigned frame of soul, trusting in the Lord my God & my Father.

Saturday First day of November 1783 . . . We are going what is called an Inland Passage and expect to be Several days aboard. We go mostly with the tides, and find that we have made Some way. . . . Find the weather to be like what Jacob speaks of, and his Situation is mine at present. In the day I suffer the heat of a very hot dry air and schorching Sun, and in the night, the froast pinches & distresses me, but my greatest trouble is, the horrid, profane, cursing & Swearing of the Patroon or Captain, who is often acknowledging his fault, & Continually repeating it. My trust is in the Lord, yet cannot help being Somewhat dull & melancholy. . . .

[275] *Monday November 3d* . . . Early in the forenoon, we got into St. Helena Sound, and having a Small breeze of wind, got up to Mrs. Hatchers landing about four O Clock. Her Nephew James Ferguson, whom she has left that plantation, and Some other young men with him, when they Saw Browns

Galley coming up their Creek, expected I was aboard, & came to meet me, at the Landing, here I was received in the kindest manner, and got a most hearty welcome, got all my things ashore here, and a Comfortable evening with my remaining friends, though could not help being affected, when reflecting on the many Social & pleasant hours I had formerly passed in this place with good old Mr. & Mrs. Hatcher, and that part of my family, who are now in a better world, was also affected at hearing of the dreadful horrid ravages of war in this parish & Neighbourhood. Was in a humble, Serious, thankful frame of soul.

Tuesday November 4 . . . Mr. Ferguson Sent a fellow on horseback to my plantation, to Inform of my being here, with a Letter to Mr. Lambert desiring him, to Send for me & my luggage, and that if he was not at home, Mr. Hamilton, the next Neighbour would open the Letter, & direct my Negroes, what to do, Mr. Lambert was not at home, Mr. Hamilton opened the Letter, & proposed to send his own wagon tomorrow, but my Negro Jamy contrived better, & sent my own ox cart, with Six oxen, and the best horse left in the plantation, which Indeed is a very poor Small Sorry creature, such a one, as in former times, I would have been ashamed to have rode, the British & the American armies, having carried off all my fine breed of horses, and Several hundred head of Cattle, they came to me about Seven O Clock at night, this afternoon drank tea with old Mrs. Kelsal, at her place in this Neighbourhood. Was all day entertained with the account of the most horrid transactions [276] of the British Army & the Loyalists, during the war, which, while it affected & distressed me, at the Same time, filled me with grateful thoughts of the Divine goodness, in sending me to, & keeping me & mine in Britain, while these things were going on here.

Wednesday November 5 . . . After Breakfast got the cart put in order, which it much needed, Loaded & Sent away by Eleven O Clock. At twelve, I set out on horseback by myself, Mr. Ferguson having in the morning gone for Beaufort to attend the Circuit Judges keep Court there. I rode around by my old parsonage or manse, which is standing, stopped on the road & viewed it, for Some time, with a heart ready to burst, at the Remembrance of past times, there my Dear children were born, there they & their Ever Dear Mother died, there, I had many a sweet, pleasant & comfortable, many a sick, melancholy & Sorrowful hour. Proceeded all alone, to my old meeting house, at Stoney Creek, which, to the Surprize of many, is left Standing, while they, that is the British burnt the Grand Episcopal church, at Sheldon, the most Elegant Country church, in this state, and Lighted from my horse. Viewed the tomb, where the Bodies of my Dear Jeany Muir, Sacheverel, Archibald & Jeany Simpson the Mother & the children, lie Interred.[16] Was greatly affected, yet could not drop a tear, but heaved many a deep fetched sigh, from a troubled breast. Went into my old study house, Sat Some time, in mournful Silence, kneeled down, & offered up fervent prayers & praises to God. Praised the Lord for His Sparing mercy to me & mine, and for bringing me back again to this Land. Prayed for grace, wisdom & council to myself, while in this Country, and that might yet again be made useful in it. Prayed for the present Minister, Mr. James Gourlay, whose Circumstances in Scotland being Somewhat peculiar, I prevailed with, to come to America, proceeded with a heart full with the most tender feelings, past the Stoney Creek store, all was desolation and indeed all the way, there was a gloomy Solitariness. Every field, Every plantation showed marks of ruin & devastation, not a person to be met with in the roads, all was gloomy. Called on Mrs. Dixon, Sister to my friend Mr. DeSaussure, who now a widow lives at old Mr. Garnears place, she was not at home. Met a Gentleman, Captain Williamson, there who I had Seen in Charleston, who is about Setting up a store at [277] Stoney Creek, & lives with Mrs. Dixon. He had Dined on such fare as the plantation afforded before I got there. I was very hungry, & dined comfortably on two Eggs, & salt without any butter & corn Journey cake bread. Had a kind of Brandy & water for Drink. Proceeded homeward. All the way, marks of desolation & destruction on every Side of the high road. My poor little horse went very slowly, overtook a Negro who knew me & would not part with me, till he brought me near my own house on a road through my own ground. Passed on the outside of the fence, by the Overseers & the Negro houses, which we generally call the plantation, & rode directly to my own house, but, though I knew the road to it, yet, I should never have known the place, had I been set down on it, in the night time. It is Impossible to describe in words how altered these once beautiful fields are, no Garden, no Inclosure, no mulberry, no fruit trees, nothing but wild fennel, thorny bushes, Underwood, & Briars, to be Seen, and a very ruinous habitation. Some of my Negroes were at work in the woods. They Saw me & run with transports of joy, holding me by the knees as I sat on horseback, and Directly run off, to the plantation to give notice to Mr. Lambert, & some Gentlemen with him, that I was come. When I got up to the house, found none there but good old Bess, long ago superannuated, (upwards of Eighty years of age) who came

creeping to the yard, and embracing my knees kissed them often, & holding up her Eyes, praised God for my return & prayed fervently for blessings
on me & on my family in Scotland. Immediately all the other Negroes were
with me, having quitted left their work, in the Barn & in the woods, & came
running with the wildest transports of joy. I took every one of them by the
hand, holding their hands in mine, with the greatest familiarity, but, that
would not Satisfy them, they broke through all restraints, cast their arms
around my Shoulders & held me fast, then cast themselves on their knees,
& grasping mine, thanked God for my return, & prayed aloud, for blessings
on me & my family. Then starting up, they stepped to a Distance, and looked
with amazement, crying they hoped, that they were not deceived, & that
it was really me, made many Inquiries [278] after their young Mistresses, &
their good Mama, as they called the present Mrs. Simpson, for they had heard
by my letters to the attornies, how happy the children were in their Mother
in Law, who has been a kind parent, and not a step mother to them, and
often, cried why had I not brought them, was I ever going to leave my poor
Negroes who had stayed on the plantation when the British wanted them to
go away, and abused the two who had left me & gone with Colonel Moncrief.[17] Again & again they held me by the knees, & wanted to carry me, in
their arms, or on shoulders over to the plantation, where the Overseer, and
the Negroes have their houses, & where the work is carried on. The Gentlemen with Mr. Lambert were Mr. Mitchell, who left Charleston the day
before I did, & has been at his lower plantation, and the Reverend Mr. Henderson of Wilton who has accompanied Mr. Mitchell from his Wilton plantation. As there was nothing to be got at my former dwelling house, I went
over to Mr. Lambert, who has lived for this year past in the Overseers house,
they were all come out to meet me, and for Some time stood amazed, pleased
& affected with the wild transports of the Negroes & the tumultuous welcome they gave me. It was Some time before we got them composed, as soon
as the cart arrived, I gave every one of them a Small quantity of Rum & told
them I had presents of a better kind to give them in a few days. Drank tea
& supped with Misters Mitchell & Henderson, was very Sorry to see Mr.
Lambert in a condition, not at all like himself. Poor man how greatly is he
fallen, how strangely is he altered. It passed over with his being suddenly
overcome & taken sick, with the joy of seeing me on my own plantation,
He could neither drink tea nor sup with us. Left them directly after Supper,
& returned to my dwelling house, which is now by far the meanest looking

house of the two. Carried Rose, a very faithful wench, & my Dear Betsys nurse, with a mulatoe boy to wait on me, was in a humble, thoughtful, praising frame of soul, after secret & family prayer, retired to rest, trusting in the Lord.

Thursday November 6 Though pretty well lodged in my own house, which is very much out of repair, yet did not sleep much. Was full of reflections on the wonders of Divine providence, towards most unworthy me, could not avoid a [279] very Serious thoughtful turn of mind, when thinking of my Dear family in Scotland, and the poor accommodations, I at present have, when compared to what I have for Some years been used unto, saw all Gods dealings with me, to be mercy & goodness, Slept towards the morning and got up refreshed, & Enlarged in prayer & praises. As Mr. Mitchell is very lame, with a many years Rhuematism, I went over and Breakfasted with him & Mr. Henderson, at the house Mr. Lambert lives, which is much Enlarged since I went away, is completely Sashed and in good Order, & well furnished. Visited the barn, there is a good Crop brought in, & fifteen barrels of rice beat out. My fine rice machine which cost me a good deal of money, and the house over it is Intirely destroyed, and many marks of destruction on what houses are left standing. Stayed & Dined here. Parted with Mr. Mitchell after breakfast, who went over to his Indian Land plantation. Parted with Reverend Mr. Henderson after dinner, who went to his own house at Wilton. Have been Informed for the first time, that when he went to live at Wilton my attorneys allowed him to Carry away a good deal of table & bed linnen, a feather bed and household furniture from my house, after he had lived Some years in my house, & preached to this people. I every day find that great Liberties has been used with my Interest, and that my plantation, in the late distressing times, was a Common good, used for the good of the publick, and that not only the armies lived upon it, but numbers of families that were drove from Georgia, lived here on the produce of the plantation, for many months together, Sometimes Sixteen & twenty families, and that when my dwelling house, the Overseers house, the Machine house and all the Negro houses were full, they Camped & hutted in the fields, to the number of two hundred persons at a time, and took what was at hand, So that besides the large quantities of Corn, rice, potatoes & pease they used, the number of Cattle, sheep & hogs killed is almost Incredible, In these respects I am thought to be the greatest sufferer by the war of any person in this large parish, I will have [280] occasion to mention particulars more fully afterwards. Went and Drank tea, with Mr. Hamilton, who now lives where Mr. Jonathan Donnom lived, and was very kindly received. In the Evening, Several of the Negroes brought me a present of fowls & Eggs, for there is not a fowl of any kind on the plantation belonging to me. Mr. Lambert, who lives in what was called the Overseers house, whose Negroes plants on shares with mine, for which he Overlooks the plantation affairs, has a great abundance of all Sorts. I offered to pay the Negroes for what they brought, but they would accept of nothing. It is pleasant to see them so grateful & attached to a Master. They Indeed lived Easy and comfortable, to what many of their Colour do, and much more comfortably not only than the generality of the Servants in Britain, but much more so than thousands of the farmers or Country people as we call them in Scotland. Happy very happy should I be, if I could be useful to their souls. . . .

Friday November 7 Had a very comfortable nights rest, was helped in prayer & praise, both mornings and Evenings with what family I have here, viz., Old Bess quite bowed down with age and Infirmities, whose kindness to my children, Engages me to take care of her, as a child, rather than a servant, a little Girle who stays with her, whose Mother is dead, Rose, & a little boy Tom, to attend on me. Spent the forenoon in writting, about twelve O Clock Mr. Lambert sent me notice, that the Reverend Mr. Gourlay from Indian Land, was come the length of his house to visit me. They both Dined with me, Mr. Gourlay looks much altered & old like, but is very brisk & lively, to what he used to be, when I saw him in Scotland. He lives at Mr. Mains plantation, and has acted as a teacher of a few boys as well as Minister at Stoney Creek. He as all other Presbyterian ministers was prevented from preaching, while the British army was in these parts, had much discourse together, about his friends in Scotland, went Over & Drank tea, at Mr. Lamberts, stayed till seven at night, and left Mr. Gourlay to sleep there, who pays great attention to Mr. Lambert and is often with him, and by report is to be his heir. Mr. Lambert appears to me, to be greatly altered, not to the better. It may be dotage, and the Infirmities of old age, there is a great appearance of great backsliding & decay in religion in it, and that to a very great degree, which grieves & distresses me, to be a witness of, may it make me humble and watchful, against the like, and O may the Lord graciously quicken, revive renew & restore his backslidden servant Mr. John Lambert, to [281] the love of his youth, & the love of his first Espousals. . . .

Lords day November 9 This has been both a Comfortable & a melancholy Sabbath to my soul, on different accounts, had the Lords very gracious & comfortable presence with my soul both in publick & private duties, yet had causes of grief and distress. As there was a very strong froast, and the weather Dark & foggy, and the people used only to one Sermon for Some years past, when they get any, which is very seldom, I did not go out till Eleven O Clock, Rode by Mr. Lamberts house, where I lighted expecting him to go with me, but was Surprized to find that his horse was not got out of the field, nor did he appear dressed for going to publick worship. He said the boy was out hunting for his horse and at the same time made grievous Complaints of being very much Indisposed, & unable to ride, with a very distressing disorder (the piles), upon which I advised him to stay at home and proceeded by myself & boy running before me. Was much affected, to see all about the meeting house grown up in bushes, like a wilderness, and the house itself without window shutters, every appearance, was that of a place forsaken & desolate. However there were several people gathered, about half past twelve I began publick worship, and was most comfortably assisted in every part of it, there appeared to be between forty & fifty white people, and as many Negroes, the Lord Enabled me to deliver his word in the power & demonstration of his Holy Spirit, but very few of the Congregation, who were almost all strangers to me, seemed to understand anything of the matter. The Lord enabled me to plead & wrestle fervently in prayer, both before & after Sermon. Preached with great freedom & Enlargement from John 21:26, last [282] Clause. Some few appeared much affected among the white people, and more among the Negroes. All were Serious, & Seemed amazed & Surprized at the manner of delivery, but there appeared much more of a kind of gazing stupidity, than anything else. Of the white people present besides Mr. Hamiltons family, & Mr. Mitchell, who came over from Indian Land on his way home, I saw only four persons whose faces I knowed, So that this Congregation appears to be wholly broke up, being either dead or removed to the back Country to get out of the way of the army, as Mr. Hamilton did, to the Waxaws, where the British army also penetrated and there he suffered much, & returned only since Charleston was evacuated. Baptized a Child, for one Greeves, to whom I had baptized children formerly. Was glad to have the opportunity of doing it in publick, & was well assisted to faithfulness, in administering this Sacrament. Gave notice, that God willing, I shall preach at Stoney Creek, Indian Land next Sabbath, Mr. Gourlay the pastor having invited me to do so. Mr. Mitchell came with me to Mr. Lamberts, where I dined & drank tea with them, found Mr. Lambert still complaining, but better, went home in the Evening, happy to get by myself, after having Spent too much time in worldly conversation. Was grieved & distressed on that & other accounts. Was sensible of the workings of Indwelling Sin in myself, and alas saw nothing but the form and hardly the form of Godliness in Some others, went to my house in a humble mourning frame of soul, and was helped to lie low before the Lord in dust & ashes, and to plead for a downpouring of the holy Spirit on myself & others, and that He who has brought back the temporal, would bring back the Spiritual Captivity of this unhappy Land.

Monday November 10 . . . Went over & breakfasted with [283] Mr. Mitchell at Mr. Lamberts, and had some discourse with Mr. Lambert, about his going to live in town, as he seems much Inclined to do so, if I go to stay there, while I remain in this state, and Indeed he does not seem fit, either to have the charge of his own negroes or mine. . . . Agreed to Endeavour to make up, a difference which has Subsisted for Some time, between him, and his Neighbour Mr. Hamilton. . . .

Tuesday November 11 . . . After four O Clock went over to Mr. Hamiltons. Drank tea there with his family, a worthy, good well disposed family & for which I have a great regard. Mentioned, my desire & design to make up the difference between him & Mr. Lambert, to which he very readily agreed, though both Mr. Mitchell & I think he has been Injured [284] and that Mr. Lambert has been too hasty, yet as there has been faults on both Sides, I have proposed a mutual agreement without any retrospect, and to this they have both agreed, being both of them, very unhappy in their minds because of their Conduct in this affair, and they are at present living So unlike Christians & Neighbours. I expect them to Dine with me on Thursday. . . .

Wednesday November 12 1783 Did not sleep so comfortably last night, as would have wished to have done. . . . It was a very cold froasty night, my Circumstances very lonesome and the Situation of my house most exposed upon a high hill for this country, though most delightful & pleasant for an Inland place, though bounded by the River, out of Sight, yet there is Something remarkably wild & Romantick in it, and more so, when Considered what a family I have in Scotland. Was in a humble, serious frame of soul, helped in prayer, comforted by reading the Scriptures. . . . In the afternoon was Engaged in several family affairs for which I am altogether unfit, and my

Negroes have for these years past lived in such a way, as to make it very un-comfortable to me. Mr. Lambert had killed a young Cow, one half of it was for me, but how to cut it up and Salted, I knew not. [285] Mr. Lambert has been used to do these things, in such a way, as to one Directly from Britain is rather disgusting, though these things do not as yet, in the least fret or vex me, yet they make me melancholy & sink my Spirits, when I think of my Dear family, & how it is with them, yet being, I know, in the way of my duty, and resigned, cheerful & even comforted. . . .

Thursday November 13 . . . [286] Mr. Lambert came over, fretted at a few lines of a letter, he had yesterday received from Mr. Hamilton and Seemed determined not to meet with Mr. Hamilton at my house today, though both parties had agreed to Dine with me. It was Some time, before I could per-suade Mr. Lambert that he had mistaken the design of Mr. Hamilton writ-ting him yesterday, and that to me it appeared, to be the very reverse of what he understood it, and was evidently Intended to promote the design of their meeting at my house. He stayed with me till Eleven O Clock. In about half an hour, Mr. Hamilton came and in about an hour more his two Sons in Law, Mr. White who lives at the Waxaws and Mr. Pepper who lives in Geor-gia, both of whom I had Invited, and before one O Clock Mr. Lambert re-turned. Mr. Hamilton & he as was agreed upon shook hands and behaved to one another with great civility, & good manners so that I hope their quar-rel is removed, and I expect that they are both to deliver up to me the angry ill natured letters they had wrote to one another, which I am to destroy, and they are henceforth to live together as becomes Christians, good men, and good Neighbours. We all Dined very comfortably together. The two young men left us Early. Mr. Hamilton stayed till near five O Clock in free & affa-ble conversation with Mr. Lambert, & went home to his family. Mr. Lam-bert drank tea with me & left me about seven at night, so that this day, although employed in a good work, and such as I can reflect on with plea-sure, yet has been in a great measure lost, as to what I intended in my pri-vate Concerns. Lord help me to Improve time usefully & wisely.

Friday November 14 . . . [287] Have this day been much grieved & troubled, that can get no letters forward to Charleston and am afraid that Captain Bowie in the ship Glasgow will Sail for Clyde before I Can get any letters sent down to him. I have not a horse to ride out, any where, I have not a boy fit to wait on me. Every person, every family in both parishes, and through all the District or Country appear to be in the Same Situation. No body comes to See me, for none have horses. All Society Seems at an End. Every person keeps close in their own plantations. Robberies & murders are often Committed on the publick rodes, the people that remain, have been peeled, pillaged & plundered, poverty, want & hardships appear in almost every Countenance, a dark melancholy gloom prevails everywhere, and the morals of the people almost Intirely extirpated. A General discontent, dissatisfaction & distrust of their present rulers and of one another, prevails through the Country. In Charleston they appear to be more happy. I am greatly disappointed Since I came to the Country, and could not have believed, that these distresses were so great had I not Seen. It is too Evident that the British army came here to plunder & not to fight or Conquer the people, far less to conciliate them to Submit to the British Government. The appearance of the whole Country shows it here, and the vast fortunes that the officers of the British army have realized in Britain and carried home with them, shows it there. Shall be greatly troubled, if I lose the opportunity of sending off my letters by the ship going directly for Greenock, and yet I am afraid it will be the case, as I dare not even venture to send a fellow to town by land as will alarm and distress my family much. This makes me wish I had stayed longer in Charleston, had no Idea that the Country was in such a dismal Situation. May the Lord Council & direct me in all my ways. . . .

Lords day November 16 . . . [288] Was up Early and had the Lords gracious and comfortable presence in secret & preparatory duties. Got a horse from Mr. Hamilton, who with Mr. Lambert & Some others Set off about ten O Clock, and got to the meetinghouse half an hour after Eleven. We did not begin until twelve O Clock. Such of my old friends and acquaintances, expressed great pleasure at Seeing me once more among them. Was grieved & distressed to see so great a Change, the meeting yard all grown up with thorns & Briars, almost to the doors of the house, the Inside of which is much broke down. Everything about very desolate like. Had the Lords most gracious presence & assistance both in prayers and in the Sermon, preached with fullness & freedom, from Col: 1:2 middle clause, Grace be unto you, the Congregation consisted of about seventy white people, and a greater number of Negroes, all very attentive and serious. The greatest part were strangers or young people grown up, this was said to be a large Congregation, and more it was Said would have been out, had my preaching there been more generally known, for Mr. Gourlay had only mentioned in private to a few.

It was on different accounts both a melancholy and a Comfortable time to my soul. After service, was Invited by severals to Spend the night with them, but as did not choose to Change my bed in such extreme cold weather, I dined with Mr. John Cuthbert a son of Dr. Cuthbert, a very comely young man, and I am told a very Sober, promising youth. He now lives where his Father did, and which was formerly Mr. Hutsons place. Young Mr. John Bull & Some others Dined with us. . . .

Monday November 17 . . . Was in a humble frame of soul, but rather dead [289] & lifeless, than otherwise and lost the forenoon in sloth & listless Idleness, was like a Silly Dove that has no heart. Am daily seeing more & more of the little trust that is to be put in man, and that my professed friends have made free, very free with my Estate. These things distress me, in different views & on different accounts. May the Lord forgive those who have wronged me, and be himself my portion and happiness. Went over by Invitation & Dined at Mr. Hamiltons, a worthy honest man, and a near Neighbour who has been a very great sufferer in the war. Spent the afternoon in agreeable Conversation with him & his good family. Returned home just before dark, where was Informed that Mr. Lambert had stayed last night at Mrs. Mains, where Mr. Gourlay is Entertained at free lodgings, and, that Mr. Gourlay was come along with Mr. Lambert to lodge with him, in his way to Charleston. This I esteemed as a very providential opportunity to forward my Letters for my Dear family in Scotland. Went over, Spent the Evening & Supped with them. Gave Mr. Gourlay my packet of letters, who promised to deliver them, and returned about nine at night to my own house. Mr. Gourlay is indeed greatly altered, several things dropped from him in Conversation this Evening, which Surprized & astonished me, and were far, from what I hoped for & expected. May the Lord yet pour down his grace & Spirit on ministers & people in this poor, very poor & most unhappy Land.

Tuesday November 18 . . . Wrote another letter, & sent to Mr. Gourlay for Charleston, & afterwards wrote a letter to Mrs. Jonathan Donnom who now lives at the Waxaws, her son James is dead, her son Isaac a very decent young man, has lately been down this way, & is this day returning to his mother & a young Sister.[18] Did Some necessary business giving out to the Negroes what useful presents I had purchased for them. Spent Some time in [290] necessary writting, went Over & drank Coffee with Mr. Lambert, and through a part of the Evening were engaged looking over some papers, concerning the

Stock & provisions taken off my Estate, by families from Georgia of whom Some thing may yet be recovered. . . .[19]

Wednesday November 19 . . . Set about looking Over a large bundle of papers, that found upon one of the Shelves left standing, and although I found none of any Consequence yet, as most of them were copies of letters, I had formerly wrote, was reminded of many tender Circumstances, and was often much affected, with a kind of pleasing melancholy, and found this was both very necessary and useful to keep my mind from flagging & sinking into a kind of listless Idleness, & vacuity of thought & action. Was the greatest part of this day alone, & by myself, and I think for the First time, discovered, that such a Situation was painful & disagreeable, and that I wearied much, and longed to be in a more Social way, to be more among Society, & more actively Employed in doing & receiving good. I found myself restless & uneasy, I frequently got up and looked towards the gate, that leads to my house from the publick road, as if I expected to see Somebody coming, though I had really no such thought and had no reason to expect any person. At other times I walked out and looked towards the plantation as if I expected Mr. Lambert, or Somebody, to come that way, and as often, did I look out, the other way, towards Mr. Hamiltons as if I expected him, or Some of his family. This I did as it were mechanically, without thinking what I did, or expecting any person whatsoever, at last I checked myself, and began to think, what I was [291] doing, why I was so restless, why I went out so often and kept looking along these different roads, and Immediately discovered, that I was unhappy to be in such a wilderness, all alone, Having none in the house with me excepting Old Bess quite Superannuated, perhaps the oldest woman in this state black or white, has for some years been a Burthen to herself, and an object of pure Charity to me, Rose, an honest virtuous wench, but slow & not very tractable, and two children, about Six or Seven years of age. This part of the country is almost quite broke up, and the few Inhabitants are Either Overseers on some Gentlemens Estates, Intire strangers to me, or, Some who were very young when I left this Country, and all in general, in such low reduced Circumstances, that they think it would be presuming, should they call on me. The people on the Indian Land Side are many of them in very much the Same Condition, the Neighbourhood, much changed, most of my old friends dead or otherwise removed, the few remaining very much reduced in their Circumstances, very few horses in this part of the Country. It is with the greatest difficulty such as are willing to attend on publick worship, can get it done, hardly such a thing as a Chair, or one horse chaise to be Seen, and these so plain & coarse without any painting and made by Negro house Carpenters, that are much like the Covered Carts, we formerly used for Carrying our Children to School, for these reasons I am all alone without being visited by any, and for want of a horse I cannot ride out. Thus I became sensible, of my wearying and saw the necessity of Endeavouring to Change my present mode of life, and that must if possible get into Some more active way. At the Same time, could not but consider myself as in a bad frame of soul, when could not be Easy & happy with my books, of which I have still many left, though many are taken away, and with access to the Lord my God & Saviour in Secret duties, and at the Same was sensible, that I had neglected some particular duties in which I ought to have been Engaged, such as a day of solemn prayer, of Solemn praise, of solemn, and express renewing of Covenant acceptance of God Father, Son & Holy Ghost, and Solemn express dedication of myself in Every Character & Relation, to God & his service through the blessed Mediator, that had fallen from some good resolutions, with respect to a methodical way of living, of dividing, Spending & improving my time, that had given too much way, to late Sitting at [292] reading & writting, in the night season, which occasions late rising in the morning, that had daily lost too much time, in thinking upon this, & the other Scheme, about my temporal affairs without fixing upon any plan, or doing what was Immediately necessary, that, though I am entirely Submissive, as to the losses I have met with, from both the armies during the war, and that I have sustained, by great numbers of destitute families, driven from Charleston [Purisburgh] & Midway in Georgia, and their own homes, in both states, living for many months together in and about my plantation, yet, that I had spent too much time in reflecting on & murmuring, because of the very shameful & extraordinary Liberties, that some of my professed Friends have all along, both in peace & war, taken with my Substance & Interest, on which they had lived, and greatly helped themselves, while I & my poor children were reduced to distress and great hardships in Scotland, there, I was running in debt, & here, they were advancing themselves by my Interest, while, though the war was raging in other States, ways & means, could have been easily found, to have sent me, such a part of my own, as would have been greatly for my relief, and now, the devastation & destruction, by the war being brought into this state, has occasioned such a loss of papers, receipts & vouchers, such a general confusion, that little or nothing can be recovered, so that it is much the same as if a general bankruptcy had taken place. I say I was made sensible that while reflecting upon these actions of my professed friends, Some of whom are dead, & Some still alive, has troubled me, & too much of my time, has been Spent in thinking how little trust, is to be put in Creatures, that by this I have been too forgetful of the Divine goodness in preserving So much of my Interest, & Subject as is left, and that after so long an absence, and that in times of so great confusion, I ought to Consider all I have left, as clear gain, as the special peculiar Gift of a most merciful providence, that I ought to be more in praising & thanking God, my heavenly Father, for what I have left, than in murmuring for what I have lost, and especially in blessing God for laying his restraints so remarkably on my Servants the Negroes, and that although Some of the persons, who had the care of my affairs have been left to themselves so far as to do what they ought not to have done & what I hope & think they would not have done in more peaceable times, yet that they have been So far restrained, as not to ruin [293] all my subject, which they might have done, but the Lord restrained them. Being sensible of these things, I went to a throne of grace, & was helped to pour out my soul to the Lord . . . Afterwards read the Scriptures, with comfort & Edification, which were comforting & strengthening to my soul, and then came to the following deliberate Resolutions, that I shall, when alone, never allow myself to be Idle, but shall Endeavour to be constantly Employed, with head or hands, as much as possible to have both head & hands Engaged, which is, the best way by a Divine blessing to keep my heart Employed, or, to keep it as the Scripture directs, with all diligence. My meaning is, that by Gods grace, I will carefully guard against, musing & thinking on my family at home, or, my Circumstances here by which I lose much precious time, that I shall Endeavour to mind, what is present duty, and leave the time of my return to my family, the disposing of my Interest here, my preaching in Charleston, or my continuing in the Country, to what providence shall point out, to be my duty. In short, that I will, while by myself, be as much as possible Employed in reading & writting, or Some other necessary Concerns and will by grace be most punctual & careful, in religious duties & exercises, that with respect to my body, I will guard against late reading & writting, that when I cannot have the benefit of reading I will at times exercise myself much in walking, Sometimes in the woods & fields, but at this season, mostly in my own house, or in the piache, or piazza, in Either of which I can have a walk of near forty feet in length, as can pass through the three Rooms on a floor, and that as my poor little horse, has been carefully [294] fed, and looked after, Since I came here, I will frequently ride out and thus Endeavour, while I am in this lonesome Situation, to Improve time usefully, exercising myself unto Godliness, and useful exercises both of body & mind, and that, I will read over every Sabbath night, or next forenoon, what I have wrote in my Diary Since I came to my own house. May the Lord strengthen me, in these & every other Christian resolution. . . .

[295] *Friday November 21* . . . Sent for my horse & rode out. Called on Mr. Lambert, & lost too much time with him, in conversation about the management or rather mismanagement of my affairs, when I was off, & before the war was actually in these parts, which had much better been let alone as it served no good purpose, & raised rather resentment & uneasy reflections in my own mind. After staying too long with him, rode out the Length of a store on the hill near the meetinghouse, kept by one Morrison, an Irish man, or rather Scotch Irish, a stranger to me, come since I left these parts, but having heard of me, gave me a very kindly reception, and made Some apologies about his way of life, in retailing liquor, & keeping a Sort of tavern, as well as a store, found that is chiefly rum & Sugar, with some very coarse things, that he deals in. Met also with two young Gentlemen here, whom I knew when Children & whose parents, I had been well acquainted with, who treated me, with great respect & Civility. [296] Had Some free general conversation with them about the late troublesome times . . . The accounts by a ship from London, are that Early in the month of September the preliminary articles of a peace between Britain & Holland were signed, and that the Definitive treaty of peace, between Britain & France, Britain & Spain, Britain & the Independent United States of America was also Signed by all parties, this Indeed is great & good news, for which we in these states, and particularly in this of South Carolina, ought to be very thankful. . . .

[297] *Lords day November 23* . . . After nine O Clock Mr. Lambert sent over word, that I need not think of going to meeting for nobody would be out, and that for his own part, he could not go. I returned him answer, that for several reasons I wished to go, and was determined in it unless it should Increase to a down pouring of rain, for though it continued a Constant, wetting rain, yet it was not very heavy, and the weather very thick & gloomy. . . . Got to the meeting a few minutes after Eleven, where there was no creature, excepting one Negroe boy sent from Mr. Hamilton to put on a fire, under a shade in the yard, where I formerly preached, while the meeting

house, was a building, and the boy who went with me. Observed all the windows still in the Same condition, as this day fortnight, most of them having the hinges broke, & propped up, with poles on the outside. All this was very discouraging, and produced many melancholy thoughts. About half an hour after Eleven, Morrison who keeps the store, having seen me ride to the meeting, & not return, came to ask me to go up to his house. About twelve O Clock Mr. Hamilton, & three young men from his house came. Waited until half after twelve when there being about ten people come, I proposed, that we should stay where we were, under the shade & near the fire, and here I would give Some exhortations, & go to prayer with them, which I did, with a heart much affected and truly Engaged in the duty. Was helped to be very Earnest in prayer, pleading and wrestling with God, for mercy [298] for spiritual mercies & blessings to this state, to this Neighbourhood & this people in particular. Before I concluded there were about fifteen in all present, was very much affected myself & so were severals present and hope it was not altogether a lost service. . . .

Monday November 24 . . . Mr. Lambert came over, drank tea with me & stayed till eight O Clock. He brought me two letters from Charleston in answer to Some I sent last week by Mr. Gourlay, who returned yesterday. The one from the Misters Penman Informing me, among other things that Captain Bowie is not yet sailed, but will certainly go Soon, so that I have no chance of Sending more letters by him, and that although my rice does not get down very well, Send a barrel to my family, the other from Mr. Ohear, informing me, that the Scotch meeting or the Presbyterian Church was repairing, that there was above seven hundred guineas subscribed, and great Inquiries made to know if I would agree to be their minister, & other things, very encouraging. This night, as well as formerly, I have learned [299] from Mr. Lambert, that Mr. Mitchell my forward & pretended friend, has acted a very unbecoming part in the management of my Estate, has helped himself while I was suffering, and has particularly helped & supported Mr. Henderson, not only while he lived in my house, and preached to this people, but every year since he went to Wilton, out of what was made on my plantation, and that Mr. Henderson though the Nominal Minister of Wilton is manager or Overseer to Mr. Mitchell, whose principal plantation is near the Wilton parsonage. These things have grieved & troubled me very much, and have almost Overset, all the good resolutions, I entered into & wrote on Wednesday last the 19 Instant. May the Lord Jehovah help me, I find myself in very difficult & distressing Circumstances and on many accounts am like to be daily, more & more unhappy. . . .

Tuesday November 25 Long nights, during a good part of which I lie awake, yet blessed be God, do not weary so much in the night as through the day. I think, if ever there was any part of my life in which I might say, wearisome days, & wearisome nights are appointed me, it is now. Idle, lonesome days, are very tiresome, or wearisome, and the want of exercise through the day, I mean of active & fatiguing exercise, makes sleepless nights. . . . If ever there was a time in my life, when I could make the 119 Psalm, the Language of my soul, it is now, and particularly within these few days, I can appropriate the fifteenth verse, this is my comfort, in my affliction, for thy Word hath quickened me, and in the exercise of faith can I pray & daily, I had almost Said hourly do I pray in the words of the 49 verse, Remember the word unto thy servant [300] upon which, thou has caused me to hope, I might have mentioned, the whole of the Sixth part, Viz., the 41:2:3:4:5:6:7:8, as very language, expressing the very present exercise of my soul, or, rather the whole of this deeply experimental psalm. This morning my kind Neighbour Mr. Hamilton sent me a horse, to ride out with him to a Vendue about seven miles distant, near Godfreys Savannah. After an Early breakfast, rode out, and met Mr. Hamilton & Son, who were waiting for Mr. Lambert & me. Mr. Lambert was not ready but came about two hours after we were at the place, which was at Mr. Joseph Donnoms. The Vendue was a Sale of cloathes, books, medicine & a horse, belonging to a young Gentleman, Dr. Brown, who lodged at Mr. Donnoms, & was murdered by some Banditti, within these two months, as noticed when I was in Charleston. His Father is a Presbyterian minister in the state of Virginia. He was a very young man, of a sober good Character, but had given some offense, to a company of notorious villains, who still go about this state murdering & plundering, by his Endeavouring to Discover, the murderers of another young Gentleman Dr. Orr, murdered about four months ago, both shot, scalped, & otherwise, most barbarously used while riding on the publick road in the way of their practice, by persons who lay in the woods waiting for them. Both these murders were committed within Six miles of this house where I now live, the one Dr. Orr shot on the Indian Land Side of Saltcatcher River about four miles south of this place, the other Dr. Brown, about Six miles north on the road to Godfreys Savannah. As rode out, this day to make my observations on what people I should see at a Vendue, when so few came to publick worship,

shall only say, that the people & their manners greatly Increased my melancholy & my disgust to staying in the Country. There was a Considerable
number of people there, a few of them were of my former acquaintance, that
is to say they were the Children of my former friends, who knew me, &
whom I could Remember, and they were in truth, the only persons there who
made anything of a decent appearance. The greatest part, were a set of the
greatest ragamuffins, or ill looked, villainous Countenanced fellows I ever
Saw, most of them had been Soldiers & officers in the Southern Continental army, and no words of Banditti, etc., can convey Such an [301] Idea of
them, as their own looks and behaviour did. I met with a General respectful
behaviour from them all, and was very particularly taken notice of, by such
Gentlemen as were present, yet was greatly shocked to hear the speeches &
see the behaviour of the greatest part. The two principal murderers, were
said to be present, one of them only was pointed out to me, his behaviour,
when the Coat & vest, the unhappy youth wore when murdered, was the
most horrid & Reprobate like that can possibly be Imagined, he held up the
clothes pierced in many places with bullets & other shot, pushed his fingers
through the holes, and called out, to the Company, to see what the Rats had
done etc. etc. etc., his name is Perry, a very little man, very lively & active,
Genteely or very neatly dressed, with a Countenance so full of the most villainous meaning, and his language so horrid, his behaviour so wicked as
Cannot be expressed. The other, who goes by the name of Brown, is a more
decent looking man, and as he was not pointed out to me, and nothing
in his behaviour, appeared remarkable, I did not take any particular notice
of him.[20] Early in the afternoon Mr. Hamilton, Mr. Lambert & I, left the
place, they remarked to me, that they had not seen as much sobriety at such
a meeting for some years, and they thought, my presence had some good
effect. I answered that it might be so, but, it had particularly affected me, to
observe, that the horrid language, the prophane cursing & swearing etc. of
the Company was not the effect of liquor, but of a deep rooted habit, and
universally prevailing degeneracy of practice, and that we had just left them
when they were beginning to set in for Drinking. It was Dark before we got
home. Mr. Lambert & I, spent a good part of the night together, & it was
late before we parted. Was pleased that had rode out this day, as what I had
seen helped to Confirm me, in the remarks I have made Since in these parts,
& in what I take to be my duty with respect to staying, yet on the whole,
thought it a day poorly spent & Improved to very little purpose.

Wednesday November 26 . . . Got up in a humble, serious, thankful frame of soul, and was in hopes, that this would be a comfortable day, but alas it was all like the morning cloud, & the Early dew, that Soon passeth away. I fell into a dull, musing, melancholy way, and lost time much time Sauntering [302] & doing nothing. Had breakfast prepared, (tea, Indian Corn bread & butter) but had no appetite, could not Eat, could not Swallow and what with difficulty I got over, I soon after vomited. Ordered it to be put away, proposed this exercise, & the other to myself, but could fix on nothing. Went Sauntering about, Sometimes Sitting, Sometimes walking, Sometimes out of doors, Sometimes within, went about the form of morning duties, but alas, it was a mere formality. Was very sensible of my own weakness & Infirmity, in being reduced to this unhappy Situation, by the want of Society, and from my present lonely Circumstances. Was also very sensible that Satan the grand adversary, was very busy and active against me, and had a great hand in my present distresses by his Suggestions of past Events into my mind, Sometimes tender & affecting Circumstances of my Dear deceased whose Dear Dust lies Interred at Stoney Creek meeting Indian Land were presented to my mind, and Sometimes very tender affecting Circumstances of my Dear (I hope) living family were presented in the most lively manner, and Sometimes strange Imaginations concerning, how it might be at present with my Dear family in Scotland, so Suddenly struck & affected, that I started up, clasped my hands, & walked about, as one in terror & amazement. At Last about one O Clock I found myself ready to Choke, or burst, like one that was stifled, or Suffocated, I immediately apprehended, that I was hypt, or falling into the hypochondria, which I have always considered as a most miserable disorder, upon which I cast myself down on my knees, cried unto God to have compassion on me, to Rebuke Satan, to deliver me from my present weaknesses & distresses, to revive, quicken, Support & strengthen me by his grace & Spirit, having thus prayed & begged of God to have pity for a few minutes, I burst into a flood of tears, which to [303] or with me, is very uncommon, but at this time was sent by my heavenly Father as a most happy & seasonable relief, here I went & made Supplication, and having Continued Some time in prayer, I got up & took the Bible to read in my Ordinary, but happened to open at the 22nd chapter of Lukes Gospel, which I read, together with the two following chapters, much to my comfort & Edification, what Struck me at first was these words 22:31:32 verses, Simon Simon behold, Satan hath desired to have you, that he may Sift you, as wheat, but I have prayed for thee, that thy faith fail not, and when thou art Converted strengthen thy Brethren. Afterwards, the account of our blessed Lords Sufferings, Death resurrection, & ashension was made most comforting and Encouraging to me. Went again to prayer, and concluded with praise. After this was able to take Some dinner. About four O Clock Mr. Hamilton having been in the Rice field near my house, came up the hill, & we walked together over to Mr. Lamberts, and returned before Dark. Afterwards had a comfortable Evening. . . .

[310] *Thursday the 4th of December 1783* On Sabbath night was comfortably refreshed with sleep, got up in a humble, thankful frame of soul. Was helped in morning duties. Was afterwards made uneasy in Some sick Negroes, whose complaints I could not well understand, and knew not if there was real Sickness in the case. To be connected with them, is to me very disagreeable, and yet also very necessary in this Country & made me more than ever think of parting with them, and that also has its difficulties. Went over & Dined with Mr. Lambert, and having now got a young horse, so far broke, as for a boy to ride, I set off, with one of his boys for the Indian Land, and got to young Mr. Cuthberts at Dark, where spent the Evening agreeably with Him & another young man. On Tuesday December 2, after breakfast set out for my good old friend Mr. Postells, was in a humble serious frame of soul, obliged to ride slow, as my horses are small & weakly. Was melancholy while riding, through a long lonely path on every Side of which, saw the desolations of the war. Was helped in Ejaculatory prayer, about twelve O Clock, got to my friends house, and to my regrate found that my very particular friend Mrs. Postell was gone from home, being sent for last Thursday to see her sister, formerly Mrs. Perry & a very particular friend of mine, who was dangerously ill, this was a very sensible disappointment to me. [311] Mr. Postell, was in his field, was Soon called, & gave me a very affectionate reception, had Seen both him & her at the Stoney Creek meeting when I preached there. Soon after, Mr. Job McPherson, his wifes Brother came to Dine with him, we were Some hours together, in Conversation on the late evil times, and the great hardships, they had gone through & the great losses they had sustained in their property, and the horrid devastations made both by the British & American armies, on the quiet & peaceable Inhabitants, as they Succeeded one another, in possessing the Country, which is the common topick of Conversation in every family when visited by a stranger. Late in the afternoon, I rode home with Mr. McPherson, the whole family being very particular friends

of mine, their Mother died about two years ago, in a good old age. Got to Mr. McPhersons just at Dark and spent the evening very agreeably with him and his wife, another good friend. Was in a humble, serious, watchful frame of mind, comfortably assisted in family prayer with my friends. On Wednesday December 3 after a very comfortable nights sleep, which I believe the riding helped me to, awoke praising the Lord in a humble, heavenly frame of soul & after breakfast Mrs. McPherson rode with me, to call on her Sister in Law, the widow of a good friend of mine, Captain John McPherson, a very worthy good woman, who has the Comfort of having her only child now living, Mr. John McPherson, settled with his family very near her. Spent about an hour with my friends here, and set off for home. Was very melancholy while riding, but helped to remove it, by Ejaculatory [prayers] & praises to God, who had Sent me & mine to a Zoar,[21] while his awful Judgments were on this Land, once a very happy & flourishing, but now a pillaged & desolate Land, and what is the worse, the few Inhabitants left very much degenerated. . . .

[313] *Friday December 5* . . . Spent the forenoon mostly in writting letters to Charleston, though know of no opportunity of forwarding them. Wrote to Mr. Ohear, my purpose of being down as soon as I can get a Safe opportunity for myself & my things, my determination not to keep house in Charleston, and desire to board in his family if he can let me have a Room with a fireplace for a few months, till I may have an opportunity of returning to Britain, if spared, and about several other matters. Wrote to the Misters Penman, about Inquiring after a purchaser for my Lands & Negroes, as would willingly have my Interest turned into money. . . .

Saturday December 6th . . . In the afternoon received a message from Mr. Lambert to come over and went, found [314] that Jamy the Driver, had been drunk as he often is and behaved very ill, Endeavoured to sooth both Mr. Lambert and the fellow, and got matters made up. Visited the barn, and all the Negroe houses which are all better built & furnished than most of the farmhouses in Scotland, they have all chimneys built to their houses, fireplaces in two & three rooms, have all yards & Gardens fenced in, and live in great Ease & great plenty, having cornfields of their own, raising fowls & hogs for themselves. Had the wench Maria blooded it being near her time and complaining. Returned before Dark, in a humble serious frame of spirit. . . .

Lords day December 7 . . . Rode to the meeting house with Mr. Lambert, about eleven O Clock and at twelve, there was Something of a Congregation gathered, though Still very small, there might be about fifty white people and a few Negroes, the whole were most attentive and the greatest part of them Seemed struck with wonder, and amazement at the things that they heard, was greatly & most assisted both in prayers & in the sermon, preached with great freedom and Enlargement from Heb: 12:2 on Looking to Jesus, and was Enabled to deal faithfully, both with Saints and Sinners . . . [315] After I came down from the pulpit was applied to administer Baptism, to a child, which after conversing with the parents and inquiring into their Character, I did in the Study or retiring house before a few witnesses, in a word, this day, was something like former times in this place. After conversing with a family of my old acquaintances, rode home by Mr. Lamberts, where was very much surprized to find him have above twelve grown people to Dine with him. This is a practice he has for Some time past very much fallen into. He has been used at times, to give prayers for which he is well qualified, and to read a sermon in the meeting house, to a dozen or fifteen hearers, and to Encourage them to come out, he used to Invite most of them to Dine with him. His design is good, yet I think it is a bad practice, as it keeps both his house Negroes and mine, dressing a large feast & Entertainment on the Lords day, when they being the most knowing & Sensible, should be particularly encouraged to go to publick worship, as well as the others. I dined with them, and Immediately after Dinner, proposed to go to my own house and the whole company went off. . . .

Monday December 8 . . . [316] Was at home between seven & eight O Clock at night and at my house found Mrs. Anderson, now Mrs. Thompson, who soon after I moved to this plantation, kept house for me, and took care of my children till they went for Britain and being always very kind to me, I left her & Old Bess to take care of the house and of Sick Negroes, during my absence, if she remained Single which she did upwards of five years. During two or three years at that time Mr. Henderson now minister at Wilton lived in the house, and preached to this people. Some time in the fifth year, she was with child & so managed it, as to be very little taken notice of, till she was taken in Labour pains, & was delivered of her child in this house. She Sat at table, three times every day, with Mr. Henderson, yet he pretended never to have discovered her being with child, till she was in Labour. Others declared, & now declare that they had seen unbecoming freedoms betwixt him & her and had Suspected her being with child, but kept silence, on account of his Character, & Station in the Church. Soon after her delivery, a Magistrate was brought to the house, & she swore the Child, to one Hall a Taylor, who worked about the Neighbourhood, & had Sometimes been about this house, making cloaths for the Negroes, he acknowledged guilt, but solemnly & perseveringly affirmed that the child did not come to his time, but according to the Law of this Land, or the Law of England, he could not be allowed to take this Oath. This Oath of hers fixed the child on him, but did not satisfy people in the Neighbourhood. As soon as it was proper, to remove her, my attornies discharged her from the plantation. She found great difficulty to be received into any place, and after wandering about for near two years, in the most destitute Condition, she was after Mr. Hendersons removal to Wilton received again into this plantation but obliged for Some months, to live in a Negroe house near to the Overseers house, and at last was permitted to live in this house along with Old Bess, and Some time [317] in the Last Spring was married to her present husband Thomson a shoemaker, living about three or four miles from this. She has been sick this fall, & her husband had visited me some time ago. She had walked here this day to Inquire after my Children, & to whom she had always been very kind, and in all respects behaved well in my family, when I lived here. She also brought her child with her, a Daughter of between Six & Seven years of age, a very Decent likely Child, & well grown for her age. The childs Countenance struck me at once, she being the very picture of Henderson, who is a tall man, with a long face, the child has his Eyes, mouth & nose, and the most striking likeness I ever Saw, between a child & a parent. As it was late, and as I had a good account of her behaviour Since her misconduct, and that she has given good proof for years past of her humility & repentance, and has been for Some years past, looked upon to be a very broken hearted person and to have Some Secret grief preying upon her Spirits, and being herself a Grand Daughter of a very worthy Presbyterian minister, who came from the North of Ireland many years ago & was Settled on Port Royal, whose name was Orr, & who an old meeting house in Beaufort [sic], and as she had been always very careful of my children, for these reasons I Invited her to stay all night, and Showed the same respect to her as formerly. . . .

Tuesday December 9 . . . [318] After breakfast had some conversation with Mrs. Thomson about her misbehaviour and gave her a Suitable exhortation, at the Same time made her a Small present of Six yards of coarse Irish Linen, some tea & sugar and two Coarse handkerchiefs, and Promised her husband who is a shoemaker & tanner a barrel of Lime, which she came to solicit for, and dismissed her. . . .

Wednesday December 10 Should have mentioned above, that yesterday in conversation with Mrs. Thompson, made some very melancholy discoveries, which very much Confirmed my desire of Selling the plantation and Negroes, Learned that my substance had been very much wasted or rather taken to their own use, by professed friends and even by those who should have protected and preserved it for me. The troublesome times made many take such Liberties with my property, as could never have been thought of at other times, and not only so, but that my house, was used for the vilest purposes, Lord, give me counsel & direction what to do. . . .

[319] *Thursday December 11* . . . After Breakfast rode out with Mr. Lambert to a friend of his, where he had engaged to Dine. Called at & sat above an hour Mr. George Timmons & his wife, a Daughter of Mr. James Jordan, one of my former friends long ago in Eternity. Mr. Timmons is an overseer for Mr. Blake, his wife, the once very handsome & sprightly Polly Jordan, is very much altered, they have five children living, and are but [in] narrow straitened Circumstances, yet very happy together, and are serious good people. Mr. Jordans two sons, are living in Georgia. Afterwards proceeded to Mr. Howie[22] who has the management of all Mr. Blakes plantations with several Overseers under him. Mr. Howie is a man of large fortune himself, & yet chooses to live in this way. He appears to be a very sensible man, very Capable of business and is full of it, shows no regard to religion, behaves well and like a Gentleman to every person, and is Esteemed in the Neighbourhood, lives in great affluence and gives good Entertainments to all who visit him, and always a particular respect to Mr. Lambert and his friends. We dined with him & Some other Company, and were most genteely Entertained, found Mr. Howie very conversable, & friendly. . . .

[320] *Friday December 12* . . . In the afternoon Mr. Lambert & I walked over to Mr. Hamiltons, and spent some hours there in agreeable Conversation. Yet in walking home with Mr. Lambert, had Some uneasiness, in finding that he is not so cordially & fully, reconciled to Mr. Hamilton, as becomes them, as Christians and as I could wish, for their own Sakes, and also upon

my own account, because if I cannot sell my plantation & Negroes, I want
Mr. Lambert to live in Charleston, and that Mr. Hamilton should have the
management of this plantation, Mr. Lamberts Negroes & mine planting together, which I think, would be for the advantage of us both. But if Mr.
Lambert & Mr. Hamilton, are not cordially reconciled, it will not do, and I
know not any other I could put Over my place as have not a sufficient number of hands to Engage an Overseer, whereas Mr. Hamilton is so situated,
that he could easily take care of his own affairs & of ours also, at a moderate
expense. Sometimes Mr. Lambert agrees that we should employ Mr. Hamilton and that he himself will live in Charleston, & leave the most of his people to plant with mine, both his & mine, are too few, to Engage an Overseer
for them alone. At other times Mr. Lamberts speaks of his going to Georgia,
with his people, & purchase a settlement and Sometimes of his living on the
place himself, so that I am often troubled & know not what to think. May
the [321] Lord Jehovah my God & Father, give me council & direction from
himself. . . .

[322] *Lords day December 14* . . . Went over to Mr. Lamberts, half past ten,
at Eleven we set out for the meeting house and were among the first there,
afterwards people came in much greater numbers than I expected, and by
twelve O Clock there was a decent Congregation, larger than any I have seen
in the Country. At twelve O Clock, began publick worship, and preached
from Psl: 119:60 with great fullness, freedom & Earnestness to a very Serious
and attentive Congregation. Had the Lords most gracious help & assistance,
and it appeared to be a good time, a season of grace & power. Baptized Mr.
Timmonses child, a grand Daughter of my good old friend Mr. James Jordan. Mr. John Roberts another of my former friends was present from a very
Considerable distance, he was my Clerk this day, as he formerly used to be,
so that we had Singing in publick worship of God, which is the first time
Since I Came to Saltcatcher. Mr. William Lambright formerly my Overseer
in this place, afterwards married to a daughter of Mr. Samuel Wilkins, a considerable fortune, but much reduced in the time of the late war, came from
Coosawhatchie to See me. After sermon, in which I was much fatigued, he
came to Mr. Lamberts & Dined with us, Drank tea there, when I came home
& Mr. Lambright went to sleep at Mr. Hamiltons. He appears [323] to be a
very Sober sensible good Christian. He was ever Since I knowed him well disposed, and I think is greatly Improved both in the rational & the Christian

life. He has been much harassed by the British and met with great losses during the war, but is still blessed with the Comfort of his wife, a Son & a daughter. Spent the Evening in reading & writting. . . .

Monday December 15 . . . Was Employed in writting a letter to Mr. John Smith at Coosawhatchie, as an apology for my not visiting his family, which Indeed has not been in my power. I have now got two young horses of a very Small breed broke, so that I could ride about the Neighbourhood, but they are not fit, to carry me to any distance, and at present there is a great fresh in Saltcatcher River, so that they cannot be made to Enter the ferry boat, and I cannot possibly get over, without very great danger. Wrote also to Mr. John Cuthbert, son to the Doctor, acquainting him, that I could not possibly visit his Father & Mother at Beaufort, unless I was assisted to go over & return this week, being determined to go to Charleston, next week, or as soon as Mr. Blakes sloop which Eldridge Commands, returned. . . . Stayed about half an hour at Pattersons who keeps the ferry, an old acquaintance, who was once a very great professor of religion, but like many others in this state & in this Neighbourhood has become a very great backslider, if not an [324] apostate from religion altogether, however I was very respectfully received by him and his family. He excused with his having been very Sick this fall, and but just recovering, as the reason of his not being at sermon Since I have preached in the parts. Stayed about an hour in friendly Conversation with him, encouraging him to attend on publick worship when he has opportunity & ability. Came round by Morrisons at the hill. . . . At this place, I also met with a Captain McNeil, who is married to Mrs. Griffiths that was and now lives at her place, over the River, her Children by her former husband are in England whither Mr. Griffiths had carried his family during the late unhappy war. Captain McNeil who appears to be but a young man, is from the North of Ireland of Scotch parents, says his mothers name was Montgomery and that he was a relation of Mrs. McVicars in Liverpool, of Mrs. Tuckers in Greenock and of Mrs. John Hunters, that he was related to these families both by his Father & Mothers Side, but could not tell what the relation was, that he was very Intimately acquainted with Mrs. McVicar, that he had been in Greenock about two years ago, and gave me a very particular account of Mrs. John Crawford, Jeany Tucker that was, of Miss Sally Tucker, and of several others, which made me Conclude, that he is Some distant relation of my Dear Mrs. Simpsons. He is about Setting up a store at this place in Company with Some other Gentlemen, and sets out for Charleston tomorrow, or I should have visited him soon at his own house, being formerly acquainted with his wife. Stayed here & dined with him & some other Gentlemen, after Dinner went home, in a humble watchful frame of soul. . . .

[329] *Lords day December 21* Another Solitary Sabbath, Confined from preaching, Lord when, O when shall I be restored, to my more stated & usual labors, in thy Vineyard, had Some refreshing sleep in the night, yet felt poorly in the morning, the pain over my Loins rather increased, the pain in my Side [330] troublesome & uneasy, was in hopes that the Sciatic or Rheumatism, would have freed me from pleauratick stitches, but it is not so. Got up at the usual time, rather late for a Sabbath morning, was well assisted in prayer & Supplication . . . After Dark received a Message from the plantation, that there was great disturbance there, by the Driver Jamy & his wife Moriah fighting, that he had beat & turned her out of Doors, and that my presence was very necessary. Accordingly I went over, found Mr. Lambert very much Indisposed, (and Indeed he has lost all authority in the plantation, and is not minded either by his own Negroes nor mine). After some time, I got matters between these worthless creatures, who are both of them very wicked, and very vile, made up, partly by threats, & partly by Soothing, and Jamy took home his wife, with many promises on both Sides to behave well to one another. Stayed about two hours with Mr. Lambert and returned, Sick, heart Sick, of having anything to do with Negroes, and Confirmed, in my Desire to sell all, if the Lord will give an opportunity. Was in a humble, serious, devout frame of soul. . . .

Monday December 22 . . . [331] In the forenoon looking over my Cloathes & what books I have left, packing up my Chest for Charleston. Was very melancholy & dejected, at the thoughts of leaving this place & the people hereabouts, who have no prospect of Enjoying the Gospel, & what is still worse, no desire after it. . . .

Wednesday December 24 . . . Was obliged to go over, to the plantation & give Some directions about the Negroes having their Christmas holly days. Appointed mine to have one Bull, & Mr. Lamberts another, to have three Gallons of Rum among them, one Bull killed tomorrow, the other on Friday, that on Saturday, they should be called out an hour after Sunrise, to Cut firewood, and do a few trifling things so that they might be altogether in some order for work on Monday, for from Wednesday night, till Saturday morning their whole time will be spent in Drinking, dancing, madness and wickedness. Left them all pleased & Satisfied. Spent the Evening usefully and Comfortably by myself. . . .

[332] *Friday December 26* . . . Received a letter from Mr. Ohear dated the 13 Instant, Informing me among other particulars that the repairs of the Presbyterian Church would be nearly done by the first of January, and that my return to the City was most earnestly and anxiously desired, that the Reverend Mr. Hollinshead the minister for the [333] Independent Church is come in from Philadelphia,[23] with his family and is very much Esteemed by his people, and that he agrees to my proposal of lodging at his house etc., all which gave me great Satisfaction (should have mentioned, on Tuesday afternoon while Mr. Hamilton & I were at Mr. Lamberts, Mr. Mitchells second son William, came there on his way to the Indian Land, & brought a letter for me from his Father giving me much the Same Information, about the Presbyterian church, and the Independent minister as above, with a pressing request in name of the Presbyterian church, to return to the Charleston as soon as possible. The young man Informed me that the roads were exceedingly bad, that he had been Some days in getting from Charleston, this length, but being a youth & desirous to spend Christmas, with his Mothers relations at Indian Land, he had come, though in some places at the risk of his life. Mr. Lambert & I sent a Negroe fellow on Wednesday to see him safe over Saltcatcher ferry, & through the fresh which is very great). Returned from Morrisons to Mr. Lamberts, thankful for the accounts I had received from Charleston, and spent the Evening at home by myself. . . .

Saturday December 27 . . . Was through the forenoon, looking Over my books & pamphlets, burnt many fragments, put up those, in a trunk, I wish to have sent to Charleston, and left the rest, many valuable books in English, Latin, Greek & Hebrew to be sold at Vendue, most of them being much hurted in their binding, and expect very little for them, yet it would be only [334] an expense and to no purpose for me to have them sent down to the City, where Second hand books Sell only as waist paper, and to carry them to Scotland would cost more than they are worth. . . .

Lords day December 28 . . . Early in the morning raised the Negroe Rose, and drank some boiled milk with Sugar. Afterwards slept till ten O Clock, got up very much Indisposed. Was helped in prayer, & crying unto the Lord, afterwards Spent about two hours among my books & pamphlets, it being a work of necessity. Dined with Mr. Lambert, where met with an old acquaintance, a Mr. Arthurly, who Sometime after the war was begun fled to the Creek Indians and lived among them, till lately, heard very dismal accounts from Him, of the past times. . . .

Monday December 29 . . . Was all the forenoon packing up my things, was much Interrupted with Company, Mr. Lambert, [335] Mr. Arthurly and Mr. Gourlay, who stayed Dinner, Mr. Lambert wants to Employ Arthurly, as an Overseer, & is much set upon it, whereas I thought, he had agreed to Engage Mr. Hamilton, but find his quarrel with him is not yet over. In the afternoon went & took my leave of Mrs. Hamilton, who has been very neighbourly Since I came here, afterwards Settled Some accounts with Mr. Lambert, who I thought was rather sharp, & selfish, and did not act, as I expected, which among many other things makes me wish to get quit of the plantation & Negroes if I can do it conveniently, so as not to hurt my family. Lord grant it, for thy glorious name Sake, if it is thy holy & blessed will.

Tuesday December 30 A very stormy night of wind & rain, which Continued until ten O Clock this forenoon, and though the wind fell & the rain stopped, yet it was dark & Cloudy all day. At Eleven, Set off from my own house, with the Ox Cart & my things. Mr. James Hamilton & his son James went with me. At 12 O Clock took a young man, a nephew of Eldridges named George into the boat & set off with three oars, young Mr. James Hamilton went with me, we were about five hours, on the water, and rowed upwards of thirty miles, got aboard of the Schooner, before Six O Clock, found that the patroon or Captain Eldridge had not taken in all his loading & must stay here another day. Was in a comfortable frame of soul, praying to & hoping in God. . . .

1784

[349] *Thursday January 22*[24] Had a very sleepless night. Have for some time been much troubled with a pain in my left Jaw, which is always worst in the night, and has broke my rest often Since my return to the City, and I believe is owing to what I Suffered on my passage from Saltcatcher. Last night, it was so violent, that I was obliged to get up about two O Clock, light a candle &

hold Spirits in my mouth, which afforded me Some Ease . . . Visited Mrs. Thomas, whose Daughter a young Lady, has been very bad of a fever, & is not yet out of danger, Stayed about three quarters of an hour & prayed by her. The Scarlet fever & Sore throat prevails much in the place. In the afternoon made several Calls. A Sad accident fell out, a boy about nine or ten years of age, fired a musket from his Fathers shop door & shot a little sister about four or five years of age, through the breast who died Instantly, wounded another Sister a young Lady of about fifteen, through the right hand cross ways, and shot another very amiable young Lady of seventeen under the left Jaw & tore the Cheek in a most dreadful manner, the only Child of the next door neighbour. My heart bleeds for the poor parents & the wounded persons. May the God of all grace [350] support & comfort them. . . .

Friday January 23 . . . My pain increased so much that after some sleepless hours in bed, I got up and rubbed where the pain was most tormenting with rum & my Gums, with Laudanum. Afterwards kept reading till about four O Clock, when fell asleep, and wakened about Seven much refreshed. . . . In the Evening Captain Ewing & Mr. Crawford who lives with Dr. Turnbull[25] called & Drank tea with me at my lodgings, a very cold night with a constant sleeting kind of rain. I was obliged to Entertain them in the hall, where there is Sometimes a Small fire kept, the family having for these ten days past, no firewood but they borrow in very Small quantities, and which is burnt chiefly in their own bedroom, and in old Mrs. Ohears room, who is at this time Sick. I have for these Eight days past Employed a friend to get me a cord of wood at my own expense, but the weather being so bad, little is brought to the City, and the demand, So great, that he has not as yet, been able to procure it. I never Suffered So much with cold in my life, and though I am obliged to walk in my room, when Engaged in study & preparatory duties, yet cannot write anything, my hands being almost constantly benumbed. . . .

Saturday January 24 Last night was on several counts one of the most distressing nights, I ever passed through. About nine O Clock the pain in my Jaw, my Ear & teeth began to be very grievous & distressing. . . . I cannot possibly describe the torment & misery I was in for several hours, got at the Small case where I have Some rum, and bathed my Cheek with it, poured it into my Ear, held it in my mouth, and used every mean in my power, which gave Some temporary ease, but still it returned more violent than ever so that

I was in a most miserable Condition, wretched and unhappy to a [351] a very great degree . . . At nine O Clock, when was sent for to breakfast, the family were struck and amazed at my very pale & distressed appearance, and expressed great concern for me. I had fully designed to send for a physician and have a tooth drawn, which is a little affected, but was very unwilling to disappoint the Congregation tomorrow, and tried Laudanum & Camphere, which by the blessing of God gave me great ease, upon which I determined to fall to study & preparatory duties, and though was often ready to break off, & send for the physician yet persevered, and had a tolerably easy day. But what was far more desirable, had much of the Lords gracious & most Comfortable presence. . . .

Lords day January 25 . . . Last night when going to bed, took a dose of Furlington say twenty drops, and Eleven drops of a Laudanum, in hopes of getting Some sleep, yet it was near morning before I slept, but what I got was very comfortable & refreshing. . . . After breakfast, went to my friend Mr. Desaussures, where a good fire & a warm room was ready for me. Preached both parts of the day from Heb: 13:5 Last Clause, He hath said, I will never leave thee, nor forsake thee, with the Lord Jehovahs most comfortable presence, help & assistance, delivered many heartfelt & experimental truths to a most serious and attentive Congregation, so that this appeared to be a great & a good day of the Son of God, the Son of Man, many were greatly moved, and the power & the [352] glory of God appeared to be amongst us. Yet there were others, particularly Some young tradesmen from Scotland whose behaviour I was told was rather offensive. I did not see them, or would have taken notice of it, great is the dissipation of manners, and the Contempt of religion at present in this place, and among none more, or so much as among the Scotch Merchants & tradesmen. . . .

[353] *Thursday January 28*[26] . . . In the afternoon was Engaged in some necessary business, in writting to, & seeking after one Walker,[27] a factor, who Some years ago sold ninety Six barrels of my Rice, and two barrels of Indigo for about four hundred pounds Sterling and has Embezzled the money, I have been Endeavouring to bring him, to give Some account, ever since I came into this State, and this afternoon found that he has lately been put in Jail, so that all will be lost, which is another addition to the many losses I have met with, during the late troublesome times, wrote him a letter, and Informed my attorney where he is. . . .

Friday January 30 . . . About four O Clock, received a packet, containing a letter from my Dear Mrs. Simpson, one from Betsy, one from my sister, & one from Mr. Johnston[28] informing, that a letter from Susie was aboard of the flora Captain Rankin, said to be in sight of the Bar, and that on the nineteenth of November, they were all well & happy, praise, praise be to God for his mercies to them & me. Cannot tell how happy & Comfortable this made me, they had received my letter of the ninth of September by Captain Stead on the 29th of October, & also my letter dated off Bermudas some time before we got here, read [354] these Dear letters over & over, and could not Sufficiently express my Gratitude and thankfulness to God my chiefest Joy. . . .

Lords day first day of February 1784 . . . Preached both parts of the day, with great fullness and freedom from Psalm 27:13 to a very serious & attentive auditory, the blessing and power of God appeared to accompany his word. Saw severals very much affected & in tears. . . . In the evening baptized my Land Lords child at home, a Daughter of about ten weeks old. The people here are in no hurry to have their children Baptized, the people in Scotland run to the other extream. I think both are wrong. Some friends were present, it was a solemn time and the Lord was with us. . . .

Monday February 2 . . . Was in the forenoon employed in writting, and in the middle of the day aboard of John McIvers Brigg. They are to return in about a Month, am anxiously desirous to go with them, could I possibly do it, but can get nothing done in Settling my temporal affairs, meet with so much delay, so many excuses, and so much villainy in Some of whom better things was to be expected, that I am heartsick of it, and long to get away, as my attornies can do everything as well without as with my being in the state, and as for my official duties, the Presbyterian church are so backward, that I am grieved to see it, and have little hope of doing good among them.

Tuesday February 3 . . . Still doing all I can to get my affairs settled, but making little or no progress. This day got my account from Mr. Mitchell, a very different one, from what I Expected, and from what he had formerly promised, both by write, and by his own declarations. [355] May the Lord bring me out of these difficulties, and if it is His holy will return me to my family and friends in Scotland. . . .

Thursday February 5 . . . This Evening I married Mr. John Reid of this City to Miss Elizabeth Penny, by a License directed to me, from the Ordinary of this district, all professions & denominations of the Protestant religion being now and having the Same privileges which the church of England had formerly, excepting that the State maintains none. Every denomination, the church of England as well as others, maintain their own Clergy. Received as is usual in this place the Complement of a piece of money, blessed be the Lord that gives me to find favour with many here, and makes me most acceptable as a minister of the Gospel. . . .

Saturday February 7 . . . About twelve O Clock, walked out and met with the young Mr. Laird Son of David in Port Glasgow, Just arrived in the flora Captain Rankin, whom I also met with on the Street, went aboard of the ship lying out in the Stream, and received a large packet of letters from my Dear family and friends. . . . [356] I received two letters from Mrs. Simpson & Betsy, two from Susy, one from Mr. Forrest[29] & one from Mr. Johnston the latest of them dated the third of December 1783. By these letters, I am Informed, that my Dear Mrs. Simpson has been bad with the St. Anthonys fire, or the Rose in her leg, but was recovered and again in good health, that my Dear Girles have been very dutiful to her, that they live in much peace & love together and that they are all in good health, & great hopes of my being home soon, that Susy is much pressed by Mr. Johnston to marry him, that she though well pleased with him refuses marriage before I return, that her Mama insists on her marrying and will take me in her own hand. I had given my Consent before I left Scotland, and am very well pleased it should take place, and doubt not but it is, or will be done, by this time. My prayer is, that God may bless them together, & make them blessings to one another. . . .

[357] *Tuesday February 10* . . . Got Mr. Mitchell to make Some alterations in his account, in my favour, by private hints I had received when in the Country, made Sad discoveries into the baseness of his Conduct, and the rottenness [358] of his heart & all under the Mask of a religious profession & friendship for me, but cannot now help myself. Late in the afternoon visited & Drank tea with Mr. Daniel Legaree who I believe is a worthy good man and has been long Confined with sickness. . . .

Wednesday February 11 . . . Through most of the day engaged in writting to my Dear family, on the Important concern of Susies Marriage with Mr. Johnston to which I have now again, as formerly, given my most free & hearty consent, and advised Susy to marry when they please, this has ever since the time he proposed it given me much thought & Sent to me often to a throne of grace. Have every reason to be pleased & Satisfied with it, and humbly hope that God will bless them. In the middle of the day was aboard of Captain Rankins ship, who is very much of a Gentleman. Am very desirous to return to Britain with him. In the Evening Drank tea at Dr. Ramsays where were several Gentlemen of the first Rank in this & some other states. From their Conversation, I learned that there is much disorder & Confusion in all the states, and no good understanding among the states themselves, that the general Congress has very little authority, that the publick Credit is likely to be much, very much hurted, by the Selfishness, dishonesty, unjustice, & resentment against Great Britain, and her adherents that universally prevails among many in the Legislature of every state, and as to Individuals very little honour or honesty with regard to their private debts, is to be met with in any state, all which, confirmed me in my resolution to return to Scotland as soon as possible, if the Lord shall be pleased to carry me there, and to withdraw my little Interest as soon as it can be done. The Reverend Mr. Hollingshead & I, went & returned together, and were very melancholy at the Representation of publick & private affairs which we heard, and the truth of which we were fully Convinced. Spent the rest of the Evening in my lodging, till late, in study for Sabbath, with the Lords gracious presence. There are frequent Robberies of Cellars & stores, almost Every night in this City, and although, the Intendant & Trustees, who are the Magistrates of the City, have Set up Lamps, Established a City watch and Issued many good Ordinances, yet these & other villanies Still prevail very much. This week is the Charleston races, great numbers of young people are come from the Country to be present at them, the town is full of Company and of many fine horses. Much money has been spent & gambled away, much fraud & wickedness committed, while the great body of the people through the whole state and especially in the Country are in very wretched distressed Circumstances. All principles of honour & common honesty seem to be gone, and religion almost wholly vanished, except in the City, where there are still a good many [359] who attend the preaching of the Gospel, and are desirous of living as becomes Christians, & good Citizens, which good Spirit It is hoped will gradually Spread & prevail over the state, peace, order, decency & good Government be in time restored through all the United States, Grant it O God, Grant it for Christs sake. . . .

Thursday February 12 . . . Late in the afternoon Drank tea at my friend Mr. DeSaussures, who is with his wife & youngest daughter returned from the Country from Indian Land, which is still in the Same Situation as when I left it, no Society, no regard to religion or publick worship, many disorders prevailing & Robberies frequently up the Saltcatcher. Supped at my lodgings & sat up pretty late in study & preparation for Sabbath. . . .

Friday February 13 Early this morning was called upon to visit a man said to be sick or distracted, got up and went out as soon as I could, found it to be Mr. Bellamy Crawford, in a high delirium, without any fever. Endeavoured to soothe & quiet him, and got liberty to pray with him. Was grieved to see such poverty & wretchedness in his family, who I had formerly Seen in the greatest affluence, and all brought on Evidently by his own misconduct. . . .

Saturday February 14 . . . In the Evening visited poor Mr. Crawford. Found him still in the same very unhappy situation, He still knew me, yet appeared every now & then to be perfectly delirious. Was informed that last night he had Six very severe Convulsion fits, apprehended that these would return & carry him off. Prayed with him, called upon Some others, Drank tea at home, and sat up late. . . .

Lords day February 15 . . . [360] After sermon went to visit Mr. Crawford, & was told he had another convulsion fit this morning & died in it, at seven O Clock, having most part of the night been bound with cords and held by five men in the bed, returned & Spent the Evening in my lodgings, quite Overcome with the Labours of yesterday & this day. . . .

Monday February 16 . . . At five O Clock attended at Mr. Crawfords burying, in the Independent churchyard, Mr. Hollingshead spoke a little & prayed at the grave, this is the second funeral I have attended with him, and have been much pleased, & Edified with his excellent discourses & prayers, short and Substantial. He appears to be a Gentleman of great prudence & piety, a fine speaker and of a very warm, tender & affectionate heart. . . .

[363] *Monday First day of March 1784* . . . In the forenoon, along with Mr. Brodie, waited upon the Sheriff of this District & allowed Liberty to visit Some Criminals under sentence of Death. Visited a mulatoe fellow and two Negroes in the Sugar house prison. Discoursed & prayed with the mullatoe, who wept much & was greatly affected, afterwards Discoursed & prayed with the two Negroes who were serious & thankful. They are to die on the Wednesday next, for house breaking. They appear to be Something penitent, but very ignorant. Afterwards visited two white men in the prevosts prison who are to be executed next Friday for Robbery in the Country. They appeared to be very serious & much affected, but more Ignorant than the other three. Was well assisted in discoursing & praying with them, felt myself much spent & fatigued with these exercises, and the Long walk I had to take between the two prisons. Learned that Mr. Hollingshead had been twice with the two white men but not with the others. In the afternoon packed up a trunk of books to go home in McIvers brigg, to sail this week for Greenock. It grieves & distresses me much that I cannot get my affairs so settled as to go home in her. . . .

Tuesday March 2 . . . [364] At twelve O Clock, went to the prevost, discoursed & prayed with the two white Criminals, they were very thankful, appeared serious & much affected, but still extremely Ignorant, and to have exercise of mind about their Salvation. One of the Jailors wept while I was discoursing & praying, and all present showed much concern. I then went out to the Sugar house prison, discoursed & prayed with the mullatoe & the two Negroes. They also were much affected, appear to have more knowledge than the white men and have been praying much Since yesterday, took my leave of them expecting to see them no more, was well assisted in these duties. Dined with Mr. Boggie & his wife whom I lately married, after Dinner being distressed with a headache walked out to the skirts of the City, and made Some calls. Drank tea at Captain Grants, whose Lady is lately come from Scotland by way of London. She appears to be a serious sensible woman. Captain Rankin was with us. He is very desirous that I should go home with him, and that is what I very much desire, but as he leaves this place soon to go to Savannah I am afraid I shall not get him Overtaken, however Intend to try for it. . . .

Thursday March 4 . . . Visited the white criminals, (having heard that the mullattoe & Negroes were reprieved) found them still very Insensible of their own misery, but humble & thankful for my services, seemingly serious & in tears, Little concerned for their Eternal Salvation, but earnest & anxious about life. Said much to them, prayed most fervently with & for them, and was enabled to deal faithfully in every part of this duty. . . .

[365] *Friday March 5* . . . At ten O Clock I went out to visit, the white Criminals, resolved to take my leave of them & not attend them to the Gallows. Gave them all the Instruction I could, but to very little purpose. Desired them to pray. The youngest of them repeated the Lords prayer, the other could not repeat it, I spoke much, prayed, & began to take my leave. They then plead so pitifully & Earnestly that I would walk with them to their execution, and begged all the Gentlemen in the Room to Intercede with me, to go with them, upon which I Consented, and having spoke to the Sheriff, walked to the Gallows with them, Surrounded by a Guard of Constables, all armed, both their Coffins in a Cart before us, and a great multitude of people. Kept still Instructing them, and praying with them, causing them to repeat Sentence by Sentence after me. At the Gallows, they Said very little, owned the Justice of their sentence & prayed a few words, I addressed the multitude, who behaved well & were very Silent & attentive. I prayed for Some time, took my leave of the Criminals, who were put into the cart, which was soon drawn from under them, and they were launched into Eternity. Was well assisted in these duties, in which was Engaged about an hour and a half. . . .[30]

[366] *Lords day March 7* . . . Preached in the forenoon with the Lords most remarkable presence & assistance from Rom: 3:21, to a very Decent, serious & attentive Congregation . . . Acquainted them that there would be no service in the afternoon, returned directly to my Lodging, and at four O Clock took a vomit. Was made most excessively Sick for about four hours. Mr. Thomas Miles stayed with me all the time, & was very helpful to me, and I at Last got comfortably through this violent & very distressing operation. Was in a cheerful, Contented, & Comfortable frame of mind. . . .

Thursday March 11 . . . Have also been very much perplexed in my mind, about returning with Captain Rankin, which though attended with many difficulties, and with great expenses, yet think it is my duty, to go with a Gentleman, who I have every reason to expect will be kind & friendly on the passage. Have got all my affairs now in Such a way, that Mr. Penman can easily settle them. The depreciation of the paper Dollars in this state, during the late horrid & most ruinous war, is several thousand pounds sterling out my pocket, and have very little to receive for Eight years past, these things have been very depressing to my Spirits, especially Since my health so visibly declines, yet my trust is in the Lord my God and Everlasting portion. . . . [367] Have had three opportunities of writting to Mr. Lambert at the plantation, desiring him to send up horses to Purisburgh for me at the End of next week, as I hope to get from Savannah there by that time. Have also wrote to my Dear Mrs. Simpson enclosing a bill for one hundred pounds sterling and been these four days as much Engaged in business, as weak in body. Will admit, have in general been rather melancholy and distressed both in body & mind, but still helped to the exercise of faith & hope in God my heavenly Father.

Saturday March 13 This day after many Struggles in my mind, so that was Sometimes in an agony of Inward distress, put all my things aboard of Captain Rankin. Have wrote a Letter by another Vessel for London to Mr. Johnston, Informing him of the Bill Sent off, to Mrs. Simpson, lest her letter should be lost, and put the Second & third Coppies of the Bill into Mr. Penmans hands, was both yesterday & this day so weak & repeatedly seized with faintings, that gave over all thoughts of preaching next Sabbath, and as Captain Rankin proposes to go out tomorrow morning, went aboard of his ship this Evening, after having put several necessaries aboard. He has Engaged, that I am to pay ten guineas for my staying in the Cabin, and at Savannah to pay for my part of Cabin stores, the Same with the other Cabin passengers, but am not to pay my ten guineas for the ship, until I get to Port Glasgow & pay it to the Owners, if they think proper to take it, and that I pay nothing for my passage round to Savannah, was yesterday morning while in bed from three O Clock till Seven, in an agony of distress about leaving this Church without preaching next Sabbath, & staying Some time longer with them, but my great weakness & faintings through the day cleared up my duty and Convinced me that I could not do it, and have this day been more easy & Comfortable in my mind. . . .

[371] *Monday March 22* . . . At eight we anchored Close by Savannah Bluff. At ten the Captain & other Gentlemen went ashore. I stayed, intending not to go out till the afternoon. Was for Some time melancholy, had another Conflict in my mind, whether or not providence, called me here, at 12 O

Clock, the Captain returned & told me, I was Invited to Dine ashore with him. I was dressed & at One, went on shore. Called on my old acquaintance Mrs. Watts, formerly Miss Jeany Ferguson on Port Royal, who often lived for months together in my family at Indian Land, & was comfortably married to a ship Carpenter in this place, she has been a Widow these nine years, has two children living, a boy & girle, she keeps Lodgers & sustains a most excellent Character and is Indeed a very prudent, sensible & truly good woman. She received me, with the greatest kindness & friendship. Sat about an hour, acquainted her, where I was to Dine, she pressed me, to make her house, my home, whenever I choose to live on shore. . . . Visited my old Friend Mr. Zublys meeting house, which is in a very ruinous Condition, and has a Chimney in the middle of it, having been an Hospital, Mr. Zubly died Some years ago, having in last days acted a very Inconsistent part, changing Sides, from the Congress, to the British, & died despised by both, yet I am persuaded he was a real good man, and that he is now in the kingdom of heaven. Visited the church of England, also in a ruinous Condition, Coming out of the church I was called to come by a white Lad, who said, he was come from Purisburgh with a boat & two Negroes & was to Inquire for a Gentleman, coming from Charleston & going to his plantation at Saltcatcher, that his boy & two horses were at Purisburgh, He named the boy Hercules & myself. I told him, I was the person he looked for. He said, he was to return tomorrow, about ten O Clock. I agreed to go up in the Canoe with him, showed him where the Ship lay & promised to pay him generously. Thought myself very fortunate in meeting with him, went aboard, looked out what things I would like with me, & spent the Evening very agreeably with the Captain. . . .

Tuesday March 23 Got up early in a thankful frame of mind. . . . Got all my things ready to go with the boat for Purisburgh, but, it is now 12 O Clock and they have not called for me, stayed aboard all this day, waiting for the white Lad, but he did not call, this Surprized me however was composed & resigned to the will of providence. . . .

[372] *Wednesday 24* . . . After Breakfast, went on shore Inquiring for a passage. Am greatly obliged to Captain Cousins. Was yesterday, & several times this day in company with Mr. Alexander Morrison of Greenock, who makes a very poor, mean, shabby appearance, he has been frequently aboard of our ship. After much searching, Captain Cousins found a man, who had come

down the River in a Small Cannoe, with two Oars, who is to return this Evening or tomorrow morning & is very willing to let me have a passage. Captain Cousins carried me, to the man, whose name is Manners, & lives at Black Swamp, about thirty miles above Purisburgh, & appears to be remarkably civil & discreet. I engaged to go with him, if he did not go, before tomorrow, as I dare not venture, to be all night, on the water in an Open boat. Was afterwards mostly on board, being exceedingly distressed with Rheumatick pains, & very great Swelling in my feet & legs, up to my knees, & so full of pain, that it is with great difficulty I can walk. . . .

Thursday March 25 1784 Had a very uneasy night. . . . Have received much kindness from Captain Rankin, who has shown much care of, & great tenderness for me. He provided me with two bottles of Rum, a large piece of Boiled beef, & Several large Bisket, I gave 14 pence for his two Small loaves of wheat Bread. Left four guineas with the Captain, & the keys of my chest, & trunks, took what things I thought might need, in my portmanteau & went into the very small Canoe, half past eight in the morning. We took in another passenger, a Mr. Grubs, the owner, Mr. Manners steered with a paddle, Mr. Grubs & I sat down on small pieces of wood, in the bottom of the Cannoe. Two Negroes, with short oars, rowed us along at an Easy rate, as long as the tide helped us. Afterwards, It was very hard work going against the stream. We crossed the River about fourteen times, to keep by the Marsh & clear of the current. At 12 O Clock we went ashore, at Mulberry Grove, with another Cannoe in our Company, Dined all together under a fine shady tree, one O Clock, set off, & laboured hard against the stream, there being a very great fresh in the River. The Master of the other Canoe, fired at & killed a very large alligator sleeping on the Bank, the Ball Entered under one of his shoulders, at half past four, put ashore, at Yamassee, stayed about twenty minutes. Half past eight, got to Purisburgh, the two Canoes were to go two to three miles farther before they camped on shore. Mr. Manners, who had behaved with great Civility, & is a very Sensible Conversible man, refused to take anything for my passage, but allowed me, to give the two Negroes what I pleased, I gave Each of them a Dollar, for which both He & they were very thankful, they Carried up my portmanteau, Saddle, Bridle & Surtout Coat to the house at the North End of Purisburgh, where my horses & Negro Hercules have been waiting Since Friday last. Found the house almost a wreck, but as the night was fair & agreeably warm, I was better Lodged than I expected at my first going into it, Everything appeared very poor & dirty. They had no bread of any kind, but Corn hominy, they had good Rum & good water, I had brought half of a Small loaf from the Canoe. I supped on two Eggs, without any butter, I was happy & thankful, blessing the Lord for my safe passage up this long & dangerous River, where accidents are almost weekly happening & that my servant & horses had waited for me. O bless the Lord O my soul, bless his holy name forever & for ever, amen & amen.

[inside back cover] Christ is all and in all.

Notes

1. This is a continuation of volume 7 of the diary, which Simpson began in 1769. The first portion of volume 7 is included in part 1 of this edition. The pages in the manuscript and in the microfilm are out of order for volume 7 of Simpson's diary. I have renumbered the pages here to reflect their correct order, as Simpson originally wrote them. The numbers in brackets are the correctly ordered pages; the numbers in parentheses denote the order of these same pages in the current manuscript and microfilm.

2. Mrs. Green was the widow of Anglican minister John Green, who came to South Carolina in 1762 and settled in St. Helena Parish until his death in 1765; Weis, *Colonial Clergy,* 79.

3. James Pierce.

4. This page is creased in the center, making many words in the middle of page illegible. I have reconstructed much of it based on the overall context and the logic of the sentences, placing uncertain words in brackets.

5. Fives was an English version of handball played on a court with three walls.

6. Garden or Gordon; Simpson rarely used this name. Simmons may refer to John Simmons, a subscriber at Indian Land; see "Minutes and Accounts," Stoney Creek Papers.

7. Godfrey's Savannah. Mrs. B was Martha Brown, cousin to John Hunt; Holcomb, *South Carolina Marriages,* 269. To avoid confusion with her sister in-law, who was also Mrs. Brown, I have retained Simpson's shortened use of her name throughout the diary.

8. William Hayne; Simmons, "Records of Willtown," 37–38.

9. Richard Hutson, son and heir of the Reverend William Hutson.

10. Mary Cater; on this letter, see the entry for October 13, 1771.

11. The reference is to twelfth-century French theologian Peter Abelard and his tragic love affair with the maiden Heloise d'Argenteuil.

12. Dr. James Reid (1701–1769), physician and assemblyman; Waring, *History of Medicine,* 388.

13. Or "be never taken that in my way." Simpson's specific meaning is not clear.

14. Probably Robert Russel (fl. 1692). The sermon on Joshua was part of his collection entitled *Seven Sermons.*

15. Simpson gives different dates as to the year of his birth, but he began his diary in 1748, in his fourteenth year and before his birthday, which would place his birth year at 1734. He would have been thirty-six in 1770.

16. Probably John Grimball, whose name appears in several land transactions alongside the names of Peter and Elias Robert, into whose family he had married; Colonial Plat Books (Copy Series), 13:91.

17. Simpson left a detailed account of this fascinating presbytery meeting, but since Howe reproduced most of it, I have omitted it here due to space constraints. See Howe, *Presbyterian Church,* 1:380–87.

18. The "stranger young minister's" admission to presbytery membership was a key point of contention at the meeting, but Simpson did not identify him by name, and no one matching his description appears in the historical record.

19. James Donnom, widower of Mrs. Holmes's sister.

20. Elias Roberts.

21. Joseph Brailsford; Colonial Plat Books (Copy Series), 9:227.

22. Brother of Mrs. Shaw and son of old Mrs. McTier.

23. Probably James Patterson; see "Minutes and Accounts," Stoney Creek Papers.

24. William Lambright; see the entry for December 14, 1783.

25. Isaac Watts (1674–1748), English nonconformist and revivalist, who was best known as a composer of popular and, at least in Presbyterian circles, controversial psalms and hymns.

26. Mrs. George Threadcraft.

27. James Donnom.

28. "E. J." is Elias Jaudon. "J. R." refers to John Roberts, a brother of Elias and Peter Roberts; Colonial Plat Books (Copy Series), 20:135.

29. Peter Roberts, brother of Elias Roberts.

30. Joseph Donnom, whose father had sent him out to sea; see the entry for November 8, 1769 in part 1.

31. Joseph Glover (1719–1783), militia officer and wealthy planter, owned some 5,550 acres in St. Bartholomew Parish; Glover, *Narratives of Colleton County,* 85–88.

32. The words beginning "as to her estate" to the end of the sentence appear to have been inserted later.

33. Steele (1672–1729) was an English man of letters, who cofounded the *Spectator.*

34. Jonathan Wilkins.

35. I have not been able to identify this author.

36. Mrs. Clark ran a tavern at Saltcatcher Bridge.

37. George Timmons, brother of Thomas Timmons.

38. John Bunyan (1628–1688), author of *Pilgrim's Progress.* Several editions of Bunyan's works had been published by 1770.

39. James Jordan.

40. Mrs. Graves was the sister of Mrs. DeSaussure and the widow Prioleau. Her connection to Betsy Clifford and her husband, who lived in Ponpon, is not known.

41. The Wando River, location of Cainhoy Presbyterian Church; Martin, *Names and Places*, 57.

42. Charles Brown; "Minutes and Accounts," Stoney Creek Papers.

43. John Tonge (1729–1773) came to South Carolina from England in 1759 and served as Anglican rector at St. Paul Parish until his death; Weis, *Colonial Clergy*, 92.

44. Simpson errs here; the passage he quotes is Psalm 119:71.

45. Andrew Maybank; Conveyance Books (Public Register), 3LO:251.

46. The following four pages are seriously torn at both edges. Despite the difficulties this presented, I have retained this interesting and important scene. To avoid the repeated use of [illegible] in this passage, I have used ellipses instead.

47. Thomas Halyburton (1674–1712), Scottish minister and theologian, whose engagement to a woman fell through when she secretly married another man. See *Memoirs of the Reverend Thomas Halyburton*, 275–78.

48. The original manuscript shows that two loose leaves, numbered here as pages 123–26 and entitled "Notes of Some Sermons Indian Land October 28 1762," were inserted into the diary here. These pages include the text of only one sermon, based on 1 Samuel 3:18, "And He said, It is the Lord, let him do what seemeth him good," along with an epitaph for and description of the death of Simpson's son Sacheverell. That epitaph is included here at the end of volume 7.

49. Probably Frederick Daser, a Lutheran minister ordained in Charleston in 1770 and ordained in the Church of England in 1774; Weis, *Colonial Clergy*, 75.

50. Nancy Fletcher.

51. Dr. Benjamin Wilply of Godfrey's Savannah, partner with Dr. Robert Osborne, who sold drugs at Saltcatcher Bridge; Waring, *History of Medicine*, 381, 388, 390.

52. Either Mrs. Perry or Mrs. Postell; they were sisters.

53. Possibly the wife of Robert Fairchild of St. Helena Parish; Warren, *Jury Lists*, 54.

54. Enos McLd, whom Simpson had visited on September 17 and who had sent Simpson a message the night before asking him to perform the funeral.

55. The writing is not clear here; "widow B and" could be "widow Barr" or otherwise.

56. During the war Carson ran afoul of the Revolutionary government and was returned to Britain; see Simpson's Journal, 10:127, 167.

57. For the plat to this tract, see Colonial Plat Books (Copy Series), 20:206.

58. Chehaw was no remote backwater; it was situated on Port Royal Island near the mouth of the Combahee River.

59. Isaac Hayne (1745–1781), planter and patriot officer, who was captured and hanged by the British in 1781; Bowden, "Isaac Hayne," 434.

60. Richard Wayne; Conveyance Books (Register of Mesne Conveyance), 11:254. Also see the entry for July 29, 1770.

61. George Ingles; Colonial Plat Books (Copy Series), 17:264.

62. Simpson probably means "Mrs. P that was C." He is referring to Jeany Clifford, daughter of Mrs. Clifford. Her deceased husband, Mr. P, was Thomas Poole. "Register of Marriage Licenses Granted," 36. Because Simpson variously referred to them as Mr. P, Mr. PC, Mrs. P, and Mrs. PC, I have not expanded their names in the text in hopes of avoiding further confusion.

63. Archibald Calder; Memorial Books (Copy Series), 10:225

64. Simmons, "Records of Willtown," 39.

65. Charles Palmer and William Starling were both subscribers at Indian Land; "Minutes and Accounts," Stoney Creek Papers.

66. Here and elsewhere, it appears to be Ganolke. The name does not appear in other historical records.

67. Arthur Peronneau had married Hutson's older sister, Mary; Hutson's younger brother was Thomas. See Barnwell, "Dr. Henry Woodward," 38.

68. Thomas Shubrick; Memorial Books (Copy Series), 2:267, 324.

69. The Falklands Crisis.

70. Stephen Bull (d. 1800), known as Bull of Sheldon, was a supporter of the parish church and connected to one of the most powerful families in the province. He was a colonial and state legislator and a brigadier general in the patriot militia; Rowland, "Bull, Stephen," 105.

71. Edward Ellington, who served Anglican churches in St. Bartholomew, St. Helena, and St. James Goose Creek parishes before removing to Savannah in 1793, where he died; Weis, *Colonial Clergy*, 76.

72. William Romaine (1714–1795), Anglican evangelical and associate of Whitefield; Shenton, *"An Iron Pillar."*

73. Possibly Griffith Jones, Welsh evangelical preacher and supporter of Whitefield's revivals; Lambert, *Inventing the "Great Awakening,"* 152.

74. Philipp Melanchthon (1497–1560), German theologian, reformer, and colleague of Luther.

75. Wife of Joseph Brailsford; see the entry for June 5, 1770. Simpson did not record the details surrounding her marriage.

76. John Beaty; Memorial Books (Copy Series), 14:127.

77. William Russel was a trustee at Indian Land; see the entry for April 29, 1771. William Orr was an Anglican minister who settled successively at St. Philip's Church and St. Paul, St. Helena, and St. John Parishes from 1736 until his death in 1755; Weis, *Colonial Clergy*, 86.

78. James Postell, and Daniel and William Blake; Conveyance Books (Public Register), 4BO:199.

79. Thomas Doolittle (1630–1707), English divine and author of *A Treatise Concerning the Lord's Supper* (1665).

80. Probably Edward Griffith; Colonial Plat Books (Copy Series), 11:254. Miss S.M. is Sally Murry.

81. Probably Benjamin Haskins; Judgment Rolls (Court of Common Pleas), 74A:576A.

82. John Roberts, Thomas Hamilton, Thomas Lambright.

83. See Duffy, *Epidemics,* 134.

84. Probably Isaac Haynes; see the entry for April 22, 1771.

85. The Brandfords of Wilton.

86. Dr. Peter Spence was a physician and later a Loyalist; Waring, *History of Medicine,* 316.

87. Betsy Hutson; see the entry for August 26, 1771.

88. The following epitaph was on one of two loose pages inserted into the middle of the volume. See note 48, above.

Volume 8

1. Father Omnipotent, Eternal God.

2. Like volume 7, this volume is written in Simpson's abbreviated form, but the pages are smaller and the writing generally more legible. Simpson's method here was to write on only one side of each page to the end, then flip the book to continue on the other side to the front.

3. Ponpon.

4. This trust deed, drawn up in 1772, has survived; see "Minutes and Accounts," Stoney Creek Papers.

5. In all likelihood this is the son of old John Cuthbert, both of whom are mentioned in the entry for September 11, 1771. Simpson also mentions a young John Cuthbert in the entry for November 16, 1783; this was the son of Dr. James Cuthbert.

6. Mrs. Dixon was a sister of Henry DeSaussure; Mrs. Graves was a sister of Mrs. Henry DeSaussure.

7. Thomas Henderson (b. 1740), who was ordained at Saltcatcher after Simpson's removal to Scotland. He served congregations at Edisto Island, Saltcatcher, and Wilton; Weis, *Colonial Clergy,* 80.

8. James Janeway, seventeenth-century Puritan author, who published *A Token for Children, Being an Exact Account of the Conversion, Holy and Exemplary Lives, and Joyful Deaths of Several Young Children* in 1671.

9. Phillip Doddridge; see the entry for January 1, 1770 in part 1 of this edition.

10. John Rogers or Rodgers was a leader in the Synod of New York and Philadelphia; Klett, *Minutes,* 478.

11. John Willison (1680–1750), minister at South Church, Presbytery of Dundee, was an evangelical who sympathized with the Seceders. The reference is to his *Sacramental Catechism, or, A Familiar Instructor for Young Communicants,* first printed in 1720; Scott, *Fasti Ecclesiae Scoticanae* (hereafter *FES*), 5:320–21.

12. John Thomas (1746–1771) served the Independent Congregation in Charleston from 1767 until his death; Weis, *Colonial Clergy,* 92.

13. Probably the widow of Gilbert Pepper, who disappeared from the historical record after 1762; Memorial Books (Copy Series), 14:149.

14. Or Bochim; see the book of Judges, chapter 2.

15. On Monday Simpson had traveled about fifty miles up the Saltcatcher to see the oldest son of Jonathan Donnom, who had been severely injured by a horse. He returned on Wednesday.

16. Probably William Burkitt (1650–1703), Church of England clergyman and devotional author.

17. Probably the widow of David Jeffreys; Memorial Books (Copy Series), 14:57.

18. Josiah Smith (1704–1781), minister at the Independent Congregation in Charleston from 1734 to 1749, who supported Whitefield during the heady days of the Great Awakening and published widely on religious subjects; Weis, *Colonial Clergy,* 90.

19. Hugh Alison came to South Carolina from Pennsylvania around 1761 and served congregations at Williamsburg and James Island until his death in 1781; Weis, *Colonial Clergy,* 71.

20. The son of Captain and Mrs. John Scott; see the entry for September 4, 1771.

21. Polly was apparently the nickname of Mary; Hetty was the nickname of Esther, who was about nineteen years old at the time; Barnwell, "Dr. Henry Woodward," 38.

22. Simpson's is just one of three accounts of Richardson's death. For an analysis, see Moore, "Mysterious Death of William Richardson."

23. Yet he does give such an account. In the three following pages Simpson gives a day-by-day description of an extended and life-threatening illness; for ten days he suffered from a high fever and excessive vomiting, during which time he was given up for dead. By October 13 he was well enough to resume his diary. I have omitted the details of his illness but included the social problems that fell out from his failed proposal to Miss Murry.

24. William Tennent III did arrive and served the Independent Congregation in Charleston and the Provincial Congress from 1772 until his death in 1777; Weis, *Colonial Clergy,* 92.

25. The profligate young man was William Garner; *South Carolina Gazette and Country Journal,* December 24, 1771.

VOLUME II

1. Simpson had sailed from Greenock, Scotland, on July 2 aboard an unnamed ship under Captain Grindlay. It was a long and trying voyage. Grindlay had little experience in American waters and had never sailed to South Carolina. Simpson was disgusted with the behavior of the captain, crew, and cabin passengers in particular,

and he was continually frustrated in his efforts to enforce Sabbath observance or even hold public worship services. He kept a detailed record of his voyage, filling over eighty pages in his journal, but space constraints have not permitted it to be included here.

2. One of the passengers on the voyage with Simpson, possibly John Cunningham from Crawford's Dyke near Port Glasgow; Tait, *Directory,* 100.

3. Daniel DeSaussure, formerly of Beaufort; his brother Henry of Indian Land died during Simpson's absence.

4. David Ramsay (1749–1815), physician, statesman, and the preeminent historian of the Revolution of his generation; Cote, *Dictionary,* 287.

5. John Witherspoon (1723–1794), Scottish Presbyterian minister who came to America in 1768 to serve as president of Princeton College. He was a signatory to the Declaration of Independence. Scott, *FES,* 3:174–75.

6. The attorney Benjamin Guerard (d. 1788) served as a colonial assemblyman, patriot militia officer, state representative, and, during the difficult years immediately following the war, as governor; Lockhart, "Guerard, Benjamin," 419.

7. Oliphant and Scot were two passengers with whom Simpson had sailed. Based on the public records, James and Edward Penman began practicing law in Charleston near the close of the war; Simpson did not mention them as his attorneys in the earlier volumes.

8. John Mitchell, an old friend; see the entry for October 24, 1769 in part 1 of this edition. Mrs. Edwards was Rebecca Donnom Edwards, youngest daughter of Simpson's deceased friend, James Donnom, and wife of John Edwards, Jr., Charleston merchant and later director of the Bank of South Carolina; Fernhagen, "John Edwards," 21.

9. James Gourlay (1732–1802) was ordained in 1765 at Tillicoultry, Presbytery of Dunblane, Scotland. In 1772 he was deposed after confessing to immorality. The following year, apparently on Simpson's advice, he went to South Carolina and settled at Indian Land, where he served until his death. Scott, *FES,* 4:362; Weis, *Colonial Clergy,* 78–79.

10. His mother's name was Margaret O'hear; Judgment Rolls (Court of Common Pleas), 153A:911A.

11. The remainder of this page and the four pages that follow it are blank. The next entry is a date more than one month later.

12. In 1776 Simpson married Jean McLean Wallace of Greenock; see volume 10 of his journals, the entry for November 11, 1776.

13. Josiah Smith, Jr. (1731–1826), son of the late minister of the Independent Congregation in Charleston and a prominent merchant, banker, and state assemblyman; Cote, *Dictionary,* 325.

14. Probably James Skirving (d. 1787), planter, physician, and assemblyman. Edgar and Bailey, *Biographical Directory,* 2:619–20.

15. The state constitution of 1778 established Protestantism as the state religion but did not provide regular financial support to any church. Brinsfield, *Religion and Politics*, 122–24.

16. The Prince William Parish church at Sheldon was indeed one of the finest in the province; it was restored after the War for Independence but burned again during or just after the Civil War. Its ruins are still standing, as is the churchyard at Stoney Creek, though the markers for Simpson's family members are lost.

17. James Moncrief was the chief engineer for the British in the southern campaign. He reportedly recruited some eight hundred slaves for military duty and took them to freedom when the British evacuated. McCrady, *South Carolina in the Revolution*, 661, 674.

18. The Donnoms established their family line in the Waxhaws; see Crockett, *Old Waxhaw Graveyard.*

19. Simpson filed claims for livestock, corn, and rations totaling over 110 pounds sterling. Accounts Audited, file number 7016.

20. James Booth was convicted for these murders, not Perry or Brown. For a fuller description, see Rowland, Moore, and Rogers, *History of Beaufort County,* 255.

21. Genesis 19:21–25.

22. Or Horrie.

23. William Hollingshead (1748–1815) was a native of Pennsylvania; he served the Independent Congregation in Charleston from 1783 until his death. See Howe, *Presbyterian Church,* 1:457–58, 564–65.

24. Pages 336–39 of volume II include entries from December 31, 1783, to January 4, 1784, during which time Simpson was aboard Eldridge's sloop. The journey to Charleston was fraught with problems and delays, which Simpson described in detail. The entry for January 4 ends abruptly, and the following ten pages are blank. When the journal resumes here, more than two weeks have elapsed, and Simpson is back in Charleston, lodging with Mrs. O'hear.

25. Dr. Andrew Turnbull (d. 1792), physician in Charleston from 1781 until his death. Waring, *History of Medicine,* 321.

26. Simpson makes an error in the date here; Thursday was actually January 29. He corrects himself on March 1.

27. Alexander Walker, who seemed to be liquidating his assets in 1784 before announcing his return to his business as factor; see the *South-Carolina Weekly Gazette,* June 2, 1784, and September 29, 1784.

28. Adam Johnston (1757–1830) began courting Simpson's daughter Susy before Simpson left Scotland. They married before he returned and had one son, Archibald Simpson Johnston. Susy died sometime thereafter, and her son eventually inherited Simpson's South Carolina estate. *Greenock Advertiser,* November 16, 1819, and August 10, 1830; Index of Births, Marriages, and Deaths, Watt Library, Greenock, Scotland.

29. John Forrest (1742–1822) was the minister at the main parish church in Port Glasgow; Simpson led a separate congregation in the parish at Newark Chapel. Scott, *FES,* 3:218.

30. The two condemned men were Thomas McDowell and Tobias Sykes; *South-Carolina Weekly Gazette,* March 6, 1784.

Works Cited

Manuscripts and Archival Records in the South Carolina Department of Archives and History, Columbia, South Carolina

Accounts Audited of Claims Growing Out of the Revolution in South Carolina, 1775–1856
Colonial Plat Books (Copy Series), 1731–1775
Conveyance Books (Public Register), 1719–1776
Conveyance Books (Register of Mesne Conveyance), 1776–1785
Judgment Rolls (Court of Common Pleas), 1703–1790
Memorial Books (Copy Series), 1731–1778
Stoney Creek Independent Presbyterian Church (McPhersonville, S.C.) Papers, 1722–1910

Other Manuscripts and Archival Sources

Index of Births, Marriages, and Deaths in Greenock, Scotland. Watt Library, Greenock, Scotland.
Simpson, Archibald. Journals and Sermons, 1748–1784. Charleston Library Society, Charleston, South Carolina.

Printed Primary Sources

Crockett, Nancy. *Old Waxhaw Graveyard.* Lancaster, S.C.: privately printed, 1965.
Greenock Advertiser.
Halyburton, Thomas. *Memoirs of the Reverend Thomas Halyburton.* Glasgow: Chalmers and Collins, 1825.
Holcomb, Brent H. *South Carolina Marriages, 1688–1799.* Baltimore: Genealogical Publishing Company, 1995.
Klett, Guy S., ed. *Minutes of the Presbyterian Church in America, 1706–1788.* Philadelphia: Presbyterian Historical Society, 1976.
"Register of Marriage Licenses Granted, December, 1765, to August, 1766." *South Carolina Historical and Genealogical Magazine* 22 (January 1921): 34–36.
Simmons, Slann L. C. "Records of the Willtown Presbyterian Church, 1738–1741." Pts. 1 and 2. *South Carolina Historical Magazine* 62 (January 1961): 33–50; 62 (April 1961): 107–63.
South Carolina Gazette, and Country Journal.

South-Carolina Weekly Gazette.

Tait, John. *John Tait's Directory for the City of Glasgow, Villages of Anderston, Calton, and Gorbals; also for the Towns of Paisley, Greenock, Port-Glasgow, and Kilmarnock, from the 15th of May 1783, to the 15th of May, 1784.* Glasgow: By the author, 1783.

Warren, Mary Bondurant, comp. *South Carolina Jury Lists, 1718 through 1783.* Danielsville, Ga.: Heritage Papers, 1977.

SECONDARY SOURCES

Barnwell, Joseph W. "Dr. Henry Woodward, the First English Settler in South Carolina, and Some of His Descendants." *South Carolina Historical and Genealogical Magazine* 8 (January 1907): 29–41.

Bowden, David K. "Hayne, Isaac." In *The South Carolina Encyclopedia,* edited by Walter Edgar, 434–35. Columbia: University of South Carolina Press, 2006.

Brinsfield, John Wesley. *Religion and Politics in Colonial South Carolina.* Easley, S.C.: Southern Historical Press, 1983.

Cote, Richard N., ed. *Dictionary of South Carolina Biography.* Easley, S.C.: Southern Historical Press, 1985.

Duffy, John. *Epidemics in Colonial America.* Baton Rouge: Louisiana State University Press, 1953.

Edgar, Walter, and N. Louise Bailey. *Biographical Directory of the South Carolina House of Representatives: The Commons House of Assembly, 1692–1775.* Columbia: University of South Carolina Press, 1977.

Fernhagen, Mary Pringle. "John Edwards and Some of His Descendants." *South Carolina Historical Magazine* 55 (January 1954): 15–21.

Glover, Beulah. *Narratives of Colleton County: The Land Lying between the Edisto and Combahee Rivers.* Walterboro, S.C.: privately printed, 1962.

Howe, George. *History of the Presbyterian Church in South Carolina.* 2 vols. Columbia, S.C.: Duffie & Chapman, 1870–83.

Lambert, Frank. *Inventing the "Great Awakening."* Princeton, N.J.: Princeton University Press, 1999.

Lockhart, Matthew A. "Guerard, Benjamin." In *The South Carolina Encyclopedia,* edited by Walter Edgar, 410. Columbia: University of South Carolina Press, 2006.

Martin, Joseph B. *Guide to Presbyterian Ecclesiastical Names and Places in South Carolina, 1685–1985.* Charleston: South Carolina Historical Society, 1989.

McCrady, Edward. *History of South Carolina in the Revolution.* New York: Macmillan, 1902.

Moore, Peter N. "The Mysterious Death of William Richardson: Kinship, Female Vulnerability, and the Myth of Supernaturalism in the Southern Backcountry." *North Carolina Historical Review* 80 (July 2003): 279–96.

Rowland, Lawrence S. "Bull, Stephen." In *The South Carolina Encyclopedia,* edited by Walter Edgar, 105. Columbia: University of South Carolina Press, 2006.

Rowland, Lawrence S., Alexander Moore, and George C. Rogers, Jr. *The History of Beaufort County, South Carolina,* vol. 1, *1514–1861.* Columbia: University of South Carolina Press, 1996.

Scott, Hew. *Fasti Ecclesiae Scoticanae: The Succession of Ministers in the Church of Scotland from the Reformation.* 8 vols. Edinburgh: Tweeddale Court, 1915–50.

Shenton, Tim. *"An Iron Pillar": The Life and Times of William Romaine.* Darlington, U.K.: Evangelical Press, 2004.

Waring, Joseph I. *A History of Medicine in South Carolina, 1670–1825.* [Charleston:] South Carolina Medical Association, 1964.

Weis, Frederick Lewis. *The Colonial Clergy of Virginia, North Carolina, and South Carolina.* Baltimore: Genealogical Publishing Company, 1976.

Index

Abelard, Peter, 12, 295n11

agriculture. *See* indigo production; plantations; rice production

Aimy (slave), 169–70

alcoholic beverages. *See* drunkenness; food and drink; taverns

Alison, Hugh, 211–12, 300n19

American Revolution: Carson's business during, 297n56; Charleston during and after, viii, 244–52, 262, 265; Edmonds's preaching on, 250; evacuation from South Carolina during, 244, 249, 281; Hayne hanged by British during, 297n59; losses to and use of Simpson's plantation during, 254, 257–58, 263, 263–66, 268–69, 276, 283, 302n19; Moncrief's southern campaign during, 302n17; peace treaty following, 267; plantations during and after, 254–58, 261–62, 264–67, 302n19; plunder by British and American armies during, 262, 272, 278; Presbyterian ministers during, 258; religious decline in South Carolina after, 247, 258, 274, 276, 278, 283, 286–87; in Saltcatcher, 254; Simpson in Scotland during, viii; slaves as soldiers for British during, 256, 302n17; South Carolina after, viii, 244–52, 254–59, 261–67, 272–73, 290; veterans of, 248–49, 270

Anabaptists, 24, 47, 89, 230, 238. *See also* Baptists.

Anderson, Mr. (tailor), 156

Anderson, Mrs.: and care for sick slaves, 274; child of, 275; and family duties in Simpson household, 187; gifts of Simpson to, 275–76; as housekeeper for Simpson, 156–57, 274, 275; illness of,

275; and Lord's Supper, 203; marriage of, to Thompson, 275; pastoral care of, 275; pregnancy and childbirth of, 274–75; at Simpson's plantation during American Revolution, 274–76

Anglicans, 90, 140, 240–42, 297n43, 298n77, 298nn71–72

Arthurly, Mr., 281

Ashepooh, 22, 141

Atcheson, William, 251

Atkins, James, 134, 136

Atkins, Mr. and Mrs., 54

Atkins, Thomas, 134

B, Mr. J, 171

B, Mr., 80

B, Mrs. (Mrs. Martha Brown, later Wilkins): agony and distress of, over Simpson's courtship, 74–77; character and personality of, 31, 46; child of, 46, 60, 74, 99; estate of, 46, 60, 74; failed courtship of Simpson and, vii, 68–72, 80–81; friends' encouragement of Simpson's courtship of, 28–29; friendship between Simpson and, 6, 28, 30–32, 80–82, 91, 98–99, 151, 229; gossip and mistaken views of courtship between Simpson and, 6, 28–32; and Griffith's criticisms of Simpson, 228–29; illness of, 99, 163, 220; marriage of, to Wilkins, 98–99; pregnancy and miscarriage of, 151, 163; return of rings and correspondence between Simpson and, 70, 71, 76, 80–81; Simpson's courtship of, 45–46, 52–56, 68–77; as slave owner, 68; and Jonathan Wilkins, 52–53, 55–57, 68–73, 75–77, 81–82, 91

B, widow (or widow Barr), 91, 297n55